His Divine Grace
A.C. Bhaktivedanta Swami Prabhupāda

Plate 1 The Lord assumed the gigantic form of a boar and fought with the demon Hiraṇyākṣa. *(p. 338)*

Plate 2 Dhruva Mahārāja is benedicted by the Personality of Godhead. *(p. 350)*

Plate 3 To help the demigods, the primeval Lord assumed the incarnation of a gigantic tortoise, swimming in the ocean of milk. *(p. 358)*

Plate 4 The Personality of Godhead Narasiṁhadeva killed the demon Hiraṇyakaśipu by piercing him with His nails. *(p. 359)*

Plate 5 After hearing the elephant's plea, the Lord cut the mouth of the crocodile to save the elephant. *(p. 364)*

Plate 6 Bali Mahārāja was very glad to receive the Lord's remaining step on his head. *(p. 366)*

Plate 7 Lord Rāmacandra appeared along with His eternal consort Sītā, brother Lakṣmaṇa and servant Hanumān. *(p. 375)*

Plate 8 In order to diminish the burden of the world, Lord Kṛṣṇa appeared with His immediate expansion Lord Balarāma. *(p. 381)*

Plate 9 The Lord sucked the breast of the Pūtanā witch along with her life air, and the demon's gigantic body fell down. *(p. 383)*

Plate 10 At the age of three months, Lord Kṛṣṇa killed the Sakaṭāsura demon, who had remained hidden behind a cart. *(p. 383)*

Plate 11 A demon of the name Śaṅkhacūḍa tried to kidnap Kṛṣṇa's cowherd damsels. *(p. 391)*

Plate 12 At the end of Kali-yuga the Lord appeared as the supreme chastiser. *(p. 397)*

Śrīmad-Bhāgavatam

ALL GLORY TO ŚRĪ GURU AND GAURĀṄGA

Śrīmad-Bhāgavatam

of

KṚṢṆA-DVAIPĀYANA VYĀSA

अहमेवासमेवाग्रे नान्यद् यत् सदसत् परम् ।
पश्चादहं यदेतच्च योऽवशिष्येत सोऽस्म्यहम् ॥३२॥

aham evāsam evāgre
nānyad yat sad-asat param
paścād ahaṁ yad etac ca
yo'vaśiṣyeta so'smy aham (p. 507)

OTHER BOOKS by
His Divine Grace A.C. Bhaktivedanta Swami Prabhupāda

Bhagavad-gītā As It Is

Teachings of Lord Caitanya

Kṛṣṇa, the Supreme Personality of Godhead (2 volumes)

Śrī Īśopaniṣad

Easy Journey to Other Planets

Kṛṣṇa Consciousness: The Topmost Yoga System

The Nectar of Devotion

The Kṛṣṇa Consciousness Movement is the Genuine Vedic Way

Back to Godhead Magazine (Founder)

Śrīmad-Bhāgavatam

Second Canto
"The Cosmic Manifestation"

(Part Two–Chapters 7-10)

With the Original Sanskrit Text,
Its Roman Transliteration, Synonyms,
Translation and Elaborate Purports by

His Divine Grace
A.C. Bhaktivedanta Swami Prabhupāda
Founder-Ācārya of the International Society for Krishna Consciousness

THE BHAKTIVEDANTA BOOK TRUST
New York · Los Angeles · London · Bombay

Readers interested in the subject matter of this book are invited by the International Society for Krishna Consciousness to correspond with its Secretary.

International Society for Krishna Consciousness
3959 Landmark Street
Culver City, California 90230

Library of Congress Catalogue Card Number: 70-127183
International Standard Book Number: 0-912776-35-8

Printed by Dai Nippon Printing Co., Ltd., Tokyo, Japan

TABLE OF CONTENTS

CHAPTER EIGHT
Questions by King Parīkṣit

CHAPTER NINE
Answers by Citing the Lord's Version

CHAPTER TEN
Bhāgavatam Is The Answer

Appendixes

CHAPTER SEVEN

Scheduled Incarnations with Specific Functions

TEXT 1

ब्रह्मोवाच

यत्रोद्यतः क्षितितलोद्धरणाय बिभ्रत्
क्रौडीं तनुं सकलयज्ञमयीमनन्तः ।
अन्तर्महार्णव उपागतमादिदैत्यं
तं दंष्ट्रयाद्रिमिव वज्रधरो ददार ॥ १ ॥

brahmovāca
yatrodyataḥ kṣiti-taloddharaṇāya bibhrat
krauḍīṁ tanuṁ sakala-yajña-mayīm anantaḥ
antar-mahārṇava upāgatam ādi-daityaṁ
taṁ daṁṣṭrayādrim iva vajra-dharo dadāra

brahmā uvāca—Lord Brahmā said; *yatra*—at that time (when); *udyataḥ*—attempted; *kṣiti-tala*—the earthly planet; *uddharaṇāya*—for the matter of lifting; *bibhrat*—assumed; *krauḍīm*—pastimes; *tanum*—form; *sakala*—total; *yajña-mayīm*—all-inclusive sacrifices; *anantaḥ*—the Unlimited; *antar*—within the universe; *mahā-arṇave*—the great Garbha Ocean; *upāgatam*—having arrived at; *ādi*—the first; *daityam*—demon; *tam*—him; *daṁṣṭrayā*—by the tusk; *adrim*—the flying mountains; *iva*—like; *vajra-dharaḥ*—the controller of the thunderbolts; *dadāra*—pierced.

TRANSLATION

Lord Brahmā said: At the time when the unlimitedly powerful Lord assumed the form of a boar as a pastime, just to lift up the earthly planet, which was drowned in the great ocean of the universe called the Garbhodaka, the first demon [Hiraṇyākṣa] appeared, and the Lord pierced him with His tusk.

PURPORT

Since the beginning of creation, the demons and the demigods or the Vaiṣṇavas are always the two classes of living beings to dominate the planets of the universes. So Lord Brahmā is the first demigod, and Hiraṇyākṣa is the first demon in this universe. Only under certain conditions do the planets float as weightless balls in the air, and as soon as these conditions are disturbed, the planets may fall down in the Garbhodaka Ocean which covers half the universe. The other half is the spherical dome within which the innumerable planetary systems exist. The floating of the planets in the weightless air is due to the inner constitution of the globes, and the modernized drilling of the earth to exploit oil from within is a sort of disturbance by the modern demons resulting in a greatly harmful reaction of the floating condition of the earth. A similar disturbance was created formerly by the demons headed by Hiraṇyākṣa (the great exploiter of the gold rush), and the earth was detached from its weightless condition and fell down into the Garbhodaka Ocean. The Lord, as the maintainer of the whole creation of the material world, therefore assumed the gigantic form of a boar with a proportionate snout and picked up the earthly planet from within the water of Garbhodaka. Śrī Jayadeva Gosvāmī, the great Vaiṣṇava poet, sang as follows:

vasati daśana-śikhare dharaṇī tava lagnā
śaśini kalaṅka-kaleva nimagnā
keśava dhṛta-sūkara-rūpa
jaya jagadīśa hare.

"O Keśava! O Supreme Lord who has assumed the form of a boar! O Lord! The earthly planet rested on Your tusks, and it appeared like the moon engraved with spots."

Such is the symptom of an incarnation of the Lord. The incarnation of the Lord is not the concocted idea of a fanciful class of men who create an incarnation out of imagination. The incarnation of the Lord appears under certain extraordinary circumstances like the above-mentioned occasion, and the incarnation performs a task which is not even imaginable by the tiny brain of mankind. The modern creators of the many cheap incarnations may take note of the factual incarnation of God as the gigantic boar with a suitable snout to carry the earthly planet.

When the Lord appeared to pick up the earthly planet, the demon of the name Hiraṇyākṣa tried to create a disturbance in the methodical functions of the Lord, and therefore he was killed by being pierced by the Lord's tusk. According to Śrīla Jīva Gosvāmī, the demon Hiraṇyākṣa was killed by the hand of the Lord. Therefore his version is that after being killed by the hand of the Lord, the demon was pierced by the tusk, and Śrīla Viśvanātha Cakravartī Ṭhākur confirms this version.

TEXT 2

जातो रुचेरजनयत् सुयमान् सुयज्ञ
आकूतिसूनुरमरानथ दक्षिणायाम् ।
लोकत्रयस्य महतीमहरद् यदार्तिं
स्वायम्भुवेन मनुना हरिरित्यनूक्तः ॥ २ ॥

jāto rucer ajanayat suyamān suyajña
ākūti-sūnur amarān atha dakṣiṇāyām
loka-trayasya mahatīm aharad yadārtiṁ
svāyambhuvena manunā harir ity anūktaḥ

jātaḥ—was born; *ruceḥ*—of the wife of Prajāpati; *ajanayat*—gave birth; *suyamān*—headed by Suyama; *suyajñaḥ*—Suyajña; *ākūti-sūnur*—of the son of Ākūti; *amarān*—the demigods; *atha*—thus; *dakṣiṇāyām*—unto the wife of the name Dakṣiṇā; *loka*—the planetary systems; *trayasya*—of the three; *mahatīm*—very great; *aharat*—diminished; *yat*—all those; *ārtim*—distresses; *svāyambhuvena*—by the Manu named Svāyambhuva; *manunā*—by the father of mankind; *hariḥ*—Hari; *iti*—thus; *anūktaḥ*—named.

TRANSLATION

The Prajāpati first begot Suyajña, in the womb of his wife Ākūti, and then Suyajña begot demigods, headed by Suyama, in the womb of his wife Dakṣiṇā. Suyajña, as the Indradeva, diminished very great miseries in the three planetary systems (upper, lower and intermediate), and because he so diminished the miseries of the universe, he was later called Hari by the great father of mankind, namely Svāyambhuva Manu.

PURPORT

In order to guard against the invention of unauthorized incarnations of God by the fanciful less intelligent persons, the name of the father of the bona fide incarnations is also mentioned in the authorized revealed scriptures. No one, therefore, can be accepted as an incarnation of the Lord if his father's name, as well as the name of the village or place in which he appears, is not mentioned by the authorized scriptures. In the *Bhāgavata-Purāṇa* the name of the Kalki incarnation, which is to take place in almost

400,000 years, is mentioned along with the name of His father and the name of the village in which He will appear. A sane man, therefore, does not accept any cheap edition of incarnation without reference to the authorized scriptures.

TEXT 3

जज्ञे च कर्दमगृहे द्विज देवहूत्यां
स्त्रीभिः समं नवभिरात्मगतिं स्वमात्रे ।
ऊचे ययात्मशमलं गुणसङ्गपङ्क-
मस्मिन् विधूय कपिलस्य गतिं प्रपेदे ॥ ३ ॥

jajñe ca kardama-gṛhe dvija devahūtyāṁ
strībhiḥ samaṁ navabhir ātmagatiṁ sva-mātre
ūce yayātma-śamalaṁ guṇa-saṅga-paṅkam
asmin vidhūya kapilasya gatiṁ prapede

jajñe—took birth; *ca*—also; *kardama*—the Prajāpati named Kardama; *gṛhe*—in the house of; *dvija*—O *brāhmaṇa; devahūtyām*—in the womb of Devahūti; *strībhiḥ*—by women; *samam*—accompanied by; *navabhiḥ*—by nine; *ātma-gatim*—spiritual realization; *sva-mātre*—unto His own mother; *ūce*—uttered; *yayā*—by which; *ātma-śamalam*—coverings of the spirit soul; *guṇa-saṅga*—associated with the modes of nature; *paṅkam*—mud; *asmin*—this very life; *vidhūya*—being washed off; *kapilasya*—of Lord Kapila; *gatim*—liberation; *prapede*—achieved.

TRANSLATION

The Lord then appeared as the Kapila incarnation, being the son of the prajāpati brāhmaṇa Kardama and his wife Devahūti, along with nine other women [sisters]. He spoke to His mother about self-realization, by which, in that very lifetime, she became fully cleansed of the mud of the material modes and thereby achieved liberation, the path of Kapila.

PURPORT

The instructions of Lord Kapila to His mother Devahūti are fully described in the Third Canto (Chapters 25-30) of the *Śrīmad-Bhāgavatam,* and anyone who follows the instructions can achieve the same liberation obtained by Devahūti. The Lord spoke *Bhagavad-gītā*, and thereby Arjuna achieved self-realization, and even today anyone who follows the path of Arjuna can also attain the same benefit as Śrī Arjuna. The scriptures are meant for this purpose. Foolish unintelligent persons make their own interpretations by imagination and thus mislead their followers, causing them to remain in the dungeon of material existence. However, simply by following the instructions imparted by Lord Kṛṣṇa or Lord Kapila, one can obtain the highest benefit, even today.

The word *ātma-gatim* is significant in the sense of perfect knowledge of the Supreme. One should not be satisfied simply by knowing the qualitative equality of the Lord and the living being. One should know the Lord as much as can be known by our limited knowledge. It is impossible for the Lord to be known perfectly as He is, even by such liberated persons as Śiva or Brahmā, so what to speak of other demigods or men in this world. Still, by following the principles of the great devotees and the instructions available in the scriptures, one can know to a considerable extent the features of the Lord. His Lordship Kapila, the incarnation of the Lord, instructed His mother fully about the personal form of the Lord, and thereby she realized the personal form of the Lord and was able to achieve a place in the *Vaikuṇṭhaloka* where Lord Kapila predominates. Every incarnation of the Lord has His own abode in the spiritual sky. Therefore Lord Kapila also has His separate Vaikuṇṭha planet. The spiritual sky is not void. There are innumerable Vaikuṇṭha planets, and in each of them the Lord, by His innumerable expansions, predominates, and the pure devotees who are there also live in the same style as the Lord and His eternal associates.

When the Lord descends personally or by His personal plenary expansions, such incarnations are called *aṁśa, kalā, guṇa, yuga,* and *manvantara* incarnations, and when the Lord's associates descend by the order of the Lord, such incarnations are called *śaktyāveśa* incarnations. But in all cases all the incarnations are supported by the invulnerable statements of the authorized scriptures, and not by any imagination of some self-interested propagandist. Such incarnations of the Lord, in either of the above categories, always declare the Supreme Personality of Godhead to be the ultimate truth. The impersonal conception of the supreme truth is just a process of negation of the form of the Lord from the mundane conception of the supreme truth.

The living entities, by their very constitution, are spiritually as good as the Lord, and the only difference between them is that the Lord is always supreme and pure, without contamination by the modes of material nature, whereas the living entities are apt to be contaminated by association with the material modes of goodness, passion and ignorance. This contamination by the material modes can be washed off completely by knowledge, renunciation and devotional service. Devotional service to the Lord is the ultimate issue, and therefore those who are directly engaged in the devotional service of the Lord do not only acquire the necessary knowledge in spiritual science, but also attain detachment from material connection and are thus promoted to the kingdom of God by complete liberation, as is stated in the *Bhagavad-gītā* (Bg. 14.26):

māṁ ca yo 'vyabhicāreṇa
bhakti-yogena sevate
sa guṇān samatītyai 'tan
brahma-bhūyāya kalpate

Even in the nonliberated stage, a living entity can be directly engaged in the transcendental loving service of the Personality of Godhead Lord Kṛṣṇa or His plenary expansions Rāma, Narasiṁha, etc. Thus, with the proportionate improvement of such transcendental devotional service, the devotee makes definite progress in the matter of *brahma-gati,* or *ātma-gati,* and ultimately attains *kapilasya gati,* or the abode of the Lord, without difficulty. The antiseptic potency of devotional service to the Lord is so great that it can neutralize the material infection even in the present life of a devotee. A devotee does not need to wait for his next birth for complete liberation.

TEXT 4

अत्रेरपत्यमभिकाङ्क्षत आह तुष्टो
दत्तो मयाहमिति यद् भगवान् स दत्तः ।
यत्पादपङ्कजपरागपवित्रदेहा
योगर्द्धिमापुरुभयीं यदुहैहयाद्याः ॥ ४ ॥

atrer apatyam abhikāṅkṣata āha tuṣṭo
datto mayāham iti yad bhagavān sa dattaḥ
yat-pāda-paṅkaja-parāga-pavitra-dehā
yogarddhim āpur ubhayīṁ yadu-haihayādyāḥ

atreḥ—of the sage Atri; *apatyam*—issue; *abhikāṅkṣataḥ*—having prayed for; *āha*—said it; *tuṣṭaḥ*—being satisfied; *dattaḥ*—given over; *mayā*—by me; *aham*—myself; *iti*—thus; *yat*—because; *bhagavān*—the Personality of Godhead; *saḥ*—He; *dattaḥ*—Dattātreya; *yat-pāda*—one whose feet; *paṅkaja*—lotus; *parāga*—dust; *pavitra*—purified; *dehāḥ*—body; *yoga*—mystic; *ṛddhim*—opulence; *āpuḥ*—got; *ubhayīm*—for both the worlds; *yadu*—the father of the Yadu dynasty; *haihaya-ādyāḥ*—and others, like King Haihaya.

TRANSLATION

The great sage Atri prayed for offspring, and the Lord, being satisfied with him, promised to incarnate as Atri's son, Dattātreya [Datta, the son of Atri]. And by the grace of the lotus feet of the Lord, many Yadus, Haihayas, etc., became so purified that they obtained both material and spiritual blessings.

PURPORT

Transcendental relations between the Personality of Godhead and the living entities are eternally established in five different affectionate humors, which are known as *śānta, dāsya, sakhya, vātsalya* and *mādhurya.* The sage Atri was related with the Lord in the affectionate *vātsalya* humor, and therefore, as a result of his devotional perfection, he was inclined to have the Personality of Godhead as his son. The Lord accepted his prayer, and He gave Himself as the son of Atreya. Such a relation of sonhood between the Lord and His pure devotees can be cited in many instances. And because the Lord is unlimited, He has an unlimited number of father-devotees. Factually the Lord is the father of all living entities, but out of transcendental affection and love between the Lord and His devotees, the Lord takes more pleasure in becoming the son of a devotee than in becoming one's father. The father actually serves the son, whereas the son only demands all sorts of services from the father; therefore a pure devotee who is always inclined to serve the Lord wants Him as the son, and not as the father. The Lord also accepts such service from the devotee, and thus the devotee becomes more than the Lord. The impersonalists desire to become one with the Supreme, but the devotee becomes more than the Lord, surpassing the desire of the greatest monist. Parents and other relatives of the Lord achieve all mystic opulences automatically because of their intimate relationship with the Lord. Such opulences include all details of material enjoyment, salvation and mystic powers. Therefore, the devotee of the Lord does not seek them separately, wasting his valuable time in life. The valuable time of one's life must therefore be fully engaged in the transcendental loving service of the Lord. Then other desirable achievements are automatically gained. But even after obtaining such achievements one should be on guard against the pitfall of offenses at the feet of the devotees. The vivid example is Haihaya, who achieved all such perfection of devotional service but, because of his offense at the feet of a devotee, was killed by Lord Paraśurāma. The Lord became the son of the great sage Atri and became known as Dattātreya.

TEXT 5

तप्तं तपो विविधलोकसिसृक्षया मे
आदौ सनात् स्वतपसः स चतुःसनोऽभूत् ।
प्राक्कल्पसम्प्लवविनष्टमिहात्मतत्त्वं
सम्यग् जगाद मुनयो यदचक्षतात्मन् ॥५॥

taptaṁ tapo vividha-loka-sisṛkṣayā me
ādau sanāt sva-tapasaḥ sa catuḥ-sano 'bhūt
prāk-kalpa-samplava-vinaṣṭam ihātma-tattvaṁ
samyag jagāda munayo yad acakṣatātman

taptam—having undergone austerities; *tapaḥ*—penance; *vividha-loka*—different planetary systems; *sisṛkṣayā*—desiring to create; *me*—of mine; *ādau*—at first; *sanāt*—from the Personality of Godhead; *sva-tapasaḥ*—by dint of my own penances; *saḥ*—He, the Lord; *catuḥ-sanaḥ*—the four bachelors named Sanat-kumāra, Sanaka, Sanandana and Sanātana; *abhūt*—appeared; *prāk*—previous; *kalpa*—creation; *samplava*—in the inundation; *vinaṣṭam*—devastated; *iha*—in this material world; *ātma*—the spirit; *tattvam*—truth; *samyak*—in complete; *jagāda*—became manifested; *munayaḥ*—sages; *yat*—that which; *acakṣata*—saw clearly; *ātman*—the spirit.

TRANSLATION

In order to create different planetary systems I had to undergo austerities and penance, and the Lord, thus being pleased with me, in-

carnated in four sanas [Sanaka, Sanatkumāra, Sanandana and Sanātana]. In the previous creation the spiritual truth was devastated, but the four sanas explained it so nicely that the truth at once became clearly perceived by the sages.

PURPORT

In the *Viṣṇu-sahasra-nāma* prayers there is a mention of the Lord's name as *sanāt* and *sanātanatama.* The Lord and the living entities are both qualitatively *sanātanam,* or eternal, but the Lord is *sanātanatama* or the eternal in the superlative degree. The living entities are positively *sanātanam,* but not superlatively because the living entities are apt to fall to the atmosphere of noneternity also. Therefore, the living entities are quantitatively different from the superlative *sanātana,* the Lord.

The word *san* is also used in the sense of charity; therefore when everything is given up in charity unto the Lord, the Lord reciprocates by giving Himself unto the devotee. This is confirmed in the *Bhagavad-gītā* also (Bg. 4.11): *ye yathā māṁ prapadyante.* Brahmājī wanted to create the whole cosmic situation as it was in the previous millennium, and because, in the last devastation, knowledge of the Absolute Truth was altogether erased from the universe, he desired that the same knowledge again be renovated; otherwise there would be no meaning in the creation. Because there is prime necessity for transcendental knowledge, the ever-conditioned souls are given a chance for liberation in every millennium of creation. This mission of Brahmājī was fulfilled by the grace of the Lord when the four *sanas,* namely Sanaka, Sanatkumāra, Sanandana, and Sanātana, appeared as his four sons. These four *sanas* were incarnations of the knowledge of the Supreme Lord, and as such they explained transcendental knowledge so explicitly that all the sages could at once assimilate this knowledge without the least difficulty. By following in the footsteps of the four Kumāras, one can at once see the Supreme Personality of Godhead within oneself.

TEXT 6

धर्मस्य दक्षदुहितर्यजनिष्ट मूर्त्यां
नारायणो नर इति स्वतपःप्रभावः ।
दृष्ट्वात्मनो भगवतो नियमावलोपं
देव्यस्त्वनङ्गपृतना घटितुं न शेकुः ॥ ६ ॥

dharmasya dakṣa-duhitary-ajaniṣṭa mūrtyāṁ
nārāyaṇo nara iti sva-tapaḥ prabhāvaḥ
dṛṣṭvātmano bhagavato niyamāvalopaṁ
devyas tv anaṅga-pṛtanā ghaṭituṁ na śekuḥ

dharmasya—of Dharma (the controller of religious principles); *dakṣa*—Dakṣa, one of the Prajāpatis; *duhitari*—unto the daughter; *ajaniṣṭa*—took birth; *mūrtyām*—of the name Mūrti; *nārāyaṇaḥ*—Nārāyaṇa; *naraḥ*—Nara; *iti*—thus; *sva-tapaḥ*—personal penances; *prabhāvaḥ*—strength; *dṛṣṭvā*—by seeing; *ātmanaḥ*—of His own; *bhagavataḥ*—of the Personality of Godhead; *niyama-avalopam*—breaking the vow; *devyaḥ*—celestial beauties; *tu*—but; *anaṅga-pṛtanāḥ*—companion of Cupid; *ghaṭitum*—to happen; *na*—never; *śekuḥ*—made possible.

TRANSLATION

In order to exhibit His personal way of austerity and penance, He appeared in twin forms as Nārāyaṇa and Nara in the womb of Mūrti, the wife of Dharma and the daughter of Dakṣa. Celestial beauties, the companions of Cupid, went to try to break His vows, but they were unsuccessful, for they saw that many beauties like them were emanating from Him, the Personality of Godhead.

PURPORT

The Lord, being the source of everything that be, is the origin of all austerities and penances also. Great vows of austerity are undertaken by sages to achieve success in self-realization. Human life is meant for such *tapasya*, with the great vow of celibacy or *brahmacarya. In the rigid life of tapasya, there is no place for the association of woman.* And because human life is meant for *tapasya*, for self-realization, factual human civilization, as conceived by the system of *sanātana-dharma* or the school of four castes and four orders of life, prescribes rigid dissociation from woman in three stages of life. In the order of gradual cultural development, one's life may be divided in four divisions: celibacy, household life, retirement, and renunciation. During the first stage of life, up to twenty-five years of age, a man may be trained as a *brahmacārī* under the guidance of a bona fide spiritual master just to understand that woman is the real binding force in the material existence. If anyone wants to get freedom from the material bondage of conditional life, he must get free from the attraction for the form of woman. Woman, or the fair sex, is the enchanting principle for the living entities, and the male form, especially of the human being, is meant for self-realization. The whole world is moving under the spell of womanly attraction, and as soon as a man becomes united with a woman, he at once becomes a victim of material bondage under a tight knot. The desires for lording it over the material world, under the intoxication of a false sense of lordship, specifically begin just after the man's unification with a woman. The desires for acquiring a house, possessing land, having children and becoming prominent in society, the affection for community and the place of birth, and the hankering for wealth, which are all like the phantasmagoria or illusory dreams of life, encumber a human being, and he is thus impeded in his progress toward self-realization, the real aim of life. The *brahmacārī*, or a boy from the age of five years, especially from the higher castes, namely from the scholarly parents (the *brāhmaṇas),* the administrative parents (the *kṣatriyas),* or the mercantile or productive parents (the *vaiśyas),* is trained until twenty-five years of age under the care of a bona fide *guru* or teacher, and under strict observance of discipline he comes to understand the values of life along with taking specific training for livelihood. The *brahmacārī* is then allowed to go home and enter householder life and get married to a suitable woman. But there are many *brahmacārīs* who do not go home to become householders but continue the life of *naiṣṭhika-brahmacārīs,* without any connection with women. They accept the order of *sannyāsa,* or the renounced order of life, knowing well that combination with women is an unnecessary burden that checks self-realization. Since sex desire is very strong at a certain stage of life, the *guru* may allow the *brahmacārī* to marry; this license is given to a *brahmacārī* who is unable to continue the way of *naiṣṭhika-brahmacarya,* and such discriminations are possible for the bona fide *guru.* A program of so-called family planning is needed. The householder who associates with woman under scriptural restrictions, after a thorough training of *brahmacarya,* cannot be a householder like cats and dogs. Such a householder, after fifty years of age, would retire from the association of woman as a *vānaprastha* to be trained up to live alone without the association of woman. When the practice is complete, the same retired householder becomes a *sannyāsī,* strictly separate from woman, even from his married wife. Studying the whole scheme of disassociation from women, it appears that a woman is a stumbling block for self-realization, and the Lord appeared as Nārāyaṇa to teach the principle of womanly disassociation with a vow in life. The demigods, being envious of the austere life of the rigid *brahmacārīs,* would try to cause them to break their vows by dispatching soldiers of Cupid. But in the case of the Lord, it became an unsuccessful attempt when the celestial beauties saw that the Lord can produce innumerable such beauties by His mystic internal potency, so there was no need to be attracted by others externally. There is a common proverb that a confectioner is never attracted by sweetmeats. The confectioner, who is always manufacturing sweetmeats, has very little desire to eat them; similarly, the Lord, by His pleasure potential powers, can produce innumerable spiritual beauties and not be the least attracted by the false beauties of material creation. One who does not know, foolishly alleges that Lord Kṛṣṇa enjoyed women in His *rāsa-līlā* in Vṛndāvana, or with His sixteen thousand married wives at Dvārakā.

TEXT 7

कामं दहन्ति कृतिनो ननु रोषदृष्ट्या
रोषं दहन्तमुत ते न दहन्त्यसह्यम् ।
सोऽयं यदन्तरमलं प्रविशन् बिभेति
कामः कथं नु पुनरस्य मनः श्रयेत ॥ ७ ॥

kāmaṁ dahanti kṛtino nanu roṣa-dṛṣṭyā
roṣaṁ dahantam uta te na dahanty asahyam
so 'yaṁ yad antaram alaṁ praviśan bibheti
kāmaḥ kathaṁ nu punar asya manaḥ śrayeta

kāmam—lust; *dahanti*—chastises; *kṛtinaḥ*—great stalwarts; *nanu*—but; *roṣa-dṛṣṭyā*—by wrathful glance; *roṣam*—wrath; *dahantam*—being overwhelmed; *uta*—although; *te*—they; *na*—cannot; *dahanti*—subjugate; *asahyam*—intolerable; *saḥ*—that; *ayam*—Him; *yat*—because; *antaram*—within; *alam*—however; *praviśan*—entering; *bibheti*—is afraid of; *kāmaḥ*—lust; *katham*—how; *nu*—as a matter of fact; *punaḥ*—again; *asya*—His; *manaḥ*—mind; *śrayeta*—take shelter of.

TRANSLATION

Great stalwarts like Lord Śiva can, by their wrathful glance, overcome lust and vanquish him, yet they cannot be free from the overwhelming effects of their own wrath. Such wrath can never enter into the heart of

Him [the Lord], who is above all this. So how can lust take shelter in His mind?

PURPORT

When Lord Śiva was engaged in severely austere meditation, Cupid, the demigod of lust, threw his arrow of sex desire, and Lord Śiva, thus being angry at him, glanced at Cupid in great wrath, and at once the body of Cupid was annihilated. Although Lord Śiva was so powerful, he was unable to get free from the effects of such wrath. But in the behavior of Lord Viṣṇu there is no incidence of such wrath at any time. On the contrary, Bhṛgu Muni tested the tolerance of the Lord by purposely kicking His chest, but instead of being angry at Bhṛgu Muni the Lord begged his pardon, saying that Bhṛgu Muni's leg might have been badly hurt due to His chest being too hard. The Lord has the sign of the foot of *Bhṛgu-pāda* as the mark of tolerance. The Lord, therefore, is never affected by any kind of wrath, so how can there be any place for lust, which is less strong than wrath? When lust or desire is not fulfilled, there is the appearance of wrath, but in the absence of wrath how can there by any place for lust? The Lord is known as *āpta-kāmaḥ,* or one who can fulfill His desires by Himself. He does not require anyone's help to satisfy His desires. The Lord is unlimited, and therefore His desires are also unlimited. All living entities but the Lord are limited in every respect; how then can the limited satisfy the desires of the unlimited? The conclusion is that the Absolute Personality of Godhead has neither lust nor anger, and even if there is sometimes a show of lust and anger by the Absolute, it should be considered an absolute benediction.

TEXT 8

विद्धः सपत्न्युदितपत्रिभिरन्ति राज्ञो
बालोऽपि सन्नुपगतस्तपसे वनानि ।
तस्मा अदाद् ध्रुवगतिं गृणते प्रसन्नो
दिव्याः स्तुवन्ति मुनयो यदुपर्यधस्तात् ॥ ८ ॥

viddhaḥ sapatny-udita-patribhir anti rājño
bālo 'pi sann upagatas tapase vanāni
tasmā adād dhruva-gatiṁ gṛṇate prasanno
divyāḥ stuvanti munayo yad upary-adhastāt

viddhaḥ—pinched by; *sapatni*—a co-wife; *udita*—uttered by; *patribhiḥ*—by sharp words; *anti*—just before; *rājñaḥ*—of the king; *bālaḥ*—a boy; *api*—although; *san*—being so; *upagataḥ*—took to; *tapase*—severe penances; *vanāni*—in a great forest; *tasmai*—therefore; *adāt*—gave as a reward; *dhruva-gatim*—a path to the Dhruva planet; *gṛṇate*—on being prayed for; *prasannaḥ*—being satisfied; *divyāḥ*—denizens of higher planets; *stuvanti*—do pray; *munayaḥ*—great sages; *yat*—thereupon; *upari*—up; *adhastāt*—down.

TRANSLATION

Being insulted by sharp words spoken by the co-wife of the king, even in his presence, Prince Dhruva, though only a boy, took to severe penances in the forest. And the Lord, being satisfied by his prayer, awarded him the Dhruva planet, which is worshiped by great sages, both upward and downward.

PURPORT

When he was only five years old, Prince Dhruva, a great devotee and the son of Mahārāja Uttānapāda, was sitting on the lap of his father. His stepmother did not like the King's patting her stepson, so she dragged him out, saying that he could not claim to sit on the lap of the King because he was not born out of her womb. The little boy felt insulted by this act of his stepmother. Nor did his father make any protest, for he was too attached to his second wife. After this incidence, Prince Dhruva went to his own mother and complained. His real mother also could not take any step against this insulting behavior, so she wept. The boy inquired from his mother how he could sit on the royal throne of his father, and the poor queen replied that only the Lord could help him. The boy inquired where the Lord could be seen, and the queen replied that it is said that the Lord is sometimes seen by great sages in the dense forest. The child prince decided to go into the forest to perform severe penances in order to achieve his objective.

Prince Dhruva performed a stringent type of penance under the instruction of his spiritual master, Śrī Nārada Muni, who was specifically deputed for this purpose by the Personality of Godhead. Prince Dhruva was initiated by Nārada to chant the hymn composed of eighteen letters, namely *om namo bhagavate vāsudevāya,* and Lord Vāsudeva incarnated Himself as Pṛśnigarbha, the Personality of Godhead with four hands, and awarded the Prince a specific planet above the seven stars. Prince Dhruva, after achieving success in his undertakings, saw the Lord face to face, and he was satisfied that all his needs were fulfilled.

The planet awarded to Prince Dhruva Mahārāja is a fixed Vaikuṇṭha planet, installed in the material atmosphere by the will of the Supreme Lord Vāsudeva. This planet, although within the material world, will not be annihilated at the time of devastation, but will remain fixed in its place. And, because it is a Vaikuṇṭha planet never to be annihilated, it is worshiped even by the denizens of the seven stars situated below the Dhruva planet, as well as the planets which are even above the Dhruva planet. Maharṣi Bhṛgu's planet is situated above the Dhruva planet.

So the Lord incarnated Himself as Pṛśnigarbha just to satisfy a pure devotee of the Lord. And this perfection was achieved by Prince Dhruva simply by chanting the hymn mentioned above, after being initiated by another pure devotee, Nārada. A serious personality can thus achieve the highest perfection of meeting the Lord and attain his objective simply by being guided by a pure devotee, who automatically approaches by dint of one's serious determination to meet the Lord by all means.

The description of Prince Dhruva's activities can be read in detail in the Fourth Canto of *Śrīmad-Bhāgavatam.*

TEXT 9

यद्वेनमुत्पथगतं द्विजवाक्यवज्र-
निष्प्लुष्टपौरुषभगं निरये पतन्तम् ।
त्रात्वार्थितो जगति पुत्रपदं च लेभे
दुग्धा वसूनि वसुधा सकलानि येन ॥ ९ ॥

yad venam utpatha-gataṁ dvija-vākya-vajra
niṣpluṣṭa-pauruṣa-bhagaṁ niraye patantam
trātvārthito jagati putra-padaṁ ca lebhe
dugdhā vasūni vasudhā sakalāni yena

yat—when; *venam*—unto King Vena; *utpatha-gatam*—going astray from the righteous path; *dvija*—of the *brāhmaṇas; vākya*—words of cursing; *vajra*—thunderbolt; *niṣpluṣṭa*—being burnt by; *pauruṣa*—great deeds; *bhagam*—opulence; *niraye*—into hell; *patantam*—going down; *trātvā*—by delivering; *arthitaḥ*—so being prayed for; *jagati*—on the world; *putra-padam*—the position of the son; *ca*—as well as; *lebhe*—achieved; *dugdhā*—exploited; *vasūni*—produce; *vasudhā*—the earth; *sakalāni*—all kinds of; *yena*—by whom.

TRANSLATION

Mahārāja Vena went astray from the path of righteousness, and the brāhmaṇas chastised him by the thunderbolt curse. By this King Vena was burnt with his good deeds and opulence and was en route to hell. The Lord, by His causeless mercy, descended as his son, by the name of Pṛthu, delivered the condemned King Vena from hell, and exploited the earth by drawing all kinds of crops as produce.

PURPORT

According to the system of *varṇāśrama-dharma,* the pious and learned *brāhmaṇas* were the natural guardians of society. The *brāhmaṇas,* by their learned labor of love, would instruct the administrator kings how to rule the country in complete righteousness, and thus the process would go on as a perfect welfare state. The kings or the *kṣatriya* administrators would always consult the council of learned *brāhmaṇas.* They were never autocratic monarchs. The scriptures like *Manu-saṁhitā* and other authorized books of the great sages were guiding principles for ruling the subjects, and there was no need for less intelligent persons to manufacture a code of law in the name of democracy. The less intelligent mass of people have very little knowledge of their own welfare, as the child has very little knowledge of its future well-being. The experienced father guides the innocent child towards the path of progress, and the childlike mass of people need similar guidance. The standard welfare codes are already there in the *Manu-saṁhitā* and other Vedic literatures. The learned *brāhmaṇas* would advise the king in terms of those standard books of knowledge and with reference to the particular situation of time and place. Such *brāhmaṇas* were not paid servants of the king, and therefore they had the strength to dictate to the king on the principles of scriptures. This system continued even up to the time of Mahārāja Candragupta, and the *brāhmaṇa* Cāṇakya was his unpaid prime minister.

Mahārāja Vena did not adhere to this principle of ruling, and he disobeyed the learned *brāhmaṇas.* The broad-minded *brāhmaṇas* were not self-interested, but looked to the interest of complete welfare for all the subjects. They wanted to chastise King Vena for his misconduct and so prayed to the Almighty Lord as well as cursed the king.

Long life, obedience, good reputation, righteousness, prospects of being promoted to higher planets, and blessings of great personalities are all vanquished simply by disobeying a great soul. One should strictly try to follow in the footsteps of great souls. Mahārāja Vena became a king, undoubtedly due to his past deeds of righteousness, but because he willfully neglected the great souls, he was punished by the loss of all the abovementioned acquisitions. In the *Vāmana Purāṇa,* the history of Mahārāja Vena and his degradation are fully described. When Mahārāja Pṛthu heard about the hellish condition of His father, Vena, who was suffering from leprosy in the family of a *mleccha,* he at once brought the former king to Kurukṣetra for his purification and relieved him from all sufferings.

Mahārāja Pṛthu, the incarnation of God, descended by the prayer of the *brāhmaṇas* to restore the disorders on earth. He produced all kinds of crops. But, at the same time, He performed the duty of a son who delivers the father from hellish conditions. The word *putra* means one who delivers from hell, called *put.* That is a worthy son.

TEXT 10

नाभेरसावृषभ आस सुदेविसूनु-
यों वै चचार समदृग् जडयोगचर्याम् ।
यत्पारमहंस्यमृषयः पदमामनन्ति
स्वस्थः प्रशान्तकरणः परिमुक्तसङ्गः॥१०॥

nābher asāv ṛṣabha āsa sudevi-sūnur
yo vai cacāra sama-dṛg jaḍa-yoga-caryām
yat pāramahaṁsyam ṛṣayaḥ padam āmananti
svasthaḥ praśānta-karaṇaḥ parimukta-saṅgaḥ

nābheḥ—by Mahārāja Nābhi; *asau*—the Personality of Godhead; *ṛṣabhaḥ*—Ṛṣabha; *āsa*—became; *sudevi*—Sudevī; *sūnuḥ*—the son of; *yaḥ*—who; *vai*—certainly; *cacāra*—performed; *sama-dṛk*—equibalanced; *jaḍa*—material; *yoga-caryām*—performance of *yoga; yat*—which; *pāramahaṁsyam*—the highest stage of perfection; *ṛṣayaḥ*—the learned sages; *padam*—situation; *āmananti*—do accept; *svasthaḥ*—self-reposed; *praśānta*—suspended; *karaṇaḥ*—the material senses; *parimukta*—perfectly liberated; *saṅgaḥ*—material contamination.

TRANSLATION

The Lord appeared as the son of Sudevī, the wife of King Nābhi, and was known as Ṛṣabhadeva. He performed materialistic yoga to equibalance the mind. This stage is also accepted as the highest perfectional situation of liberation, wherein one is situated in one's self and is completely satisfied.

PURPORT

Out of many types of mystic performances for self-realization, the process of *jaḍa-yoga* is also one accepted by authorities. This *jaḍa-yoga* involves practicing becoming like a dumb stone without being affected by material reactions. Just as a stone is indifferent to all kinds of attacks and reattacks of external situations, similarly one practices *jaḍa-yoga* by tolerating voluntary infliction of pain upon the material body. Such *yogīs*, out of many self-infliction methods, practice plucking out the hairs on their head, without shaving and without any instrumental help. But the real purpose of such *jaḍa-yoga* practice is to get free from all material affection and to be completely situated in the self. At the last stage of his life, Emperor Ṛṣabhadeva wandered like a dumb madman without being affected by all kinds of bodily mistreatment. Seeing him like a madman, wandering naked with long hair and a long beard, less intelligent children and men in the street used to spit on him and urinate on his body. He used to lie in his own stool and never move. But the stool of his body was flavored like the smell of fragrant flowers, and a saintly person would recognize him as a *paramahaṁsa,* one in the highest state of human perfection. One who is not able to make his stool fragrant should not, however, imitate Emperor Ṛṣabhadeva. The practice of *jaḍa-yoga* was possible by Ṛṣabhadeva and others on the same level of perfection, but such an uncommon practice is impossible for an ordinary man.

The real purpose of *jaḍa-yoga,* as mentioned here in this verse, is *praśānta-karaṇaḥ,* or subduing the senses. The whole process of *yoga,* under whatever heading it may be, is to control the unbridled material senses and thus prepare oneself for self-realization. In this age specifically, this *jaḍa-yoga* cannot be of any practical value, but on the other hand the practice of *bhakti-yoga* is feasible because it is just suitable for this age. The simple method of hearing from the rightful source of *Śrīmad-Bhāgavatam* will lead one to the highest perfectional stage of *yoga.* Ṛṣabhadeva was the son of King Nābhi and the grandson of King Āgnīdhra, and he was the father of King Bharata, after whose name this planet earth was called *Bhāratavarṣa.* Ṛṣabhadeva's mother was also known as Merudevī, although her name is mentioned here as Sudevī. It is sometimes proposed that Sudevī was another wife of King Āgnīdhra, but since King Ṛṣabhadeva is mentioned elsewhere as the son of Merudevī, it is clear that Merudevī and Sudevī are the same person under different names.

TEXT 11

सत्रे ममास भगवान् हयशीरषाथो
साक्षात् स यज्ञपुरुषस्तपनीयवर्णः ।
छन्दोमयो मखमयोऽखिलदेवतात्मा
वाचो बभूवुरुशतीः श्वसतोऽस्य नस्तः ॥ ११ ॥

satre mamāsa bhagavān haya-śīraṣātho
sākṣāt sa yajña-puruṣas tapanīya-varṇaḥ
chandomayo makhamayo'khila-devatātmā
vāco babhūvur uśatīḥ śvasato'sya nastaḥ

satre—in the sacrificial ceremony; *mama*—of mine; *āsa*—appeared; *bhagavān*—the Personality of Godhead; *haya-śīraṣā*—with His horselike head; *atha*—thus; *sākṣāt*—directly; *saḥ*—He; *yajña-puruṣaḥ*—the person who is pleased by performances of sacrifice; *tapanīya*—golden; *varṇaḥ*—hue; *chandomayaḥ*—personified Vedic hymns; *makhamayaḥ*—personified sacrifices; *akhila*—all that be; *devatā-ātmā*—soul of the demigods; *vācaḥ*—sounds; *babhūvaḥ*—become audible; *uśatīḥ*—very pleasing to hear; *śvasataḥ*—while breathing; *asya*—His; *nastaḥ*—through the nostrils.

TRANSLATION

The Lord appeared as the Hayagrīva incarnation in the sacrifice performed by Brahmā. He was the personified sacrifices, and the hue of His body was golden. He is the personified Vedas as well, and the Supersoul of all demigods. When He breathed, all the sweet sounds of the Vedic hymns came out of His nostrils.

PURPORT

The Vedic hymns are generally meant for sacrifices to be performed by the fruitive workers who also want to satisfy the demigods to achieve their fruitive result. But the Lord is the personified sacrifices and personified Vedic hymns. Therefore one who is directly a devotee of the Lord is a person who has automatically both served the purposes of sacrifices and pleased the demigods. The devotees of the Lord may not perform any sacrifice or may not please the demigods as per Vedic injunctions, and still the devotee is on a higher level than the fruitive workers or the worshipers of different demigods.

TEXT 12

मत्स्यो युगान्तसमये मनुनोपलब्धः
क्षोणीमयो निखिलजीवनिकायकेतः ।
विस्रंसितानुरुभये सलिले मुखान्मे
आदाय तत्र विजहार ह वेदमार्गान् ॥१२॥

matsyo yugānta-samaye manunopalabdhaḥ
kṣoṇīmayo nikhila-jīva-nikāya-ketaḥ
visraṁsitān uru-bhaye salile mukhān me
ādāya tatra vijahāra ha veda-mārgān

matsyaḥ—incarnation of the fish; *yuga-anta*—at the end of the millennium; *samaye*—at the time of; *manunā*—the would-be Vaivasvata Manu; *upalabdhaḥ*—seen; *kṣoṇīmayaḥ*—up to the earthly planets; *nikhila*—all; *jīva*—living entities; *nikāya-ketaḥ*—shelter for; *visraṁsitān*—emanating from; *uru*—great; *bhaye*—out of fear; *salile*—in the water; *mukhāt*—from the mouth; *me*—mine; *ādāya*—having taken to; *tatra*—there; *vijahāra*—enjoyed; *ha*—certainly; *veda-mārgān*—all the *Vedas*.

TRANSLATION

At the end of the millennium, the would-be Vaivasvata Manu, of the name Satyavrata, would see that the Lord in the fish incarnation is the shelter of all kinds of living entities, up to those in the earthly planet. Out

of fear of the vast water, at the end of the millennium, the Vedas come out of my [Brahmā's] mouth, and the Lord enjoys those vast waters and protects the Vedas.

PURPORT

During one day of Brahmā, there are fourteen Manus, and at the end of each Manu, there is devastation up to the earthly planets, and the vast water is fearful even to the personality of Brahmā. So in the beginning of the would-be Vaivasvata Manu, such devastation would be seen by him. There would be many other incidences also, such as the killing of the famous Śaṅkhāsura, etc. This foretelling is by past experience of Brahmājī, who knew that in that fearful devastating scene, the *Vedas* would come out of his mouth, but the Lord in His fish incarnation not only would save all living entities, namely the demigods, animals, man and the great sages, but would also save the *Vedas*.

TEXT 13

क्षीरोदधावमरदानवयूथपाना-
मुन्मथ्नताममृतलब्धय आदिदेवः ।
पृष्ठेन कच्छपवपुर्विदधार गोत्रं
निद्राक्षणोऽद्रिपरिवर्तकषाणकण्डूः ॥१३॥

kṣīrodadhāv amara-dānava-yūthapānām
unmathnatām amṛta-labdhaya ādi-devaḥ
pṛṣṭhena kacchapa-vapur vidadhāra gotraṁ
nidrākṣaṇo'dri-parivarta-kaṣāṇa-kaṇḍūḥ

kṣīra—milk; *udadhau*—in the ocean of; *amara*—the demigods; *dānava*—the demons; *yūtha-pānām*—of the leaders of both hosts; *unmathnatām*—while churning; *amṛta*—nectar; *labdhaya*—for gaining; *ādi-devaḥ*—the primeval Lord; *pṛṣṭhena*—by the backbone; *kacchapa*—tortoise; *vapuḥ*—body; *vidadhāra*—assumed; *gotram*—the Mandara Hill; *nidrākṣaṇaḥ*—while partly sleeping; *adri-parivarta*—rolling the hill; *kaṣāṇa*—scratching; *kaṇḍūḥ*—itching.

TRANSLATION

The primeval Lord then assumed the tortoise incarnation in order to serve as a resting place [pivot] for the Mandara Mountain, which was acting as a churning rod. The demigods and demons were churning the ocean of milk with the Mandara Mountain in order to extract nectar. The mountain moved back and forth, scratching the back of Lord Tortoise, who, while partly sleeping, was experiencing an itching sensation.

PURPORT

Although it is not in our experience, there is a milk ocean within this universe. It is accepted even by the modern scientist that there are hundreds and hundreds of thousands of planets hovering over our heads, and each of them has different kinds of climatic conditions. *Śrīmad-Bhāgavatam* gives much information which may not tally with our present experience. But as far as Indian sages are concerned, knowledge is received from the Vedic literatures, and the authorities accept without any hesitation that we should look through the pages of authentic books of knowledge *(śāstra-cakṣusvat).* So we cannot deny the existence of the ocean of milk as stated in the *Śrīmad-Bhāgavatam* unless and until we have experimentally seen all the planets hovering in space. Since such an experiment is not possible, naturally we have to accept the statement of *Śrīmad-Bhāgavatam* as it is because it is so accepted by spiritual leaders like Śrīdhara Svāmī, Jīva Gosvāmī, Viśvanātha Cakravartī and others. The Vedic process is to follow in the footsteps of great authorities, and that is the only process for knowing that which is beyond our imagination.

The primeval Lord, being all-powerful, can do whatever He likes, and therefore His assuming the incarnation of a tortoise or a fish for serving a particular purpose is not at all astonishing. Therefore we should not have any hesitation whatsoever in accepting the statements of the authentic scriptures like *Śrīmad-Bhāgavatam.*

The gigantic work of churning the milk ocean by combined effort of the demigods and the demons required a gigantic resting ground or pivot for the gigantic Mandara Hill. Thus to help the attempt of the demigods the primeval Lord assumed the incarnation of a gigantic tortoise, swimming in the ocean of milk. At the same time, the mountain scratched His backbone as He was partly sleeping and thus relieved His itching sensation.

TEXT 14

त्रैपिष्टपोरुभयहा स नृसिंहरूपं
कृत्वा भ्रमद्भ्रुकुटिदंष्ट्रकरालवक्त्रम् ।
दैत्येन्द्रमाशु गदयाभिपतन्तमारा-
दूरौ निपात्य विददार नखैः स्फुरन्तम् ॥१४॥

trai-piṣṭaporu-bhaya-hā sa nṛsiṁha-rūpaṁ
kṛtvā bhramad-bhrukuṭi-daṁṣṭra-karāla-vaktram
daityendram āśu gadayābhipatantam
ārād ūrau nipātya vidadāra nakhaiḥ sphurantam

trai-piṣṭapa—the demigods; *uru-bhaya-hā*—one who vanquishes great fears; *saḥ*—He, the Personality of Godhead; *nṛsiṁha-rūpam*—assuming the incarnation Nṛsiṁha; *kṛtvā*—doing so; *bhramat*—by rolling; *bhru-kuṭi*—eyebrows; *daṁṣṭra*—teeth; *karāla*—greatly fearful; *vaktram*—mouth; *daitya-indram*—the king of the demons; *āśu*—immediately; *gadayā*—with club in hand; *abhipatantam*—while falling down; *ārāt*—nearby; *ūrau*—on the thighs; *nipātya*—placing on; *vidadāra*—pierced; *nakhaiḥ*—by the nails; *sphurantam*—while challenging.

TRANSLATION

The Personality of Godhead assumed the incarnation of Narasiṁhadeva in order to vanquish the great fears of the demigods. He killed the king of the demons [Hiraṇyakaśipu], who challenged the Lord with a club in his hand, by placing the demon on His thighs and piercing him with His nails, rolling His eyebrows in anger and showing His fearful teeth and mouth.

PURPORT

The history of Hiraṇyakaśipu and his great devotee son Prahlāda Mahārāja is narrated in the Seventh Canto of *Śrīmad-Bhāgavatam.* Hiraṇyakaśipu became very powerful by material achievements and thought himself to be immortal by the grace of Brahmājī. Brahmājī declined to award him the benediction of immortality because he himself is not an immortal being. But Hiraṇyakaśipu derived Brahmājī's benediction in a roundabout way, almost equal to becoming an immortal being. Hiraṇyakaśipu was sure that he would not be killed by any man or demigod or by any kind of known weapon, nor would he die in day or night. The Lord, however, assumed the incarnation of half-man and half-lion, which was beyond the imagination of a materialistic demon like Hiraṇyakaśipu, and thus, keeping pace with the benediction of Brahmājī, the Lord killed him. He killed him on His lap, so that he was killed neither on the land nor on the water nor in the sky. He was pierced by Narasiṁha's nails, which were beyond the human weapons imaginable by Hiraṇyakaśipu. The literal meaning of Hiraṇyakaśipu is one who is after gold and soft bedding, the ultimate aim of all materialistic men. Such demonic men, who have no relationship with God, gradually become puffed up by material acquisitions and begin to challenge the authority of the Supreme Lord and torture those who are devotees of the Lord. Prahlāda Mahārāja happened to be the son of Hiraṇyakaśipu, and because he was a great devotee, his father tortured him to the best of his ability. In this extreme situation, the Lord assumed the incarnation of Narasiṁhadeva, and just to finish the enemy of the demigods, the Lord killed Hiraṇyakaśipu in a manner which was beyond the demon's imagination. Materialistic plans of godless demons are always frustrated by the all-powerful Lord.

TEXT 15

अन्तःसरस्युरुबलेन पदे गृहीतो
ग्राहेण यूथपतिरम्बुजहस्त आर्तः ।
आहेदमादिपुरुषाखिललोकनाथ
तीर्थश्रवः श्रवणमङ्गलनामधेय ॥१५॥

antaḥ-sarasy uru-balena pade gṛhīto
grāheṇa yūtha-patir ambuja-hasta ārtaḥ
āhedam ādi-puruṣākhila-loka-nātha
tīrtha-śravaḥ śravaṇa-maṅgala-nāmadheya

antaḥ-sarasi—within the river; *uru-balena*—by superior strength; *pade*—leg; *gṛhītaḥ*—being taken up; *grāheṇa*—by the crocodile; *yūtha-patiḥ*—of the leader of the elephants; *ambuja-hastaḥ*—with a lotus flower in the hand; *ārtaḥ*—greatly aggrieved; *āha*—addressed; *idam*—like this; *ādi-puruṣa*—the original enjoyer; *akhila-loka-nātha*—the Lord of the universe; *tīrtha-śravaḥ*—

as famous as a place of pilgrimage; *śravaṇa-maṅgala*—all good simply by hearing the name; *nāma-dheya*—whose holy name is worth chanting.

TRANSLATION

The leader of the elephants, whose leg was attacked in the river by a crocodile of superior strength, was much aggrieved. Taking a lotus flower in his trunk, he addressed the Lord, saying, 'O original enjoyer, Lord of the universe! O deliverer, as famous as the place of pilgrimage! All are purified simply by hearing Your holy name, which is worthy to be chanted.'

PURPORT

The history of delivering the leader of the elephants, whose leg was attacked in the river by the superior strength of a crocodile, is described in the Eighth Canto of *Śrīmad-Bhāgavatam (Bhāg.* 8.2.4). Since the Lord is absolute knowledge, there is no difference between His holy name and the Personality of Godhead. The leader of the elephants was much distressed when he was attacked by the crocodile. Although the elephant is always stronger than the crocodile, the latter is stronger than the elephant when it is in the water. And because the elephant was a great devotee of the Lord in his previous birth, he was able to chant the holy name of the Lord by dint of his past good deeds. Every living entity is always distressed in this material world because this place is such that in every step one has to meet with some kind of distress. But one who is supported by his past good deeds engages himself in the devotional service of the Lord, as is confirmed in the *Bhagavad-gītā* (Bg. 7.19). Those who are supported by impious acts cannot be engaged in the devotional service of the Lord, even though they are distressed. This is also confirmed in the *Bhagavad-gītā* (Bg. 7.15). The Personality of Godhead Hari appeared at once on the back of His eternal bearer Garuḍa and delivered the elephant.

The elephant was conscious of his relation with the Supreme Lord. He addressed the Lord as *ādi-puruṣa,* or the original enjoyer. Both the Lord and the living beings are conscious and are therefore enjoyers, but the Lord is the original enjoyer because He is the creator of everything. In a family, both the father and his sons are undoubtedly enjoyers, but the father is the original enjoyer, and the sons are subsequent enjoyers. A pure devotee knows well that everything in the universe is the property of the Lord, and a living entity can enjoy a thing as ordained by the Lord. A living being cannot even touch a thing which is not alloted to him. This idea of the original enjoyer is explained very nicely in the *Īśopaniṣad.* One who knows this difference between the Lord and himself never accepts anything without first offering it to the Lord.

The elephant addressed the Lord as *akhila-loka-nātha,* or the Lord of the universe, and as such He is the Lord of the elephant also. The elephant, being a pure devotee of the Lord, specifically deserved to be saved from the attack of the crocodile, and because it is a promise of the Lord that His devotee will never be vanquished, it was quite befitting that the elephant called upon the Lord to protect him, and the merciful Lord also at once responded. The Lord is the protector of everyone, but He is the first protector of one who acknowledges the superiority of the Lord without being so falsely proud as to deny the superiority of the Lord or to claim to be equal to Him. He is ever superior. A pure devotee of the Lord knows this difference between the Lord and himself. Therefore a pure devotee is given first preference because of his full dependence, whereas the person who denies the existence of the Lord and declares himself the Lord is called *asura,* and as such he is given protection by the strength of limited power subject to the sanction of the Lord. Since the Lord is superior to everyone, His perfection is also superior. No one can imagine it.

The elephant addressed the Lord as *tīrtha-śravaḥ,* or "famous as the place of pilgrimage." People go to places of pilgrimage in order to be delivered from the reactions of unknown sinful acts. But one can be freed from all sinful reactions simply by remembering His holy name. The Lord is therefore as good as the holy places of pilgrimage. One can be free from all sinful reactions after reaching a place of pilgrimage, but one can have the same benefit at home or at any place simply by chanting the holy name of the Lord. For a pure devotee, there is no need to go to the holy place of pilgrimage. He can be delivered from all sinful acts simply by remembering the Lord in earnestness. A pure devotee of the Lord never commits any sinful acts, but because the whole world is full of the sinful atmosphere, even a pure devotee may commit a sin unconsciously, as a matter of course. One who commits sinful acts consciously cannot be worthy of becoming a devotee of the Lord, but a pure devotee who unconsciously does something sinful is certainly delivered by the Lord because a pure devotee remembers the Lord always.

The Lord's holy name is called *śravaṇa-maṅgala.* This means that everything auspicious is received simply by hearing the holy name. In another place in *Śrīmad-Bhāgavatam,* His holy name is described as *puṇya-śravaṇa-*

kīrtana. It is a pious act simply to chant and hear all about the Lord. The Lord descends on this earth and acts like others in connection with the activities of the world just to create subject matter for hearing about Him; otherwise the Lord has nothing to do in this world, nor has He any obligation to do anything. He comes out of His own causeless mercy and acts as He desires, and the *Vedas* and *Purāṇas* are full of descriptions of His different activities so that people in general may naturally be eager to hear and read something about His activities. Generally, however, the modern fictions and novels of the world occupy a greater part of people's valuable time. Such literatures cannot do good to anyone; on the contrary, they agitate the young mind unnecessarily and increase the modes of passion and ignorance, leading to increasing bondage to the material conditions. The same aptitude for hearing and reading is better utilized in hearing and reading of the Lord's activities. This will give one all around benefit.

It is concluded, therefore, that the holy name of the Lord and things in relation with Him are always worth hearing, and therefore He is called here in this verse *nāma-dheya,* or one whose holy name is worth chanting.

TEXT 16

श्रुत्वा हरिस्तमरणार्थिनमप्रमेय-
श्चक्रायुधः पतगराजभुजाधिरूढः ।
चक्रेण नक्रवदनं विनिपाट्य तस्मा-
द्धस्ते प्रगृह्य भगवान् कृपयोज्जहार ॥१६॥

śrutvā haris tam araṇārthinam aprameyaś
cakrāyudhaḥ patagarāja-bhujādhirūḍhaḥ
cakreṇa nakra-vadanaṁ vinipāṭya tasmādd
haste pragṛhya bhagavān kṛpayojjahāra

śrutvā—by hearing; *hariḥ*—the Personality of Godhead; *tam*—him; *araṇa-arthinam*—one who is in need of help; *aprameyaḥ*—the unlimitedly powerful Lord; *cakra*—wheel; *āyudhaḥ*—equipped with His weapon; *pataga-rāja*—the king of the birds (Garuḍa); *bhuja-adhirūḍhaḥ*—being seated on the wings of; *cakreṇa*—by the wheel; *nakra-vadanam*—the mouth of the crocodile; *vinipāṭya*—cutting in two; *tasmāt*—from the mouth of the crocodile; *haste*—in the hands; *pragṛhya*—taking hold of the trunk; *bhagavān*—the

Personality of Godhead; *kṛpayā*—out of causeless mercy; *ujjahāra*—delivered him.

TRANSLATION

The Personality of Godhead, after hearing the elephant's plea, felt that he needed His immediate help, for he was in great distress. Thus at once the Lord appeared there on the wings of the king of birds, Garuḍa, fully equipped with His weapon, the wheel [cakra]. And with the wheel He cut to pieces the mouth of the crocodile to save the elephant, and He delivered the elephant by lifting him by his trunk.

PURPORT

The Lord resides in His Vaikuṇṭha planet. No one can estimate how far away this planet is situated. It is said, however, that anyone trying to reach that planet by airships or by mindships, traveling for millions of years, will find it still unknown. Modern scientists have invented airships which are material, and a still finer material attempt is made by the *yogīs* to travel by mindships. The *yogīs* can reach any distant place very quickly with the help of mindships. But neither the airship nor the mindship has access into the kingdom of God in the Vaikuṇṭhaloka, situated far beyond the material sky. Since this is the situation, how was it possible for the prayers of the elephant to be heard from such an unlimitedly distant place, and how could the Lord at once appear on the spot? These things cannot be calculated by human imagination. All this was possible by the unlimited power of the Lord, and therefore the Lord is described here as *aprameya,* for not even the best human brain can estimate His powers and potencies by mathematical calculation. The Lord can hear from such a distant place, He can eat from there, and He can appear simultaneously in all places at a moment's notice. Such is the omnipotency of the Lord.

TEXT 17

ज्यायान् गुणैरवरजोऽप्यदितेः सुतानां
लोकान् विचक्रम इमान् यदथाधियज्ञः।
क्ष्मां वामनेन जगृहे त्रिपदच्छलेन
याच्ञामृते पथि चरन् प्रभुभिर्न चाल्यः॥१७॥

jyāyān guṇair avarajo'py aditeḥ sutānāṁ
lokān vicakrama imān yad athādhiyajñaḥ
kṣmāṁ vāmanena jagṛhe tripadacchalena
yācñām ṛte pathi caran prabhubhir na cālyaḥ

jyāyān—the greatest; *guṇaiḥ*—by qualities; *avarajaḥ*—transcendental; *api*—although He is so; *aditeḥ*—of Aditi; *sutānām*—of all the sons known as Ādityas; *lokān*—all the planets; *vicakrame*—surpassed; *imān*—in this universe; *yat*—one who; *atha*—therefore; *adhiyajñaḥ*—the Supreme Personality of Godhead; *kṣmām*—all the lands; *vāmanena*—in the incarnation of Vāmana; *jagṛhe*—accepted; *tri-pada*—three steps; *chalena*—by pretention; *yācñām*—begging; *ṛte*—without; *pathi caran*—passing over the right path; *prabhubhiḥ*—by authorities; *na*—never to be; *cālyaḥ*—to be bereft of.

TRANSLATION

The Lord, although transcendental to all material modes, still surpassed all qualities of the sons of Aditi, known as the Ādityas. The Lord appeared as the youngest son of Aditi. And because He surpassed all the planets of the universe, He is the Supreme Personality of Godhead. On the pretense of asking for a measurement of three footsteps of land, He took away all the lands of Bali Mahārāja. He asked simply because without begging, no authority can take one's rightful possession.

PURPORT

The history of Bali Mahārāja and his charity to Vāmanadeva is described in the Eighth Canto of *Śrīmad-Bhāgavatam*. Bali Mahārāja conquered all the planets of the universe by rightful possession. A king can conquer other kings by strength, and such possession is considered to be rightful. So Bali Mahārāja possessed all the lands of the universe, and he happened to be charitably disposed toward the *brāhmaṇas*. The Lord therefore pretended to be a beggar *brāhmaṇa,* and He asked for a measurement of three footsteps of land from Bali Mahārāja. The Lord, as the proprietor of everything, could take from him all the lands that Bali Mahārāja possessed, but He did not do so because Bali Mahārāja possessed all those lands by king's rights. While Bali Mahārāja was asked by Lord Vāmana for such small charity, the spiritual master of Bali Mahārāja, namely Śukrācārya, objected to this proposal because he knew that Vāmanadeva was Viṣṇu

Himself, pretending to be a beggar. Bali Mahārāja did not agree to abide by the order of his spiritual master when he understood that the beggar was Viṣṇu Himself, and he at once agreed to give Him in charity the land requested. By this agreement Lord Vāmana covered all the lands of the universe with His first two steps and then asked Bali Mahārāja where to place the third step. Bali Mahārāja was very glad to receive the Lord's remaining step upon his head, and thus Bali Mahārāja, instead of losing everything that he possessed, was blessed by the Lord's becoming his constant companion and doorman. So, by giving everything to the cause of the Lord, one does not lose anything, but he gains everything that he could never otherwise expect.

TEXT 18

नार्थो बलेरयमुरुक्रमपादशौच-
मापः शिखा धृतवतो विबुधाधिपत्यम्।
यो वै प्रतिश्रुतमृते न चिकीर्षदन्य-
दात्मानमङ्ग मनसा हरयेऽभिमेने ॥१८॥

nārtho baler ayam urukrama-pāda-śaucam
āpaḥ śikhā-dhṛtavato vibudhādhipatyam
yo vai pratiśrutam ṛte na cikīrṣad anyad
ātmānam aṅga manasā haraye' bhimene

na—never; *arthaḥ*—of any value in comparison with; *baleḥ*—of strength; *ayam*—this; *urukrama-pāda-śaucam*—the water washed from the feet of the Personality of Godhead; *āpaḥ*—water; *sikhā-dhṛtavataḥ*—of one who has kept it on his head; *vibudha-adhipatyam*—supremacy over the kingdom of the demigods; *yaḥ*—one who; *vai*—certainly; *pratiśrutam*—what was duly promised; *ṛte na*—besides that; *cikīrṣat*—tried for; *anyat*—anything else; *ātmānam*—even his personal body; *aṅga*—O Nārada; *manasā*—within his mind; *haraye*—unto the Supreme Lord; *abhimene*—dedicated.

TRANSLATION

Bali Mahārāja, who put on his head the water washed from the lotus feet of the Lord, did not think of anything else besides his promise, in

spite of being forbidden by his spiritual master. The king dedicated his own personal body to fulfill the measurement of the Lord's third step. For such a personality, even the kingdom of heaven, which he conquered by his strength, was of no value.

PURPORT

Bali Mahārāja, by gaining the transcendental favor of the Lord in exchange for his great material sacrifice, was able to have a place in the Vaikuṇṭhaloka with equal or greater facilities of eternal enjoyment; therefore he was not at all the loser by sacrificing the kingdom of heaven, which he possessed by his material strength. In other words, when the Lord snatches away one's hard-earned material possessions and favors one with His personal transcendental service for eternal life, bliss and knowledge, such taking away by the Lord should be considered a special favor upon such a pure devotee.

Material possessions, however alluring they may be, cannot be permanent possessions. Therefore one has to voluntarily give up such possessions, or one has to leave such possessions at the time of quitting this material body. The sane man knows that all material possessions are temporary, and the best use of such possessions is to engage them in the service of the Lord so that the Lord may be pleased with him and award him a permanent place in His *param dhāma.*

In the *Bhagavad-gītā,* the *param dhāma* of the Lord is described as follows:

nirmāna-mohā jita-saṅga-doṣā
adhyātma-nityā vinivṛtta-kāmāḥ
dvandvair vimuktāḥ sukha-duḥkha-saṁjñair
gacchanty amūḍhāḥ padam avyayaṁ tat

na tad bhāsayate sūryo
na śaśāṅko na pāvakaḥ
yad gatvā na nivartante
tad dhāma paramaṁ mama (Bg. 15.5-6)

One who possesses more in this material world, in the shape of houses, land, children, society, friendship and wealth, possesses these things only for the time being. One cannot possess all this illusory paraphernalia, created by *māyā*, permanently. Such a possessor is more illusioned in the matter of his self-realization; therefore one should possess less or nothing, so that he may be free from artificial prestige. We are contaminated in the material world by association with the three modes of material nature. Therefore, the more one is spiritually advanced by devotional service to the Lord, in exchange for his temporary possessions, the more one is freed from the attachment of material illusion. And to achieve this stage of life one must be firmly convinced about spiritual existence and its permanent effects. To know exactly the permanency of spiritual existence, one must voluntarily practice to possess less or the minimum only to maintain the material existence without any difficulty. One should not create artificial needs. That will help one to be satisfied with the minimum. Artificial needs of life are activities of the senses. The modern advancement of civilization is based on these activities of the senses, or, in other words, it is the civilization of sense gratification. Perfect civilization is the civilization of *ātmā*, or the soul proper. The civilized man of sense gratification is on an equal level with animals because animals cannot go beyond the activities of the senses. Above the senses there is the mind. The civilization of mental speculation is also not the perfect stage of life because above the mind there is the intelligence, and the *Bhagavad-gītā* gives us information of the intellectual civilization. The Vedic literatures give different directions for the human civilization, including the civilization of the senses, of the mind, of intelligence, and the civilization of the soul proper. The *Bhagavad-gītā* primarily deals with the intelligence of man, leading one to the progressive path of the civilization of the spirit soul. And *Śrīmad-Bhāgavatam* is the complete human civilization dealing with the subject matter of the soul proper. As soon as a man is raised to the status of the civilization of the soul, he is fit to be promoted to the kingdom of God, and the kingdom of God is described in the *Bhagavad-gītā* as per the above verses.

The primary information of the kingdom of God informs us that there is no need of sun nor moon nor of electricity, which are all necessary in this material world of darkness. And the secondary information of the kingdom of God explains that anyone able to reach that kingdom by adoption of the civilization of the soul proper, or, in other words, by the method of *bhakti-yoga*, attains the highest perfection of life. One is then situated in the permanent existence of the soul, with full knowledge of transcendental loving service for the Lord. Bali Mahārāja accepted this civilization of the soul in exchange for his great material possession and thus became fit for promotion to the kingdom of God. The kingdom of heaven, which he achieved by dint of his material power, was considered most insignificant in comparison with the kingdom of God.

Those who have attained the comforts of material civilization, made for sense gratification, should try to attain the kingdom of God by following in the footsteps of Bali Mahārāja, who exchanged his acquired material strength, adopting the process of *bhakti-yoga* as recommended in the *Bhagavad-gītā* and further explained in the *Śrīmad-Bhāgavatam.*

TEXT 19

तुभ्यं च नारद भृशं भगवान् विवृद्ध-
भावेन साधुपरितुष्ट उवाच योगम् ।
ज्ञानं च भागवतमात्मसतत्त्वदीपं
यद्वासुदेवशरणा विदुरञ्जसैव ॥१९॥

tubhyaṁ ca nārada bhṛśaṁ bhagavān vivṛddha-
bhāvena sādhu parituṣṭa uvāca yogam
jñānaṁ ca bhāgavatam ātma-satattva-dīpaṁ
yad vāsudeva-śaraṇā vidur añjasaiva

tubhyam—unto you; *ca*—also; *nārada*—O Nārada; *bhṛśam*—very nicely; *bhagavān*—the Personality of Godhead; *vivṛddha*—developed; *bhāvena*—by transcendental love; *sādhu*—your goodness; *parituṣṭaḥ*—being satisfied; *uvāca*—described; *yogam*—service; *jñānam*—knowledge; *ca*—also; *bhāgavatam*—the science of God and His devotional service; *ātma*—the self; *satattva*—with all details; *dīpam*—just like the light in the darkness; *yat*—that which; *vāsudeva-śaraṇāḥ*—those who are souls surrendered unto Lord Vāsudeva; *viduḥ*—know them; *añjasā*—perfectly well; *eva*—as it is.

TRANSLATION

O Nārada, you were taught about the science of God and His transcendental loving service by the Personality of Godhead in His incarnation of Haṁsāvatāra. He was very much pleased with you, due to your intense proportion of devotional service. He also explained unto you, lucidly, the full science of devotional service, which is especially understandable by persons who are souls surrendered unto Lord Vāsudeva, the Personality of Godhead.

PURPORT

The devotee and devotional service are two correlative terms. Unless one is inclined to be a devotee of the Lord, he cannot enter into the intracacies of devotional service. Lord Śrī Kṛṣṇa wanted to explain the *Bhagavad-gītā,* which is the science of devotional service, unto Śrī Arjuna because Arjuna was not only a friend of Lord Kṛṣṇa, but was a great devotee as well. The whole process is that all living entities, being constitutionally parts and parcels of the supreme living being, the Absolute Personality of Godhead, have proportionately minute independence of action also. So the preliminary qualification for entering into the devotional service of the Lord is that one become a willing cooperator, and as such one should voluntarily cooperate with persons who are already engaged in the transcendental devotional service of the Lord. By cooperating with such persons, the prospective candidate will gradually learn the techniques of devotional service, and with the progress of such learning one becomes proportionately free from the contamination of material association. Such a purificatory process will establish the prospective candidate in firm faith and gradually elevate him to the stage of transcendental taste for such devotional service. Thus he acquires a genuine attachment for the devotional service of the Lord, and his conviction carries him on to the point of ecstasy, just prior to the stage of transcendental love.

Such knowledge of devotional service may be divided into two sections, namely preliminary knowledge of the nature of devotional service and the secondary knowledge of execution. *Bhāgavatam* is in relation with the Personality of Godhead, His beauty, fame, opulence, dignity, attraction and transcendental qualities which attract one towards Him for exchange of love and affection. There is a natural affinity of the living entity for the loving service of the Lord. This affinity becomes artificially covered by the influence of material association, and *Śrīmad-Bhāgavatam* helps one very genuinely remove that artificial covering. Therefore it is particularly mentioned herein that *Śrīmad-Bhāgavatam* acts like the lamp of transcendental knowledge. These two sections of transcendental knowledge in devotional service become revealed to a person who is a soul surrendered unto Vāsudeva; as it is said in the *Bhagavad-gītā* (Bg. 7.19), such a great soul, fully surrendered unto the lotus feet of Vāsudeva, is very, very rare.

TEXT 20

चक्रं च दिक्ष्वविहतं दशसु स्वतेजो
मन्वन्तरेषु मनुवंशधरो बिभर्ति ।
दुष्टेषु राजसु दमं व्यदधात् स्वकीर्तिं
सत्ये त्रिपृष्ठ उशतीं प्रथयंश्चरित्रैः ॥२०॥

cakraṁ ca dikṣv avihataṁ daśasu sva-tejo
manvantareṣu manu-vaṁśa-dharo bibharti
duṣṭeṣu rājasu damaṁ vyadadhāt sva-kīrtiṁ
satye tri-pṛṣṭha uśatīṁ prathayaṁś caritraiḥ

cakram—the Sudarśana wheel of the Lord; *ca*—as well as; *dikṣu*—in all directions; *avihatam*—without being deterred; *daśasu*—ten sides; *sva-tejaḥ*—personal strength; *manvantareṣu*—in different incarnations of Manu; *manu-vaṁśa-dharaḥ*—as the descendant of the Manu dynasty; *bibharti*—rules over; *duṣṭeṣu*—unto the miscreants; *rājasu*—upon the kings of that type; *damam*—subjection; *vyadadhāt*—performed; *sva-kīrtim*—personal glories; *satye*—in the Satyaloka planet; *tri-pṛṣṭhe*—the three planetary systems; *uśatīm*—glorious; *prathayan*—established; *caritraiḥ*—characteristics.

TRANSLATION

As the incarnation of Manu, the Lord became the descendant of the Manu dynasty and ruled over the miscreant kingly order, subjecting them by His powerful wheel weapon. Undeterred in all circumstances, His rule was characterized by His glorious fame, which spread over the three lokas, and above them up to the planetary system of the Satyaloka, the topmost in the universe.

PURPORT

We have already discussed the incarnations of Manu in the First Canto. In one day of Brahmā there are fourteen Manus, changing one after another. In that way there are 420 Manus in a month of Brahmā and 5,040 Manus in one year of Brahmā. Brahmā lives for one hundred years in his calculation, and as such there are 504,000 Manus in the jurisdiction of one Brahmā. And there are innumerable Brahmās, and all of them live only during one breathing period of Mahā-Viṣṇu. So we can just imagine how the incarnations of the Supreme Lord work all over the material worlds, which comprehend only one-fourth of the total energy of the Supreme Personality of Godhead.

The Manvantara incarnation chastises all the miscreant rulers of different planets with as much power as that of the Supreme Personality of Godhead, who punishes the miscreants with His wheel weapon. The Manvantara incarnations disseminate the transcendental glories of the Lord.

TEXT 21

धन्वन्तरिश्च भगवान् स्वयमेव कीर्ति-
नाम्ना नृणां पुरुरुजां रुज आशु हन्ति ।
यज्ञे च भागममृतायुरवावरुन्ध
आयुष्यवेदमनुशास्त्यवतीर्य लोके ॥२१॥

dhanvantariś ca bhagavān svayam eva kīrtir
nāmnā nṛṇāṁ puru-rujāṁ ruja āśu hanti
yajñe ca bhāgam amṛtāyur-avāvarundha
āyuṣya-vedam anuśāsty avatīrya loke

dhanvantariḥ—the incarnation of God named Dhanvantari; *ca*—and; *bhagavān*—the Personality of Godhead; *svayam eva*—personally Himself; *kīrtiḥ*—fame personified; *nāmnā*—by the name; *nṛṇām puru-rujām*—of the diseased living entities; *rujaḥ*—diseases; *āśu*—very soon; *hanti*—cures; *yajñe*—in the sacrifice; *ca*—also; *bhāgam*—share; *amṛta*—nectar; *āyuḥ*—duration of life; *ava*—from; *avarundhe*—obtains; *āyuṣya*—of duration of life; *vedam*—knowledge; *anuśāsti*—directs; *avatīrya*—incarnating; *loke*—in the universe.

TRANSLATION

The Lord in His incarnation of Dhanvantari very quickly cures the diseases of the ever diseased living entities simply by His fame personified, and due to Him only the demigods achieve long duration of life. Thus the Personality of Godhead becomes ever glorified. He also exacted a share from the sacrifices, and it is He only who inaugurated the medical science or the knowledge of medicine in the universe.

PURPORT

As stated in the beginning of the *Śrīmad-Bhāgavatam*, everything emanates from the ultimate source of the Personality of Godhead; it is therefore understood in this verse that medical science or knowledge in medicine was also inaugurated by the Personality of Godhead in His incarnation Dhanvantari, and thus the knowledge is recorded in the *Vedas*. The *Vedas* are the source of all knowledge, and thus knowledge in medical science is also there for the perfect cure of the diseases of the living entity. The embodied living entity is diseased by the very construction of his body. The body is the symbol of diseases. The disease may differ from one variety to another, but disease must be there just as there is birth and death for everyone. So, by the grace of the Personality of Godhead, not only diseases of the body and mind are cured, but also the soul is relieved of the constant repetition of birth and death. The name of the Lord is also called *bhavauṣadhi*, or the source of curing the disease of material existence.

TEXT 22

क्षत्रं क्षयाय विधिनोपभृतं महात्मा
ब्रह्मध्रुगुज्झितपथं नरकार्तिलिप्सु ।
उद्धन्त्यसाववनिकण्टकमुग्रवीर्य-
स्त्रिःसप्तकृत्व उरुधारपरश्वधेन ॥२२॥

kṣatraṁ kṣayāya vidhinopabhṛtaṁ mahātmā
brahma-dhrug ujjhita-pathaṁ narakārti-lipsu
uddhanty asāv avanikaṇṭakam ugra-vīryas
triḥ-sapta-kṛtva urudhāra-paraśvadhena

kṣatram—the royal order; *kṣayāya*—for the matter of diminishing; *vidhinā*—by destination; *upabhṛtam*—increased in proportion; *mahātmā*—the Lord in the form of the great sage Paraśurāma; *brahma-dhruk*—the ultimate truth in Brahman; *ujjhita-patham*—those who have given up the path of Absolute Truth; *naraka-ārti-lipsu*—desirous to suffer pain in hell; *uddhanti*—exacts; *asau*—all those; *avanikaṇṭakam*—thorns of the world; *ugra-vīryaḥ*—awfully powerful; *triḥ-sapta*—thrice seven times; *kṛtvaḥ*—performed; *urudhāra*—very sharp; *paraśvadhena*—by the great chopper.

TRANSLATION

When the ruling administrators, who are known as the kṣatriyas, turned astray from the path of Absolute Truth, being desirous to suffer in hell, the Lord, in His incarnation as the sage Paraśurāma, uprooted those unwanted kings, who appeared as the thorns of the earth. Thus He thrice seven times uprooted the kṣatriyas with His keenly sharpened chopper.

PURPORT

The *kṣatriyas,* or the ruling administrators of any part of the universe, either on this planet or on other planets, are factually the representatives of the Almighty Personality of Godhead, and they are meant to lead the subjects towards the path of God realization. Every state and its administrators, regardless of the nature of the administration—monarchy or democracy, oligarchy or dictatorship or autocracy—have the prime responsibility to lead the citizens toward God realization. This is essential for all human beings, and it is the duty of the father, spiritual master, and ultimately the state to take up the responsibility to lead the citizens towards this end. The whole creation of material existence is made for this purpose, just to give a chance to the fallen souls who rebelled against the will of the Supreme Father and thus became conditioned by material nature. The force of material nature gradually leads one to a hellish condition of perpetual pains and miseries. Those going against the prescribed rules and regulations of conditional life are called *brahmojjhita-pathas,* or persons going against the path of the Absolute Truth, and they are liable to be punished. Lord Paraśurāma, the incarnation of the Personality of Godhead, appeared in such a state of worldly affairs and killed all the miscreant kings twenty-one times. Many *kṣatriya* kings fled away at that time from India to other parts of the world, and according to the authority of the *Mahābhārata,* the kings of Egypt originally migrated from India because of Paraśurāma's program of chastisement. The kings or administrators are similarly chastised in all circumstances whenever they become godless and plan a godless civilization, and that is the order of the Almighty.

TEXT 23

असत्प्रसादसुमुखः कलया कलेश
इक्ष्वाकुवंश अवतीर्य गुरोर्निदेशे ।

तिष्ठन् वनं सदयितानुज आविवेश
यस्मिन् विरुध्य दशकन्धर आर्तिमार्च्छत्॥२३॥

asmat-prasāda-sumukhaḥ kalayā kaleśa
ikṣvāku-vaṁśa avatīrya guror nideśe
tiṣṭhan vanaṁ sa-dayitānuja āviveśa
yasmin virudhya daśa-kandhara ārtim ārcchat

asmat—unto us, beginning from Brahmā down to the insignificant ant; *prasāda*—causeless mercy; *sumukhaḥ*—so inclined; *kalayā*—with His plenary extensions; *kaleśaḥ*—the Lord of all potencies; *ikṣvāku*—Mahārāja Ikṣvāku, in the dynasty of the sun; *vaṁse*—family; *avatīrya*—by descending in; *guroḥ*—of the father or spiritual master; *nideśe*—under the order of; *tiṣṭhan*—being situated in; *vanam*—in the forest; *sa-dayitā-anujaḥ*—along with His wife and younger brother; *āviveśa*—entered in; *yasmin*—unto whom; *virudhya*—being rebellious; *daśa-kandharaḥ*—Rāvaṇa, who had ten heads; *ārtim*—great distress; *ārcchat*—achieved.

TRANSLATION

Due to His causeless mercy upon all living entities within the universe, the Supreme Personality of Godhead, along with His plenary extensions, appeared in the family of Mahārāja Ikṣvāku as the Lord of His internal potency, Sītā. Under the order of His father, Mahārāja Daśaratha, He entered the forest and lived there for considerable years with His wife and younger brother. Rāvaṇa, who was very materially powerful, with ten heads on His shoulders, committed a great offense against Him and was thus ultimately vanquished.

PURPORT

Lord Rāma is the Supreme Personality of Godhead, and His brothers, namely Bharata, Lakṣmaṇa and Śatrughna, are His plenary expansions. All four brothers were *Viṣṇu-tattva* and were never ordinary human beings. There are many unscrupulous and ignorant commentators on *Śrīmad Rāmāyaṇa* who present the younger brothers of Lord Rāmacandra as ordinary living entities. But here in the *Śrīmad-Bhāgavatam,* the most authentic scripture on the science of Godhead, it is clearly stated that His brothers were His plenary expansions. Originally Lord Rāmacandra is the incarnation of Vāsudeva, Lakṣmaṇa is the incarnation of Saṅkarṣaṇa, Bharata is the incarnation of Pradyumna, and Śatrughna is the incarnation of Aniruddha, expansions of the Personality of Godhead. Lakṣmījī Sītā is the internal potency of the Lord and is neither an ordinary woman nor the external potency incarnation of Durgā. Durgā is the external potency of the Lord, and she is associated with Lord Śiva.

As stated in the *Bhagavad-gītā* (Bg. 4.7), the Lord appears when there is discrepancy in the discharge of factual religiousness, and Lord Rāmacandra also appeared under the same circumstances, accompanied by His brothers, who are expansions of the Lord's internal potency, and by Lakṣmījī Sītādevī.

Lord Rāmacandra was ordered by His father, Mahārāja Daśaratha, to leave home for the forest under awkward circumstances, and the Lord, as the ideal son of His father, carried out the order, even on the occasion of His being declared the King of Ayodhyā. One of His younger brothers, Lakṣmaṇajī, desired to go with Him, and so also His eternal wife, Sītājī, desired to go with Him. The Lord agreed to both of them, and all together they entered the Daṇḍakāraṇya Forest, to live there for fourteen years. During their stay in the forest, there was some quarrel between Rāmacandra and Rāvaṇa, and the latter kidnapped the Lord's wife, Sītā. The quarrel ended in the vanquishing of the greatly powerful Rāvaṇa, along with all his kingdom and family.

Sītā is Lakṣmījī, or the goddess of fortune, but she is never to be enjoyed by any living being. She is meant for being worshiped by the living being along with her husband, Śrī Rāmacandra. A materialistic man like Rāvaṇa does not understand this great truth, but on the contrary he wants to snatch Sītādevī from the custody of Rāma and thus incurs great miseries. The materialists, who are after opulence and material prosperity, may take lessons from the *Rāmāyaṇa* that the policy of exploiting the nature of the Lord without acknowledging the supremacy of the Supreme Lord is the policy of Rāvaṇa. Rāvaṇa was very advanced materially, so much so that he turned his kingdom, Laṅkā, into pure gold, or full material wealth. But because he did not recognize the supremacy of Lord Rāmacandra and defied Him by stealing His wife Sītā, Rāvaṇa was killed and all his opulence and power destroyed.

Lord Rāmacandra is a full incarnation with six opulences in full, and He is therefore mentioned in this verse as *kaleśaḥ,* or master of all opulence.

TEXT 24

यस्मा अदादुदधिरूढभयाङ्गवेपो
मार्गं सपद्यरिपुरं हरवद् दिधक्षोः ।
दूरे सुहृन्मथितरोषसुशोणदृष्ट्या
तातप्यमानमकरोरगनक्रचक्रः ॥२४॥

yasmā adād udadhi rūḍha-bhayāṅga-vepo
mārgaṁ sapady ari-puraṁ haravad didhakṣoḥ
dūre suhṛn-mathita-roṣa-suśoṇa-dṛṣṭyā
tātapyamāna-makaroraga-nakra-cakraḥ

yasmai—unto whom; *adāt*—gave; *udadhiḥ*—the great Indian Ocean; *rūḍha-bhaya*—affected by fear; *aṅga-vepaḥ*—bodily trembling; *mārgam*—way; *sapadi*—quickly; *ari-puram*—the city of the enemy; *haravat*—like that of Hara (Mahādeva); *didhakṣoḥ*—desiring to burn into ashes; *dūre*—at a long distance; *su-hṛt*—intimate friend; *mathita*—being aggrieved by; *roṣa*—in anger; *su-śoṇa*—red-hot; *dṛṣṭyā*—by such a glance; *tātapyamāna*—burning in heat; *makara*— sharks;*uraga*— snakes;*nakra*— crocodiles;*cakraḥ*—circle.

TRANSLATION

The Personality of Godhead Rāmacandra, being aggrieved for His distant intimate friend [Sītā], glanced over the city of the enemy Rāvaṇa with red-hot eyes like those of Hara [who wanted to burn the kingdom of heaven]. The great ocean, trembling in fear, gave Him His way because its family members, the aquatics like the sharks, snakes and crocodiles, were being burnt by the heat of the angry red-hot eyes of the Lord.

PURPORT

The Personality of Godhead has every sentiment of a sentient being, like all other living beings, because He is the chief and original living entity, the supreme source of all other living beings. He is the *nitya,* or the chief eternal amongst all other eternals. He is the chief one, and all others are the dependent many. The many eternals are supported by the one eternal, and thus both the eternals are qualitatively one. Due to such oneness, both the eternals have constitutionally a complete range of sentiments, but the difference is that the sentiments of the chief eternal are different in quantity from the sentiments of the dependent eternals. When Rāmacandra was angry and showed His red-hot eyes, the whole ocean became heated with that energy, so much so that the acquatics within the great ocean felt the heat, and the personified ocean trembled in fear and offered the Lord an easy path for reaching the enemy's city. The impersonalists will see havoc in this red-hot sentiment of the Lord because they want to see negation in perfection. Because the Lord is absolute, the impersonalists imagine that in the absolute the sentiment of anger, which resembles mundane sentiments, must be conspicuous by absence. Due to a poor fund of knowledge, they do not realize that the sentiment of the Absolute Person is transcendental to all mundane concepts of quality and quantity. Had Lord Rāmacandra's sentiment been of mundane origin, how could it disturb the whole ocean and its inhabitants? Can any mundane red-hot eye generate heat in the great ocean? These are factors to be distinguished in terms of the personal and impersonal conception of the Absolute Truth. As it is said in the beginning of the *Śrīmad-Bhāgavatam,* the Absolute Truth is the source of everything, so the Absolute Person cannot be devoid of the sentiments that are reflected in the temporary mundane world. Rather, the different sentiments found in the Absolute, either in anger or in mercy, have the same qualitative influence, or, in other words, there is no mundane difference of value because these sentiments are all on the absolute plane. Such sentiments are definitely not absent in the Absolute, as the impersonalists think, making their mundane estimation of the transcendental world.

TEXT 25

वक्षःस्थलस्पर्शरुग्नमहेन्द्रवाह-
दन्तैर्विडम्बितककुब्जुष ऊढहासम् ।
सद्योऽसुभिः सह विनेष्यति दारहर्तु-
र्विस्फूर्जितैर्धनुष उच्चरतोऽधिसैन्ये ॥२५॥

vakṣaḥ-sthala-sparśa-rugna-mahendra-vāha-
dantair viḍambita-kakubjuṣa ūḍha-hāsam
sadyo'subhiḥ saha vineṣyati dāra-hartur
visphūrjitair dhanuṣa uccarato'dhisainye

vakṣaḥ-sthala—chest; *sparśa*—touched by; *rugna*—broken; *mahā-indra*—the King of heaven; *vāha*—the conveyor; *dantaiḥ*—by the trunk; *viḍambita*—illuminated; *kakubjuṣaḥ*—all directions thus being served; *ūḍha-hāsam*—overtaken by laughter; *sadyaḥ*—within no time; *asubhiḥ*—by the life; *saha*—along with; *vineṣyati*—was killed; *dāra-hartuḥ*—of the one who kidnapped the wife; *visphūrjitaiḥ*—by the tingling of the bow; *dhanuṣaḥ*—bow; *uccarataḥ*—strolling fast; *adhisainye*—in the midst of the fighting soldiers of both sides.

TRANSLATION

When Rāvaṇa was engaged in the battle, the trunk of the elephant which carried the King of heaven, Indra, broke in pieces, having collided with the chest of Rāvaṇa, and the scattered broken parts illuminated all directions. Rāvaṇa therefore felt proud of his prowess and began to loiter in the midst of the fighting soldiers, thinking himself the conqueror of all directions. But his laughter, overtaken by joy, along with his very air of life, suddenly ceased with the tingling sound of the bow of Rāmacandra, the Personality of Godhead.

PURPORT

However powerful a living being may be, when he is condemned by God no one can save him, and, similarly, however weak one may be, if he is protected by the Lord no one can annihilate him.

TEXT 26

भूमेः सुरेतरवरूथविमर्दितायाः
क्लेशव्ययाय कलया सितकृष्णकेशः ।
जातः करिष्यति जनानुपलक्ष्यमार्गः
कर्माणि चात्ममहिमोपनिबन्धनानि ॥२६॥

bhūmeḥ suretara-varūtha-vimarditāyāḥ
kleśa-vyayāya kalayā sita-kṛṣṇa-keśaḥ
jātaḥ kariṣyati janānupalakṣya-mārgaḥ
karmāṇi cātma-mahimopanibandhanāni

bhūmeḥ—of the entire world; *sura-itara*—other than godly persons; *varūtha*—soldiers; *vimarditāyāḥ*—distressed by the burden; *kleśa*—miseries; *vyayāya*—for the matter of diminishing; *kalayā*—along with His plenary expansion; *sita-kṛṣṇa*—not only beautiful but also black; *keśaḥ*—with such hairs; *jātaḥ*—having appeared; *kariṣyati*—would act; *jana*—people in general; *anupalakṣya*—rarely to be seen; *mārgaḥ*—path; *karmāṇi*—activities; *ca*—also; *ātma-mahima*—glories of the Lord Himself; *upanibandhanāni*—in relation to.

TRANSLATION

When the world is overburdened by the fighting strength of kings who have no faith in God, the Lord, just to diminish the distressed condition of the world, descends with His plenary portion. The Lord comes in His original form, with beautiful black hair. And just to expand His transcendental glories, He acts extraordinarily. No one can properly estimate how great He is.

PURPORT

This verse is especially describing the appearance of Lord Kṛṣṇa and His immediate expansion, Lord Baladeva. Both Lord Kṛṣṇa and Lord Baladeva are one Supreme Personality of Godhead. The Lord is omnipotent, and He expands Himself in innumerable forms and energies, and the whole unit is known as the one Supreme Brahman. Such extensions of the Lord are divided into two divisions, namely personal and differential. Personal expansions are called the *Viṣṇu-tattvas,* and the differential expansions are called the *jīva-tattvas.* And in such expansional activity, Lord Baladeva is the first personal expansion of Kṛṣṇa, the Supreme Personality of Godhead.

In the *Viṣṇu Purāṇa,* as well as in the *Mahābhārata,* both Kṛṣṇa and Baladeva are mentioned as having beautiful black hair, even in Their advanced age. The Lord is called *anupalakṣya-mārgaḥ* or, in still more technical Vedic terms, *avāṅ-manasa-gocara:* one who is never to be seen or realized by the limited sense perception of the people in general. In the *Bhagavad-gītā* it is said by the Lord, *nāhaṁ prakāśaḥ sarvasya yogamāyā samāvṛtaḥ* (Bg. 7.25). In other words, He reserves the right of not being exposed to anyone and everyone. Only the bona fide devotees can know Him by His specific symptoms, and out of such many, many symptoms, one symptom is mentioned here in this verse, that the Lord is *sita-kṛṣṇa-keśaḥ,* or one who is observed always with beautiful black hair. Both Lord

Kṛṣṇa and Lord Baladeva have such hair on Their heads, and thus even in advanced age They appeared like young boys sixteen years old. That is the particular symptom of the Personality of Godhead. In the *Brahma-saṁhitā* it is stated that although He is the oldest personality among all the living entities, still He always looks like a new, youthful boy. That is the characteristic of a spiritual body. The material body is symptomized by birth, death, old age and diseases, but the spiritual body is conspicuous by the absence of those symptoms. Living entities who reside in the Vaikuṇṭhalokas in eternal life and bliss have the same type of spiritual body, without being affected by any signs of old age. It is described in the *Bhāgavatam* (Canto Six) that the party of Viṣṇudūtas who came to deliver Ajāmila from the clutches of the party of Yamarāja appeared like youthful boys, corroborating the description in this verse. It is ascertained thus that the spiritual bodies in the Vaikuṇṭhalokas, either of the Lord or of the other inhabitants, are completely distinct from the material bodies of this world. Therefore, when the Lord descends from that world to this world, He descends in His spiritual body of *Ātma-māyā* or internal potency, without any touch of the *bahiraṅgā-māyā* or external material energy. The allegation that the impersonal Brahman appears in this material world by accepting a material body is quite absurd. Therefore the Lord, when He comes here, has not a material body, but a spiritual body. The impersonal *brahmajyoti* is only the glaring effulgence of the body of the Lord, and there is no difference in quality between the body of the Lord and the impersonal ray of the Lord, called *brahmajyoti.*

Now the question is why the Lord, who is omnipotent, comes here to diminish the burden of the world, created by the unscrupulous kingly order. Certainly the Lord does not need to come here personally for such purposes, but He actually descends to exhibit His transcendental activities in order to encourage His pure devotees, who want to enjoy life by chanting the glories of the Lord. In the *Bhagavad-gītā* it is stated (Bg. 9.13-14) that the *mahātmās,* great devotees of the Lord, take pleasure in chanting of the activities of the Lord. All Vedic literatures are meant for turning one's attention towards the Lord and His transcendental activities. Thus the activities of the Lord, in His dealings with worldly people, create a subject matter for discussion by His pure devotees.

TEXT 27

तोकेन जीवहरणं यदुलूकिकाया-
स्त्रैमासिकस्य च पदा शकटोऽपवृत्तः ।

यद् रिङ्गतान्तरगतेन दिविस्पृशोर्वा
उन्मूलनं त्वितरथार्जुनयोर्न भाव्यम्॥२७॥

tokena jīva-haraṇaṁ yad ulūki-kāyās
trai-māsikasya ca padā śakaṭo'pavṛttaḥ
yad riṅgatāntaragatena divi-spṛśor vā
unmūlanaṁ tv itarathārjunayor na bhāvyam

tokena—by a child; *jīva-haraṇam*—killing a living being; *yat*—one which; *ulūki-kāyāḥ*—assumed the giant body of a demon; *trai-māsikasya*—of one who is only three months old; *ca*—also; *padā*—by the leg; *śakaṭaḥ upavṛttaḥ*—turned over the cart; *yat*—one who; *riṅgatā*—while crawling; *antara-gatena*—being overtaken; *divi*—high in the sky; *spṛśoḥ*—touching; *vā*—either; *unmūlanam*—uprooting; *tu*—but; *itarathā*—anyone else than; *arjunayoḥ*—of the two *arjuna* trees; *na bhāvyam*—was not possible.

TRANSLATION

There is no doubt about Lord Kṛṣṇa's being the Supreme Lord, otherwise how was it possible for Him to kill a giant demon like Pūtanā when He was just on the lap of His mother, to overturn a cart with His leg when He was only three months old, to uproot a pair of arjuna trees, so high that they touched the sky, when He was only crawling. All these activities are not possible for anyone other than the Lord Himself.

PURPORT

One cannot manufacture a God by one's mental speculation or by numerical votes, as has become a practice for the less intelligent class of men. God is God eternally, and an ordinary living entity is eternally a part and parcel of God. God is one without a second, and the ordinary living entities are many without number. All such living entities are maintained by God Himself, and that is the verdict of the Vedic literatures. When Kṛṣṇa was on the lap of His mother, the demon Pūtanā appeared before His mother and prayed to nurture the child in her lap. Mother Yaśodā agreed, and the child was transferred onto the lap of Pūtanā, who was in the garb of a respectable lady. Pūtanā wanted to kill the child by smearing poison on the nipple of her breast. But when everything was complete, the Lord sucked her breast along with her very air of life, and the demon's gigantic body, said to be as long as six miles, fell down. But Lord Kṛṣṇa did not need to expand Himself to the length of the she-demon Pūtanā, although He was quite competent to extend Himself more than six miles long. In His Vāmana incarnation He posed Himself as a dwarf *brāhmaṇa,* but when He took possession of His land, promised by Bali Mahārāja, He expanded His footstep to the top end of the universe, extending over thousands and millions of miles. So it was not very difficult for Kṛṣṇa to perform a miracle by extending His bodily feature, but He had no desire to do it because of His deep filial love for His mother, Yaśodā. If Yaśodā would have seen Kṛṣṇa in her lap extending six miles to cope with the she-demon Pūtanā, then the natural filial love of Yaśodā would have been hurt because in that way Yaśodā would come to know that her so-called son, Kṛṣṇa, was God Himself. And with the knowledge of the Godhead of Kṛṣṇa, Yaśodā mayī would have lost the temper of her love for Kṛṣṇa as a natural mother. But as far as Lord Kṛṣṇa is concerned, He is God always, either as a child on the lap of His mother, or as the coverer of the universe, Vāmanadeva. He does not require to become God by undergoing severe penances, although some men think of becoming God in that way. By undergoing severe austerities and penances, one cannot become one or equal with God, but one can attain most of the godly qualities. A living being can attain godly qualities to a large extent, but he cannot become God; whereas Kṛṣṇa, without undergoing any type of penance, is God always, either in the lap of His mother or growing up or at any stage of growth.

So at the age of only three months He killed the Śakaṭāsura who remained hidden behind a cart in the house of Yaśodāmayī. And when He was crawling and was disturbing His mother from doing household affairs, the mother tied Him with a grinding pestle, but the naughty child dragged the pestle up to a pair of very high *arjuna* trees in the yard of Yaśodāmayī, and when the pestel was stuck in between the pair of trees, they fell down with a horrible sound. When Yaśodāmayī came to see the happenings, she thought that her child was saved from the falling trees by the mercy of the Lord, without knowing that the Lord Himself, crawling in her yard, had wreaked the havoc. So that is the way of reciprocation of love affairs between the Lord and His devotees. Yaśodāmayī wanted to have the Lord as her child, and the Lord played exactly like a child in her lap, but at the same time played the part of the Almighty Lord whenever it was so required. The beauty of such pastimes was that the Lord fulfilled everyone's desire. In the case of felling the gigantic *arjuna* tree, the Lord's mission was to deliver the two sons of Kuvera, who were condemned to become trees by the curse of Nārada, as well as to play like a crawling child in the yard of Yaśodā, who took transcendental pleasure in seeing such activities of the Lord in the very yard of her home.

The Lord in any condition is Lord of the universe, and He can act as such in any form, gigantic or small, as He likes.

TEXT 28

यद् वै व्रजे व्रजपशून् विषतोयपीतान्
पालांस्त्वजीवयदनुग्रहदृष्टिवृष्ट्या ।
तच्छुद्धयेऽतिविषवीर्यविलोलजिह्व-
मुच्चाटयिष्यदुरगं विहरन् ह्रदिन्याम् ॥२८॥

yad vai vraje vraja-paśūn viṣatoya-pītān
pālāṁs tv ajīvayad anugraha-dṛṣṭi-vṛṣṭyā
tac-chuddhaye'ti-viṣa-vīrya-vilola-jihvam
uccāṭayiṣyad uragaṁ viharan hradinyām

yat—one who; *vai*—certainly; *vraje*—at Vṛndāvana; *vraja-paśūn*—the animals thereof; *viṣa-toya*—poisoned water; *pītān*—those who drank; *pālān*—the cowherd men; *tu*—also; *ajīvayat*—brought to life; *anugraha-dṛṣṭi*—merciful glance; *vṛṣṭyā*—by the showers of; *tat*—that; *śuddhaye*—for purification; *ati*—exceedingly; *viṣa-vīrya*—highly potent poison; *vilola*—lurking; *jihvam*—one who has such a tongue; *uccāṭayiṣyat*—severely punished; *uragam*—unto the snake; *viharan*—taking it as a pleasure; *hradinyām*—in the river.

TRANSLATION

Then also when the cowherd boys and their animals drank the poisoned water of the River Yamunā, and after the Lord [in His childhood] revived them by His merciful glance, just to purify the water of the River Yamunā He jumped into it as if playing and chastised the venomous Kāliya snake,

which was lurking there, its tongue emitting waves of poison. Who can perform such Herculean tasks but the Supreme Lord?

TEXT 29

तत् कर्म दिव्यमिव यन्निशि निःशयानं
दावाग्निना शुचिवने परिदह्यमाने ।
उन्नेष्यति व्रजमतोऽवसितान्तकालं
नेत्रे पिधाप्य सबलोऽनधिगम्यवीर्यः ॥२९॥

tat karma divyam iva yan niśi niḥśayānaṁ
dāvāgninā śuci-vane paridahyamāne
unneṣyati vrajam ato'vasitānta-kālaṁ
netre pidhāpya sabalo'nadhigamya-vīryaḥ

tat—that; *karma*—activity; *divyam*—superhuman; *iva*—like; *yat*—which; *niśi*—at night; *niḥśayānam*—sleeping carefreely; *dāva-agninā*—by the flare of the forest fire; *śuci-vane*—in the dry forest; *paridahyamāne*—being set ablaze; *unneṣyati*—would deliver; *vrajam*—all the inhabitants of Vraja; *ataḥ*—hence; *avasita*—surely; *anta-kālam*—last moments of life; *netre*—on the eyes; *pidhāpya*—simply by closing; *sabalaḥ*—along with Baladeva; *anadhigamya*—unfathomable; *vīryaḥ*—prowess.

TRANSLATION

On the very night of the day of the chastisement of the Kāliya snake, when the inhabitants of Vrajabhūmi were sleeping carefreely, there was a forest fire ablaze due to dry leaves, and it appeared that all the inhabitants were sure to meet their death. But the Lord, along with Balarāma, saved them simply by closing His eyes. Such are the superhuman activities of the Lord.

PURPORT

Although in this verse the Lord's activity has been described as superhuman, it should be noted that the Lord's activities are always superhuman, and that distinguishes Him from the ordinary living being. Uprooting a gigantic banyan or *arjuna* tree and extinguishing a blazing forest fire simply by closing one's eyes are certainly impossible by any kind of human endeavor. But not only are these activities amazing to hear, but in fact all other activities of the Lord, whatever He may do, are all superhuman, as is confirmed in the *Bhagavad-gītā* (Bg. 4.9). And whoever knows the superhuman activities of the Lord, due to their very transcendental nature, becomes eligible to enter the kingdom of Kṛṣṇa, and as such, after quitting this present material body, the knower of the transcendental activities of the Lord goes back home, back to Godhead.

TEXT 30

गृह्णीत यद् यदुपबन्धममुष्य माता
शुल्बं सुतस्य न तु तत् तदमुष्य माति ।
यज्जृम्भतोऽस्य वदने भुवनानि गोपी
संवीक्ष्य शङ्कितमनाः प्रतिबोधितासीत् ॥३०॥

gṛhṇīta yad yad upabandham amuṣya mātā
śulbaṁ sutasya na tu tat tad amuṣya māti
yaj jṛmbhato 'sya vadane bhuvanāni gopī
saṁvīkṣya śaṅkita-manāḥ pratibodhitāsīt

gṛhṇīta—by taking up; *yat yat*—whatsoever; *upabandham*—ropes for tying; *amuṣya*—His; *mātā*—mother; *śulbam*—ropes; *sutasya*—of her son; *na*—not; *tu*—however; *tat tat*—by and by; *amuṣya*—His; *māti*—was sufficient; *yat*—that which; *jṛmbhataḥ*—opening the mouth; *asya*—of Him; *vadane*—in the mouth; *bhuvanāni*—the worlds; *gopī*—the cowherd woman; *saṁvīkṣya*—so seeing it; *śaṅkita-manāḥ*—doubtful in mind; *pratibodhitā*—convinced in a different way; *āsīt*—was so done.

TRANSLATION

When the cowherd woman [Kṛṣṇa's foster mother, Yaśodā] was trying to tie the hands of her son with ropes, she found the rope to be always insufficient in length, and when she finally gave up, Lord Kṛṣṇa, by and by, opened His mouth, wherein the mother found all the universes situated. Seeing this, she was doubtful in her mind, but she was convinced in a different manner of the mystic nature of her son.

PURPORT

One day Lord Kṛṣṇa as the naughty child disturbed His mother Yaśodā, and she began to tie up the child with ropes just to punish Him. But no matter how much rope she used, she found it always insufficient. Thus she became fatigued, but in the meantime the Lord opened His mouth, and the affectionate mother saw within the mouth of her son all the universes situated together. The mother was astonished, but out of her deep affection for Kṛṣṇa she thought that the Almighty Godhead Nārāyaṇa had kindly looked after her son just to protect Him from all the continuous calamities happening to Him. Because of her deep affection for Kṛṣṇa, she could never think that her very son was Nārāyaṇa, the Personality of Godhead Himself. That is the action of *yogamāyā,* the internal potency of the Supreme Lord, which acts to perfect all the pastimes of the Lord with His different types of devotees. Who could play such wonders without being God?

TEXT 31

नन्दं च मोक्ष्यति भयाद् वरुणस्य पाशाद्
गोपान् बिलेषु पिहितान् मयसूनुना च।
अह्न्याप‍ृतं निशि शयानमतिश्रमेण
लोकं विकुण्ठमुपनेष्यति गोकुलं स्म ॥३१॥

nandaṁ ca mokṣyati bhayād varuṇasya pāśād
gopān bileṣu pihitān maya-sūnunā ca
ahny āpṛtaṁ niśi śayānam atiśrameṇa
lokaṁ vikuṇṭham upaneṣyati gokulaṁ sma

nandam—unto Nanda (the father of Kṛṣṇa); *ca*—also; *mokṣyati*—saves; *bhayāt*—from the fear of; *varuṇasya*—of Varuṇa, the demigod of water; *pāśāt*—from the clutches of; *gopān*—the cowherd men; *bileṣu*—in the caves of the mountain; *pihitān*—placed; *maya-sūnunā*—by the son of Maya; *ca*—also; *ahni āpṛtam*—being very engaged during the daytime; *niśi*—at night; *śayānam*—lying down; *atiśrameṇa*—because of hard labor; *lokam*—planet; *vikuṇṭham*—the spiritual sky; *upaneṣyati*—He awarded; *gokulam*—the highest planet; *sma*—certainly.

TRANSLATION

Lord Kṛṣṇa saved His foster father Nanda Mahārāja from the fear of the demigod Varuṇa and released the cowherd boys from the caves of the mountain, for they were placed there by the son of Maya. Also, to the inhabitants of Vṛndāvana, who were busy working during daytime and sleeping soundly at night because of their hard labor in day, Lord Kṛṣṇa awarded promotion to the highest planet in the spiritual sky. All these acts are transcendental and certainly prove without any doubt His Godhood.

PURPORT

Nanda Mahārāja, the foster father of Lord Kṛṣṇa, went to take his bath in the River Yamunā in the dead of night, mistakenly thinking that the night was already over; thus the demigod Varuṇa took him to the Varuṇa planet just to have a look at the Personality of Godhead Lord Kṛṣṇa, who appeared there to release the father. Actually there was no arrest of Nanda Mahārāja by Varuṇa because the inhabitants of Vṛndāvana were always engaged in thinking of Kṛṣṇa, in constant meditation on the Personality of Godhead in a particular form of *samādhi,* or trance of *bhakti-yoga.* They had no fear of the miseries of material existence. In the *Bhagavad-gītā* it is confirmed that to be in association with the Supreme Personality of Godhead by full surrender in transcendental love frees one from the miseries inflicted by the laws of material nature. Here it is clearly mentioned that the inhabitants of Vṛndāvana were extensively busy in the hard labor of their day's work, and due to the day's hard labor they were engaged in sound sleep at night. So practically they had very little time to devote to meditation or to the other paraphernalia of spiritual activities. But factually they were engaged in the highest spiritual activities only. Everything done by them was spiritualized because everything was dovetailed in their relationship with Lord Śrī Kṛṣṇa. The central point of activities was Kṛṣṇa, and as such the so-called activities in the material world were saturated with spiritual potency, and that is the advantage of the way of *bhakti-yoga.* One should discharge one's duty on Lord Kṛṣṇa's behalf, and all one's actions will be saturated with Kṛṣṇa thought, the highest pattern of trance in spiritual realization.

TEXT 32

गोपैर्मखे प्रतिहते व्रजविप्लवाय
देवेऽभिवर्षति पशून् कृपया रिरक्षुः ।

धर्तोच्छिलीन्ध्रमिव सप्त दिनानि सप्त-
वर्षो महीध्रमनघैककरे सलीलम् ॥३२॥

gopair makhe pratihate vraja-viplavāya
deve 'bhivarṣati paśūn kṛpayā rirakṣuḥ
dhartocchilīndhram iva sapta-dināni sapta-
varṣo mahīdhram anaghaikakare salīlam

gopaiḥ—by the cowherd men; *makhe*—in offering a sacrifice to the King of heaven; *pratihate*—being hampered; *vraja-viplavāya*—for devastating the whole existence of Vrajabhūmi, the land of Kṛṣṇa's pastimes; *deve*—by the King of heaven; *abhivarṣati*—having poured down heavy rain; *paśūn*—the animals; *kṛpayā*—by causeless mercy upon them; *rirakṣuḥ*—desired to protect them; *dharta*—held up; *ucchilīndhram*—uprooted as an umbrella; *iva*—exactly like that; *sapta-dināni*—continuously for seven days; *sapta-varṣaḥ*—although He was only seven years old; *mahīdhram*—the Govardhana Hill; *anagha*—without being tired; *ekakare*—in one hand only; *salīlam*—playfully.

TRANSLATION

When the cowherd men of Vṛndāvana stopped offering sacrifice to the heavenly King, Indra, under instruction of Kṛṣṇa, the whole tract of land known as Vraja was threatened to be washed away by constant heavy rains for seven days. Lord Kṛṣṇa, out of His causeless mercy upon the inhabitants of Vraja, held up the hill known as Govardhana with one hand only, although He was only seven years old. He did this to protect the animals from the onslaught of water.

PURPORT

Children play with an umbrella generally known as a frog's umbrella, and Lord Kṛṣṇa, when He was seven years old only, could snatch the great hill known as the Govardhana Parvata at Vṛndāvana and hold it for seven days continually with one hand, just to protect the animals and the inhabitants of Vṛndāvana from the wrath of Indra, the heavenly King, who was denied sacrificial offering by the inhabitants of Vrajabhūmi.

Factually there is no need of offering sacrifices to the demigods for their services if one is engaged in the service of the Supreme Lord. Sacrifices recommended in the Vedic literature for satisfaction of the demigods are a sort of inducement to the sacrificers just to realize the existence of higher authorities. The demigods are engaged by the Lord as controlling deities of the material affairs, and according to the *Bhagavad-gītā*, when a demigod is worshiped the process is accepted as the indirect method for worshiping the Supreme Lord. But when the Supreme Lord is worshiped directly there is no need of worshiping the demigods or offering them sacrifices as is recommended in particular circumstances. Lord Kṛṣṇa therefore advised the inhabitants of the Vrajabhūmi not to offer any sacrifices to the heavenly King Indra. But Indra, not knowing Lord Kṛṣṇa in Vrajabhūmi, was angry at the inhabitants of Vrajabhūmi and tried to avenge the offense. But, competent as the Lord was, He saved the inhabitants and animals of Vrajabhūmi by His personal energy and proved definitely that anyone who is directly engaged as a devotee of the Supreme Lord need not satisfy any other demigods, however great, even to the level of Brahmā or Śiva. Thus this incidence definitely proved without a doubt that Lord Kṛṣṇa is the Personality of Godhead and He was so in all circumstances, as a child on the lap of His mother, as a boy seven years old, and as an old man of 125 years of age. In either case He was never on the level of the ordinary man, and even in His advanced age He appeared a young boy sixteen years old. These are the particular features of the transcendental body of the Lord.

TEXT 33

क्रीडन् वने निशि निशाकररश्मिगौर्यां
रासोन्मुखः कलपदायतमूर्च्छितेन ।
उद्दीपितस्मररुजां व्रजभृद्वधूनां
हर्तुर्हरिष्यति शिरो धनदानुगस्य ॥३३॥

krīḍan vane niśi niśākara-raśmi-gauryāṁ
rāsonmukhaḥ kala-padāyata-mūrcchitena
uddīpita-smara-rujāṁ vraja-bhṛd-vadhūnāṁ
hartur hariṣyati śiro dhanadānugasya

krīḍan—while engaged in His pastimes; *vane*—in the forest of Vṛndāvana; *niśi*—nocturnal; *niśākara*—the moon; *raśmi-gauryām*—white moonshine; *rāsa-unmukhaḥ*—desiring to dance with; *kala-padāyata*—accompanied by sweet songs; *mūrcchitena*—and melodious music; *uddīpita*—awakened; *smara-rujām*—sex desires; *vraja-bhṛt*—the inhabitants of Vrajabhūmi; *vadhū-nām*—of the wives; *hartuḥ*—of the kidnappers; *hariṣyati*—will vanquish; *śiraḥ*—the head; *dhanada-anugasya*—of the follower of the rich Kuvera.

PURPORT

When the Lord was engaged in His pastimes of the rāsa dance in the forest of Vṛndāvana, enlivening the sexual desires of the wives of the inhabitants of Vṛndāvana by sweet and melodious songs, a demon of the name Śaṅkhacūḍa, a rich follower of the treasurer of heaven [Kuvera], kidnapped the damsels, and the Lord severed his head from his trunk.

TRANSLATION

We should carefully note that the statements described herein are the statements of Brahmājī to Nārada, and He was speaking to Nārada of events that would happen in future during the advent of Lord Kṛṣṇa. The pastimes of the Lord are known to the experts who are able to see past, present and future, and Brahmājī, being one of them, foretold what would happen in the future. The killing of Śaṅkhacūḍa by the Lord is a more recent incident, after *rāsa-līlā,* and not exactly a simultaneous affair. In the previous verses we have seen also that the Lord's engagement in the forest fire affairs was described along with His pastimes of punishing the Kāliya snake, and similarly the pastimes of the *rāsa* dance and the killing of Śaṅkhacūḍa are also described herein. The adjustment is that all these incidences would take place in the future, after the time when it was being foretold by Brahmājī to Nārada. The demon Śaṅkhacūḍa was killed by the Lord during His pastimes at Horikā in the month of Phālgunī, and the same ceremony is still observed in India by the burning of the effigy of Śaṅkhacūḍa one day prior to the Lord's pastimes at Horikā generally known as *Holi.*

Generally the future appearance and the activities of the Lord or His incarnations are foretold in the scriptures, and thus the pseudo-incarnations are unable to cheat persons who are in the knowledge of the events as they are described in the authoritative scriptures.

TEXTS 34-35

ये च प्रलम्बखरदर्दुरकेश्यरिष्ट-
मल्लेभकंसयवनाः कपिपौण्ड्रकाद्याः ।
अन्ये च शाल्वकुजबल्वलदन्तवक्र-
सप्तोक्षशम्बरविदूरथरुक्मिमुख्याः ॥३४॥
ये वा मृधे समितिशालिन आत्तचापाः
काम्बोजमत्स्यकुरुसृञ्जयकैकयाद्याः ।
यास्यन्त्यदर्शनमलं बलपार्थभीम-
व्याजाह्वयेन हरिणा निलयं तदीयम् ॥३५॥

ye ca pralamba-khara-dardurakeśy-ariṣṭa-
mallebha-kaṁsa-yavanāḥ kapi-pauṇḍrakādyāḥ
anye ca śālva-kuja-balvala-dantavakra-
saptokṣa-śambara-vidūratha-rukmi-mukhyāḥ

ye vā mṛdhe samiti-śālina āttacāpāḥ
kāmboja-matsya-kuru-sṛñjaya-kaikayādyāḥ
yāsyanty adarśanam alaṁ bala-pārtha-bhīma-
vyājāhvayena hariṇā nilayaṁ tadīyam

ye—all those; *ca*—totally; *pralamba*—the demon named Pralamba; *khara*—Gardhavāsura; *dardura*—Bakāsura; keśī—the Keśī demon; *ariṣṭa*—the demon Ariṣṭāsura; *malla*—a wrestler in the court of Kaṁsa; *ibha*—Kuvalayāpīḍa; *kaṁsa*—the King of Mathurā and the maternal uncle of Kṛṣṇa; *yavanāḥ*—the kings of Persia and other adjoining places; *kapi*—Dvivida; *pauṇḍraka-ādyāḥ*—Pauṇḍraka and others; *anye*—others; *ca*—as much as; *śālva*—King Śālva; *kuja*—Narakāsura; *balvala*—King Balvala; *dantavakra*—the brother of Śiśupāla, a dead rival of Kṛṣṇa's; *saptokṣa*—King Saptokṣa; *śambara*—King Śambara; *vidūratha*—King Vidūratha; *rukmi-mukhyāḥ*—the brother of Rukmiṇī, the first Queen of Kṛṣṇa at Dvārakā. *ye*—all those; *vā*—either; *mṛdhe*—in the battlefield; *samiti-śālinaḥ*—all very powerful; *ātta-cāpāḥ*—well equipped with bows and arrows; *kāmboja*—the King of Kāmboja; *matsya*—the King of Dvarbhaṅga; *kuru*—the sons of Dhṛtarāṣṭra; *sṛñjaya*—King Sṛñjaya; *kaikaya-ādyāḥ*—the King of Kekaya and others; *yāsyanti*—would attain; *adarśanam*—impersonal merging within the *brahmajyoti; alam*—what to speak of; *bala*—Baladeva, the elder brother of

Kṛṣṇa; *pārtha*—Arjuna; *bhīma*—the second Pāṇḍava; *vyāja-āhvayena*—by the false names; *hariṇā*—by Lord Hari; *nilayam*—the abode; *tadīyam*—of Him.

TRANSLATION

All demonic personalities like Pralamba, Dhenuka, Baka, Keśī, Ariṣṭa, Cāṇūra, Muṣṭika, Kuvalayāpīḍa elephant, Kaṁsa, Yavana, Narakāsura, and Pauṇḍraka, and great marshals like Śālva, Dvivida monkey, and Balvala, Dantavakra, the seven bulls, Śambara, Vidūratha and Rukmī, as also great warriors like Kāmboja, Matsya, Kuru, Sṛñjaya and Kekaya, would all fight vigorously, either with the Lord Hari directly or with Him under His names of Baladeva, Arjuna, Bhīma, etc. And the demons, thus being killed, would attain either the impersonal brahmajyoti or His personal abode in the Vaikuṇṭha planets.

PURPORT

All manifestations, both in the material and spiritual worlds, are demonstrations of the different potencies of Lord Kṛṣṇa. The Personality of Godhead Baladeva is His immediate personal expansion, and Bhīma, Arjuna, etc., are His personal associates. The Lord would appear (and He does so whenever He appears) with all His associates and potencies. Therefore the rebellious souls, like the demons and demoniac men, mentioned by names like Pralamba, etc., would be killed either by the Lord Himself or by His associates. All these affairs will be clearly explained in the Tenth Canto. But we should know well that all the above-mentioned living entities killed would attain salvation either by being merged in the *brahmajyoti* of the Lord or being allowed to enter into the abodes of the Lord called Vaikuṇṭhas. This is already explained by Bhīṣmadeva (First Canto). All persons who participated in the Battlefield of Kurukṣetra or otherwise with the Lord or with Baladeva, etc., would be benefitted by attaining spiritual existence according to the situation of the mind at the time of death. Those who recognized the Lord would enter Vaikuṇṭha, and those who estimated the Lord as a powerful being only would attain salvation by merging into the spiritual existence of the impersonal *brahmajyoti* of the Lord. But every one of them would get release from material existence. Since such is the benefit of those who played with the Lord inimically, one can imagine what would be the position of those who devoutly served the Lord in transcendental relationship with Him.

TEXT 36

कालेन मीलितधियामवमृश्य नृणां
स्तोकायुषां स्वनिगमो बत दूरपारः ।
आविर्हितस्त्वनुयुगं स हि सत्यवत्यां
वेदद्रुमं विटपशो विभजिष्यति स्म ॥३६॥

kālena mīlita-dhiyām avamṛśya nṛṇāṁ
stokāyuṣāṁ sva-nigamo bata dūra-pāraḥ
āvirhitas tv anuyugaṁ sa hi satyavatyāṁ
veda-drumaṁ viṭa-paśo vibhajiṣyati sma

kālena—in course of time; *mīlita-dhiyām*—of the less intelligent persons; *avamṛśya*—considering the difficulties; *nṛṇām*—of humanity at large; *stoka-āyuṣām*—of the short-living persons; *sva-nigamaḥ*—the Vedic literatures compiled by him; *bata*—exactly; *dūra-pāraḥ*—greatly difficult; *āvirhitaḥ*—having appeared as; *tu*—but; *anuyugam*—in terms of the age; *saḥ*—He, the Lord; *hi*—certainly; *satyavatyām*—in the womb of Satyavatī; *veda-drumam*—the desire tree of the *Vedas; viṭa-paśaḥ*—by division of branches; *vibhajiṣyati*—would divide; *sma*—as it were.

TRANSLATION

The Lord Himself in His incarnation as the son of Satyavatī [Vyāsadeva] would consider His compilation of the Vedic literature to be very difficult for the less intelligent persons with short life, and thus He would divide the tree of Vedic knowledge into different branches, according to the circumstances of the particular age.

PURPORT

Herein Brahmā mentions the future compilation of *Śrīmad-Bhāgavatam* for the short-lived persons of the Kali age. As explained in the First Canto, the less intelligent persons of the age of Kali would be not only short-lived, but also perplexed with so many problems of life due to the awkward situation of the godless human society. Advancement of material comforts of the body is activity in the mode of ignorance according to the laws of material nature. Real advancement of knowledge means progress of knowledge in self-realization. But in the age of Kali the less intelligent men mistakenly consider the short lifetime of one hundred years (now factually reduced to about forty or sixty years) to be all in all. They are less intelligent because they have no information of the eternity of life, and they identify with the temporary material body existing for forty years and consider it the only basic principle of life. Such persons are described as equal to the asses and bulls. But the Lord, as the compassionate father of all living beings, imparts unto them the vast Vedic knowledge in short treatises like the *Bhagavad-gītā* and, for the graduates, the *Śrīmad-Bhāgavatam*. The *Purāṇas* and the *Mahābhārata* are also similarly made by Vyāsadeva for the different types of men in the modes of material nature. But none of them are independent of the Vedic principles.

TEXT 37

देवद्विषां निगमवर्त्मनि निष्ठितानां
पूर्भिर्मयेन विहिताभिरदृश्यतूर्भिः ।
लोकान् घ्नतां मतिविमोहमतिप्रलोभं
वेषं विधाय बहु भाष्यत औपधर्म्यम्‌॥३७॥

deva-dviṣāṁ nigama-vartmani niṣṭhitānāṁ
pūrbhir mayena vihitābhir adṛśya-tūrbhiḥ
lokān ghnatāṁ mati-vimoham atipralobhaṁ
veṣaṁ vidhāya bahu bhāṣyata aupadharmyam

deva-dviṣām—of those who were envious of the devotees of the Lord; *nigama*—the *Vedas; vartmani*—on the path of; *niṣṭhitānām*—of the well situated; *pūrbhiḥ*—by rockets; *mayena*—made by the great scientist Maya; *vihitābhiḥ*—made by; *adṛśya-tūrbhiḥ*—unseen in the sky; *lokān*—the different planets; *ghnatām*—of the killers; *mati-vimoham*—bewilderment of the mind; *atipralobham*—very attractive; *veṣam*—dress; *vidhāya*—having done so; *bahu bhāṣyate*—would talk very much; *aupadharmyam*—subreligious principles.

TRANSLATION

When the atheists, after being well versed in the Vedic scientific knowledge, would annihilate inhabitants of different planets, flying unseen in the sky on well-built rockets prepared by the great scientist Maya, the Lord would bewilder their minds by dressing Himself attractively as Buddha and would preach on subreligious principles.

PURPORT

This incarnation of Lord Buddha is not exactly the same Buddha incarnation as we have in the present history of mankind. According to Śrīla Jīva Gosvāmī, the Buddha incarnation mentioned in this verse appeared in a different Kali age. In the duration of life of one Manu there are more than seventy-two Kali-yugas, and in one of them the particular type of Buddha mentioned here would appear. Lord Buddha incarnates at a time when the people are most materialistic and preaches common-sense religious principles. Such *ahiṁsā* is not a religious principle itself, but it is an important quality for persons who are actually religious. It is a common-sense religion because one is advised to do no harm to any other animal or living being because such harmful actions are equally harmful to him who does the harm. But before learning these principles of nonviolence one has to learn two other principles, namely to be humble and to be prideless. Unless one is humble and prideless, one cannot be harmless and nonviolent. And after being nonviolent one has to learn tolerance and simplicity of living. One must offer respects to the great religious preachers and spiritual leaders and also train the senses for controlled action, learning to be unattached to family and home, and enacting devotional service to the Lord, etc. At the ultimate stage one has to accept the Lord and become His devotee; otherwise there is no religion. In religious principles there must be God in the center; otherwise simple moral instructions are simply subreligious principles, generally known as *upadharma,* or nearness to religious principles.

TEXT 38

यर्ह्यालयेष्वपि सतां न हरेः कथाः स्युः
पाषण्डिनो द्विजजना वृषला नृदेवाः ।

स्वाहा स्वधा वषडिति स्म गिरो न यत्र
शास्ता भविष्यति कलेर्भगवान् युगान्ते ॥३८॥

yarhy ālayeṣv api satāṁ na hareḥ kathāḥ syuḥ
pāṣaṇḍino dvija-janā vṛṣalā nṛdevāḥ
svāhā svadhā vaṣaḍ iti sma giro na yatra
śāstā bhaviṣyati kaler bhagavān yugānte

yarhi—when it would so happen; *ālayeṣu*—in the residence of; *api*—even; *satām*—civilized gentlemen; *na*—no; *hareḥ*—of the Personality of Godhead; *kathāḥ*—topics; *syuḥ*—would take place; *pāṣaṇḍinaḥ*—atheists; *dvija-janāḥ*—persons declaring themselves to be the higher three classes *(brāhmaṇas, kṣatriyas* and *vaiśyas); vṛṣalāḥ*—the lower class *śūdras; nṛ-devāḥ*—ministers of the government; *svāhā*—hymns to perform sacrifices; *svadhā*—the ingredients to perform sacrifices; *vaṣaṭ*—the altar of sacrifice; *iti*—all these; *sma*—shall; *giraḥ*—words; *na*—never; *yatra*—anywhere; *śāstā*—the chastiser; *bhaviṣyati*—would appear; *kaleḥ*—of the Kali age; *bhagavān*—the Personality of Godhead; *yuga-ante*—at the end of.

TRANSLATION

Thereafter, at the end of Kali-yuga, when there would exist no topics on the subject of God, even at the residences of so-called saints and respectable gentlemen of the three higher castes, and when the power of government would be transferred to the hands of ministers elected from the lowborn śūdra class or those less than them, and when there would be nothing known of the techniques of sacrifice, even by word, at that time the Lord would appear as the supreme chastiser.

PURPORT

The symptoms of the worst conditions of the material world, at the last stage of this age, called Kali-yuga, are stated herein. The sum and substance of such conditions is godlessness. Even the so-called saints and higher castes of the social orders, generally known as the *dvija-janas* or the twice-born, will become atheists. As such, all of them will practically forget even the holy name of the Lord, and what to speak of His activities. The higher castes of society, namely the intelligent class of men guiding the destinies of the social orders, the administrative class of men guiding the law and order of the society, and the productive class of men guiding the economic development of the society, must all be properly well versed in knowledge of the Supreme Lord, knowing factually His name, quality, pastimes, entourage, paraphernalia and personalities. The saints and the higher castes or orders of the society are judged by their proportion of knowledge in the science of God, or *tattva-jñāna,* and not by any kind of birthright or bodily designations. Such designations, without any knowledge of the science of God and practical knowledge of devotional service, are considered to be but decorations of dead bodies. And when there is too much inflation of these decorated dead bodies in society, there develop so many anomalies in the progressive, peaceful life of the human being. Because of the lack of training or culture in the upper section of the social orders, they are no more to be designated as the *dvija-janas,* or the twice-born. The significance of being twice-born has been explained in many places in these great literatures, and again one is being reminded herewith that birth, executed by the sex life of the father and the mother, is called animal birth. But such animal birth and progress of life on the animal principles of eating, sleeping, fearing and mating (without any scientific culture of spiritual life) is called the *śūdra* life, or, to be more explicit, the uncultured life of the lower class of men. It is stated herein that the governmental power of the society in the Kali-yuga would be passed over to the uncultured, godless laborer classes of men, and thus the *nṛdevas* (or the ministers of the government) would be the *vṛṣalas,* or the uncultured lower-class men of society. No one can expect any peace and prosperity in a human society full of uncultured lower classes of men. The symptoms of such uncultured social animals are already in vogue, and it is the duty of the leaders of men to take note of it and try to reform the social order by introducing the principles of twice-born men trained in the science of God consciousness. This can be done by expanding the culture of *Śrīmad-Bhāgavatam* all over the world. In the degraded condition of the human society, the Lord incarnates as the Kalki *avatāra* and kills all the demonic without mercy.

TEXT 39

सर्गे तपोऽहमृषयो नव ये प्रजेशाः
स्थानेऽथ धर्ममखमन्वमरावनीशाः ।

अन्ते त्वधर्महरमन्युवशासुराद्या
मायाविभूतय इमाः पुरुशक्तिभाजः ॥३९॥

sarge tapo'ham ṛṣayo nava ye prajeśāḥ
sthāne'tha dharma-makha-manv-amarāvanīśāḥ
ante tv adharma-hara-manyuvaśāsurādyā
māyā-vibhūtaya imāḥ puru-śakti-bhājaḥ

sarge—in the beginning of the creation; *tapaḥ*—penance; *aham*—myself; *ṛṣayaḥ*—sages; *nava*—nine; *ye prajeśāḥ*—those who would generate; *sthāne*—in the middle while maintaining the creation; *atha*—certainly; *dharma*—religion; *makha*—Lord Viṣṇu; *manu*—the father of mankind; *amara*—the demigods deputed to control the affairs of maintenance; *avanīśāḥ*—and the kings of different planets; *ante*—at the end; *tu*—but; *adharma*—irreligion; *hara*—Lord Śiva; *manyu-vaśa*—subjected to anger; *asura-ādyāḥ*—atheists, the enemies of the devotees; *māyā*—energy; *vibhūtayaḥ*—powerful representatives; *imāḥ*—all of them; *puru-śakti-bhājaḥ*—of the Supreme Powerful Lord.

TRANSLATION

At the beginning of creation there is penance, myself [Brahmā], the Prajāpatis, and great sages who generate; then, during the maintenance of the creation, there is Lord Viṣṇu, the demigods with controlling powers, and the kings of different planets. But at the end there is irreligion, and then Lord Śiva and the atheists full of anger, etc. All of them are different representative manifestations of the energy of the supreme power, the Lord.

PURPORT

The material world is created by the energy of the Lord, which is manifested in the beginning of the creation by the penance of Brahmājī, the first living being in the creation, and then there are the nine Prajāpatis, known as great sages. In the stage when the creation is maintained, there are devotional service to Lord Viṣṇu, or factual religion, the different demigods, and the kings of different planets who maintain the world. At last, when the creation is preparing to wind up, there is first the principle of irreligion, then Lord Śiva along with the atheists, full of anger. But all of them are but different manifestations of the Supreme Lord. Therefore Brahmā, Viṣṇu and Mahādeva (Śiva) are different incarnations of the different modes of material nature. Viṣṇu is the Lord of the mode of goodness. Brahmā is the lord of the mode of passion, and Śiva is the lord of the mode of ignorance. Ultimately, the material creation is but a temporary manifestation meant to give the chance of liberation to the conditioned souls who are entrapped in the material world, and one who develops the mode of goodness under the protection of Lord Viṣṇu has the greatest chance of being liberated by following the Vaiṣṇava principles and thus being promoted to the kingdom of God, no more to return to this miserable material world.

TEXT 40

विष्णोर्नु वीर्यगणनां कतमोऽर्हतीह
यः पार्थिवान्यपि कविर्विममे रजांसि ।
चस्कम्भ यः स्वरहसास्खलता त्रिपृष्ठं
यस्मात् त्रिसाम्यसदनादुरु कम्पयानम् ॥४०॥

viṣṇor nu vīrya-gaṇanāṁ katamo'rhatīha
yaḥ pārthivāny api kavir vimame rajāṁsi
caskambha yaḥ sva-rahasāskhalatā tri-pṛṣṭhaṁ
yasmāt tri-sāmya-sadanād uru-kampayānam

viṣṇoḥ—of Lord Viṣṇu; *nu*—but; *vīrya*—prowess; *gaṇanām*—in the matter of accounting; *katamaḥ*—who else; *arhati*—is able to do it; *iha*—in this world; *yaḥ*—one who; *pārthivāni*—the atoms; *api*—also; *kaviḥ*—great scientist; *vimame*—might have counted; *rajāṁsi*—particles; *caskambha*—could catch; *yaḥ*—one who; *sva-rahasā*—by His own leg; *askhalatā*—without being hampered; *tri-pṛṣṭham*—the topmost planetary space; *yasmāt*—by which; *tri-sāmya*—the neutral state of the three modes; *sadanāt*—up to that place; *uru-kampayānam*—moving very greatly.

TRANSLATION

Who can describe completely the prowess of Viṣṇu? Even the scientist, who might have counted the particles of the atoms of the universe, cannot

do so. Because it is He only who, in His form of Trivikrama, moved His leg effortlessly beyond the topmost planet, Satyaloka, up to the neutral state of the three modes of material nature. And all were moved.

PURPORT

The highest scientific advancement of the material scientist is atomic energy. But the material scientist is not able to have an estimation of the particles of atoms contained in the whole of the universe. But even if one is able to count such atomic particles or is able to roll up the sky, like one's bedding, even then one is unable to estimate the extent of the prowess and energy of the Supreme Lord. He is known as Trivikrama because once, in His incarnation of Vāmana, He expanded His leg beyond the highest planetary system of Satyaloka and reached the neutral state of the modes of nature called the covering of the material world. There are seven layers of material coverings over the material sky, and the Lord could penetrate even those coverings. And with His toe He made a hole through which the water of the Causal Ocean filters into the material sky, and the current is known as the sacred Ganges, which purifies the planets of the three worlds. In other words, no one is equal to the transcendentally powerful Viṣṇu. He is omnipotent, and no one is equal to or greater than Him.

TEXT 41

नान्तं विदाम्यहममी मुनयोऽग्रजास्ते
मायाबलस्य पुरुषस्य कुतोऽवरा ये ।
गायन् गुणान् दशशतानन आदिदेवः
शेषोऽधुनापि समवस्यति नास्य पारम् ॥४१॥

nāntaṁ vidāmy aham amī munayo'gra-jās te
māyā-balasya puruṣasya kuto'varā ye
gāyan guṇān daśa-śatānana ādi-devaḥ
śeṣo'dhunāpi samavasyati nāsya pāram

na—never; *antam*—end; *vidāmi*—do I know; *aham*—myself; *amī*—and all those; *munayaḥ*—great sages; *agra-jāḥ*—born prior to yourself; *te*—you; *māyā-balasya*—of the omnipotent; *puruṣasya*—of the Personality of Godhead; *kutaḥ*—what to speak of others; *avarāḥ*—born after us; *ye*—those; *gāyan*—by singing; *guṇān*—the qualities; *daśa-śata-ānanaḥ*—one who has ten hundred faces; *ādi-devaḥ*—the first incarnation of the Lord; *śeṣaḥ*—known as Śeṣa; *adhunā*—up to date; *api*—even; *samavasyati*—can achieve; *na*—not; *asya*—of Him; *pāram*—limit.

TRANSLATION

Neither myself nor all the sages who were born before you know fully the omnipotent Personality of Godhead. So what can others, who are born after us, know about Him? Even the first incarnation of the Lord, namely Śeṣa, has not been able to reach the limit of such knowledge, although He is describing the qualities of the Lord with ten hundred faces.

PURPORT

The omnipotent Personality of Godhead has primarily three potential manifestations, namely internal, external, and marginal potencies, with unlimited expansions of these three energies. As such, the potential expansions can never be calculated by anyone because even the Personality of God Himself, as the incarnation of Śeṣa, could not estimate the potencies, although He has been describing them continually with His one thousand faces.

TEXT 42

येषां स एष भगवान् दययेदनन्तः
सर्वात्मनाश्रितपदो यदि निर्व्यलीकम् ।
ते दुस्तरामतितरन्ति च देवमायां
नैषां ममाहमिति धीः श्वशृगालभक्ष्ये ॥४२॥

yeṣāṁ sa eṣa bhagavān dayayed anantaḥ
sarvātmanāśrita-pado yadi nirvyalīkam
te dustarām atitaranti ca deva-māyāṁ
naiṣāṁ mamāham iti dhīḥ śva-śṛgāla-bhakṣye

yeṣām—unto those only; *saḥ*—the Lord; *eṣaḥ*—the; *bhagavān*—the Personality of Godhead; *dayayet*—does bestow His mercy; *anantaḥ*—the unlimited potential; *sarva-ātmanā*—by all means without reservation; *āśrita-padaḥ*—surrendered soul; *yadi*—if such surrender; *nirvyalīkam*—without pretention; *te*—those only; *dustarām*—insurmountable; *atitaranti*—can overcome; *ca*—and the paraphernalia; *deva-māyām*—diverse energies of the Lord; *na*—not; *eṣām*—of them; *mama*—mine; *aham*—myself; *iti*—thus; *dhīḥ*—conscious; *śva*—dogs; *śṛgāla*—jackals; *bhakṣye*—in the matter of eating.

TRANSLATION

But anyone who is specifically favored by the Supreme Lord, the Personality of Godhead, due to unalloyed surrender unto the service of the Lord, can overcome the insurmountable ocean of illusion and can understand the Lord also. But those who are attached to this body, which is meant to be eaten up at the end by dogs and jackals, cannot do so.

PURPORT

The unalloyed devotees of the Lord know the glories of the Lord in the sense that they can understand how great the Lord is and how great is His expansion of diverse energy. Those who are attached to the perishable body can hardly enter into the realm of the science of Godhead. The whole materialistic world, based on the conception of the material body as the self, is ignorant of the science of God. The materialist is always busy working for the welfare of the material body, not only of his own but also that of his children, kinsmen, communitymen, countrymen, etc. They have many branches of philanthropic and altruistic activities from a political, national, and international angle of vision, but none of the field work can go beyond the jurisdiction of the misconception of identifying the material body with the spirit soul. Unless, therefore, one is saved from the wrong conception of the body and the soul, there is no knowledge of Godhead, and unless there is knowledge of God, all advancement of material civilization, however dazzling, should be considered to be a failure.

TEXTS 43-45

वेदाहमङ्ग परमस्य हि योगमायां
यूयं भवश्च भगवानथ दैत्यवर्यः ।
पत्नी मनोः स च मनुश्च तदात्मजाश्च
प्राचीनबर्हिर्ऋभुरङ्ग उत ध्रुवश्च ॥४३॥
इक्ष्वाकुरैलमुचुकुन्दविदेहगाधि-
रघ्वम्बरीषसगरा गयनाहुषाद्याः ।
मान्धात्रलर्कशतधन्वनुरन्तिदेवा
देवव्रतो बलिरमूर्त्तरयो दिलीपः ॥४४॥
सौभर्युतङ्कशिबिदेवलपिप्पलाद-
सारस्वतोद्धवपराशरभूरिषेणाः ।
येऽन्ये विभीषणहनूमदुपेन्द्रदत्त-
पार्थार्ष्टिषेणविदुरश्रुतदेववर्याः ॥४५॥

vedāham aṅga paramasya hi yoga-māyāṁ
yūyaṁ bhavaś ca bhagavān atha daitya-varyaḥ
patnī manoḥ sa ca manuś ca tad-ātmajāś ca
prācīnabarhir ṛbhur aṅga uta dhruvaś ca

ikṣvākur aila-mucukunda-videha-gādhi-
raghv-ambarīṣa-sagarā gaya-nāhuṣādyāḥ
māndhātralarka-śatadhanvanu-rantidevā
devavrato balir amūrttarayo dilīpaḥ

saubharyutaṅka-śibi-devala-pippalāda-
sārasvatoddhava-parāśara-bhūriṣeṇāḥ
ye'nye vibhīṣaṇa-hanūmad-upendradatta-
pārthārṣṭiṣeṇa-vidura-śrutadeva-varyāḥ

veda—know it; *aham*—myself; *aṅga*—O Nārada; *paramasya*—of the Supreme; *hi*—certainly; *yoga-māyām*—potency; *yūyam*—yourself; *bhavaḥ*—Śiva; *ca*—and; *bhagavān*—the great demigod; *atha*—as also; *daitya-varyaḥ*—Prahlāda Mahārāja, the great devotee of the Lord born in the family of the atheist; *patnī*—Śatarūpā; *manoḥ*—of Manu; *saḥ*—he; *ca*—also; *manuḥ*—

Svāyambhuva; *ca*—and; *tat-ātmajāḥ ca*—and his children like Priyavrata, Uttānapāda, Devahūti, etc.

TRANSLATION

O Nārada, although the potencies of the Lord are unknowable and immeasurable, still, because we are all surrendered souls, we know how He acts through yogamāyā potencies. And, similarly, the all-powerful Śiva, the great king of the atheist family, namely Prahlāda Mahārāja, Svāyambhuva Manu, his wife Śatarūpā, his sons and daughters like Priyavrata, Uttānapāda, Ākūti, Devahūti, Prasūti, etc., Prācīnabarhi, Ṛbhu, Aṅga the father of Vena, Mahārāja Dhruva, Ikṣvāku, Aila, Mucukunda, Mahārāja Janaka, Gādhi, Raghu, Ambarīṣa, Sagara, Gaya, Nāhuṣa, Māndhātā, Alarka, Śatadhanu, Anu, Rantideva, Bhīṣma, Bali, Amūrtaraya, Dilīpa, Saubhari, Utaṅka, Śibi, Devala, Pippalāda, Sārasvata, Uddhava, Parāśara, Bhūriṣeṇa, Vibhīṣaṇa, Hanūmān, Śukadeva Gosvāmī, Arjuna, Ārṣṭiṣena, Vidura, Śrutadeva, etc., all also know the potencies of the Lord.

PURPORT

All the great devotees of the Lord, as mentioned above, who flourished in the past or present, and all devotees of the Lord who will come in the future, are aware of the different potencies of the Lord along with the potency of His name, quality, pastimes, entourage, personality, etc. And how do they know? Certainly it is not by mental speculation, nor by any attempt by dint of limited instruments of knowledge. By the limited instruments of knowledge (either senses or the material instruments like microscopes and telescopes) one cannot even fully know the Lord's material potencies, which are manifested before our eyes. For example there are many millions and billions of planets far, far beyond the scientist's calculation. But these are only the manifestations of the Lord's material energy. What can the scientist hope to know of the spiritual potency of the Lord by such material efforts? Mental speculations, by adding some dozens of "if's" and "maybe's," cannot aid the advancement of knowledge—on the contrary, such mental speculation will only end in despair by dismissing the case abruptly and declaring the nonexistence of God. The sane person, therefore, ceases to speculate on subjects beyond the jurisdiction of his tiny brain, and as a matter of course he tries to learn to surrender unto the Supreme Lord, who alone can lead one to the platform of real knowledge. In the *Upaniṣads* it is clearly said that the Supreme Personality of Godhead can never be known simply by working very hard and taxing the good brain, nor can He be known simply by mental speculation and jugglery of words. The Lord is knowable only by one who is a surrendered soul. Herein Brahmājī, the greatest of all material living beings, acknowledges this truth. Therefore, the fruitless spoiling of energy by pursuing the path of experimental knowledge must be given up. One should gain knowledge by surrendering unto the Lord and by acknowledging the authority of the persons mentioned herein. The Lord is unlimited and, by the grace of the *yogamāyā,* helps the surrendered soul to know Him proportionately with the advance of one's surrendering process.

TEXT 46

ते वै विदन्त्यतितरन्ति च देवमायां
स्त्रीशूद्रहूणशबरा अपि पापजीवाः ।
यद्यद्भुतक्रमपरायणशीलशिक्षा-
स्तिर्यग्जना अपि किमु श्रुतधारणा ये ॥४६॥

te vai vidanty atitaranti ca deva-māyāṁ
strī-śūdra-hūṇa-śabarā api pāpa-jīvāḥ
yady adbhuta-krama-parāyaṇa-śīla-śikṣās
tiryag-janā api kim u śruta-dhāraṇā ye

te—such persons; *vai*—undoubtedly; *vidanti*—do know; *atitaranti*—surpass; *ca*—also; *deva-māyām*—the covering energy of the Lord; *strī*—such as women; *śūdra*—the laborer class of men; *hūṇa*—the mountaineers; *śabarāḥ*—the Siberians, or those lower than the *śūdras; api*—although; *pāpa-jīvāḥ*—sinful living beings; *yadi*—provided; *adbhuta-krama*—one whose acts are so wonderful; *parāyaṇa*—those who are devotees; *śīla*—behavior; *śikṣāḥ*—trained up by, *tiryak-janāḥ*—even those who are not human beings; *api*—also; *kim*—what; *u*—to speak of; *śruta-dhāraṇāḥ*—those who have taken to the idea of the Lord by hearing about Him; *ye*—those.

TRANSLATION

Surrendered souls, even from the groups leading sinful lives, such as the woman, the laborer class, the mountaineers, the Siberians, etc., or

even the birds and beasts, can also know about the science of Godhead and become liberated from the clutches of the illusory energy by surrendering unto the pure devotees of the Lord and by following in their footsteps in devotional service.

PURPORT

Sometimes there are inquiries as to how one can surrender unto the Supreme Lord. In the *Bhagavad-gītā* (Bg. 18.66) the Lord asked Arjuna to surrender unto Him, and therefore persons unwilling to do so question as to where God is and to whom they should surrender. The answer to such questions or inquiries is given herein very properly. The Personality of Godhead may not be present before one's eyes, but if one is sincere in wanting such guidance the Lord will send a bona fide person who can guide one properly back to home, back to Godhead. There is no need of material qualifications for making progress in the path of spiritual realization. In the material world, when one accepts some particular type of service, he is required to possess some particular type of qualification also. Without this one is unfit for such service. But in the devotional service of the Lord the only qualification required is surrender. Surrendering oneself is in one's own hand. If one likes, he can surrender immediately without any delay, and that begins his spiritual life. The bona fide representative of God is as good as God Himself. Or, in other words, the loving representative of the Lord is more kind and more easy to approach. A sinful soul cannot approach the Lord directly, but such a sinful man can very easily approach a pure devotee of the Lord. And if one agrees to put himself under the guidance of such a devotee of the Lord, he can also understand the science of God and can also become like the transcendental pure devotee of the Lord and thus get his liberation back to Godhead, back home for eternal happiness.

So realization of the science of Godhead and relief from the unnecessary, useless struggle for existence are not at all difficult for the willing candidate. But they are very difficult for persons who are not surrendered souls but only simple, profitless speculators.

TEXT 47

शश्वत् प्रशान्तमभयं प्रतिबोधमात्रं
शुद्धं समं सदसतः परमात्मतत्त्वम् ।
शब्दो न यत्र पुरुकारकवान् क्रियार्थो
माया परैत्यभिमुखे च विलज्जमाना

तद् वै पदं भगवतः परमस्य पुंसो
ब्रह्मेति यद् विदुरजस्रसुखं विशोकम् ॥४७॥

śaśvat praśāntam abhayaṁ pratibodha-mātraṁ
śuddhaṁ samaṁ sad-asataḥ paramātma-tattvam
śabdo na yatra puru-kārakavān kriyārtho
māyā paraity abhimukhe ca vilajjamānā
tad vai padaṁ bhagavataḥ paramasya puṁso
brahmeti yad vidur ajasra-sukhaṁ viśokam

śaśvat—eternal; ***praśāntam***—without disturbance; ***abhayam***—without fear; ***pratibodha-mātram***—a consciousness opposed to the material counterpart; ***śuddham***—uncontaminated; ***samam***—without distinction; ***sat-asataḥ***—of the cause and effect; ***paramātma-tattvam***—the principle of primeval cause; ***śabdaḥ***—speculative sound; ***na***—not; ***yatra***—where there is; ***puru-kārakavān***—resulting in fruitive action; ***kriyā-arthaḥ***—for the matter of sacrifice; ***māyā***—illusion; ***paraiti***—flies away; ***abhimukhe***—in front of; ***ca***—also; ***vilajjamānā***—being ashamed of; ***tat***—that; ***vai***—is certainly; ***padam***—ultimate phase; ***bhagavataḥ***—of the Personality of Godhead; ***paramasya***—of the Supreme; ***puṁsaḥ***—of the person; ***brahma***—the Absolute; ***iti***—thus; ***yat***—which; ***viduḥ***—known as; ***ajasra***—unlimited; ***sukham***—happiness; ***viśokam***—without grief.

TRANSLATION

What is realized as the Absolute Brahman is full of unlimited bliss without grief. That is certainly the ultimate phase of the supreme enjoyer, the Personality of Godhead. He is eternally void of all disturbances, without any fear, complete consciousness as opposed to matter, uncontaminated, without any distinction, the principle primeval cause of all causes and effects, in whom there is no sacrifice for fruitive activities, and in whom the illusory energy does not stand.

PURPORT

The supreme enjoyer, Personality of Godhead, is the Supreme Brahman or the *summum bonum* because of His being the supreme cause of all causes. The conception of impersonal Brahman realization is the first step, due to His distinction from the illusory conception of material existence. In other words, impersonal Brahman is a feature of the Absolute distinct from the material variegatedness, just as light is a conception distinct from its counterpart, darkness. But the light has its variegatedness, which is seen by those who further advance in the light, and thus the ultimate realization of Brahman is the source of the Brahman light, the Supreme Personality of Godhead, the *summum bonum* or the ultimate source of everything. Therefore, meeting the Personality of Godhead includes the realization of the impersonal Brahman as realized at first in contrast with material inebriety. The Personality of Godhead is the third step of Brahman realization. As explained in the First Canto, one must understand all three features of the Absolute—Brahman, Paramātmā, and Bhagavān.

Pratibodha-mātram is just the opposite conception of material existence. In matter there are material miseries, and thus in the first realization of Brahman there is the negation of such material inebrieties and a feeling of eternal existence distinct from the pangs of birth and death, disease and old age. That is the primary conception of impersonal Brahman.

The Supreme Lord is the Supreme Soul of everything, and therefore in the supreme conception affection is realized. The conception of affection is due to the relationship of soul to soul. A father is affectionate to his son because there is some relationship of nearness between the son and the father. But that sort of affection in the material world is full of inebriety. When the Personality of Godhead is met, the fullness of affection becomes manifested because of the reality of the affectionate relationship. He is not the object of affection by material tinges of body and mind, but He is the full, naked uncontaminated object of affection for all living entities because He is the Supersoul or Paramātmā within everyone's heart. In the liberated state of affairs, the full-fledged affection for the Lord is awakened.

As such, there is an unlimited flow of happiness, everlasting, without any fear of being broken as we have experienced here in the material world. The relationship with the Lord is never broken; thus there is no grief and no fear. Such happiness is inexplicable by words, and there can be no attempt to generate such happiness by fruitive activities by arrangement and sacrifices. But we must know also that happiness, unbroken happiness, exchanged with the Supreme Person, the Personality of Godhead as described in this verse, transcends the impersonal conception of the *Upaniṣads*. In the *Upaniṣads* the description is more or less negation of the material conception of things, but this is not denial of the transcendental senses of the Supreme Lord. Herein also the same is affirmed in the statements about the material elements; they are all transcendental, free from all contamination of material identification. And also the liberated souls are not devoid of senses; otherwise there cannot be any reciprocation of unhampered spiritual happiness exchanged between them in spontaneous unbroken joy. All the senses, both of the Lord and of the devotees, are without any material contamination. They are so because they are beyond the material cause and effects, as it is clearly mentioned herein *(sad-asataḥ param).* The illusory material energy cannot work there, being ashamed before the Lord and His transcendental devotees. In the material world the sense activities are not without grief, but here it is clearly said that the senses of the Lord and the devotees are without any grief. There is a distinct difference between the material and spiritual senses. And it should be understood without denying the spiritual senses because of a material conception.

The senses in the material world are surcharged with material ignorance. In every way the authorities have recommended purification of the senses from the material conception. In the material world the senses are manipulated for individual and personal satisfaction, whereas in the spiritual world the senses are properly used for the purpose for which they were originally meant, namely the satisfaction of the Supreme Lord. Such sensual activities are natural, and therefore sense gratification there is uninterrupted and unbroken by material contamination because the senses are spiritually purified. And such satisfaction of the senses is equally shared by the transcendental reciprocators. Since the activities are unlimited and constantly increasing, there is no scope for material attempts or artificial arrangements. Such happiness of transcendental quality is called *brahma-saukhyam,* which will be clearly described in the Fifth Canto.

TEXT 48

सध्र्यङ् नियम्य यतयो यमकर्तहेतिं
जह्युः स्वराडिव निपानखनित्रमिन्द्रः ॥४८॥

sadhryaṅ niyamya yatayo yama-karta-hetiṁ
jahyuḥ svarāḍ iva nipāna-khanitram indraḥ

sadhryaṅ—artificial mental speculation or meditation; *niyamya*—controlling; *yatayaḥ*—the mystics; *yama-karta-hetim*—the process of spiritual culture; *jahyuḥ*—are given up; *svarāṭ*—fully independent; *iva*—as; *nipāna*—well; *khanitram*—trouble for digging; *indraḥ*—the controlling demigod supplying rains.

TRANSLATION

In such a transcendental state there is no need of artificial control of the mind, mental speculation or meditation, as performed by the jñānīs and yogīs. Such processes are given up, as the heavenly King, Indra, does not take the trouble to dig a well.

PURPORT

A poor man in want of water digs a well and undertakes the trouble of digging. Similarly, those who are poor in transcendental realization speculate on the mind or meditate by controlling the senses. But they do not know that such control of the senses and achievement of spiritual perfection are simultaneously made possible as soon as one is factually engaged in the transcendental loving service of the Supreme Person, the Personality of Godhead. It is for this reason that the great liberated souls also desire to be associated in hearing and chanting the activities of the Lord. The example of Indra is very appropriate in this connection. King Indra of heaven is the controlling deity or demigod for arranging clouds and supplying rains in the universe, and as such he does not have to take the trouble to dig a well for his personal water supply. For him, digging a well for a water supply is simply ludicrous. Similarly, those who are factually engaged in the loving service of the Lord have attained the ultimate goal of life, and for them there is no need of mental speculation to find out the true nature of God or His activities. Nor do such devotees have to meditate upon the imaginary or real identity of the Lord. Because they are factually engaged in the transcendental loving service of the Lord, the Lord's pure devotees have already achieved the results of mental speculation and meditation. The real perfection of life is therefore to be engaged in the transcendental loving service of the Lord.

TEXT 49

स श्रेयसामपि विभुर्भगवान् यतोऽस्य
भावस्वभावविहितस्य सतः प्रसिद्धिः ।
देहे स्वधातुविगमेऽनुविशीर्यमाणे
व्योमेव तत्र पुरुषो न विशीर्यतेऽजः ॥४९॥

sa śreyasām api vibhur bhagavān yato'sya
bhāva-svabhāva-vihitasya sataḥ prasiddhiḥ
dehe sva-dhātu-vigame'nuviśīryamāṇe
vyomeva tatra puruṣo na viśīryate'jaḥ

saḥ—He; *śreyasām*—all auspiciousness; *api*—also; *vibhuḥ*—the master; *bhagavān*—the Personality of Godhead; *yataḥ*—because; *asya*—of the living entity; *bhāva*—natural modes; *sva-bhāva*—own constitution; *vihitasya*—performances; *sataḥ*—all good work; *prasiddhiḥ*—ultimate success; *dehe*—of the body; *sva-dhātu*—forming elements; *vigame*—being vanquished; *anu*—after; *viśīryamāṇe*—having given up; *vyoma*—sky; *iva*—like; *tatra*—thereupon; *puruṣaḥ*—the living entity; *na*—never; *viśīryate*—becomes vanquished; *ajaḥ*—due to being unborn.

TRANSLATION

The Personality of Godhead is the supreme master of everything auspicious because the results of whatever actions are performed by the living being, either in the material or spiritual existence, are awarded by the Lord. As such, He is the ultimate benefactor. Every individual living entity is unborn, and therefore even after the annihilation of the material elementary body, the living entity exists, exactly like the air within the body.

PURPORT

The living entity is unborn and eternal, and as it is confirmed in the *Bhagavad-gītā* (Bg. 2.30), the living entity is not exhausted even though the material elementary body is vanquished. As long as the living entity is in the material existence, actions performed by him are rewarded in the next life, or even in the present life. Similarly, in his spiritual life also actions are rewarded by the Lord by the five kinds of liberation. Even the impersonalist cannot achieve the desired merging into the existence of the Supreme without being favored by the Supreme Personality of Godhead. It is confirmed in the *Bhagavad-gītā* also (Bg. 4.11) that the Lord awards similar results, as one desires, in one's present life. The living entities are given freedom to make their choice, and the Lord awards them accordingly.

It is the duty of everyone, therefore, to worship devoutly only the Personality of Godhead to achieve his desired goal. The impersonalist, instead of speculating or meditating, can directly execute the routine devotional service of the Lord and thus easily obtain the desired goal.

The devotees, however, are naturally inclined to become associates of the Lord without being merged in the spiritual existence, as conceived by the impersonalist. The devotees, therefore, following their constitutional instincts, achieve the desired goal of becoming servitors, friends, fathers, mothers or conjugal lovers of the Lord. The devotional service of the Lord involves nine transcendental processes of hearing and chanting, etc., and by performing such easy and natural devotional services the devotees achieve the highest perfectional results, far, far superior to merging into the existence of the Brahman. The devotees are, therefore, never advised to indulge in speculating upon the nature of the Supreme, or artificially meditating on the void.

One should not, however, misunderstand that after the annihilation of this present body there is no body by which one can associate with the Lord face to face. The living entity is unborn. It is not that he is manifest with the creation of the material body. On the other hand, it is true that the material body develops only by the desire of the living entity. The evolution of the material body is due to such desires of the living being. According to the desires of the living being, the material body develops. So from the spirit soul the material body comes into existence, generated from the living force. As the living being is eternal, so he exists just like the air within the body. Air is within and without the body. Therefore when the external covering, the material body, is vanquished, the living spark, like the air within the body, continues to exist. And by the direction of the Lord, because He is the ultimate benefactor, the living entity is at once awarded the necessary spiritual body befitting his association with the Lord in the manner of *sārūpya* (equal bodily feature), *sālokya* (equal facility to live in the same planet with the Lord), *sārṣṭi* (equal possession of opulence like the Lord), and *sāmīpya* (equal association with the Lord).

The Lord is so kind that even if a devotee of the Lord cannot fulfill the complete course of devotional service unalloyed and uncontaminated by material association, he is given another chance in the next life by being awarded a birth in the family of a devotee or rich man so that without being engaged in the struggle for material existence, the devotee can finish the remaining purification of his existence and thus immediately, after relinquishing the present body, go back home, back to Godhead. This is confirmed in the *Bhagavad-gītā*.

In this connection detailed information is available in the *Bhagavat-sandarbha* of Śrīla Jīva Gosvāmī Prabhupāda. Once achieving the spiritual existence, the devotee is eternally situated there, as already discussed in the previous verse.

TEXT 50

सोऽयं तेऽभिहितस्तात भगवान् विश्वभावनः ।
समासेन हरेर्नान्यदन्यस्मात् सदसच्च यत् ॥५०॥

so'yaṁ te'bhihitas tāta
bhagavān viśva-bhāvanaḥ
samāsena harer nānyad
anyasmāt sad-asac ca yat

saḥ—that; *ayam*—the same; *te*—unto you; *abhihitaḥ*—explained by me; *tāta*—my dear son; *bhagavān*—the Personality of Godhead; *viśva-bhāvanaḥ*—the creator of the manifested worlds; *samāsena*—in brief; *hareḥ*—without Hari, the Lord; *na*—never; *anyat*—anything else; *anyasmāt*—being the cause of; *sat*—manifested or phenomenal; *asat*—noumenal; *ca*—and; *yat*—whatever there may be.

TRANSLATION

My dear son, I have now explained in brief the Supreme Personality of Godhead, who is creator of the manifested worlds. Without Him, Hari, the Lord, there are no other causes of the phenomenal and noumenal existences.

PURPORT

As we have generally the experience of the temporary, material world and conditioned souls trying to lord it over the material worlds, so Brahmājī explained to Nāradadeva that this temporary world is the work of the external potency of the Lord, and the conditioned souls struggling here for existence are the marginal potency of the Supreme Lord Personality of Godhead, and but for Him, Hari, the Supreme Lord, there is no other cause for all these phenomenal activities. He is the primeval cause of all causes. This does not mean, however, that the Lord Himself is distributed impersonally. He is aloof from all these interactions of the external and marginal potencies. In the *Bhagavad-gītā,* it is confirmed

(Bg. 9.4) that by His potencies alone He is present everywhere and anywhere, and everything that is manifested rests on His potency only, but He, as the Supreme Personality of Godhead, is always aloof from them. The potency and the potent are simultaneously one and different from one another.

One should not deprecate the Supreme Lord for the creation of this miserable world, just as one should not blame the king for creating a prisonhouse in the government. The prisonhouse is a necessary institution of the establishment of the government for those who are disobedient to the laws of the government. Similarly, this material world, full of miseries, is a temporary creation of the Lord for those who have forgotten Him and are trying to lord it over the false manifestation. He, however, is always anxious to get the fallen souls back home, back to Godhead, and for this He has given so many chances to the conditioned souls via the authoritative scriptures, His representatives, and personal incarnations also. Since He has no direct attachment to this material world, He is not to be blamed for its creation.

TEXT 51

इदं भागवतं नाम यन्मे भगवतोदितम् ।
संग्रहोऽयं विभूतीनां त्वमेतद् विपुलीकुरु ॥५१॥

idaṁ bhāgavataṁ nāma
yan me bhagavatoditam
saṅgraho'yaṁ vibhūtīnāṁ
tvam etad vipulīkuru

idam—this; *bhāgavatam*—the science of Godhead; *nāma*—of the name; *yat*—that which; *me*—unto me; *bhagavata*—by the Personality of Godhead; *uditam*—enlightened; *saṅgrahaḥ*—is the accumulation of; *ayam*—His; *vibhūtīnām*—of the diverse potencies; *tvam*—your good self; *etat*—this science of Godhead; *vipulī*—expand; *kuru*—do it.

TRANSLATION

O Nārada, this science of God, Śrīmad-Bhāgavatam, was spoken to me in a nutshell by the Supreme Personality of Godhead, and it was spoken in

a nutshell as the accumulation of His diverse potencies. Please expand this science yourself.

PURPORT

The *Bhāgavatam* in a nutshell, spoken in about half a dozen verses by the Personality of Godhead, as it will appear ahead, is the science of God, and it is the potential representation of the Personality of Godhead. He, being absolute, is nondifferent from the science of God, *Śrīmad-Bhāgavatam.* Brahmājī received this science of Godhead from the Lord directly, and he handed over the same to Nārada, who in his turn ordered Śrīla Vyāsadeva to expand it. So the transcendental knowledge of the Supreme Lord is not mental speculation by the mundane wranglers, but is uncontaminated, eternal, perfect knowledge beyond the jurisdiction of material modes. The *Bhāgavata Purāṇa* is therefore the direct incarnation of the Lord in the form of transcendental sound, and one should receive this transcendental knowledge from the bona fide representative of the Lord in the chain of disciplic succession from the Lord to Brahmājī, from Brahmājī to Nārada, from Nārada to Vyāsa, from Vyāsadeva to Śukadeva Gosvāmī, from Śukadeva Gosvāmī to Sūta Gosvāmī, as the ripened fruit of the Vedic tree drops from one hand to another without being broken by falling suddenly from the high branch down to the earth. Therefore unless one hears the science of Godhead from the bona fide representative of the disciplic succession, as above mentioned, it will be a difficult job for one to understand the theme of the science of Godhead. It should never be heard from the professional *Bhāgavatam* reciters who earn their livelihood by gratifying the senses of the audience.

TEXT 52

यथा हरौ भगवति नृणां भक्तिर्भविष्यति ।
सर्वात्मन्यखिलाधारे इति सङ्कल्प्य वर्णय ॥५२॥

yathā harau bhagavati
nṛṇāṁ bhaktir bhaviṣyati
sarvātmany akhilādhāre
iti saṅkalpya varṇaya

yathā—as much as; *harau*—unto the Personality of Godhead; *bhagavati*—unto the Lord; *nṛṇām*—for human beings; *bhaktiḥ*—devotional service; *bhaviṣyati*—become enlightened; *sarva-ātmani*—the Absolute Whole; *akhila-ādhāre*—unto the *summum bonum; iti*—thus; *saṅkalpya*—by determination; *varṇaya*—describe.

TRANSLATION

Please describe the science of Godhead with determination and in a manner by which it will be quite possible for the human being to develop transcendental devotional service unto the Personality of Godhead Hari, the Supersoul of every living being and the summum bonum source of all energies.

PURPORT

Śrīmad-Bhāgavatam is the philosophy of devotional service and the scientific presentation of man's relationship with the Supreme Personality of Godhead. Prior to the age of Kali there was no need for such a book of knowledge to know the Lord and His potential energies, but with the beginning of the age of Kali the human society became gradually influenced by four sinful principles, namely illegitimate connection with women, intoxication, gambling and unnecessary killing of animals. Because of these basic sinful acts, gradually man became forgetful of his eternal relation with God. Therefore man became blind, so to speak, to his ultimate goal of life. The ultimate goal of life is not to pass a life of irresponsibility like the animals and indulge in a polished way in the four animal principles, namely eating, sleeping, fearing and mating. For such a blind human society in the darkness of ignorance, *Śrīmad-Bhāgavatam* is the torchlight to see things in proper perspective. Therefore it was necessary to describe the science of God from the very beginning, or from the very birth of the phenomenal world.

As we have already explained previously, *Śrīmad-Bhāgavatam* is so scientifically presented that any sincere student of this great science will be able to understand the science of God simply by reading it with attention or simply by regularly hearing it from the bona fide speaker. Everyone is hankering after happiness in life, but in this age, blind as they are, the members of human society have no proper vision that the Personality of Godhead is the reservoir of all happiness because He is the ultimate source of everything: *janmādasya yataḥ*. Happiness in complete perfection without hindrance can be achieved only by our devotional relationship with Him. And it is only by His association that we can get rid of the distressful material existence. Even those who are after the enjoyment of this material world can also take shelter of the great science of *Śrīmad-Bhāgavatam,* and they will be successful at the end. Nārada is therefore requested or ordered by his spiritual master to present this science with determination and in good plan. Nārada was never advised to preach the principles of *Bhāgavatam* to earn a livelihood, but he was ordered by his spiritual master to take the matter very seriously in a missionary spirit.

TEXT 53

मायां वर्णयतोऽमुष्य ईश्वरस्यानुमोदतः ।
शृण्वतः श्रद्धया नित्यं माययात्मा न मुह्यति॥५३॥

māyāṁ varṇayato'muṣya
īśvarasyānumodataḥ
śṛṇvataḥ śraddhayā nityaṁ
māyayātmā na muhyati

māyām—affairs of the external energy; *varṇayataḥ*—while describing; *amuṣya*—of the Lord; *īśvarasya*—of the Personality of Godhead; *anumodataḥ*—thus appreciating; *śṛṇvataḥ*—thus hearing; *śraddhayā*—with devotion; *nityam*—regularly; *māyayā*—by the illusory energy; *ātmā*—the living entity; *na*—never; *muhyati*—becomes illusioned.

TRANSLATION

Activities of the Lord, in association with His different energies, should be described, appreciated and heard in accordance with the teachings of the Supreme Lord. If this is done regularly with devotion and respect, one is sure to get out of the illusory energy of the Lord."

PURPORT

The science of learning a subject matter seriously is different from the sentiments of the fanatics. The fanatics or the fools may consider the

Lord's activities in relation with external energy useless for them, and they may falsely claim to be higher participants in the internal energy of the Lord, but factually the Lord's activities, either in relation with the external energy or with the internal energy, are equally good. On the other hand, those who are not completely free from the clutches of the external energy of the Lord should devoutly hear regularly about the activities of the Lord in relation with the external energy. They should not foolishly jump up to the activities of the internal energy, falsely attracted by the Lord's internal potential activities like His *rāsa-līlā.* The cheap reciters of the *Bhāgavatam* are very much enthusiastic about the Lord's internal potential activities, and the pseudo-devotees, absorbed in material sense enjoyment, falsely jump to the stage of liberated souls and thus fall down deeply into the clutches of external energy.

Some of them think that to hear about the pastimes of the Lord means to hear about His activities with the *gopīs* or about His pastimes like uplifting the Govardhana Hill, etc., and they have nothing to do with the Lord's plenary expansions as the *puruṣāvatāras* and Their pastimes of creation, maintenance, or annihilation of the material worlds. But a pure devotee knows that there is no difference between the pastimes of the Lord, either in *rāsa-līlā* or in creation, maintenance or destruction of the material world. Rather, the description of such activities of the Lord as *puruṣāvatāras* are specifically meant for persons who are in the clutches of the external energy. *Rāsa-līlā,* etc., are meant for the liberated souls and not for the conditioned souls. The conditioned souls, therefore, must hear the Lord's pastimes in relationship with the external energy with appreciation and devotion, and such acts are as good as the hearing of *rāsa-līlā* in the liberated stage. A conditioned soul should not imitate the activities of liberated souls. Lord Śrī Caitanya never indulged in hearing the *rāsa-līlā* with ordinary men.

In the *Śrīmad-Bhāgavatam,* the science of God, the first nine cantos prepare the ground for hearing the Tenth Canto. This will be further explained in the last chapter of this canto. In the Third Canto it will be more explicit. A pure devotee of the Lord, therefore, must begin reading or hearing *Śrīmad-Bhāgavatam* from the very beginning, and not from the Tenth Canto. We have several times been requested by some so-called devotees to take up the Tenth Canto immediately, but we have refrained from such an action because we wish to present *Śrīmad-Bhāgavatam* as the science of Godhead and not as a sensuous understanding for the conditioned souls. This is forbidden by such authorities as Śrī Brahmājī. By reading and hearing *Śrīmad-Bhāgavatam* as a scientific presentation, the conditioned souls will gradually be promoted to the higher status of transcendental knowledge after being freed from the illusory energy based on sense enjoyment.

Thus end the Bhaktivedanta purports of the Second Canto, Seventh Chapter, of the Śrīmad-Bhāgavatam, *entitled "Scheduled Incarnations with Specific Functions."*

CHAPTER EIGHT

Questions by King Parīkṣit

TEXT 1

राजोवाच
ब्रह्मणा चोदितो ब्रह्मन् गुणाख्यानेऽगुणस्य च ।
यस्मै यस्मै यथा प्राह नारदो देवदर्शनः ॥ १ ॥

rājovāca
brahmaṇā codito brahman
guṇākhyāne 'guṇasya ca
yasmai yasmai yathā prāha
nārado deva-darśanaḥ

rājā—the King; *uvāca*—inquired; *brahmaṇā*—by Lord Brahmā; *coditaḥ*—being instructed; *brahman*—O learned *brāhmaṇa* (Śukadeva Gosvāmī); *guṇa-ākhyāne*—in narrating the transcendental qualities; *aguṇasya*—of the Lord, who is without material qualities; *ca*—and; *yasmai yasmai*—and whom; *yathā*—as much as; *prāha*—explained; *nāradaḥ*—Nārada Muni; *deva-darśanaḥ*—one whose audience is as good as that of any demigod.

TRANSLATION

King Parīkṣit inquired from Śukadeva Gosvāmī: How did Narada Muni, whose hearers are as fortunate as those instructed by Lord Brahmā, explain the transcendental qualities of the Lord, who is without material qualities, and before whom did he speak?

PURPORT

Devarṣi Nārada was directly instructed by Brahmājī, who was also directly instructed by the Supreme Lord; therefore the instructions imparted by Nārada to his various disciples are as good as those of the Supreme Lord. That is the way of understanding Vedic knowledge. It comes down from the Lord by disciplic succession, and this transcendental knowledge is distributed to the world by this descending process.

There is no chance, however, to receive the Vedic knowledge from mental speculators. Therefore, wherever Nārada Muni goes, he represents himself as authorized by the Lord, and his appearance is as good as that of the Supreme Lord. Similarly, the disciplic succession which strictly follows the transcendental instruction is the bona fide chain of disciplic succession, and the test for such bona fide spiritual masters is that there should be no difference between the instruction of the Lord originally imparted to His devotee and that which is imparted by the authority in the line of disciplic succession. How Nārada Muni distributed the transcendental knowledge of the Lord will be explained in later cantos.

It will appear also that the Lord existed prior to the material creation, and therefore His transcendental name, quality, etc., do not represent any material quality. Whenever, therefore, the Lord is described as *aguṇa,* or without any quality, it does not mean that He has no quality, but that He has no material quality, such as the modes of goodness, passion, or ignorance, as the conditioned souls have. He is transcendental to all material conceptions, and thus He is described as *aguṇa.*

TEXT 2

एतद् वेदितुमिच्छामि तत्त्वं तत्त्वविदां वर ।
हरेरद्भुतवीर्यस्य कथा लोकसुमङ्गलाः ॥ २ ॥

etad veditum icchāmi
tattvaṁ tattva-vidāṁ vara
harer adbhuta-vīryasya
kathā loka-sumaṅgalāḥ

etat—all these; *veditum*—just understand; *icchāmi*—do I wish; *tattvam*—the truth; *tattva-vidām*—of those who are well versed in the matter of Absolute Truth; *vara*—the great; *hareḥ*—of the Lord; *adbhuta-vīryasya*—of the one who possesses wonderful potencies; *kathāḥ*—narrations; *loka*—for all planets; *su-maṅgalāḥ*—auspicious.

TRANSLATION

The King said: I wish to know. Narrations concerning the Lord, who possesses wonderful potencies, are certainly auspicious for living beings in all planets.

PURPORT

Śrīmad-Bhāgavatam, which is full of narration of the activities of the Supreme Lord, is auspicious for all living beings residing in every planet.

One who takes it as belonging to a particular sect is certainly mistaken. *Śrīmad-Bhāgavatam* is certainly a very dear scripture for the devotees of the Lord, but it is auspicious even for the nondevotees also because it explains that even the nondevotees hovering under the spell of material energy can be delivered from such clutches if they hear with devotion and attention the narration of the *Śrīmad-Bhāgavatam* from the right source representing the Lord by disciplic succession.

TEXT 3

कथयस्व महाभाग यथाहमखिलात्मनि ।
कृष्णे निवेश्य निःसङ्गं मनस्त्यक्ष्ये कलेवरम् ॥ ३ ॥

kathayasva mahābhāga
yathāham akhilātmani
kṛṣṇe niveśya niḥsaṅgaṁ
manas tyakṣye kalevaram

kathayasva—please continue speaking; *mahābhāga*—O greatly fortunate one; *yathā*—as much as; *aham*—I; *akhila-ātmani*—unto the Supreme Soul; *kṛṣṇe*—unto Lord Śrī Kṛṣṇa; *niveśya*—having placed; *niḥsaṅgam*—being freed from material qualities; *manaḥ*—mind; *tyakṣye*—may relinquish; *kalevaram*—body.

TRANSLATION

O greatly fortunate Śukadeva Gosvāmī, please continue narrating Śrīmad-Bhāgavatam so that I can place my mind upon the Supreme Soul, Lord Kṛṣṇa, and, being completely freed from material qualities, thus relinquish this body.

PURPORT

To be fully engaged in hearing the transcendental narration described in the text of *Śrīmad-Bhāgavatam* means to be constantly associated with the Supreme Soul Śrī Kṛṣṇa. And to be constantly associated with the Supreme Lord Kṛṣṇa means to be liberated from the qualities of matter. Lord Kṛṣṇa is like the sun, and the material contamination is like the darkness. As darkness is dissipated in the presence of the sun, so to be constantly engaged in the association of the Lord Śrī Kṛṣṇa means to be uncontaminated by the material qualities. Contamination by material qualities is the cause of repeated birth and death, and liberation from material qualities is transcendence. Mahārāja Parīkṣit is now a realized soul by this secret of liberation through the grace of Śukadeva Gosvāmī, for the latter informed the King that the highest perfection of life is to be in remembrance of Nārāyaṇa at the end of life. Mahārāja Parīkṣit was destined to give up his body at the end of seven days, and thus he decided to continue the remembrance of the Lord by His association with the topic of *Śrīmad-Bhāgavatam,* and thus to quit his body in full consciousness of the presence of the Lord Śrī Kṛṣṇa, the Supreme Soul.

The hearing of *Śrīmad-Bhāgavatam* performed by the professional men is different from the transcendental hearing of Mahārāja Parīkṣit. Mahārāja Parīkṣit was a soul realized in the Absolute Truth, Śrī Kṛṣṇa, the Personality of Godhead. The fruitive materialist is not a realized soul; he wants to derive some material benefit from his so-called hearing of *Śrīmad-Bhāgavatam.* Undoubtedly such an audience, hearing *Śrīmad-Bhāgavatam* from the professional men, can derive some material benefit as desired by them, but that does not mean that such a pretense of hearing *Śrīmad-Bhāgavatam* for a week is as good as that of Mahārāja Parīkṣit.

It is the duty of the sane to hear *Śrīmad-Bhāgavatam* from a self-realized soul without being duped by professional men, and one should continue such hearing till the end of one's life so that one can actually have the transcendental association of the Lord and thus be liberated simply by hearing *Śrīmad-Bhāgavatam.*

Mahārāja Parīkṣit had already given up all his connections with his kingdom and family, the most attractive features of materialism, but still he was conscious of his material body. He wanted to be free of such bondage also by the constant association of the Lord.

TEXT 4

शृण्वतः श्रद्धया नित्यं गृणतश्च स्वचेष्टितम् ।
कालेन नातिदीर्घेण भगवान् विशते हृदि ॥ ४ ॥

śṛṇvataḥ śraddhayā nityaṁ
gṛṇataś ca sva-ceṣṭitam
kālena nātidīrgheṇa
bhagavān viśate hṛdi

śṛṇvataḥ—of those who hear; *śraddhayā*—in earnestness; *nityam*—regularly, always; *gṛṇataḥ*—taking the matter; *ca*—also; *sva-ceṣṭitam*—seriously by one's own endeavor; *kālena*—duration; *na*—not; *atidīrgheṇa*—very prolonged time; *bhagavān*—the Personality of Godhead Śrī Kṛṣṇa; *viśate*—becomes manifest; *hṛdi*—within one's heart.

TRANSLATION

Persons who hear Śrīmad-Bhāgavatam regularly and are always taking the matter very seriously will have the Personality of Godhead Śrī Kṛṣṇa manifested in their hearts within a short time.

PURPORT

Cheap devotees or the material devotees of the Lord are very much desirous to see the Lord personally without making any requisite qualification. Such third-grade devotees should know well that material attachment and seeing the Lord eye to eye cannot go together. It is not such a mechanical process that the professional *Bhāgavatam* reciters can do the job on behalf of the third-grade materialist pseudo-devotee. The professional men are useless in this connection because they are neither self-realized nor interested in the liberation of the audience. They are simply interested in maintaining the material establishment of family attachment and earning some material benefits out of the profession. Mahārāja Parīkṣit had no more than seven days to live, but for others Mahārāja Parīkṣit personally recommends that one should hear *Śrīmad-Bhāgavatam* regularly, *nityam*, always by one's own effort and with serious devotion also. That will help one to see the Lord Śrī Kṛṣṇa manifested in one's heart within no time.

The pseudo-devotee, however, is very anxious to see the Lord by his whims, not making any serious effort to hear *Śrīmad-Bhāgavatam* regularly and without detachment from material benefit. That is not the way recommended by an authority like Mahārāja Parīkṣit, who heard and benefitted by hearing *Śrīmad-Bhāgavatam.*

TEXT 5

प्रविष्टः कर्णरन्ध्रेण स्वानां भावसरोरुहम् ।
धुनोति शमलं कृष्णः सलिलस्य यथा शरत् ॥ ५ ॥

praviṣṭaḥ karṇa-randhreṇa
svānāṁ bhāva-saroruham
dhunoti śamalaṁ kṛṣṇaḥ
salilasya yathā śarat

praviṣṭaḥ—thus being entered; *karṇa-randhreṇa*—through the holes of the ears; *svānām*—according to one's liberated position; *bhāva*—constitutional relationship; *saraḥ-ruham*—the lotus flower; *dhunoti*—cleanses; *śamalam*—material qualities like lust, anger, avarice, hankering, etc.; *kṛṣṇaḥ*—Lord Kṛṣṇa, the Supreme Personality of Godhead; *salilasya*—of the reservoir of waters; *yathā*—as it were; *śarat*—the autumn season.

TRANSLATION

The sound incarnation of Lord Kṛṣṇa, the Supreme Soul [i.e. Śrīmad-Bhāgavatam], entering into the heart of a self-realized devotee, sits on the lotus flower of his loving relationship and thus cleanses the dust of material association, such as lust, anger, hankerings, etc., and acts like the autumnal rains upon the pools of muddy water.

PURPORT

It is said that a single pure devotee of the Lord can deliver all the fallen souls of the world, and thus one who is actually in the confidence of a pure devotee like Nārada or Śukadeva Gosvāmī and thus empowered by one's spiritual master, as Nārada was by Brahmājī, can not only deliver himself from the clutches of *māyā,* or illusion, but can deliver the whole world by his pure and empowered devotional strength. The comparison to the autumnal rain which falls on the muddy reservoirs of water is very appropriate. During the rainy season, all waters of the rivers become muddy, but in the month of July-August, the autumn season, when there is a slight rainfall, the muddy waters of the rivers all over the world become at once clear. By addition of some chemical, a small reservoir of water like that of the metropolitan waterworks tanks, etc., can be cleared, but by such a tiny effort it is not possible to clear up all the reservoirs of water like the rivers, etc. Similarly, a powerful pure devotee of the Lord can deliver not only his personal self but also many others in his association.

In other words, the cleansing of the polluted heart by other methods (like culture of empiric knowledge or mystic gymnastics) can simply cleanse one's own heart, but devotional service to the Lord is so powerful that it can cleanse the hearts of the people in general, by the devotional service of the pure empowered devotee. A true representative of the Lord like Nārada, Śukadeva Gosvāmī, Lord Caitanya, the six Gosvāmīs and later Śrīla Bhaktivinode Ṭhākur or Śrīmad Bhaktisiddhānta Sarasvatī Ṭhākur, etc., can deliver all people by their empowered devotional service.

By sincere efforts to hear *Śrīmad-Bhāgavatam* one realizes his constitutional relationship with the Lord in the transcendental humor of servitude, friendship, paternal affection or conjugal love, and by such self-realization one becomes situated at once in the transcendental loving service of the Lord. All such pure devotees like Nārada were not only self-realized souls, but they were engaged in preaching work automatically by spiritual impetus, and thus they delivered many poor souls entangled in the material modes. They became so powerful because they sincerely followed the *Bhāgavatam* principles by regular hearing and worshiping. By such actions the accumulated material lusts, etc., become cleansed by the personal endeavor of the Lord within the heart. The Lord is always within the heart of the living being, but He becomes manifested by one's devotional service.

Purification of the heart by culture of knowledge or mystic *yoga* may be all right for the time being for an individual person, but it is like cleansing the stagnant water in small quantity by chemical processes. Such clarification of water may stand for the time being and the sediments settle down, but by a slight agitation everything becomes muddy. The idea is that devotional service to the Lord is the only method of cleansing the heart for good. Whereas other methods may be superficially good for the time being, there is a risk of becoming muddy again due to agitation of the mind. Devotional service to the Lord, with specific attention for hearing *Śrīmad-Bhāgavatam* regularly and always, is the best recommended method for liberation from the clutches of illusion.

TEXT 6

धौतात्मा पुरुषः कृष्णपादमूलं न मुञ्चति ।
मुक्तसर्वपरिक्लेशः पान्थः स्वशरणं यथा ॥ ६ ॥

dhautātmā puruṣaḥ kṛṣṇa-
pāda-mūlaṁ na muñcati
mukta-sarva-parikleśaḥ
pānthaḥ sva-śaraṇaṁ yathā

dhauta-ātmā—a person whose heart has been cleansed; *puruṣaḥ*—the living being; *kṛṣṇa*—the Supreme Personality of Godhead; *pāda-mūlam*—the shelter of the lotus feet; *na*—never; *muñcati*—gives up; *mukta*—liberated; *sarva*—all; *parikleṣaḥ*—of all miseries of life; *pānthaḥ*—the traveler; *sva-śaraṇam*—in his own abode; *yathā*—as it were.

TRANSLATION

A pure devotee of the Lord, whose heart is once cleansed by the process of devotional service, never relinquishes the lotus feet of Lord Kṛṣṇa because they fully satisfy him, as the traveler is satisfied at home after a troubled journey.

PURPORT

One who is not a pure devotee of the Supreme Lord Kṛṣṇa is not completely cleansed in the heart. But a perfectly cleansed person never quits the devotional service of the Lord. In discharging such devotional service, as it was ordered by Brahmājī to Nārada in the preaching of *Śrīmad-Bhāgavatam*, sometimes the representative of the Lord engaged in preaching work meets various so-called difficulties of life. This was exhibited by Lord Nityānanda when He delivered the two fallen souls Jagai and Madhai, and similarly Lord Jesus Christ was crucified by the nonbelievers. But such difficulties are suffered by the devotees in preaching work very gladly because in such activities, although apparently very severe, the devotees of the Lord feel transcendental pleasure because the Lord is satisfied. Prahlāda Mahārāja suffered greatly, but still he never forgot the lotus feet of the Lord. This is because a pure devotee of the Lord is so purified in the heart that he cannot leave the shelter of Lord Kṛṣṇa in any circumstances. There is no self-interest in such service. The progress of culturing knowledge by the *jñānīs* or the bodily gymnastics by the *yogīs* are ultimately given up by the respective performers, but a devotee of the Lord cannot give up the service of the Lord, for he is ordered by his spiritual master. Pure devotees like Nārada or Nityānanda Prabhu take up the order of the spiritual master as the sustenance of life. They do not mind what becomes of the future of their lives. They take the matter very seriously as the order comes from the higher authority, from the representative of the Lord, or from the Lord Himself.

The example set herein is very appropriate. A traveler leaves home to search for wealth in far distant places, sometimes in the forest and sometimes on the ocean and sometimes on hilltops. Certainly there are many troubles for the traveler when he is in such unknown places. But all such troubles are at once mitigated as soon as the sense of his family affection is remembered, and as soon as he returns home he forgets all such troubles on the way.

A pure devotee of the Lord is exactly in a family tie with the Lord, and therefore he is undeterred in discharging his duty in full affectionate tie with the Lord.

TEXT 7

यदधातुमतो ब्रह्मन् देहारम्भोऽस्य धातुभिः ।
यदृच्छया हेतुना वा भवन्तो जानते यथा ॥ ७ ॥

yad adhātu-mato brahman
dehārambho'sya dhātubhiḥ
yadṛcchayā hetunā vā
bhavanto jānate yathā

yat—as it is; *adhātu-mataḥ*—without being materially constituted; *brahman*—O learned *brāhmaṇa; deha*—the material body; *ārambhaḥ*—the beginning of; *asya*—of the living being; *dhātubhiḥ*—by matter; *yadṛcchayā*—without cause, accidental; *hetunā*—due to some cause; *vā*—either; *bhavantaḥ*—your good self; *jānate*—as you may know it; *yathā*—so you inform me.

TRANSLATION

O learned brāhmaṇa, the transcendental spirit soul is different from the material body. Does he acquire the body accidentally or by some cause? Will you kindly explain this, for it is known to you.

PURPORT

Mahārāja Parīkṣit, being a typical devotee, is not only satisfied by confirming the importance of hearing the *Śrīmad-Bhāgavatam* from the representative of Brahmājī by disciplic succession, but he is still more anxious to establish the philosophical basis of *Śrīmad-Bhāgavatam. Śrīmad-Bhāgavatam* is the science of the Supreme Personality of Godhead, and as such all questions that may arise in the mind of a serious student must be cleared by the statements of the authority. A person on the path of devotional service may inquire from his spiritual master all about the spiritual position of God and the living beings. From the *Bhagavad-gītā*, as well as from the *Śrīmad-Bhāgavatam,* it is known that qualitatively the Lord and the living beings are one. The living being in the conditioned state of material existence is subjected to many transmigrations by continuously changing the material body. But what are the causes of such material embodiment of the part and parcel of the Lord? Mahārāja Parīkṣit inquires about this very important matter for the benefit of all classes of candidates on the path of self-realization and devotional service to the Lord.

Indirectly it is confirmed that the Supreme Being, the Lord, makes no such material changes of body. He is spiritually whole, with no difference between His body and His soul, unlike the conditioned soul. The liberated living beings, who associate with the Lord in person, are also exactly like the Lord. Only the conditioned souls awaiting liberation are subjected to change of bodies. How was the process first begun?

In the process of devotional service, the first step is to take shelter of the spiritual master and then inquire from the spiritual master all about the process. This inquiry is essential in order to be made immune to all kinds of offenses in the path of devotional service. Even if one is fixed in devotional service like Mahārāja Parīkṣit, he must still inquire from the realized spiritual master all about this. In other words, the spiritual master must also be well versed and learned so that he may be able to answer all these inquiries from the devotees. Thus one who is not well versed in the authorized scriptures and not able to answer all such relevant inquiries should not pose as a spiritual master for the matter of material gain. It is illegal to become a spiritual master if one is unable to deliver the disciple.

TEXT 8

आसीद् यदुदरात् पद्मं लोकसंस्थानलक्षणम् ।
यावानयं वै पुरुष इयत्तावयवैः पृथक् ।
तावानसाविति प्रोक्तः संस्थावयववानिव ॥ ८ ॥

āsīd yad-udarāt padmaṁ
loka-saṁsthāna-lakṣaṇam

yāvān ayaṁ vai puruṣa
iyattāvayavaiḥ pṛthak
tāvān asāv iti proktaḥ
saṁsthāvayavavān iva

āsīt—as it grew; *yat-udarāt*—from whose abdomen; *padmam*—lotus flower; *loka*—world; *saṁsthāna*—situation; *lakṣaṇam*—possessed of; *yāvān*—as it were; *ayam*—this; *vai*—certainly; *puruṣaḥ*—the Supreme Personality of Godhead; *iyattā*—measurement; *avayavaiḥ*—by embodiment; *pṛthak*—different; *tāvān*—so; *asau*—that; *iti proktaḥ*—it is so said; *saṁsthā*—situation; *avayavavān*—embodiment; *iva*—like.

TRANSLATION

If the Supreme Personality of Godhead, from whose abdomen the lotus stem sprouted, is possessed of a gigantic body according to His own caliber and measurement, then what is the specific difference between the body of the Lord and those of other common living entities?

PURPORT

One should note how Mahārāja Parīkṣit intelligently put the questions before his spiritual master for scientific understanding of the transcendental body of the Lord. It has been described in many places before this that the Lord assumed a very gigantic body, like Kāraṇodakaśāyī Viṣṇu, from whose hair pores innumerable universes have generated. The body of the Garbhodakaśāyī Viṣṇu is described as sprouting the lotus stem within which all the planets of the universe remain, and at the top of the stem there is the lotus flower on which Lord Brahmā is born. In the creation of the material world He undoubtedly assumes the gigantic body, and living entities also get bodies, big or small, according to the respective necessity. For example, an elephant gets a gigantic body according to its needs, and so also an ant gets its body according to its needs. Similarly, if the Personality of Godhead assumes a gigantic body to accomodate the universes or the planets of a particular universe, there is no difference in the principle of assuming or accepting a particular type of body in terms of necessity. A living being and the Lord cannot be distinguished simply by the difference of the magnitude of the body. So the answer depends on the specific significance of the body of the Lord, as distinguished from the body of the common living being.

TEXT 9

अजः सृजति भूतानि भूतात्मा यदनुग्रहात् ।
ददृशे येन तद्रूपं नाभिपद्मसमुद्भवः ॥ ९ ॥

ajaḥ sṛjati bhūtāni
bhūtātmā yad-anugrahāt
dadṛśe yena tad-rūpaṁ
nābhi-padma-samudbhavaḥ

ajaḥ—one who is born without a material source; *sṛjati*—creates; *bhūtāni*—all those materially born; *bhūta-ātmā*—having a body of matter; *yat*—whose; *anugrahāt*—by the mercy of; *dadṛśe*—could see; *yena*—by whom; *tat-rūpam*—His form of body; *nābhi*—navel; *padma*—lotus flower; *samudbhavaḥ*—being born of.

TRANSLATION

Brahmā, who was not born of a material source but of the lotus flower coming out of the navel abdomen of the Lord, is the creator of all those who are materially born. Of course, by the grace of the Lord, Brahmā was able to see the form of the Lord.

PURPORT

The first living creature, Brahmā, is called *ajaḥ* because he did not take his birth from the womb of a mother materially born. He was directly born from the bodily expansion of the lotus flower of the Lord. Thus it is not readily understandable whether the body of the Lord and that of Brahmā are of the same quality or different. This must also be clearly understood. One thing is, however, certain: Brahmā was completely dependent on the mercy of the Lord because after his birth he could create living beings by the Lord's grace only, and he could see the form of the Lord. Whether the form seen by Brahmā is of the same quality as that of Brahmā is a bewildering question, and Mahārāja Parīkṣit wanted to get clear answers from Śrīla Śukadeva Gosvāmī.

TEXT 10

स चापि यत्र पुरुषो विश्वस्थित्युद्भवाप्ययः ।
मुक्त्वात्ममायां मायेशः शेते सर्वगुहाशयः ॥१०॥

sa cāpi yatra puruṣo
viśva-sthity-udbhavāpyayaḥ
muktvātma-māyāṁ māyeśaḥ
śete sarva-guhā-śayaḥ

saḥ—He; *ca*—also; *api*—as He is; *yatra*—where; *puruṣaḥ*—the Personality of Godhead; *viśva*—the material worlds; *sthiti*—maintenance; *udbhava*—creation; *apyayaḥ*—annihilation; *muktvā*—without being touched; *ātma-māyām*—own energy; *māyeśaḥ*—the Lord of all energies; *śete*—does lie on; *sarva-guhā-śayaḥ*—one who lies in everyone's heart.

TRANSLATION

Please also explain the Personality of Godhead, who lies in every heart as the Supersoul and as the Lord of all energies, but is untouched by His external energy.

PURPORT

Undoubtedly the form of the Lord who was seen by Brahmā must be transcendental, otherwise how could He simply look upon the creative energy without being touched? It is understood also that the same *puruṣa* lies in the heart of every living entity. This also requires proper explanation.

TEXT 11

पुरुषावयवैर्लोकाः सपालाः पूर्वकल्पिताः ।
लोकैरमुष्यावयवाः सपालैरिति शुश्रुम ॥११॥

puruṣāvayavair lokāḥ
sa-pālāḥ pūrva-kalpitāḥ
lokair amuṣyāvayavāḥ
sa-pālair iti śuśruma

puruṣa—universal form of the Lord (*virāṭa puruṣaḥ*); *avayavaiḥ*—by different parts of the body; *lokāḥ*—the planetary system; *sa-pālāḥ*—with respective governors; *pūrva*—formerly; *kalpitāḥ*—discussed; *lokaiḥ*—by the different planetary systems; *amuṣya*—His; *avayavāḥ*—different parts of the body; *sa-pālaiḥ*—with the governors; *iti*—thus; *śuśruma*—I heard.

TRANSLATION

O learned brāhmaṇa, it was formerly explained that all the planets of the universe with their respective governors are situated in the different parts of the gigantic body of the virāṭa puruṣa. I have also heard that the different planetary systems are supposed to be in the gigantic body of the virāṭa puruṣa. But what is their actual position? Will you please explain that?

TEXT 12

यावान् कल्पो विकल्पो वा यथा कालोऽनुमीयते ।
भूतभव्यभवच्छब्द आयुर्मानं च यत् सतः ॥१२॥

yāvān kalpo vikalpo vā
yathā kālo'numīyate
bhūta-bhavya-bhavac-chabda
āyur-mānaṁ ca yat sataḥ

yāvān—as it is; *kalpaḥ*—the duration of time between creation and annihilation; *vikalpaḥ*—subsidiary creation and annihilation; *vā*—either; *yathā*—as also; *kālaḥ*—the time; *anumīyate*—is measured; *bhūta*—past; *bhavya*—future; *bhavat*—present; *śabdaḥ*—sound; *āyuḥ*—duration of life; *mānam*—measurement; *ca*—also; *yat*—which; *sataḥ*—of all living beings in all planets.

TRANSLATION

Also please explain the duration of time between creation and annihilation, and that of other subsidiary creations, as well as the nature of time, indicated by the sound of past, present and future. Also, please explain the duration and measurement of life of the different living beings known as the demigods, the human beings, etc., in different planets of the universe.

PURPORT

Past, present and future are different features of time to indicate the duration of life for the universe and all its paraphernalia, including the different living beings in different planets.

TEXT 13

कालस्यानुगतिर्या तु लक्ष्यतेऽण्वी बृहत्यपि ।
यावत्यः कर्मगतयो यादृशीर्द्विजसत्तम ॥१३॥

kālasyānugatir yā tu
lakṣyate'ṇvī bṛhaty api
yāvatyaḥ karma-gatayo
yādṛśīr dvija-sattama

kālasya—of the eternal time; *anugatiḥ*—beginning; *yā tu*—as they are; *lakṣyate*—experienced; *aṇvī*—small; *bṛhatī*—great; *api*—even; *yāvatyaḥ*—as long as; *karma-gatayaḥ*—in terms of the work performed; *yādṛśīḥ*—as it may; *dvija-sattama*—O purest of all *brāhmaṇas.*

TRANSLATION

O purest of the brāhmaṇas, please also explain the cause of the different durations of time, both short and long, as well as the beginning of time, following the course of action.

TEXT 14

यस्मिन् कर्मसमावायो यथा येनोपगृह्यते ।
गुणानां गुणिनां चैव परिणाममभीप्सताम् ॥१४॥

yasmin karma-samāvāyo
yathā yenopagṛhyate
guṇānāṁ guṇināṁ caiva
pariṇāmam abhīpsatām

yasmin—in which; *karma*—actions; *samāvāyaḥ*—accumulation; *yathā*—as far as; *yena*—by which; *upagṛhyate*—takes over; *guṇānām*—of the different modes of material nature; *guṇinām*—of the living beings; *ca*—also; *eva*—certainly; *pariṇāmam*—resultant; *abhīpsatām*—of the desires.

TRANSLATION

Then again, kindly describe how the proportionate accumulation of the resultant actions of the different modes of material nature act upon the desiring living being, promoting or degrading him among the different species of life, beginning from the demigods down to the most insignificant creatures.

PURPORT

The actions and reactions of all works in the material modes of nature, either in the minute form or in the gigantic form, are accumulated, and thus the result of such accumulated actions and reactions of *karma,* or work, become manifested in the same proportion. How such actions and reactions take place, what are the different procedures, and in what proportion they act are all the subject matter of Mahārāja Parīkṣit's inquiries from the great *brāhmaṇa,* Śukadeva Gosvāmī.

Life in the higher planets, known as the abode of the denizens of heaven, is obtained not by the strength of spacecraft (as is now being contemplated by the inexperienced scientists), but by works done in the mode of goodness.

There is even restriction on the very planet where we are now living for entrance of foreigners to a country where the citizens are more prosperous. For example, the American government has many restrictions for entrance of foreigners from less prosperous countries. The reason is that the Americans do not wish to share their prosperity with any foreigner who has not qualified himself as a citizen of America. Similarly, the same mentality is prevailing in every other planet also where there are more and more intelligent living beings residing. The higher planetary living conditions are all in the mode of goodness, and anyone desiring to enter the higher planets like the moon, sun, Venus, etc., must qualify thoroughly by activity in complete goodness.

Mahārāja Parīkṣit's inquiries are on the basis of proportionate actions of goodness which qualify one in this planet to be promoted to the highest regions of the universe.

Even on this planet of our present residence, no one can achieve a good position within the social order without being qualified with proportionate good work. No one can forcibly sit on the chair of a high court judge without being qualified for the post. Similarly, no one can enter into the higher regions of the planetary system without being qualified by good works in this life. Persons addicted to the habits of passion and ignorance have no chance of entering the higher planetary system simply by an electronic mechanism.

According to the statement of the *Bhagavad-gītā* (Bg. 9.25), persons trying to qualify themselves for promotion to the higher regions of heavenly planets can go there; similarly, persons trying for the Pitṛlokas can go there; similarly, persons trying to improve the conditions on this earth can also do that, and persons who are engaged in going back home, back to Godhead, can also achieve the result. These various actions and reactions of work in the mode of goodness are generally known as pious work with devotional service, culture of knowledge with devotional service, mystic powers with devotional service and (at last) devotional service unmixed with any other varieties of goodness. This unmixed devotional service is transcendental and is called the *parā bhakti,* which alone can promote a person to the transcendental kingdom of God. Such a transcendental kingdom is not a myth, but is as factual as the moon planet. It requires the transcendental qualities to understand the kingdom of God and God Himself.

TEXT 15

भूपातालककुब्व्योमग्रहनक्षत्रभूभृताम् ।
सरित्समुद्रद्वीपानां सम्भवश्चैतदोकसाम् ॥१५॥

bhū-pātāla-kakub-vyoma-
graha-nakṣatra-bhūbhṛtām
sarit-samudra-dvīpānāṁ
sambhavaś caitad-okasām

bhūḥ-pātāla—underneath the land; *kakub*—four sides of the heavens; *vyoma*—the sky; *graha*—the planets; *nakṣatra*—the stars; *bhūbhṛtām*—of the hills; *sarit*—the river; *samudra*—the sea; *dvīpānām*—of the islands; *sambhavaḥ*—appearance; *ca*—also; *etat*—their; *okasām*—of the inhabitants.

TRANSLATION

O best of the brāhmaṇas, please also describe how the creation of the globes throughout the universe, the four directions of the heavens, the sky, the planets, the stars, the mountains, the rivers, the seas and the islands, as well as their different kinds of inhabitants, takes place.

PURPORT

The inhabitants of different varieties of land, etc., are differently situated, and not all of them are equal in all respects. The inhabitants of the land are different from the inhabitants of the water or the sky, and similarly the inhabitants of the different planets and stars in the sky are also different from one another. No place is vacant by the laws of the Lord, but the creatures of one particular place are different from others. Even in the human society the inhabitants of the jungles or those of the desert are different from those of the cities and villages. They are so made according to different qualities of the modes of nature. Such adjustment of the laws of nature is not blind. There is a great plan behind the arrangement. Mahārāja Parīkṣit requests the great sage Śukadeva Gosvāmī to explain all these authoritatively, in accordance with proper understanding.

TEXT 16

प्रमाणमण्डकोशस्य बाह्याभ्यन्तरभेदतः ।
महतां चानुचरितं वर्णाश्रमविनिश्चयः ॥१६॥

pramāṇam aṇḍa-kośasya
bāhyābhyantara-bhedataḥ
mahatāṁ cānucaritaṁ
varṇāśrama-viniścayaḥ

pramāṇam—extent and measurement; *aṇḍa-kośasya*—of the universe; *bāhya*—outer space; *abhyantara*—inner space; *bhedataḥ*—by division of; *mahatām*—of the great souls; *ca*—also; *anucaritam*—character and activities; *varṇa*—castes; *āśrama*—orders of life; *viniścayaḥ*—specifically describe.

TRANSLATION

Also, please describe the inner and outer space of the universe by specific divisions, as well as the character and activities of the great souls, and also the characteristics of the different classifications of the castes and orders of social life.

PURPORT

Mahārāja Parīkṣit is a typical devotee of Lord Kṛṣṇa, and as such he is anxious to know the complete significance of the creation of the Lord. He wants to know the inner and outer space of the universal form. It is quite fitting for the real searcher of knowledge to know all about this. Those who are of the opinion that the devotees of the Lord are satisfied with some sentiments only can find good lessons in the inquiries of Mahārāja Parīkṣit as to how much a pure devotee is inquisitive to know things in their true perfection. The modern scientist is unable to know about the inner space of the universal horizon, and what to speak of the space which covers the universes.

Mahārāja Parīkṣit is not simply satisfied with material knowledge only. He is inquisitive about the characters and activities of the great souls or devotees of the Lord. The glories of the Lord and the glories of His devotees, combined together, comprise the complete knowledge of *Śrīmad-Bhagāvatam.* Lord Kṛṣṇa showed His mother the complete universal creation within His mouth, while she, completely charmed by her son, wanted to see the inner mouth of the Lord just to see how much earth the child had eaten. By the grace of the Lord the devotees are able to see everything in the universe within the mouth of the Lord.

The very idea of the scientific divisions of four classes of human society and four orders of life is also inquired about herewith on the basis of individual personal quality. The four divisions are exactly like the four divisions of one's personal body. The parts and parcels of the body are nondifferent from the body, but by themselves they are only parts and parcels of the body. That is the significance of the whole scientific system of four orders of castes and social orders. The value of such scientific divisions of human society can only be ascertained in terms of the proportionate development of devotional service to the Lord. Any person employed in the government service is a part and parcel of the entire government, including the president. Everyone is a government servant, but no one is the government himself. That is the position of all living entities in the government of the Supreme Lord. No one can artificially claim to the supreme position of the Lord, but everyone is meant to serve the purpose of the supreme whole.

TEXT 17

युगानि युगमानं च धर्मो यश्च युगे युगे ।
अवतारानुचरितं यदाश्चर्यतमं हरेः ॥१७॥

yugāni yuga-mānaṁ ca
dharmo yaś ca yuge yuge
avatārānucaritaṁ
yad āścaryatamaṁ hareḥ

yugāni—the different ages; *yuga-mānam*—the duration of each age; *ca*—as well as; *dharmaḥ*—the particular occupational duty; *yaḥ ca*—and which; *yuge yuge*—in each and every *yuga* or particular age; *avatāra*—the incarnation; *anucaritam*—and the activities of the incarnation; *yat*—which; *āścaryatamam*—the most wonderful activities; *hareḥ*—of the Supreme Lord.

TRANSLATION

Please explain all the different ages in the duration of the creation, and also the duration of such ages. Also tell me about the different activities of the different incarnations of the Lord in different ages.

PURPORT

Lord Kṛṣṇa is the original Personality of Godhead, and all the incarnations of the Supreme Lord, although nondifferent from Him, are emanations from the Supreme. Mahārāja Parīkṣit inquires from the great learned sage Śukadeva Gosvāmī about the different activities of such incarnations so that the incarnation of the Lord may be confirmed by His activities in the authoritative scriptures. Mahārāja Parīkṣit is not to be carried away by the sentiments of the common man to accept an incarnation of the Lord very cheaply. Instead he wished to accept the incarnation of the Lord by symptoms mentioned in the Vedic literatures and confirmed by an *ācārya* like Śukadeva Gosvāmī. The Lord descends by His internal energy without any obligation to the laws of material nature, and thus His activities are also uncommon. The specific activities of the Lord are mentioned, and one should know that the activities of the Lord and the Lord are identical due to being on the absolute plane. Thus to hear the activities of the Lord means to associate with the Lord directly, and association of the Lord directly means purification from material contamination. We have already discussed this point in the First Volume.

TEXT 18

नृणां साधारणो धर्मः सविशेषश्च यादृशः ।
श्रेणीनां राजर्षीणां च धर्मः कृच्छ्रेषु जीवताम् ॥१८॥

nṛṇāṁ sādhāraṇo dharmaḥ
saviśeṣaś ca yādṛśaḥ
śreṇīnāṁ rājarṣīṇāṁ ca
dharmaḥ kṛcchreṣu jīvatām

nṛṇām—of human society; *sādhāraṇaḥ*—general; *dharmaḥ*—religious affiliation; *sa-viśeṣaḥ*—specific; *ca*—also; *yādṛśaḥ*—as they are; *śreṇīnām*—of the particular three classes; *rājarṣīṇām*—of the saintly royal order; *ca*—also; *dharmaḥ*—occupational duty; *kṛcchreṣu*—in the matter of distressed conditions; *jīvatām*—of the living beings.

TRANSLATION

Please also explain what may generally be the common religious affiliations of human society, as well as their specific occupational duties in religion, the classification of the social orders as well as the administrative royal orders, and the religious principles for one who may be in the distressed condition of life.

PURPORT

The common religion of all classes of human beings, regardless of whosoever and whatsoever one may be, is devotional service. Even the animals may be included in devotional service to the Lord, and the best example is set by Śrī Bajrāṅgajī or Hanumān, the great devotee of Lord Śrī Rāma. As we have already discussed, even the aborigines and cannibals can also be engaged in the devotional service of the Lord if they happen to be under the guidance of a genuine devotee of the Lord. In the *Skanda Purāṇa* there is a narration that a hunter in the jungle became the most enlightened devotee of the Lord by the guidance of Śrī Nārada Muni. Therefore devotional service to the Lord can be equally shared by every living being.

Religious affiliation in terms of different countries and cultural circumstances is obviously not the common religion of the human being, but the basic principle is devotional service. Even if a particular type of religious principle does not recognize the supremacy of the Supreme Personality of Godhead, the followers still have to obey the disciplinary principles laid down by a particular leader. Such a leader of a religious sect is never the supreme leader because such a circumstantial leader comes to the position of leadership after undergoing some penance. The Supreme Personality of Godhead does not, however, require to be under disciplinary action to become leader, as we see in the activities of Lord Kṛṣṇa.

The occupational duties of the castes and the orders of society, following the principles of livelihood, also depend on the principle of devotional service. In the *Bhagavad-gītā* it is stated that a person can achieve the highest perfection of life simply by awarding the results of one's occupational duty unto the devotional service of the Lord. People following the principles of devotional service of the Lord can never be put into difficulty, and thus there cannot be any question of *āpad-dharma,* or religion in distress. As will be explained in this book by the greatest authority, Śrīla Śukadeva Gosvāmī, there is no religion save and except the devotional service of the Lord, though this may be presented in different forms.

TEXT 19

तत्त्वानां परिसंख्यानं लक्षणं हेतुलक्षणम् ।
पुरुषाराधनविधिर्योगस्याध्यात्मिकस्य च ॥१९॥

tattvānāṁ parisaṅkhyānaṁ
lakṣaṇaṁ hetu-lakṣaṇam
puruṣārādhana-vidhir
yogasyādhyātmikasya ca

tattvānām—of the elements that constitute the creation; *parisaṅkhyānam* —of the number of such elements; *lakṣaṇam*—symptoms; *hetu-lakṣaṇam*—the symptoms of the causes; *puruṣa*—complete; *ārādhana*—devotional service; *vidhiḥ*—rules and regulations; *yogasya*—cultivation of the *yoga* system; *adhyātmikasya*—spiritual methods leading to devotional service; *ca*—also.

TRANSLATION

Kindly explain all about the elementary principles of creation, the number of such elementary principles, their causes, and their development, and also the process of devotional service and the method of mystic powers.

TEXT 20

योगेश्वरैश्वर्यगतिर्लिङ्गभङ्गस्तु योगिनाम् ।
वेदोपवेदधर्माणामितिहासपुराणयोः ॥२०॥

yogeśvaraiśvarya-gatir
liṅga-bhaṅgas tu yoginām
vedopaveda-dharmāṇām
itihāsa-purāṇayoḥ

yogeśvara—the master of the mystic powers; *aiśvarya*—opulence; *gatiḥ*—advancement; *liṅga*—astral body; *bhaṅgaḥ*—detachment; *tu*—but; *yoginām* —of the mystics; *veda*—transcendental knowledge; *upaveda*—knowledge in pursuance of the *Veda* indirectly; *dharmāṇām*—of the religiosities; *itihāsa*—history; *purāṇayoḥ*—of the *Purāṇas*.

TRANSLATION

What are the opulences of the great mystics, and what is their ultimate realization? How does the perfect mystic become detached from the subtle astral body? What is the basic knowledge of the Vedic literatures, including the branches of history and the supplementary Purāṇas?

PURPORT

The *yogeśvara,* or the master of mystic powers, can exhibit eight kinds of wonders of perfection by becoming smaller than the atom or lighter than a feather, getting anything and everything he desires, going anywhere and everywhere he likes, creating even a planet in the sky, etc. There are many *yogeśvaras* having different proficiencies in these wonderful powers, and the topmost of all of them is Lord Śiva. Lord Śiva is the greatest *yogī*, and he can perform such wonderful things, far beyond the ordinary living beings. The devotees of the Lord, the Supreme Personality of Godhead, do not directly practice the process of mystic powers, but, by the grace of the Lord, His devotee can defeat even a great *yogeśvara* like Durvāsā Muni, who picked up a quarrel with Mahārāja Ambarīṣa and wanted to show the wonderful achievements of his mystic powers. Mahārāja Ambarīṣa was a pure devotee of the Lord, and thus without any effort on his part the Lord saved him from the wrath of Yogeśvara Durvāsā Muni, and the latter was obliged to beg pardon from the King. Similarly, at the time of Draupadī's precarious position, when she was attacked by the Kurus who wanted to see her naked in the open assembly of the royal order, the Lord saved her from being stripped by supplying an unlimited length of *sari* to cover her. And Draupadī knew nothing of mystic powers. Therefore the devotees are also *yogeśvara* by the unlimited power of the Lord, just as a child is powerful by the strength of the parents. They do not try to protect themselves by any artificial means, but are saved by the mercy of the parents.

Mahārāja Parīkṣit inquired from the learned *brāhmaṇa* Śukadeva Gosvāmī about the ultimate destination of such great mystics or how they attain such extraordinary powers by their own efforts or by the grace of the Lord. He inquired also about their detachment from the subtle and gross material bodies. He inquired also about the purports of the Vedic knowledge, and, as is stated in the *Bhagavad-gītā* (Bg. 15.15), the whole purport of all the *Vedas* is to know the Supreme Personality of Godhead and thus become a transcendental loving servant of the Lord.

TEXT 21

सम्प्लवः सर्वभूतानां विक्रमः प्रतिसंक्रमः ।
इष्टापूर्तस्य काम्यानां त्रिवर्गस्य च यो विधिः ॥२१॥

samplavaḥ sarva-bhūtānāṁ
vikramaḥ pratisaṅkramaḥ
iṣṭāpūrtasya kāmyānāṁ
tri-vargasya ca yo vidhiḥ

samplavaḥ—the perfect means or complete devastation; *sarva-bhūtānām*—of all living beings; *vikramaḥ*—specific power or situation; *pratisaṅkramaḥ*—ultimate destruction; *iṣṭā*—performance of Vedic rituals; *pūrtasya*—pious acts in terms of religion; *kāmyānām*—rituals for economic development; *tri-vargasya*—the three means of religion, economic development and sense satisfaction; *ca*—also; *yaḥ*—whatsoever; *vidhiḥ*—procedures.

TRANSLATION

Please explain unto me how the living beings are generated, how they are maintained, and how they are annihilated. Tell me also of the advantages and disadvantages of discharging devotional service unto the Lord. What are the Vedic rituals and injunctions of the supplementary Vedic rites, and what are the procedures of religion, economic development and sense satisfaction?

PURPORT

Samplavaḥ, in the sense of "perfect means," is employed to denote the discharging of devotional service, and *pratisamplavaḥ* means just the opposite, or that which destroys the progress of devotional service. One who is firmly situated in devotional service of the Lord can very easily execute the function of conditional life. Living the conditional life is just like plying a boat in the middle of the ocean. One is completely at the mercy of the ocean, and at every moment there is every chance of being drowned in the ocean by slight agitation. If the atmosphere is all right, the boat can ply very easily, undoubtedly, but if there is some storm, fog, wind, or cloud, there is every possibility of being drowned in the ocean. No one can control the whims of the ocean, however one may be materially well equipped. One who has crossed the oceans by ship may have sufficient experience of such dependence upon the mercy of the ocean. But one can ply over the ocean of material existence by the grace of the Lord very easily, without any fear of storm or fog. It all depends on the will of the Lord; no one can help if there is some unfortunate danger in the state of conditional life. The devotees of the Lord, however, cross the ocean of material existence without anxiety because a pure devotee is always protected by the Lord (Bg. 9.13). The Lord gives special attention to His devotees in their activities within material, conditional life. (Bg. 9.29) Therefore everyone should take shelter of the lotus feet of the Lord and be a pure devotee of the Lord by all means.

One should know, therefore, from the expert spiritual master the advantages and disadvantages of discharging devotional service, just as Mahārāja Parīkṣit asked his spiritual master Śrīla Śukadeva Gosvāmī. According to *Bhakti-rasāmṛta-sindhu*, the science of devotional service, one should not eat more than what he requires to maintain body and soul together. Vegetable diets and milk are sufficient for maintenance of the human body, and therefore one has no need to eat anything more to satisfy the palate. One should also not accumulate money to become puffed up in the material world. One should earn his livelihood easily and honestly, for it is better to become a coolie for honest livelihood than to become a great man in the society by hook and crook. There is no harm if one becomes the richest man in the world by honest dealings, but one should not sacrifice the honest means of livelihood simply to accumulate wealth. Such an endeavor is harmful to devotional service. One should not talk nonsense. A devotee's business is to earn the favor of the Lord. Therefore a devotee should always glorify the Lord in His wonderful creations. A devotee should not decry the creation of the Lord, defying Him by saying that He has created a false world. The world is not false. Factually we have to take so many things from the world for our maintenance, so how we can say that the world is false? Similarly, how can one think of the Lord as being without form? How can one become formless and at the same time have all intelligence and consciousness, direct and indirect? So there are many things for a pure devotee to learn, and he should learn them perfectly from a bona fide personality like Śukadeva Gosvāmī.

The favorable conditions for discharging devotional service are that one should be very enthusiastic in serving the Lord. The Lord in His form of Śrī Caitanya Mahāprabhu wanted the cult of devotional service to the Lord to be preached all over the world, in every nook and corner, and therefore a pure devotee's duty is to discharge this order as far as possible. Every devotee should be very enthusiastic, not only in performing his daily rituals of devotional service, but in trying to preach the cult peacefully by following in the footsteps of Lord Caitanya. If he is not superficially successful in such an attempt, he should not be deterred from the discharge of his duty. Success or failure has no meaning for a pure devotee because he is a soldier in the field. Preaching the cult of devotional service is something like declaring war against materialistic life. There are different kinds of materialists, such as the fruitive workers, the mental speculators, the mystic jugglers, and so many others. All of them are against the existence of Godhead. They would declare that they are themselves God, although in every step and in every action they are dependent on the mercy of the

Lord. Therefore a pure devotee may not associate with such gangs of atheists. A strong devotee of the Lord will not be misled by such atheistic propaganda of the nondevotees, but a neophyte devotee should be very cautious about them. A devotee should see to the right discharge of devotional service under the guidance of a bona fide spiritual master and should not stick only to the formalities. Under the direction of the bona fide spiritual master one should see how much service is being executed, and not simply in the matter of rituals. A devotee should not hanker after anything, but he should be satisfied with things that may automatically come to him by the will of the Lord. That should be the principle of a devotional life. And all these principles are easily learned under the guidance of a spiritual master like Śukadeva Gosvāmī. Mahārāja Parīkṣit inquired from Śukadeva correctly, and one should follow his example.

Mahārāja Parīkṣit inquired about the process of creation, maintenance and destruction of the material world, the process of Vedic rituals and the method of executing pious activities in terms of the supplementary *Vedas* like the *Purāṇas, Mahābhārata,* etc. As explained before, the *Mahābhārata* is the history of ancient India, and so also the *Purāṇas.* Pious acts are prescribed in the supplementary *Vedas (smṛtis),* and they are specifically mentioned in the matter of digging tanks and wells for water supply of the people in general. To implant trees on the public roads, to construct public temples and places of worship of God, to establish places of charity where the poor destitutes can be provided with foodstuff, and similar activities, are called *pūrta.*

Similarly, the process of fulfilling the natural desires for sense gratification was also inquired about by the King for the benefit of all concerned.

TEXT 22

यो वानुशायिनां सर्गः पाषण्डस्य च सम्भवः ।
आत्मनो बन्धमोक्षौ च व्यवस्थानं स्वरूपतः ॥२२॥

yo vānuśāyināṁ sargaḥ
pāṣaṇḍasya ca sambhavaḥ
ātmano bandha-mokṣau ca
vyavasthānaṁ sva-rūpataḥ

yaḥ—all those; *vā*—either; *anuśāyinām*—merged into the body of the Lord; *sargaḥ*—creation; *pāṣaṇḍasya*—of the infidels; *ca*—and; *sambhavaḥ*—appearance; *ātmanaḥ*—of the living beings; *bandha*—conditioned; *mokṣau*—being liberated; *ca*—also; *vyavasthānam*—being situated; *sva-rūpataḥ*—in an unconditioned state.

TRANSLATION

Please also explain how, merged in the body of the Lord, living beings are created, and how the infidels appear in the world. Also please explain how the unconditioned living entities exist.

PURPORT

The progressive devotee of the Lord must inquire from the bona fide spiritual master how living entities merged in the body of the Lord again come back at the time of creation. There are two kinds of living entities. There are the ever liberated unconditioned living beings as well as the ever conditioned living beings. Of the ever conditioned living beings, there are two divisions. They are the faithful and the infidels. Of the faithful there are again two divisions, namely the devotees and the mental speculators. The mental speculators desire to merge into the existence of the Lord, or to become one with the Lord, whereas the devotees of the Lord desire to keep separate identities and constantly engage in the service of the Lord. The devotees who are not fully purified, as well as the empiric philosophers, become conditioned again during the next creation for further purification. Such conditioned souls become liberated by further progress of devotional service to the Lord. Mahārāja Parīkṣit asked all these questions from the bona fide spiritual master in order to become fully equipped in the science of God.

TEXT 23

यथात्मतन्त्रो भगवान् विक्रीडत्यात्ममायया ।
विसृज्य वा यथा मायामुदास्ते साक्षिवद् विभुः॥२३॥

yathātma-tantro bhagavān
vikrīḍaty ātma-māyayā

visṛjya vā yathā māyām
udāste sākṣivad vibhuḥ

yathā—as; *ātma-tantraḥ*—independent; *bhagavān*—the Personality of Godhead; *vikrīḍati*—enjoys His pastimes; *ātma-māyayā*—by His internal potency; *visṛjya*—giving up; *vā*—as also; *yathā*—as He desires; *māyām*—the external potency; *udāste*—remains; *sākṣivat*—just as the witness; *vibhuḥ*—the almighty.

TRANSLATION

The independent Personality of Godhead enjoys His pastimes by His internal potency and at the time of annihilation gives them up to the external potency, and He remains a witness to it all.

PURPORT

Lord Śrī Kṛṣṇa, being the Supreme Personality of Godhead and fountainhead of all other incarnations, is the only independent person. He enjoys His pastimes by creation as He desires and gives them up to the external energy at the time of annihilation. By His internal potency only He kills the demon Pūtanā, even though enjoying His pastimes in the lap of His mother Yaśodā. And when He desired to leave this world He created the pastimes of killing His own family members *(Yadu-kula)* and remained unaffected by such annihilation. He is the witness of everything that is happening, and yet He has nothing to do with anything. He is independent in every respect. Mahārāja Parīkṣit desired to know more perfectly, for a pure devotee ought to know well.

TEXT 24

सर्वमेतच्च भगवन् पृच्छतो मेऽनुपूर्वशः ।
तत्त्वतोऽर्हस्युदाहर्तुं प्रपन्नाय महामुने ॥२४॥

sarvam etac ca bhagavan
pṛcchato me'nupūrvaśaḥ
tattvato'rhasy udāhartuṁ
prapannāya mahā-mune

sarvam—all these; *etat*—inquiries; *ca*—also that I have not been able to ask; *bhagavan*—O great sage; *pṛcchataḥ*—of the inquisitive; *me*—myself; *anupūrvaśaḥ*—from the beginning; *tattvataḥ*—just in accordance with the truth; *arhasi*—may kindly be explained; *udāhartum*—as you will let know; *prapannāya*—one who is surrounded; *mahā-mune*—O great sage.

TRANSLATION

O great sage, representative of the Lord, kindly satisfy my inquisitiveness in all that I have inquired from you and all that I may not have inquired from you from the very beginning of my questionings. Since I am a surrendered soul unto you, please impart full knowledge in this connection.

PURPORT

The spiritual master is always prepared to impart knowledge to the disciple and specifically when the disciple is very inquisitive. Inquisitiveness on the part of a disciple is greatly necessary for the progressive disciple. Mahārāja Parīkṣit is a typical disciple because he is perfectly inquisitive. If one is not very inquisitive about self-realization, one need not approach a spiritual master simply to make a show of discipleship. Mahārāja Parīkṣit is inquisitive, not only for all that he has inquired, but he is also anxious to know what he has not been able to inquire. Factually it is not possible for a man to inquire about everything from the spiritual master, but the bona fide spiritual master is able to enlighten the disciple in every way for the disciple's benefit.

TEXT 25

अत्र प्रमाणं हि भवान् परमेष्ठी यथात्मभूः ।
अपरे चानुतिष्ठन्ति पूर्वेषां पूर्वजैः कृतम् ॥२५॥

atra pramāṇaṁ hi bhavān
parameṣṭhī yathātma-bhūḥ
apare cānutiṣṭhanti
pūrveṣāṁ pūrva-jaiḥ kṛtam

atra—in this matter; *pramāṇam*—evidential facts; *hi*—certainly; *bhavān*—yourself; *parameṣṭhī*—Brahmā, the creator of the universe; *yathā*—as; *ātma-bhūḥ*—born directly from the Lord; *apare*—others; *ca*—only; *anutiṣṭhanti*—just to follow; *pūrveṣām*—as a matter of custom; *pūrva-jaiḥ*—knowledge suggested by a previous philosopher; *kṛtam*—having been done.

TRANSLATION

O great sage, you are as good as Brahmā, the original living being. Others follow custom only, as followed by the previous philosophical speculators.

PURPORT

It may be argued that Śukadeva Gosvāmī is not the only authority of perfect knowledge in transcendence because there are many other sages and their followers. Contemporary to Vyāsadeva or even prior to him there were many other great sages, such as Gautama, Kaṇāda, Jaimini, Kapila and Aṣṭāvakra, and all of them have presented a philosophical path by themselves. Patañjali is also one of them, and all these six great *ṛṣis* have their own way of thinking, exactly like the modern philosophers and mental speculators. The difference between the six philosophical paths put forward by the renowned sages above mentioned and that of Śukadeva Gosvāmī, as presented in the *Śrīmad-Bhāgavatam,* is that all the six sages mentioned above speak the facts according to their own thinking, but Śukadeva Gosvāmī presents the knowledge which comes down directly from Brahmājī, who is known as *ātma-bhūḥ,* or born of and educated by the Almighty Personality of Godhead.

Vedic transcendental knowledge descends directly from the Personality of Godhead. By His mercy, Brahmā, the first living being in the universe, was enlightened, and from Brahmājī, Nārada was enlightened, and from Nārada, Vyāsa was enlightened. Śukadeva Gosvāmī received such transcendental knowledge directly from his father, Vyāsadeva. Thus the knowledge, being received from the chain of disciplic succession, is perfect. One cannot be a spiritual master in perfection unless and until one has received the same by disciplic succession. That is the secret of receiving transcendental knowledge. The six great sages mentioned above may be great thinkers, but their knowledge by mental speculation is not perfect. However perfect an empiric philosopher may be in presenting a philosophical thesis, such knowledge is never perfect because it is produced by an imperfect mind. Such great sages also have their disciplic succession, but they are not authorized because such knowledge does not come directly from the independent Supreme Personality of Godhead, Nārāyaṇa. No one can be independent except Nārāyaṇa; therefore no one's knowledge can be perfect due to being dependent on the flickering mind. Mind is material, and thus knowledge presented by material speculators is never transcendental and can never become perfect. Mundane philosophers, being imperfect in themselves, disagree with other philosophers because a mundane philosopher is not a philosopher at all unless he presents his own theory. Intelligent persons like Mahārāja Parīkṣit do not recognize such mental speculators, however great they may be, but hear from the authorities like Śukadeva Gosvāmī, who is nondifferent from the Supreme Personality of Godhead by the *paramparā* system, as is specially stressed in the *Bhagavad-gītā.*

TEXT 26

न मेऽसवः परायन्ति ब्रह्मन्ननशनादमी ।
पिबतोऽच्युतपीयूषम् तद् वाक्याब्धिविनिःसृतम् ॥२६॥

na me 'savaḥ parāyanti
brahmann anaśanādamī
pibato 'cyuta-pīyūṣam
tad vākyābdhi-viniḥsṛtam

na—never; *me*—mine; *asavaḥ*—life; *parāyanti*—becomes exhausted; *brahman*—O learned *brāhmaṇa; anaśanāt amī*—because of fasting; *pibataḥ*—because of my drinking; *acyuta*—the infallible; *pīyūṣam*—nectar; *tat*—your; *vākyābdhi*—ocean of speech; *viniḥsṛtam*—flowing down from.

TRANSLATION

O learned brāhmaṇa, because of my drinking the nectar of the message of the infallible Personality of Godhead, which is flowing down from the ocean of your speeches, I do not feel any sort of exhaustion due to my fasting."

PURPORT

The disciplic succession from Brahmā, Nārada, Vyāsa and Śukadeva Gosvāmī is particularly different from others. The disciplic succession from other sages is simply a waste of time, being devoid of *Acyuta-kathā*, or the message of the infallible Lord. The mental speculators can present their theories very nicely by reason and arguments, but such reasons and arguments are not infallible because they are defeated by better mental speculators. Mahārāja Parīkṣit was not interested in the dry speculation of the flickering mind, but he was interested in the topics of the Lord because factually he felt that by hearing such a nectarean message from the mouth of Śukadeva Gosvāmī he was not feeling any exhaustion, even though he was fasting because of his imminent death.

One can indulge in hearing the mental speculators, but such hearing cannot be prolonged for any length of time. One will be exhausted very soon by hearing such hackneyed ways of thinking, and no one in the world can be satisfied simply by hearing such useless speculations. The message of the Lord, especially from a personality like Śukadeva Gosvāmī, can never be tiring, even though one may be exhausted from other causes.

In some editions of the *Śrīmad-Bhāgavatam,* the text of the last line of this verse reads *anyatra kupitād dvijāt*, which means the King might be overwhelmed by the thought of his imminent death by snakebite. The snake is also twice-born, and its anger is compared with the cursing *brāhmaṇa* boy who was without good intelligence. Mahārāja Parīkṣit was not at all afraid of death because of being fully encouraged by the message of the Lord. One who is fully absorbed in *Acyuta-kathā* can never be afraid of anything in this world.

TEXT 27

सूत उवाच
स उपामन्त्रितो राज्ञा कथायामिति सत्पतेः ।
ब्रह्मरातो भृशं प्रीतो विष्णुरातेन संसदि ॥२७॥

sūta uvāca
sa upāmantrito rājñā
kathāyām iti sat-pateḥ
brahmarāto bhṛśaṁ prīto
viṣṇurātena saṁsadi

śrī sūtaḥ uvāca—Śrīla Sūta Gosvāmī said; *saḥ*—he (Śukadeva Gosvāmī); *upāmantritaḥ*—thus being inquired; *rājñā*—by the King; *kathāyām*—in the topics of; *iti*—thus; *sat-pateḥ*—of the highest truth; *brahmarātaḥ*—Śukadeva Gosvāmī; *bhṛśam*—very much; *prītaḥ*—pleased; *viṣṇurātena*—by Mahārāja Parīkṣit; *saṁsadi*—in the meeting.

TRANSLATION

Sūta Gosvāmī said: Thus Śukadeva Gosvāmī, being invited by Mahārāja Parīkṣit to speak on topics of the Lord Śrī Kṛṣṇa with the devotees, was very much pleased.

PURPORT

Śrīmad-Bhāgavatam can only be legitimately discussed among the devotees of the Lord. As the *Bhagavad-gītā* was authoritatively discussed between Lord Kṛṣṇa and Arjuna (the Lord and the devotee respectively), similarly *Śrīmad-Bhāgavatam,* which is the postgraduate study of the *Bhagavad-gītā,* can also be discussed between the scholars and devotees like Śukadeva Gosvāmī and Mahārāja Parīkṣit. Otherwise the real taste of the nectar cannot be relished. Śukadeva Gosvāmī was pleased with Mahārāja Parīkṣit because he was not at all tired of hearing the topics of the Lord, and he was more and more anxious to hear them on and on with interest. Foolish interpreters unnecessarily tackle the *Bhagavad-gītā* and *Śrīmad-Bhāgavatam* when they have no access to the subject matter. There is no use in nondevotees' meddling with the two topmost Vedic literatures, and therefore Śaṅkarācārya did not touch *Śrīmad-Bhāgavatam* for commentation. In his commentation on the *Bhagavad-gītā,* Śrīpāda Śaṅkarācārya accepted Lord Kṛṣṇa as the Supreme Personality of Godhead, but later on he commented from the impersonalist's view. But, being conscious of his position, he did not comment on the *Śrīmad-Bhāgavatam.*

Śrīla Śukadeva Gosvāmī was protected by Lord Kṛṣṇa (vide *Brahma-vaivarta Purāṇa),* and therefore he is known as Brahmarāta, and Śrīmān Parīkṣit Mahārāja was protected by Viṣṇu, and thus he is known as the Viṣṇurāta. As devotees of the Lord, they are always protected by the Lord. It is clear also in this connection that a Viṣṇurāta should hear *Śrīmad-Bhāgavatam* from Brahmarāta and no one else because others misrepresent the transcendental knowledge and thus spoil one's valuable time.

TEXT 28

प्राह भागवतं नाम पुराणं ब्रह्मसम्मितम् ।
ब्रह्मणे भगवत्प्रोक्तं ब्रह्मकल्प उपागते ॥२८॥

prāha bhāgavataṁ nāma
purāṇaṁ brahma-sammitam
brahmaṇe bhagavat-proktaṁ
brahma-kalpa upāgate

prāha—he said; *bhāgavatam*—the science of the Personality of Godhead; *nāma*—of the name; *purāṇam*—the supplement of the *Vedas; brahma-sammitam*—just in pursuance of the *Vedas; brahmaṇe*—unto Lord Brahmā; *bhagavat-proktam*—was spoken by the Personality of Godhead; *brahma-kalpe*—the millennium in which Brahmā was first generated; *upāgate*—just in the beginning.

TRANSLATION

He just began to reply to the inquiries of Mahārāja Parīkṣit by saying that the science of the Personality of Godhead was spoken first by the Lord Himself to Brahmā when he was first born. Śrīmad-Bhāgavatam is the supplementary Vedic literature, and it is just in pursuance of the Vedas.

PURPORT

Śrīmad-Bhāgavatam is the science of the Personality of Godhead. The impersonalist always tries to misrepresent the personal feature of the Lord without knowing the science of this great knowledge, and *Śrīmad-Bhāgavatam* is in pursuance of the *Vedas* and scientific knowledge of the Personality of Godhead. To learn this science one should take shelter of the representative of Śrī Śukadeva and follow in the footsteps of Mahārāja Parīkṣit without foolishly attempting to interpret, thereby committing a great offense at the feet of the Lord. The dangerous ways of interpretations by the nondevotee class of men have played havoc in understanding the *Śrīmad-Bhagavad-gītā* and the *Śrīmad-Bhāgavatam,* and the careful student should be always alert in this matter if he at all wants to learn the science of Godhead.

TEXT 29

यद् यत् परीक्षिदृषभः पाण्डूनामनुपृच्छति ।
आनुपूर्व्येण तत्सर्वमाख्यातुमुपचक्रमे ॥२९॥

yad yat parīkṣid ṛṣabhaḥ
pāṇḍūnām anupṛcchati
ānupūrvyeṇa tat sarvam
ākhyātum upacakrame

yat yat—whatsoever; *parīkṣit*—the King; *ṛṣabhaḥ*—the best; *pāṇḍūnām*—in the dynasty of Pāṇḍu; *anupṛcchati*—goes on inquiring; *ānupūrvyeṇa*—the beginning to the end; *tat*—all those; *sarvam*—fully; *ākhyātum*—to describe; *upacakrame*—he just prepared himself.

TRANSLATION

He also prepared himself to reply to all that King Parīkṣit inquired from him. Mahārāja Parīkṣit was the best in the dynasty of the Pāṇḍus, and thus he was able to ask the right questions from the right person."

PURPORT

Mahārāja Parīkṣit asked many questions, some of them very curiously, to know things as they are, but it is not necessary for the master to answer them in the order of the disciple's inquiries, one after the other. But Śukadeva Gosvāmī, experienced teacher that he was, answered all the questions in a systematic way as they were received from the chain of disciplic succession. And he answered all of them without exception.

Thus end the Bhaktivedanta purports of the Second Canto, Eighth Chapter, of the Śrīmad-Bhāgavatam, *entitled "Questions By King Parīkṣit."*

CHAPTER NINE

Answers by Citing the Lord's Version

TEXT 1

श्रीशुक उवाच
आत्ममायामृते राजन् परस्यानुभवात्मनः ।
न घटेतार्थसम्बन्धः स्वप्नद्रष्टुरिवाञ्जसा ॥ १ ॥

śrī śuka uvāca
ātma-māyām ṛte rājan
parasyānubhavātmanaḥ
na ghaṭetārtha-sambandhaḥ
svapna-draṣṭur ivāñjasā

śrī śukaḥ uvāca—Śrī Śukadeva Gosvāmī said; *ātma*—the Supreme Personality of Godhead; *māyām*—energy; *ṛte*—without; *rajan*—O King; *parasya*—of the pure soul; *anubhava-ātmanaḥ*—of the purely conscious; *na*—never; *ghaṭeta*—it can so happen; *artha*—meaning; *sambandhaḥ*—relation with the material body; *svapna*—dream; *draṣṭuḥ*—of the seer; *iva*—like it; *añjasā*—completely.

TRANSLATION

Śrī Śukadeva Gosvāmī said: O King, unless one is influenced by the energy of the Supreme Personality of Godhead, there is no meaning to the relationship of the pure soul in pure consciousness with the material body. It is just like the dreamer seeing his own body working.

PURPORT

The question of Mahārāja Parīkṣit is perfectly answered as to how a living entity began his material life, although he is apart from the material body and mind. The spirit soul is distinct from the material conception of his life, but he is absorbed in such a material conception because of being influenced by the external energy of the Lord, called *ātma-māyā*. This is already explained in the First Canto in connection with Vyāsadeva's realization of the Supreme Lord and His external energy. The external energy is controlled by the Lord, and the living entities are controlled by the external energy—by the will of the Lord. Therefore, although the living entity is purely conscious in his pure state, he is subordinate to the will of the Lord in being influenced by the external energy of the Lord. In the *Bhagavad-gītā* also the same thing is confirmed (Bg. 15.15), that the Lord is present within the heart of every living entity, and all consciousness and forgetfulness of the living entity are influenced by the Lord.

Now the next question will automatically be made as to why the Lord influences the living entity to such consciousness and forgetfulness. The answer is that the Lord clearly wishes that every living entity be in his pure consciousness as the part and parcel of the Lord and thus be engaged in the loving service of the Lord as he is constitutionally made; but because the living entity is partially independent also, he may not be willing to serve the Lord, but may try to become as independent as the Lord is. The whole nondevotee class of living entities are all desirous of becoming equally as powerful as the Lord, although they are not fit to become so. The living entities are illusioned by the will of the Lord because they wanted to become like Him. As a person thinks of becoming a king without possessing the necessary qualification, similarly when the living entity desires to become the Lord Himself, he is put in a condition of dreaming that he is a king. Therefore the first sinful will of the living entity is to become the Lord, and the consequent will of the Lord is that the living entity forgets his factual life and thus dreams of the land of utopia where he may become one like the Lord. The child cries to have the moon from the mother, and the mother gives the child a mirror to satisfy the crying and disturbing child with the shadow of the moon. Similarly, the crying child of the Lord is given over to the shadow of the material world to lord it over as *karmī* and to give this up in frustration to become one with the Lord. Both these stages are dreaming illusions only. There is no necessity of tracing out the history when the living entity desired this. But the fact is that as soon as he desired such, he was put under the control of *ātma-māyā* by the direction of the Lord. Therefore the living entity in his material condition is dreaming falsely that this is "mine" and this is "I." The dream is that the conditioned soul thinks of his material body as "I" or falsely thinks that he is the Lord and that everything in connection with that material body is "mine." Thus in dream only the misconception of "I" and "mine" persists life after life. This continues life after life, as long as the living entity is not purely conscious of his identity as the subordinate part and parcel of the Lord.

In his pure consciousness, however, there is no such misconceived dream, and in that pure conscious state the living entity does not forget that he is never the Lord, but that he is eternally the servitor of the Lord in transcendental love.

TEXT 2

बहुरूप इवाभाति मायया बहुरूपया ।
रममाणो गुणेष्वस्या ममाहमिति मन्यते ॥ २ ॥

bahu-rūpa ivābhāti
māyayā bahu-rūpayā
ramamāṇo guṇeṣv asyā
mamāham iti manyate

bahu-rūpaḥ—multiforms; *iva*—as it were; *ābhāti*—manifested; *māyayā*—by the influence of the exterior energy; *bahu-rūpayā*—in multifarious forms; *ramamāṇaḥ*—enjoying as it were; *guṇeṣu*—in the modes of different qualities; *asyāḥ*—of the external energy; *mama*—mine; *aham*—I; *iti*—thus; *manyate*—thinks.

TRANSLATION

The illusioned living entity appears in so many forms which are offered by the external energy of the Lord, and the encaged living entity, while enjoying in the modes of material nature, misconceives, thinking in terms of "I" and "mine."

PURPORT

The different forms of the living entities are different dresses offered by the illusory external energy of the Lord according to the modes of nature desired to be enjoyed by the living being. The external material energy is represented by her three modes, namely goodness, passion and ignorance. So even in the material nature there is a chance of an independent choice by the living entity, and according to his choice the material energy offers him different varieties of material bodies. There are 900,000 varieties of material bodies in the water, two million vegetable bodies, 1,100,000 worms and reptiles, one million forms of birds, three million different bodies of beasts, and 400,000 human forms. Altogether there are 8,400,000 varieties of bodies in different planets of the universe, and the living entity is traveling by so many transmigrations according to different modes of enjoying spirit within himself. Even in one particular body the living entity changes from childhood to boyhood, from boyhood to youth, from youth to old age and from old age to another body created by his own action. The living entity creates his own body by his personal desires, and the external energy of the Lord supplies him the exact form by which he can enjoy his desires to the fullest extent. The tiger wanted to enjoy the blood of another animal, and therefore, by the grace of the Lord, the material energy supplies him the body of the tiger with facilities for enjoying blood from another animal. Similarly, a living entity desiring to get the body of a demigod in the higher planet can also get it by the grace of the Lord. And if he is intelligent enough, he can desire to get a spiritual body to enjoy the company of the Lord, and he will get it. So the minute freedom of the living entity can be fully utilized, and the Lord is so kind that he will award him the same type of body that he desires. It is like dreaming of a golden mountain. A person knows what a mountain is, and he knows also what gold is. Out of his desire only he dreams of a golden mountain, and when the dream is over he sees something else in his presence. He finds in his awakened state that there is neither gold nor a mountain, and what to speak of a golden mountain.

The different positions of the living entities in the material world under multifarious manifestations of bodies are due to the misconception of "mine" and "I." The *karmī* thinks of this world as "mine," and the *jñānī* thinks "I am" everything. The whole material conception of politics, sociology, philanthropy, altruism, etc., conceived by the conditioned souls is on the basis of this misconceived "I" and "mine," and this I and mine are products of a strong desire to enjoy material life. Identification of the body and the place where the body is obtained under different conceptions of socialism, nationalism, family affection, and so on and so forth is all due to forgetfulness of the real nature of the living entity, and the whole misconception of the bewildered living entity can be removed by the association of Śukadeva Gosvāmī and Mahārāja Parīkṣit, as all this is explained in the *Śrīmad-Bhāgavatam.*

TEXT 3

यर्हि वाव महिम्नि स्वे परस्मिन् कालमाययोः ।
रमेत गतसम्मोहस्त्यक्त्वोदास्ते तदोभयम् ॥ ३ ॥

yarhi vāva mahimni sve
parasmin kāla-māyayoḥ

rameta gata-sammohas
tyaktvodāste tadobhayam

yarhi—at any time; *vāva*—certainly; *mahimni*—in the glory; *sve*—of himself; *parasmin*—in the Supreme; *kāla*—time; *māyayoḥ*—also the material energy; *rameta*—enjoys; *gata-sammohaḥ*—being freed from misconception; *tyaktvā*—giving up; *udāste*—in fullness; *tadā*—that; *ubhayam*—both.

TRANSLATION

As soon as the living entity becomes situated in his constitutional glory and begins to enjoy the transcendence beyond time and material energy, he at once gives up the two misconceptions of life [mine and I] and thus becomes fully manifested as the pure self.

PURPORT

The two misconceptions of life, namely "I" and "mine," are verily manifested in two classes of men. In the lower state the conception of "mine" is very prominent, and in the higher state the misconception of "I" is prominent. In the animal state of life the misconception of "mine" is perceivable even in the category of cats and dogs, and they fight with one another with the same misconception of "mine." In the lower stage of human life the same misconception is also prominent in the shape of "It is my body," "It is my house," "It is my family," "It is my caste," "It is my nation," "It is my country," and so on. And in the higher stage of speculative knowledge, the same misconception of "mine" is transformed into "I am," or "It is all I am," or "I," etc. There are many classes of men comprehending the same misconception of "I" and "mine" in different color. But the real significance of such "I" can only be realized when one is situated in the consciousness of *"I am the eternal servitor of the Lord."* This is pure consciousness, and the whole Vedic literatures teach us this conception of life.

The misconception of "I am the Lord," or "I am the Supreme," is more dangerous than the misconception of "mine." Although there are sometimes directions in the Vedic literatures to think oneself one with the Lord, that does not mean that one becomes identified in every respect with the Lord. Undoubtedly there is oneness of the living entity with the Lord in many respects, but ultimately the living entity is subordinate to the Lord, and he is constitutionally meant for satisfying the senses of the Lord. The Lord therefore asks the conditioned souls to surrender unto Him. Had the living entities not been subordinate to the supreme will, why would the living entity be asked to surrender? Had the living being been equal in all respects, then why was he put under the influence of *māyā?* We have already discussed many times that the material energy is controlled by the Lord. The *Bhagavad-gītā* confirms this controlling power of the Lord over the material nature (Bg. 9.10). Can a living entity who claims to be as good as the Supreme Being control the material nature? The foolish "I" would reply that he would do so in the future. Even accepting that in the future one would be as good a controller of the material nature as the Supreme Being, then why is he now under the control of the material nature? The *Bhagavad-gītā* says that one can be freed from the control of the material nature by surrendering unto the Supreme Lord, but if there is no surrender, then the living entity will never be able to control the material nature. So this misconception of "I" must also be given up by practicing the way of devotional service or firmly being situated in the transcendental loving service of the Lord. A poor man without any employment or without any occupation may undergo so many troubles in life, but if by chance the same man gets a good service under the government, he at once becomes happy. There is no profit in denying the supremacy of the Lord, who is the controller of all energies, but one should be constitutionally situated in one's own glory, namely to be situated in the pure consciousness of being the eternal servitor of the Lord. In his conditional life the living entity is servant of the illusory *māyā,* and in his liberated state he is the pure unqualified servant of the Lord. To become untinged by the modes of material nature is the qualification for entering into the service of the Lord. As long as one is a servant of mental concoctions, one cannot be completely free from the disease of "I" and "mine."

The Supreme Truth is without any contamination of the illusory energy because He is the controller of that energy. The relative truths are apt to be engrossed with illusory energy. The best purpose is, however, served when one is directly facing the supreme truth, as when one faces the sun. The sun overhead in the sky is full of light, but when the sun is not in the visible sky, all is in darkness. Similarly, when one is face to face with the Supreme Lord, he is freed from all illusions, and one who is not so is in the darkness of illusory *māyā.* The *Bhagavad-gītā* confirms this as follows:

māṁ ca yo 'vyabhicāreṇa bhakti-yogena sevate
sa guṇān samatītyaitān brahma-bhūyāya kalpate
(Bg. 14.26)

So the science of *bhakti-yoga,* of worshiping the Lord, glorifying the Lord, hearing the *Śrīmad-Bhāgavatam* from the right sources (not from the professional man but from a person who is *Bhāgavatam* in life) and being always in the association of pure devotees, should be adopted in earnestness without being misled by misconceptions of "I" and "mine." The *karmīs* are fond of the conception of "mine," and the *jñānīs* are fond of the conception of "I," and both of them are unqualified to be free from the bondage of the illusory energy. *Śrīmad-Bhāgavatam,* and primarily the *Bhagavad-gītā,* are both meant for delivering a person from the misconception of "I" and "mine," and Śrīla Vyāsadeva transcribed them for the deliverance of the fallen souls. The living entity has to be situated in the transcendental position where there is no more influence of time nor of the material energy. In conditioned life the living entity is subjected to the influence of time in the dream of past, present and future. The mental speculator tries to conquer the influence of time by future speculation of becoming Vāsudeva or the Supreme Lord himself by means of culture of knowledge and conquering over ego. But the process is not perfect. The perfect process is to accept Lord Vāsudeva as the Supreme in everything, and the best perfection of culturing knowledge is to surrender unto Him because He is the source of everything. In that conception only can one get rid of the misconception of I and mine. Both *Bhagavad-gītā* and the *Śrīmad-Bhāgavatam* confirm it. Śrīla Vyāsadeva has specifically contributed to the illusioned living entities the science of God and the process of *bhakti-yoga* in his great literature *Śrīmad-Bhāgavatam,* and the conditioned soul should fully take advantage of this great science.

TEXT 4

आत्मतत्त्वविशुद्ध्यर्थं यदाह भगवानृतम् ।
ब्रह्मणे दर्शयन् रूपमव्यलीकव्रतादृतः ॥ ४ ॥

ātma-tattva-viśuddhy-arthaṁ
yad āha bhagavān ṛtam
brahmaṇe darśayan rūpam
avyalīka-vratādṛtaḥ

ātma-tattvam—the science of God or that of the living entity; *viśuddhi*—purification; *artham*—goal; *yat*—that which; *āha*—said; *bhagavān*—the Personality of Godhead; *ṛtam*—in reality; *brahmaṇe*—unto Lord Brahmā; *darśayan*—by showing; *rūpam*—eternal form; *avyalīka*—without any deceptive motive; *vrata*—vow; *ādṛtah*—worshiped.

TRANSLATION

O King, the Personality of Godhead, being very much pleased with Lord Brahmā because of his nondeceptive penance in bhakti-yoga, presented His eternal and transcendental form before Brahmā. And that is the objective goal for purifying the conditioned soul.

PURPORT

Ātma-tattvam is the science of both God and the living entity. Both the Supreme Lord and the living entity are known as *ātmā.* The Supreme Lord is called *Paramātmā* or *Parambrahma,* and the living entity is called the *ātmā* or the *brahma* or the *jīva.* Both the *Paramātmā* and the *jīvātmā,* being transcendental to the material energy, are called *ātmā.* So Śukadeva Gosvāmī explains this verse with the aim of purifying the truth of both the *Paramātmā* and the *jīvātmā.* Generally people have many wrong conceptions about both of them. The wrong conception of the *jīvātmā* is to identify the material body with the pure soul, and the wrong conception of *Paramātmā* is to think Him on an equal level with the living entity. But both misconceptions can be removed by one stroke of *bhakti-yoga,* just as in the sunlight both the sun and the world and everything within the sunlight are properly seen. In the darkness no one can see the sun, nor himself, nor the world. But in the sunlight one can see the sun, himself and the world around him. Śrīla Śukadeva Gosvāmī therefore says that for purification of both wrong conceptions, the Lord presented His eternal form before Brahmājī, being fully satisfied by Brahmā's nondeceptive vow of discharging *bhakti-yoga.* Except for *bhakti-yoga,* any method for realization of *ātma-tattva,* or the science of *ātmā,* will prove deceptive in the long run.

In the *Bhagavad-gītā,* the Lord says that only by *bhakti-yoga* can one know Him perfectly, and then one can enter into the science of God. Brahmājī undertook great penance in performing *bhakti-yoga,* and thus he was able to see the transcendental form of the Lord. His transcendental form is one hundred percent spiritual, and one can see Him only by spiritualized vision after proper discharge of *tapasya* or penance in pure *bhakti-yoga.* The form of the Lord which was manifested before Brahmā is not one of the forms with which we have experience in the material world. Brahmājī did not perform such severe types of penance just to see a form of material production. Therefore the question by Mahārāja Parīkṣit about the form of the Lord is answered. The form of the Lord is *sac-cid-ānanda,* or eternal, full of knowledge and full of bliss. But the material form of the living being is neither eternal, nor full of knowledge, nor blissful. That is the distinction between the form of the Lord and that of the conditioned soul. The conditioned soul, however, can regain his form of eternal knowledge and bliss simply by seeing the Lord by means of *bhakti-yoga.*

The summary is that due to ignorance the conditioned soul is encaged in the temporary varieties of material forms. But the Supreme Lord has no such temporary form like the conditioned souls. He is always possessed of an eternal form of knowledge and bliss, and that is the difference between the Lord and the living entity. One can understand this difference by the process of *bhakti-yoga.* Brahmā was then told by the Lord the gist of *Śrīmad-Bhāgavatam* in four original verses. Thus *Śrīmad-Bhāgavatam* is not a creation of the mental speculators. The sound of *Śrīmad-Bhāgavatam* is transcendental, and the resonance of *Śrīmad-Bhāgavatam* is as good as that of the *Vedas.* Thus the topic of the *Śrīmad-Bhāgavatam* is the science of both the Lord and the living entity. Regular reading or hearing of *Śrīmad-Bhāgavatam* is also performance of *bhakti-yoga,* and one can attain the highest perfection simply by the association of *Śrīmad-Bhāgavatam.* Both Śukadeva Gosvāmī and Mahārāja Parīkṣit attained perfection through the medium of *Śrīmad-Bhāgavatam.*

TEXT 5

स आदिदेवो जगतां परो गुरुः
स्वधिष्ण्यमास्थाय सिसृक्षयैक्षत ।
तां नाध्यगच्छद् दृशमत्र सम्मतां
प्रपञ्चनिर्माणविधिर्यया भवेत् ॥ ५ ॥

sa ādi-devo jagatāṁ paro guruḥ
svadhiṣṇyam āsthāya sisṛkṣayaikṣata
tāṁ nādhyagacchad dṛśam atra sammatāṁ
prapañca-nirmāṇa-vidhir yayā bhavet

saḥ—he; *ādi-devaḥ*—the first demigod; *jagatām*—of the universe; *paraḥ*—supreme; *guruḥ*—spiritual master; *svadhiṣṇyam*—his lotus seat; *āsthāya*—to find out the source of it; *sisṛkṣayā*—for the matter of creating the universal affairs; *aikṣata*—began to think; *tām*—in that matter; *na*—could not; *adhyagacchat*—understand; *dṛśam*—the direction; *atra*—therein; *sammatām*—just the proper way; *prapañca*—material; *nirmāṇa*—construction; *vidhiḥ*—process; *yayā*—as much as; *bhavet*—should be.

TRANSLATION

Lord Brahmā, the first spiritual master, supreme in the universe, could not trace out the source of his lotus seat, and while thinking of creating the material world, he could not understand the proper direction for such creative work, nor could he find out the process for such creation.

PURPORT

This verse is the prelude for explaining the transcendental nature of the form and the abode of the Lord. In the beginning of *Śrīmad-Bhāgavatam* it is already said that the Supreme Absolute Truth exists in His own abode without any touch of the deluding energy. Therefore the kingdom of God is not a myth but factually a different and transcendental sphere of planets known as the Vaikuṇṭhas. This will also be explained in this chapter.

Such knowledge of the spiritual sky far above this material sky and its paraphernalia can be known only by dint of devotional service or *bhakti-yoga.* The power of creation by Lord Brahmā was also achieved by *bhakti-yoga.* Brahmājī was bewildered in the matter of creation, and he could not even trace out the source of his own existence. But all this knowledge was fully achieved by him through the medium of *bhakti-yoga.* By *bhakti-yoga* one can know the Lord, and by knowing the Lord as the Supreme, one is able to know everything else. One who knows the Supreme knows everything else. That is the version of all *Vedas.* Even the first spiritual master of the universe was enlightened by the grace of the Lord, so who else can attain perfect knowledge of everything without the mercy of the Lord? If anyone desires to seek perfect knowledge of everything, he must seek the mercy of the Lord, and there is no other means. To seek knowledge on the strength of one's personal attempt is a sheer waste of time.

TEXT 6

स चिन्तयन् द्व्यक्षरमेकदाम्भ-
स्युपाश्रृणोद् द्विर्गदितं वचो विभुः ।
स्पर्शेषु यत्षोडशमेकविंशं
निष्किञ्चनानां नृप यद् धनं विदुः ॥ ६ ॥

sa cintayan dvyakṣaramekadāmbhasy
upāśṛṇod dvir-gaditaṁ vaco vibhuḥ
sparśeṣu yat ṣoḍaśam ekaviṁśaṁ
niṣkiñcanānāṁ nṛpa yad dhanaṁ viduḥ

saḥ—he; *cintayan*—while thus thinking; *dvi*—two; *akṣaram*—syllables; *ekadā*—once upon a time; *ambhasi*—in the water; *upāśṛṇot*—heard it nearby; *dviḥ*—twice; *gaditam*—uttered; *vacaḥ*—words; *vibhuḥ*—the great; *sparśeṣu*—of the *sparśa* letters; *yat*—which; *ṣoḍaśam*—the sixteenth; *ekaviṁśam*—and the twenty-first; *niṣkiñcanānām*—of the renounced order of life; *nṛpa*—O King; *yat*—what is; *dhanam*—wealth; *viduḥ*—as it is known.

TRANSLATION

While thus engaged in thinking, in the water, Brahmājī heard twice from nearby two syllables joined together. One of the syllables was taken from the sixteenth and the other from the twenty-first of the sparśa alphabets, and both joined to become the wealth of the renounced order of life.

PURPORT

In Sanskrit language, the consonant alphabets are divided into two divisions, namely the *sparśa-varṇas* and the *tālavya-varṇas*. From *ka* to *ma* the letters are known as the *sparśa-varṇas,* and the sixteenth of the group is called *ta,* whereas the twenty-first letter is called *pa.* So when they are joined together, the word *tapa,* or penance, is constructed. This penance is the beauty and wealth of the *brāhmaṇas* and the renounced order of life. According to *Bhāgavata* philosophy, every human being is meant simply for this *tapa* and for no other business, because by penance only can one realize his self; and self-realization, and not sense gratification, is the business of human life. This *tapa,* or penance, was begun from the very beginning of the creation, and it was first adopted by the supreme spiritual master, Lord Brahmā. By *tapasya* only can one get the profit of human life, and not by a polished civilization of animal life. The animal does not know anything except sense gratification in the jurisdiction of eat, drink, be merry and enjoy. But the human being is made to undergo *tapasya* for going back to Godhead, back to home.

When Lord Brahmā was perplexed about how to construct the material manifestations in the universe and went down within the water to find out the means and the source of his lotus seat, he heard the word *tapa* vibrated twice. To take the path of *tapa* is the second birth of the desiring disciple. The word *upāśṛṇot* is very significant. It is similar to *upanayana,* or bringing the disciple nearer to the spiritual master for the path of *tapa.* So Brahmājī was thus initiated by Lord Kṛṣṇa, and this fact is corroborated by Brahmājī himself in his book the *Brahma-saṁhitā.* In the *Brahma-saṁhitā* Lord Brahmā has sung in every verse *govindam ādi-puruṣaṁ tam ahaṁ bhajāmi.* Thus Brahmā was initiated by the Kṛṣṇa *mantra,* by Lord Kṛṣṇa Himself, and thus he became a Vaiṣṇava, or a devotee of the Lord, before he was able to construct the huge universe. It is stated in the *Brahma-saṁhitā* that Lord Brahmā was initiated into the eighteen-letter Kṛṣṇa *mantra,* which is generally accepted by all the devotees of Lord Kṛṣṇa. We follow the same principle because we belong to the Brahmā *sampradāya,* directly in the disciplic chain from Brahmā to Nārada, from Nārada to Vyāsa, from Vyāsa to Madhva Muni, from Madhva Muni to Mādhavendra Purī, from Mādhavendra Purī to Īśvara Purī, from Īśvara Purī to Lord Caitanya and gradually to His Divine Grace Bhaktisiddhānta Sarasvatī, our divine master.

One who is thus initiated in the disciplic succession is able to achieve the same result or power of creation. Chanting of this holy *mantra* is the only shelter of the desireless pure devotee of the Lord. Simply by such *tapasya,* or penance, the devotee of the Lord achieves all perfections like Lord Brahmā.

TEXT 7

निशम्य तद्वक्तृदिदृक्षया दिशो
विलोक्य तत्रान्यदपश्यमानः ।
स्वधिष्ण्यमास्थाय विमृश्य तद्धितं
तपस्युपादिष्ट इवादधे मनः ॥ ७ ॥

niśamya tad-vaktṛ-didṛkṣayā diśo
vilokya tatrānyad apaśyamānaḥ
svadhiṣṇyam āsthāya vimṛśya taddhitaṁ
tapasy upādiṣṭa ivādadhe manaḥ

niśamya—after hearing; *tat*—that; *vaktṛ*—the speaker; *didṛkṣayā*—just to find out who spoke; *diśaḥ*—all sides; *vilokya*—by seeing; *tatra*—there; *anyat*—any other; *apaśyamānaḥ*—not to be found; *svadhiṣṇyam*—on his lotus seat; *āsthāya*—sit down; *vimṛśya*—thin king; *tat*—it; *hitam*—welfare; *tapasi*—in penance; *upādiṣṭaḥ*—as he was instructed; *iva*—in pursuance of; *ādadhe*—gave; *manaḥ*—attention.

TRANSLATION

When he heard the sound, he tried to find out the speaker, searching on all sides. But when he was unable to find anyone besides himself, he thought it wise to sit down on his lotus seat firmly and give his attention to the execution of penance, as he was instructed.

PURPORT

To achieve success in life, one should follow the example of Lord Brahmā, the first living creature in the beginning of creation. After being initiated by the Supreme Lord to execute *tapasya,* he was fixed in his determination to do it and although he could not find anyone besides himself, he could rightly understand that the sound was transmitted by the Lord Himself. Brahmā was the only living being at that time because there was no other creation, and none could be found there except himself. In the beginning of the First Canto, First Chapter, first verse of the *Śrīmad-Bhāgavatam,* it is already mentioned that Brahmā was initiated by the Lord from within. The Lord is within every living entity as the Supersoul, and He initiated Brahmā because Brahmā was willing to receive the initiation. The Lord can similarly initiate everyone who is inclined to have it.

As already stated, Brahmā is the original spiritual master for the universe, and since he was initiated by the Lord Himself, the message of *Śrīmad-Bhāgavatam* is coming down by disciplic succession, and in order to receive the real message of *Śrīmad-Bhāgavatam* one should approach the current link, or spiritual master in the chain of disciplic succession. After being initiated by the proper spiritual master in that chain of succession, one should engage himself in the discharge of *tapasya* in the execution of devotional service. One should not, however, think himself on the level of Brahmā to be initiated directly by the Lord from inside because in the present age no one can be accepted to be as pure as Brahmā. The post of Brahmā to officiate in the creation in the universe is offered to the most pure living being, and unless one is so qualified one cannot expect to be treated like Brahmājī directly. But one can have the same facility through unalloyed devotees of the Lord, and scriptural instructions (as revealed in the *Bhagavad-gītā* and *Śrīmad-Bhāgavatam* especially), and also the bona fide spiritual master available to the sincere soul. The Lord Himself appears as the spiritual master to a person who is sincere in heart to serve the Lord. Therefore the bona fide spiritual master who happens to meet the sincere devotee should be accepted as the most confidential and beloved representative of the Lord. If a person is posted under the guidance of such a bona fide spiritual master, it may be accepted without any doubt that the desiring person has achieved the grace of the Lord.

TEXT 8

दिव्यं सहस्राब्दममोघदर्शनो
जितानिलात्मा विजितोभयेन्द्रियः ।
अतप्यत स्माखिललोकतापनं
तपस्तपीयांस्तपतां समाहितः ॥ ८ ॥

divyaṁ sahasrābdam amogha-darśano
jitānilātmā vijitobhayendriyaḥ
atapyata smākhila-loka-tāpanaṁ
tapas tapīyāṁs tapatāṁ samāhitaḥ

divyam—pertaining to the demigods in the higher planets; *sahasra*—one thousand; *abdam*—years; *amogha*—spotless, without a tinge of impurity; *darśanaḥ*—one who has such a vision of life; *jita*—controlled; *anila*—life; *ātmā*—mind; *vijita*—controlled over; *ubhaya*—both; *indriyaḥ*—one who has such senses; *atapyata*—executed penance; *sma*—in the past; *akhila*—all; *loka*—planet; *tāpanam*—enlightening; *tapaḥ*—penance; *tapīyān*—extremely hard penance; *tapatām*—of all the executors of penances; *samāhitaḥ*—thus situated.

TRANSLATION

Lord Brahmā underwent penances for one thousand years by the calculations of the demigods. He heard this transcendental vibration from the sky, and he accepted it as divine. Thus he controlled his mind and senses, and the penances which he executed were a great lesson for the living entities. Thus he is known as the greatest of all ascetics.

PURPORT

Lord Brahmā heard the occult sound *tapa,* but he did not see the person who vibrated the sound. And still he accepted the instruction as beneficial for him, and therefore he engaged himself in meditation for one thousand celestial years. One celestial year is equal to 6 *x* 30 *x* 12 *x* 1000 of our years. His acceptance of the sound was due to his pure vision of the absolute nature of the Lord. And due to his correct vision, he made no distinction between the Lord and the Lord's instruction. There is no difference between the Lord and sound vibration coming from Him, even though He is not personally present. The best way of understanding is to accept such divine instruction, and Brahmā, the prime spiritual master of everyone, is the living example of this process of receiving transcendental knowledge. The potency of transcendental sound is never minimized because the vibrator is apparently absent. Therefore *Śrīmad-Bhāgavatam* or the *Bhagavad-gītā* or any revealed scripture in the world is never to be accepted as an ordinary mundane sound without transcendental potency.

One has to receive the transcendental sound from the right source and accept it as a reality and prosecute the direction without any hesitation. The secret of success is to receive the sound from the right source of a bona fide spiritual master. Mundane manufactured sound has no potency, and as such, seemingly transcendental sound received from an unauthorized person also has no potency. One should be qualified enough to discern such transcendental potency, and either by discriminating or by fortunate chance if one is able to receive the transcendental sound from the bona fide spiritual master, his path of liberation is guaranteed. The disciple, however, must be ready to execute the order of the bona fide spiritual master as Lord Brahmā executed the instruction of his spiritual master, the Lord Himself. Following the order of the bona fide spiritual master is the only duty of the disciple, and this completely faithful execution of the order of the bona fide spiritual master is the secret of success.

Lord Brahmā controlled his two grades of senses by means of sense perception and sense organs because he had to engage such senses in the execution of the order of the Lord. Therefore controlling the senses means to engage them in the transcendental service of the Lord. The Lord's order descends in disciplic succession through the bona fide spiritual master, and thus execution of the order of the bona fide spiritual master is factual control of the senses. Such execution of penance in full faith and sincerity made Brahmājī so powerful that he became the creator of the universe. And because he was able to attain such power, he is called the best amongst all the *tapasvīs*.

TEXT 9

तस्मै स्वलोकं भगवान् सभाजितः
सन्दर्शयामास परं न यत्परम् ।
व्यपेतसंक्लेशविमोहसाध्वसं
स्वदृष्टवद्भिःपुरुषैरभिष्टुतम् ॥ ९ ॥

tasmai sva-lokaṁ bhagavān sabhājitaḥ
sandarśayāmāsa paraṁ na yat-param
vyapeta-saṅkleśa-vimoha-sādhvasaṁ
sva-dṛṣṭavadbhir puruṣair abhiṣṭutam

tasmai—unto him; *sva-lokam*—His own planet or abode; *bhagavān*—the Personality of Godhead; *sabhājitaḥ*—being pleased by the penance of Brahma; *sandarśayāmāsa*—manifested; *param*—the supreme; *na*—not; *yat*—of which; *param*—further supreme; *vyapeta*—completely given up; *saṅkleśa*—five kinds of material afflictions; *vimoha*—without illusion; *sādhvasam*—fearfulness of material existence; *sva-dṛṣṭavadbhiḥ*—by those who have perfectly realized the self; *puruṣaiḥ*—by persons; *abhiṣṭutam*—worshiped by.

TRANSLATION

The Personality of Godhead, being thus very much satisfied with the penance of Lord Brahmā, was pleased to manifest His personal abode, Vaikuṇṭha, the supreme planet above all others. This transcendental abode of the Lord is adored by all self-realized persons freed from all kinds of miseries and fearfulness of illusory existence.

PURPORT

The troubles of penance accepted by Lord Brahmā were certainly in the line of devotional service *(bhakti)*. Otherwise there was no chance of Vaikuṇṭha or *svalokam*, the Lord's personal abodes, becoming visible to Brahmājī. The personal abodes of the Lord, known as Vaikuṇṭhas, are neither myth nor material, as conceived by the impersonalists. But such realization of the transcendental abodes of the Lord is possible only through devotional service, and thus the devotees enter into such abodes. There is undoubtedly trouble in executing penance, but the trouble accepted in executing *bhakti-yoga* is transcendental happiness from the very beginning, whereas the trouble of penance in other processes of self-realization (namely *jñānayoga, dhyānayoga*, etc.) without any Vaikuṇṭha realization ends in trouble only and nothing more. There is no profit in biting husks without grains. Similarly, there is no profit in executing troublesome penances other than *bhakti-yoga* for self-realization.

Execution of *bhakti-yoga* is exactly like sitting on the lotus sprouted out of the abdomen of the transcendental Personality of Godhead, for Lord Brahmā was seated there. Brahmājī was able to please the Lord, and the Lord was also pleased to show Brahmājī His personal abode. Śrīla Jīva Gosvāmī narrates, in the comments of his *Krama-sandarbha* annotation of *Śrīmad-Bhāgavatam*, quotations from the *Gārga Upaniṣad*, Vedic evidence. It is said that Yājñavalkya described this transcendental abode of the Lord to Gārgī, and it is said there that the abode of the Lord is situated above the highest planet of the universe, namely Brahmaloka. This abode of the Lord, although described in the revealed scriptures like the *Bhagavad-gītā* and the *Śrīmad-Bhāgavatam*, remains only a myth for the less intelligent class of men with a poor fund of knowledge. Herein the word *svadṛṣṭavadbhi* is very significant. One who has actually realized his self realizes the transcendental form of one's self. Impersonal realization of self and the Supreme is not complete, because it is just an opposite conception of material personalities. The Personality of Godhead and the personalities of devotees of the Lord are all transcendental; they do not have material bodies. The material body is overcast with five kinds of miserable conditions, namely ignorance, material conception, attachment, hatred and absorption. As long as one is overwhelmed with these five kinds of material miseries, there is no question of entering into the Vaikuṇṭhalokas. Impersonal conception of one's self is just the negation of material personality, far from the positive existence of personal form. These personal forms of the transcendental abode will be explained in the following verses. Brahmājī also described this highest planet of the Vaikuṇṭhaloka as Goloka Vṛndāvana, where the Lord resides as a cowherd boy keeping transcendental *surabhi* cows and surrounded by hundreds and thousands of goddesses of fortune.

cintāmaṇi-prakara-sadmasu kalpavṛkṣa-
lakṣāvṛteṣu surabhīr abhipālayantam
lakṣmī-sahasra-śata-sambhrama-sevyamānaṁ
govindam ādi-puruṣaṁ tam ahaṁ bhajāmi (Bs. 5.29)

The statement of the *Bhagavad-gītā, yad gatvā na nivartante tad dhāma paramaṁ mama,* is also confirmed herewith. *Param* means transcendental Brahmā. Therefore, the abode of the Lord is also Brahma, nondifferent from the Supreme Personality of Godhead. The Lord is known as Vaikuṇṭha, and His abode is also known as Vaikuṇṭha. And such Vaikuṇṭha realization and worship can be made possible by transcendental form and sense.

TEXT 10

प्रवर्तते यत्र रजस्तमस्तयोः
सत्त्वं च मिश्रं न च कालविक्रमः ।
न यत्र माया किमुतापरे हरे-
रनुव्रता यत्र सुरासुरार्चिताः ॥१०॥

pravartate yatra rajas tamas tayoḥ
sattvaṁ ca miśraṁ na ca kāla-vikramaḥ
na yatra māyā kim utāpare harer
anuvratā yatra surāsurārcitāḥ

pravartate—prevail; *yatra*—wherein; *rajaḥ tamaḥ*—the modes of ignorance and passion; *tayoḥ*—both of them; *sattvam*—the mode of goodness; *ca*—and; *miśram*—mixture; *na*—never; *ca*—and; *kāla*—time; *vikramaḥ*—influence; *na*—neither; *yatra*—therein; *māyā*—illusory external energy; *kim*—what; *uta*—there is; *apare*—others; *hareḥ*—of the Personality of Godhead; *anuvratāḥ*—devotees; *yatra*—wherein; *sura*—the demigods; *asura*—the demons; *arcitāḥ*—worshiped.

TRANSLATION

In that personal abode of the Lord, the material modes of ignorance and passion do not prevail, nor is there any of their influence in the matter of goodness. There is no predominance of the influence of time, so what to speak of the illusory external energy that cannot enter in that region. Without discrimination, both the demigods and the demons worship the Lord as devotees.

PURPORT

The kingdom of God, or the atmosphere of Vaikuṇṭha nature, which is called the *tripād-vibhūti,* is three times bigger than the material universes and is described here, as also in the *Bhagavad-gītā,* in a nutshell. This universe, containing billions of stars and planets, is one of the billions of such universes clustered together within the compass of *mahat-tattva.* And all these millions and billions of universes combined together constitute only one fourth of the magnitude of the whole creation of the Lord. There is the spiritual sky also; beyond this sky the spiritual planets are there under the names of Vaikuṇṭha, and all of them constitute three fourths of the entire creation of the Lord. God's creations are always innumerable. Even the leaves of a tree cannot be counted by a man, nor the hairs on his head. However, foolish men are puffed up with the idea of becoming God Himself, though unable to create a hair of their own bodies. Man may discover so many wonderful vehicles of journey, but even if he reaches the moon by his much advertised spacecraft, he cannot remain there. The sane man, therefore, without being puffed up, as if he were the God of the universe, abides by the instructions of the Vedic literature, the easiest way to acquire knowledge in transcendence. So let us know through the authority of *Śrīmad-Bhāgavatam* of the nature and constitution of the transcendental world beyond the material sky. In that sky the material qualities, especially the modes of ignorance and passion, are completely absent. The mode of ignorance influences a living entity to the habit of lust and hankering, and this means that in the Vaikuṇṭhalokas the living entities are free from these two things. As confirmed in the *Bhagavad-gītā,* in the *brahma-bhūta* stage of life one becomes free from hankering and lamentation. Therefore the conclusion is that the inhabitants of the Vaikuṇṭha planets are all *brahma-bhūta* living entities, as distinguished from the mundane creatures who are all compact in hankering and lamentation. When one is not in the modes of ignorance and passion, one is supposed to be situated in the mode of goodness in the material world. Goodness in the material world also at times becomes contaminated with touches of the modes of passion and ignorance. In the Vaikuṇṭhaloka, it is unalloyed goodness only.

The whole situation there is one of freedom from the illusory manifestation of the external energy. Although illusory energy is also part and parcel of the Supreme Lord, still illusory energy is differentiated from the Lord. The illusory energy is not, however, false, as claimed by the monist philosophers. The rope accepted as a snake may be an illusion to a particular person, but the rope is a fact, and the snake is also a fact. The illusion of water on the hot desert may be illusion for the ignorant animal searching out water in the desert, but the desert and water are actual facts. Therefore the material creation of the Lord may be an illusion to the nondevotee class of men, but to a devotee even the material creation of the Lord is a fact, as the manifestation of His external energy. But this energy of the Lord is not all. The Lord has His internal energy also, which has another creation known to be the Vaikuṇṭhalokas, where there is no ignorance, no passion, no illusion and no past and present. With a poor fund of knowledge one may be unable to understand the existence of such things as the Vaikuṇṭha atmosphere, but that does not nullify its existence. That spacecraft cannot reach these planets does not mean that there are no such planets, for they are described in the revealed scriptures.

As quoted by Śrīla Jīva Gosvāmī, we can know from the *Nārada-pañcarātra* that the transcendental world or Vaikuṇṭha atmosphere is enriched with transcendental qualities. These transcendental qualities, as revealed through the devotional service of the Lord, are distinct from the mundane qualities of ignorance, passion and goodness. Such qualities are nonattainable by the nondevotee class of men. In the *Pādma Purāṇa, Uttara-khaṇḍa,* it is stated that beyond the one-fourth part of God's creation, there is the three-fourths part manifestation. The marginal line between the material manifestation and the spiritual manifestation is the Virajā River, and beyond the Virajā, which is a transcendental current flowing from the perspiration of the body of the Lord, there is the three-fourths part manifestation of God's creation. This part is eternal, everlasting, without any deterioration, and unlimited, and contains the highest perfectional stage of living conditions. In the *Sāṅkhya-kaumudī* it is stated that unalloyed goodness or transcendence is just opposite to the material modes. All living entities are eternally associated without any break, and the Lord is the chief and prime entity there. In the *Āgama Purāṇas* also, the transcendental abode is described as follows: The associated members there are free to go everywhere within the creation of the Lord, and there is no limit to such creation, particularly in the region of the three-fourths magnitude. Since the nature of that region is unlimited, there is no history of such association, nor is there end of it.

The conclusion may be drawn that because of the complete absence of the mundane qualities of ignorance and passion, there is no question of creation nor of annihilation. In the material world everything is created and everything is annihilated, and the duration of life between the creation and annihilation is temporary. In the transcendental realm there is no creation and no destruction, and thus the duration of life is eternal unlimitedly. In other words, everything in the transcendental world is everlasting, full of knowledge and bliss without any deterioration. Since there is no deterioration, there is no past, present and future in the estimation of time. It is clearly stated in this verse that the influence of time is conspicuous by its absence. The whole material existence is manifested by actions and reactions of elements which make the influence of time prominent in the matter of past, present and future. There are no such actions and reactions of cause and effects there, so the cycle of birth, growth, existence, transformations, deterioration and annihilation, or the six material changes, are not existent there. It is the unalloyed manifestation of the energy of the Lord without any illusion as experienced here in the material world. The whole Vaikuṇṭha existence proclaims that everyone there is a follower of the Lord. The Lord is the chief leader there without any competition of leadership, and the people in general are all followers of the Lord. It is confirmed in the *Vedas*, therefore, that the Lord is the chief leader, and all other living entities are subordinate to Him, as only the Lord satisfies all the needs of all other living entities.

TEXT 11

श्यामावदाताः शतपत्रलोचनाः
पिशङ्गवस्त्राः सुरुचः सुपेशसः ।
सर्वे चतुर्बाहव उन्मिषन्मणि-
प्रवेकनिष्काभरणाः सुवर्चसः ॥११॥

śyāmāvadātāḥ śata-patra-locanāḥ
piśaṅga-vastrāḥ su-rucaḥ su-peśasaḥ
sarve catur-bāhava unmiṣan-maṇi-
praveka-niṣkābharaṇāḥ su-varcasaḥ

śyāma—sky-bluish; *avadātāḥ*—glowing; *śata-patra*—lotus flower; *locanāḥ*—eyes; *piśaṅga*—yellowish; *vastrāḥ*—clothing; *su-rucaḥ*—greatly attractive; *su-peśasaḥ*—growing youthful; *sarve*—all of them; *catuḥ*—four; *bāhavaḥ*—hands; *unmiṣan*—rising luster; *maṇi*—pearls; *praveka*—superior quality; *niṣka-ābharaṇāḥ*—ornamental medallion; *su-varcasaḥ*—effulgent.

TRANSLATION

The inhabitants of the Vaikuṇṭha planets are described as having a glowing sky-bluish complexion. Their eyes resemble the lotus flower, their dress is of yellowish color and their bodily features very attractive. They are just the age of growing youths, they all have four hands, they are all nicely decorated with pearl necklaces with ornamental medallions, and they all appear to be effulgent.

PURPORT

The inhabitants in Vaikuṇṭhaloka are all personalities with spiritual bodily features not to be found in the material world. We can find the descriptions in the revealed scriptures like *Śrīmad-Bhāgavatam.* Impersonal descriptions of transcendence in the scriptures indicate that the bodily features in Vaikuṇṭhaloka are never to be seen in any part of the universe, As there are different bodily features in different places of a particular planet, or as there are different bodily features between bodies in different planets, similarly the bodily features of the inhabitants in the Vaikuṇṭhalokas are completely different from those in the material universe. For example, the four hands are distinct from two hands in this world.

TEXT 12

प्रवालवैदूर्यमृणालवर्चसः
परिस्फुरत्कुण्डलमौलिमालिनः ॥१२॥

pravāla-vaidūrya-mṛṇāla-varcasaḥ
parisphurat-kuṇḍala-mauli-mālinaḥ

pravāla—coral; *vaidūrya*—a special diamond; *mṛṇāla*—celestial lotus; *varcasaḥ*—rays; *parisphurat*—blooming; *kuṇḍala*—earring; *mauli*—heads; *mālinaḥ*—with garlands.

TRANSLATION

Some of them are effulgent like the coral and diamond in complexion and have garlands on their heads, blooming like the lotus flowers, and some wear earrings.

PURPORT

There are some inhabitants who have attained the liberation of *sārūpya*, or possessing bodily features like that of the Personality of Godhead. The *vaidūrya* diamond is especially meant for the Personality of Godhead, but one who achieves the liberation of bodily equality with the Lord is especially favored with such diamonds on the body.

TEXT 13

भ्राजिष्णुभिर्यः परितो विराजते
लसद्विमानावलिभिर्महात्मनाम् ।
विद्योतमानः प्रमदोत्तमाद्युभिः
सविद्युदभ्रावलिभिर्यथा नभः ॥१३॥

bhrājiṣṇubhir yaḥ parito virājate
lasad-vimānāvalibhir mahātmanām
vidyotamānaḥ pramadottamādyubhiḥ
sa-vidyud abhrāvalibhir yathā nabhaḥ

bhrājiṣṇubhiḥ—by the glowing; *yaḥ*—the Vaikuṇṭha-lokas; *paritaḥ*—surrounded by; *virājate*—thus situated; *lasat*—brilliant; *vimāna*—airplanes; *avalibhiḥ*—assemblage; *mahā-ātmanām*—of the great devotees of the Lord; *vidyotamānaḥ*—beautiful like the lightning; *pramada*—ladies; *uttama*—celestial; *adyubhiḥ*—by complexion; *sa-vidyut*—with electric lightning; *abhrāvalibhiḥ*—with clouds in the sky; *yathā*—as it were; *nabhaḥ*—the sky.

TRANSLATION

The Vaikuṇṭha planets are also surrounded by various airplanes, all glowing and brilliantly situated, belonging to the great mahātmās or devotees of the Lord. The ladies also are as beautiful as lightning because of

their celestial complexions, and all these combined together appear just like the sky decorated with both clouds and lightning.

PURPORT

It appears that in the Vaikuṇṭha planets there are airplanes also brilliantly glowing, and they are occupied by the great devotees of the Lord with ladies of celestial beauty as brilliant as lightning. As there are airplanes, so there must be different types of carriages also like the airplanes, but they may not be driven machines, as we have experience in this world. Because everything is of the same nature of eternity, bliss and knowledge, the airplanes and carriages are of the same quality as Brahman. As there is nothing except Brahman, so it should not be misconceived that there is only void and no variegatedness. To think like that is due to a poor fund of knowledge, otherwise no one would have such a misconception of voidness in the Brahman. As there are airplanes, ladies, and gentlemen, so there must be cities and houses and everything else just suitable to the particular planets. One should not carry the ideas of imperfection from this world to the transcendental world without taking into consideration the nature of the atmosphere, as completely free from the influence of time, etc., as described previously.

TEXT 14

श्रीर्यत्र रूपिण्युरुगायपादयोः
करोति मानं बहुधा विभूतिभिः ।
प्रेङ्खं श्रिता या कुसुमाकरानुगै-
र्विगीयमाना प्रियकर्म गायती ॥१४॥

śrīr yatra rūpiṇy urugāya-pādayoḥ
karoti mānaṁ bahudhā vibhūtibhiḥ
preṅkhaṁ śritā yā kusumākarānugair
vigīyamānā priya-karma gāyatī

śrīḥ—the goddess of fortune; *yatra*—in the Vaikuṇṭha planets; *rūpiṇī*—in her transcendental form; *urugāya*—the Lord, who is sung of by the great devotees; *pādayoḥ*—under the lotus feet of the Lord; *karoti*—does; *mānam*

—respectful services; *bahudhā*—in diverse paraphernalia; *vibhūtibhiḥ*—accompanied by her personal associates; *preṅkham*—movement of enjoyment; *śritā*—taken shelter of; *yā*—who; *kusumākara*—spring; *anugaiḥ*—by the black bees; *vigīyamānā*—being followed by the songs; *priya-karma*—activities of the dearmost; *gāyatī*-singing.

TRANSLATION

The goddess of fortune in her transcendental form is engaged in the loving service of the Lord's lotus feet, and being moved by the black bees, followers of spring, she is not only engaged in variegated pleasure—service to the Lord, along with her constant companions—but also she is engaged in singing the glories of the Lord's activities.

TEXT 15

ददर्श तत्राखिलसात्वतां पतिं
श्रियः पतिं यज्ञपतिं जगत्पतिम् ।
सुनन्दनन्दप्रबलार्हणादिभिः
स्वपार्षदाग्रैः परिसेवितं विभुम् ॥१५॥

dadarśa tatrākhila-sātvatāṁ patiṁ
śriyaḥ patiṁ yajña-patiṁ jagat-patim
sunanda-nanda-prabalārhaṇādibhiḥ
sva-pārṣadāgraiḥ parisevitaṁ vibhum

dadarśa—Brahmā saw; *tatra*—there in the Vaikuṇṭhaloka; *akhila*—entire; *sātvatām*—of the great devotees; *patim*—the Lord; *śriyaḥ*—of the goddess of fortune; *patim*—the Lord; *yajña*—sacrifice; *patim*—the Lord; *jagat*—the universe; *patim*—the Lord; *sunanda*—Sunanda; *nanda*—Nanda; *prabala*—Prabala; *arhaṇa*—Arhaṇa; *ādibhiḥ*—by them; *sva-pārṣada*—own associates; *agraiḥ*—by the foremost; *parisevitam*—being served in transcendental love; *vibhum*—the Great Almighty.

TRANSLATION

Lord Brahmā saw in the Vaikuṇṭha planet the Personality of Godhead, who is the Lord of the entire devotee community, the Lord of the goddess of fortune, the Lord of all sacrifices, and the Lord of the universe, and who

is served by the foremost servitors like Nanda, Sunanda, Prabala, and Arhaṇa, His immediate associates.

PURPORT

When we speak of the king it is naturally understood that the king is accompanied by his confidential associates, like his secretary, private secretary, aide-de-camp, ministers, advisers, etc. So also when we see the Lord we see Him with His different energies, associates and confidential servitors, etc. So the Supreme Lord, who is the leader of all living entities, the Lord of all devotee sects, the Lord of all opulences, the Lord of sacrifices and the enjoyer of everything in His entire creation, is not only the Supreme Person, but also He is always surrounded by His immediate associates, all engaged in their loving transcendental service to Him.

TEXT 16

भृत्यप्रसादाभिमुखं दृगासवं
प्रसन्नहासारुणलोचनाननम् ।
किरीटिनं कुण्डलिनं चतुर्भुजं
पीतांशुकं वक्षसि लक्षितं श्रिया ॥१६॥

bhṛtya-prasādābhimukhaṁ dṛg-āsavaṁ
prasanna-hāsāruṇa-locanānanam
kirīṭinaṁ kuṇḍalinaṁ catur-bhujaṁ
pītāṁ-śukaṁ vakṣasi lakṣitaṁ śriyā

bhṛtya—the servitor; *prasāda*—affection; *abhimukham*—favorably facing; *dṛk*—the very sight; *āsavam*—an intoxication; *prasanna*—very much pleased; *hāsa*—smile; *aruṇa*—reddish; *locana*—eyes; *ānanam*—face; *kirīṭinam*—with helmet; *kuṇḍalinam*—with earrings; *catuḥ-bhujam*—with four hands; *pītām*—yellow; *śukam*—dress; *vakṣasi*—on the chest; *lakṣitam*—marked with; *śriyā*—the goddess of fortune.

TRANSLATION

The Personality of Godhead, seen leaning favorably towards His loving servitors, His very sight intoxicating and attractive, appeared to be

very much satisfied. He had a smiling face decorated with an enchanting reddish hue. He was dressed in yellow robes and wore earrings and a helmet on his head. He had four hands, and His chest was marked with the lines of the goddess of fortune.

PURPORT

In the *Pādma Purāṇa, Uttara-khaṇḍa,* there is a full description of the *yoga-pīṭha* or the particular place where the Lord is in audience to His eternal devotees. In that *yoga-pīṭha,* the personifications of religiousness, knowledge, opulence, and renunciation are all seated at the lotus feet of the Lord. The four Vedas, namely *Ṛk, Sāma, Yajus, and Atharva,* are present there personally to advise the Lord. The sixteen energies headed by Caṇḍa are all present there. Caṇḍa and Kūmuda are the two first doorkeepers, and at the middle door there are the doorkeepers named Bhadra and Subhadra, and at the last door there are Jaya and Vijaya. There are other doorkeepers also, named Kūmuda, Kumudākṣa, Puṇḍarīka, Vāmana, Śaṅkukarṇa, Sarvanetra, Sumukha, etc. The palace is well decorated and protected by the above-mentioned doorkeepers.

TEXT 17

अध्यर्हणीयासनमास्थितं परं
वृतं चतुःषोडशपञ्चशक्तिभिः ।
युक्तं भगैः स्वैरितरत्र चाध्रुवैः
स्व एव धामन् रममाणमीश्वरम् ॥१७॥

adhyarhaṇīyāsanam āsthitaṁ paraṁ
vṛtaṁ catuḥ-ṣoḍaśa-pañca-śaktibhiḥ
yuktaṁ bhagaiḥ svair itaratra cādhruvaiḥ
sva eva dhāman ramamāṇam īśvaram

adhyarhaṇīya—greatly worshipable; *āsanam*—throne; *āsthitam*—seated on it; *param*—the Supreme; *vṛtam*—surrounded by; *catuḥ*—four, namely *prakṛti, puruṣa, mahat* and ego; *ṣoḍaśa*—the sixteen; *pañca*—the five; *śaktibhiḥ*—by the energies; *yuktam*—empowered with; *bhagaiḥ*—His opulences; *svaiḥ*—personal; *itaratra*—other minor prowesses; *ca*—also; *adhruvaiḥ*—temporary; *sva*—own; *eva*—certainly; *dhāman*—abode; *ramamāṇam*—enjoying; *īśvaram*—the Supreme Lord.

TRANSLATION

The Lord was seated on His throne and was surrounded by different energies like the four, the sixteen, the five, and the six natural opulences, along with other insignificant energies of the temporary character. But He was the factual Supreme Lord, enjoying His own abode.

PURPORT

The Lord is naturally endowed with His six opulences, namely He is the richest in wealth, He is the most powerful, He is the most famous, He is the most beautiful, He is the greatest in knowledge, and He is the greatest renouncer as well. And for His material creative energies, He is served by four, namely the principles of *prakṛti, puruṣa, mahat-tattva* and ego. He is also served by the sixteen, namely the five elements, earth, water, air, fire and sky, the five perceptive sense organs, namely the eye, ear, nose, tongue and skin, and the five working sense organs, namely the hand, the leg, the stomach, the evacuation outlet and the genitals. Together with the mind, they are sixteen in all. And the five includes the sense objects, namely form, taste, smell, sound and touch. All these twenty-five items serve the Lord in the material creation, and all of them are personally present to serve the Lord. The insignificant opulences numbering eight (the *aṣṭa-siddhis,* attained by *yogīs* for temporary overlordship) are also under His control, but He is naturally full with all such powers without any effort, and therefore He is the Supreme Lord.

The living being, by severe penance and performances of bodily exercises, can temporarily attain some wonderful power, but that does not make him the Supreme Lord. The Supreme Lord by His own potency is unlimitedly more powerful than any *yogī,* He is unlimitedly more learned than any *jñānī,* He is unlimitedly richer than any wealthy person, He is unlimitedly more beautiful than any beautiful living being, and He is unlimitedly more charitable than any philanthropist. He is above all, and no one is equal to or greater than Him. Nor can anyone reach His level of perfection in all the above powers by any amount of performance of penance or yogic demonstration. The *yogīs* are dependent on His mercy. Out of His immensely charitable disposition He can award some temporary powers to the *yogīs* because of the *yogīs'* hankering after them, but to His unalloyed devotees, who do not want anything from the Lord save and except His transcendental service, the Lord is so pleased that He gives Himself in exchange for unalloyed service.

TEXT 18

तद्दर्शनाह्लादपरिप्लुतान्तरो
हृष्यत्तनुः प्रेमभराश्रुलोचनः ।
ननाम पादाम्बुजमस्य विश्वसृग्
यत् पारमहंस्येन पथाधिगम्यते ॥१८॥

tad-darśanāhlāda-pariplutāntaro
hṛṣyat-tanuḥ prema-bharāśru-locanaḥ
nanāma pādāmbujam asya viśva-sṛg
yat pāramahaṁsyena pathādhigamyate

tat—by that audience of the Lord; *darśana*—audience; *āhlāda*—joy; *paripluta*—overwhelmed; *antaraḥ*—within the heart; *hṛṣyat*—full in ecstasy; *tanuḥ*—body; *prema-bhara*—in full transcendental love; *aśru*—tears; *locanaḥ*—in the eyes; *nanāma*—bowed down; *pādāmbujam*—under the lotus feet; *asya*—of the Lord; *viśva-sṛg*—the creator of the universe; *yat*—which; *pāramahaṁsyena*—by the great liberated soul; *pathā*—the path; *adhigamyate*—is followed.

TRANSLATION

Lord Brahmā, thus seeing the Personality of Godhead in His fullness, became overwhelmed with joy within his heart, and thus in full transcendental love and ecstasy, his eyes became full with tears of love. He thus bowed down before the Lord. That is the way of highest perfection for the living being [paramahaṁsa].

PURPORT

In the beginning of the *Śrīmad-Bhāgavatam* it is stated that this great literature is meant for the *paramahaṁsas. Param nirmatsarāṇām satām,* i.e. the *Śrīmad-Bhāgavatam* is meant for such persons who are completely free from malice. In the conditioned life the malicious life begins from the top, namely bearing malice against the Supreme Personality of Godhead. The Personality of Godhead is an established fact in all the revealed scriptures, and in the *Bhagavad-gītā* the personal feature of the Supreme Lord is especially mentioned, so much so that in the last portion of the great literature it has been emphatically stressed that one should surrender unto the Personality of Godhead to be saved from the miseries of life. Unfortunately, persons with impious backgrounds do not believe in the Personality of Godhead, and everyone wants to become God himself without any qualification. This malicious nature in the conditioned soul continues even up to the stage when a person wants to be one with the Lord, and thus even the greatest of the empiric philosophers speculating on becoming one with the Supreme Lord cannot become a *paramahaṁsa* because the malicious mind is there. Therefore the *paramahaṁsa* stage of life can only be attained by those who are fixed in the practice of *bhakti-yoga.* This *bhakti-yoga* begins if a person has the firm conviction that simply discharging devotional service to the Lord in full transcendental love can elevate him to the highest perfectional stage of life. Brahmājī believed in this art of *bhakti-yoga;* he believed in the words of the Lord to execute *tapa,* and he discharged the function with great penance and thus achieved the great success of seeing the Vaikuṇṭhalokas and the Lord also by personal experience. No one can reach the abode of the Supreme Lord by any mechanical means of the mind or machine, but one can reach the abode of the Vaikuṇṭhalokas simply by following the process of *bhakti-yoga* because the Lord can be realized only through the *bhakti-yoga* process. Lord Brahmājī was actually sitting on his lotus seat, and from there, by executing the process of *bhakti-yoga* in great seriousness, he could see the Vaikuṇṭhalokas with all variegatedness as well as the Lord in person and His associates.

Following in the footsteps of Lord Brahmā, any person, even up to this day, can attain the same perfection by following the path of the *paramahaṁsa* as recommended herein. Lord Caitanya also approved of this method of self-realization for men in this age. One should first, with all conviction, believe in the Personality of Godhead Śrī Kṛṣṇa, and without making efforts to realize Him by speculative philosophy, one should prefer to hear about Him from the *Śrīmad-Bhagavad-gītā* and later on from the text of the *Śrīmad-Bhāgavatam.* He should hear such discourses from a person *Bhāgavatam* and not from the professional man, nor from the *karmī, jñānī* or *yogī.* That is the secret of learning the science. One does not need to be in the renounced order of life; he can remain in his present condition of life, but he must search out the association of a bona fide devotee of the Lord and hear from him the transcendental message of the Lord with faith and conviction. That is the path of the *paramahaṁsa* recommended herein. Amongst various holy names of the Lord, He is called also *ajita,* or one who can never be conquered by anyone else. Yet He can be conquered by the *paramahaṁsa* path, as is practically realized and shown by the great spiritual master Lord Brahmā. Lord Brahmā has personally recommended this *paramahaṁsa-pantha* in his own words as follows:

jñāne prayāsam udapāsya namanta eva
jīvanti sanmukharitāṁ bhavadīyavārtām
sthāne sthitāḥ śruti-gatāṁ tanuvāṅmanobhir
ye prāyaśo'jita-jito'pyasi tais trilokyām

Lord Brahmā said, "O my Lord Kṛṣṇa, a devotee who abandons the path of empiric philosophical speculation aimed at becoming merged in the existence of the Supreme and engages himself in *hearing* Your glories and activities from a bona fide *sādhu,* or saint, and who lives an honest life in the occupational engagement of his social life, can conquer Your sympathy and mercy even though You are *ajita,* or unconquerable by anyone." (*Bhāg.* 10.14.3) That is the path of the *paramahaṁsas,* which was personally followed by Lord Brahmā and later on recommended by him for attaining perfect success in life.

TEXT 19

तं प्रीयमाणं समुपस्थितं कविं
प्रजाविसर्गे निजशासनार्हणम् ।
बभाष ईषत्स्मितशोचिषा गिरा
प्रियः प्रियं प्रीतमनाः करे स्पृशन् ॥१९॥

taṁ prīyamāṇaṁ samupasthitaṁ kaviṁ
prajā-visarge nija-śāsanārhaṇam
babhāṣa īṣat-smita-śociṣā girā
priyaḥ priyaṁ prīta-manāḥ kare spṛśan

tam—unto Lord Brahmā; *prīyamāṇam*—worthy of being dear; *samupasthitam*—present before; *kavim*—the great scholar; *prajā*—living entities;

visarge—in the matter of creation; *nija*—His own; *śāsana*—control; *arhaṇam*—just suitable; *babhāṣe*—addressed; *īṣat*—mild; *smita*—smiling; *śociṣā*—enlightening; *girā*—words; *priyaḥ*—the beloved; *priyam*—the counterpart of love; *prīta-manāḥ*—being very much pleased; *kare*—by the hand; *spṛśan*—shaking.

TRANSLATION

And seeing Brahmā present before Him, the Lord accepted him as worthy to create living beings, to be controlled as He desired, and thus being much satisfied with him, the Lord shook hands with Brahmā and, slightly smiling, addressed him thus.

PURPORT

The creation of the material world is not blind nor accidental. The living entities who are ever conditioned, or *nitya-bandha,* are thus given a chance for liberation under the guidance of His own representative like Brahmā. The Lord instructs Brahmā in Vedic knowledge in order to diffuse this knowledge to the conditioned souls. The conditioned souls are forgetful souls in their relationship with the Lord, and thus a period of creation and the process of dissemination of Vedic knowledge are necessary activities of the Lord. Lord Brahmā has great responsibility to deliver the conditioned souls, and therefore he is very dear to the Lord.

Brahmā also does his duty very perfectly, not only by generating the living entities but also by spreading his party for reclaiming the fallen souls. The party is called the *Brahma-sampradāya,* and any member of this party to date is naturally engaged in reclaiming the fallen souls back to Godhead, back to home. The Lord is very much anxious to get back His parts and parcels, as stated in the *Bhagavad-gītā.* No one is more dear than the one who takes the task of reclaiming the fallen souls back to Godhead.

There are many renegades from the Brahma-sampradāya whose only business is to make men more forgetful of the Lord and thus entangle them more and more in material existence. Such persons are never dear to the Lord, and the Lord sends them deeper into the darkest region of matter so that such envious demons may not be able to know the Supreme Lord.

Anyone, however, preaching the mission of the Lord in the line of *Brahma-sampradāya* is always dear to the Lord, and the Lord, being satisfied with such a preacher of the authorized *bhakti* cult, shakes hands with him in great satisfaction.

TEXT 20

श्रीभगवानुवाच
त्वयाहं तोषितः सम्यग् वेदगर्भ सिसृक्षया ।
चिरं भृतेन तपसा दुस्तोषः कूटयोगिनाम् ॥२०॥

śrī bhagavān uvāca
tvayāhaṁ toṣitaḥ samyag
veda-garbha sisṛkṣayā
ciraṁ bhṛtena tapasā
dustoṣaḥ kūṭa-yoginām—

śrī bhagavān uvāca—the all-beautiful Personality of Godhead said; *tvayā*—by you; *aham*—I am; *toṣitaḥ*—pleased; *samyak*—complete; *veda-garbha*—impregnated with the *Vedas; sisṛkṣayā*—for creating; *ciram*—for a long time; *bhṛtena*—accumulated; *tapasā*—by penance; *dustoṣaḥ*—very hard to please; *kūṭa-yoginām*—for the pseudo mystics.

TRANSLATION

The beautiful Personality of Godhead addressed Lord Brahmā: O Brahmā, impregnated with the Vedas, I am very much pleased with your long accumulated penance with the desire for creation. Hardly am I pleased with the pseudo mystics.

PURPORT

There are two kinds of penance: one for sense gratification and the other for self-realization. There are many pseudo mystics who undergo severe penances for their own satisfaction, and there are others who undergo severe penances for the satisfaction of the senses of the Lord. For example, the penances undertaken to discover nuclear weapons will never satisfy the Lord because such a penance is never satisfactory. By nature's own way, everyone has to meet death, and if such a process of death is accelerated by anyone's penances, there is no satisfaction of the Lord. The Lord wants every one of His parts and parcels to attain eternal life and bliss by coming home to Godhead, and the whole material creation is meant for that objective. Brahmā underwent severe penances for that purpose, namely to regulate the process of creation so that the Lord might be satisfied, and therefore the Lord was very much pleased with him, and for this Brahmā was impregnated with Vedic knowledge. The ultimate purpose of Vedic knowledge is to know the Lord and not to misuse the knowledge for any other purposes. Those who do not utilize Vedic knowledge for that purpose are known as *kūṭa-yogīs,* or pseudo transcendentalists who spoil their lives with ulterior motives.

TEXT 21

वरं वरय भद्रं ते वरेशं माभिवाञ्छितम् ।
ब्रह्मञ्छ्रेयःपरिश्रामः पुंसां मद्दर्शनावधिः ॥२१॥

varaṁ varaya bhadraṁ te
vareśaṁ mābhivāñchitam
brahmañ chreyaḥ-pariśrāmaḥ
puṁsāṁ mad-darśanāvadhiḥ

varam—benediction; *varaya*—just ask from; *bhadram*—auspicious; *te*—unto you; *vareśam*—the giver of all benediction; *mā (mām)*—from Me; *abhivāñchitam*—wishing; *brahman*—O Brahmā; *śreyaḥ*—the ultimate success; *pari-śrāmaḥ*—for all penances; *puṁsām*—for everyone; *mat*—My; *darśana*—realization; *avadhiḥ*—up to the limit of.

TRANSLATION

I wish you good luck. O Brahmā, you can ask from Me, the giver of all benediction, all that you may desire. You may know that the ultimate benediction, as the result of all penances, is to see Me by realization.

PURPORT

The ultimate realization of the Supreme Truth is to know and see eye to eye the Personality of Godhead. Realization of the impersonal Brahman and localized Paramātmā features of the Personality of Godhead is not ultimate realization. When one realizes the Supreme Lord, one does not struggle hard to perform such penances. The next stage of life is to discharge devotional service to the Lord just to satisfy Him. In other words, one who has realized and seen the Supreme Lord has attained all perfection because everything is included there in that highest perfectional stage. The impersonalists and the pseudo mystics, however, cannot reach this state.

TEXT 22

मनीषितानुभावोऽयं मम लोकावलोकनम् ।
यदुपश्रुत्य रहसि चकर्थ परमं तपः ॥२२॥

manīṣitānubhāvo 'yaṁ
mama lokāvalokanam
yad upaśrutya rahasi
cakartha paramaṁ tapaḥ

manīṣita—ingenuity; *anubhāvaḥ*—perception; *ayam*—this; *mama*—My; *loka*—abode; *avalokanam*—seeing by actual experience; *yat*—because; *upaśrutya*—hearing; *rahasi*—in great penance; *cakartha*—having performed; *paramam*—highest; *tapaḥ*—penance.

TRANSLATION

The highest perfectional ingenuity is the personal perception of My abodes, and this has been possible because of your submissive attitude in the performance of severe penance on My order.

PURPORT

The highest perfectional stage of life is to know the Lord by actual perception, by the grace of the Lord. This can be attained by everyone who is willing to discharge the act of devotional service to the Lord as enjoined in the revealed scriptures that are standard and accepted by the bona fide *ācāryas,* spiritual masters. For example, the *Bhagavad-gītā* is the approved Vedic literature accepted by all the great *ācāryas,* such as Śaṅkara, Rāmānuja, Madhva, Caitanya, Viśvanātha, Baladeva, Siddhānta Sarasvatī and many others. In that *Bhagavad-gītā* the Personality of Godhead, Śrī Kṛṣṇa, asks that one should always be mindful of Him, one should always be His devotee, one should always worship Him only, and one should always bow down before the Lord. And by doing so one is sure to go back home, back to Godhead, without any doubt. In other places also the same order is there, that one should give up all other engagements and fully surrender unto the Lord without any hesitation. And the Lord will give such a devotee all protection. And these are the secrets of attaining the highest perfectional stage. Lord Brahmā exactly followed these principles without any superiority complex, and thus he attained the highest perfectional stage of experiencing the abode of the Lord and the Lord Himself with all His paraphernalia. Impersonal realization of the effulgence of the body of the Lord is not the highest perfectional stage, nor is the stage of Paramātmā realization. The word *manīṣita* is significant. Everyone is falsely or factually proud of his so-called learning. But the Lord says that the highest perfectional stage of learning is to know Him and His abode, devoid of all illusion.

TEXT 23

प्रत्यादिष्टं मया तत्र त्वयि कर्मविमोहिते ।
तपो मे हृदयं साक्षादात्माहं तपसोऽनघ ॥२३॥

pratyādiṣṭaṁ mayā tatra
tvayi karma-vimohite
tapo me hṛdayaṁ sākṣād-
ātmāhaṁ tapaso'nagha

pratyādiṣṭam—ordered by; *mayā*—by Me; *tatra*—because of; *tvayi*—unto you; *karma*—duty; *vimohite*—being perplexed; *tapaḥ*—penance; *me*—Mine; *hṛdayam*—heart; *sākṣāt*—directly; *ātmā*—life and soul; *aham*—Myself; *tapasaḥ*—of one who is engaged in penance; *anagha*—O sinless one.

TRANSLATION

O Brahmā, the sinless, you may know from Me that it was I who ordered you to undergo penance at first on your being perplexed in your duty, because such penance is My heart and soul, and because of that, penance and I are nondifferent.

PURPORT

The penance by which one can see the Personality of Godhead eye to eye is to be understood as devotional service to the Lord and nothing else because only by discharging devotional service in transcendental love can one approach the Lord. Such penance is the internal potency of the Lord and is nondifferent from Him. Such acts of internal potency are exhibited by nonattachment for material enjoyment. The living entities are encaged in the conditions of material bondage because of their propensity for overlordship. But by engagement in the devotional service of the Lord one becomes detached from such enjoying spirit. The devotees automatically become detached from worldly enjoyment, and this detachment is the result of perfect knowledge. Therefore the penance of devotional service includes knowledge and detachment, and that is the manifestation of the transcendental potency.

One cannot enjoy material illusory prosperity if he desires to return home, back to Godhead. One who has no information of the transcendental bliss in the association of the Lord foolishly desires to enjoy this temporary material happiness. In the *Caitanya-caritāmṛta* it is said that if someone sincerely wants to see the Lord and at the same time wants to enjoy this material world, he is considered to be a fool only. One who wants to remain here in the material world for material enjoyment has no business entering into the eternal kingdom of God. Such a foolish devotee is favored by the Lord by His snatching all that he may possess in the material world. If such a foolish devotee of the Lord again tries to recoup his position, then the merciful Lord again snatches away all that he may have possessed. By such repeated failures in material prosperity he becomes very unpopular with his family members and friends. In the material world the family members and the friends honor persons who may be very successful in accumulating wealth by any means. The foolish devotee of the Lord is thus put into forcible penance by the grace of the Lord, and at the end the devotee becomes perfectly happy, being engaged in the service of the Lord. Therefore penance in devotional service of the Lord, either by voluntary submission or being forced by the Lord, is necessary for attaining perfection, and thus such penance is the internal potency of the Lord.

One cannot, however, be engaged in the penance of devotional service without being completely free from all sins. As is stated in the *Bhagavad-gītā*, only a person who is completely free from all reactions of sins can engage himself in the worship of the Lord. Brahmājī was sinless, and therefore he faithfully discharged the advice of the Lord, "*tapa tapa,*" and the Lord, being satisfied with him, awarded him the desired result. Therefore love and penance combined can only please the Lord, and thus one is able to attain His complete mercy. He directs the sinless, and the sinless devotee attains the highest perfection of life.

TEXT 24

सृजामि तपसैवेदं ग्रसामि तपसा पुनः ।
बिभर्मि तपसा विश्वं वीर्यं मे दुश्चरं तपः ॥२३॥

sṛjāmi tapasaivedaṁ
grasāmi tapasā punaḥ
bibharmi tapasā viśvaṁ
vīryaṁ me duścaraṁ tapaḥ

sṛjāmi—I create; *tapasā*—by the same energy of penance; *eva*—certainly; *idam*—this; *grasāmi tapasā*—I do withdraw also by the same energy; *punaḥ*—again; *bibharmi*—do maintain; *tapasā*—by penance; *viśvam*—the cosmos; *vīryam*—potency; *me*—Mine; *duścaram*—severe; *tapaḥ*—penance.

TRANSLATION

I create this cosmos by such penance, I maintain it by the same energy, and I withdraw it all by the same energy. Therefore the potential power is penance only.

PURPORT

In executing penance, one must be determined to return home, back to Godhead, and must decide to undergo all types of tribulations for that end. Even for material prosperity, name and fame, one has to undergo severe types of penance, otherwise no one can become an important figure in this material world. Why, then, are there severe types of penance for perfection of devotional service? An easygoing life and attainment of perfection in transcendental realization cannot go together. The Lord is more clever than any living entity; therefore He wants to see how painstaking the devotee is in devotional service. The order is received from the Lord, either directly or through the bona fide spiritual master, and to execute that order, however painstaking, is the severe type of penance. One who follows the principle rigidly is sure to achieve success in attaining the Lord's mercy.

TEXT 25

ब्रह्मोवाच
भगवन् सर्वभूतानामध्यक्षोऽवस्थितो गुहाम् ।
वेद ह्यप्रतिरुद्धेन प्रज्ञानेन चिकीर्षितम् ॥२४॥

śrī brahmovāca
bhagavan sarva-bhūtānām
adhyakṣo'vasthito guhām
veda hy apratiruddhena
prajñānena cikīrṣitam

śrī brahmā uvāca—Lord Brahmā said; *bhagavan*—O my Lord; *sarva*—all; *bhūtānām*—of all living entities; *adhyakṣaḥ*—director; *avasthitaḥ*—situated; *guhām*—within the heart; *veda*—know; *hi*—certainly; *apratiruddhena*—without hindrance; *prajñānena*—by superintelligence; *cikīrṣitam*—endeavors.

TRANSLATION

Lord Brahmā said: O Personality of Godhead, You are situated in every living entity's heart as the supreme director, and therefore You are aware of all endeavors by Your superior intelligence, without any hindrance whatsoever.

PURPORT

The *Bhagavad-gītā* confirms that the Lord is situated in everyone's heart as the witness, and as such He is the supreme director of sanction. The director is not the enjoyer of the fruits of action, but without His sanction no one can enjoy. For example, in a prohibited area a habituated drunkard puts forward his application to the director of drinking, and the director, considering his case, sanctions only a certain amount of liquor for drinking. Similarly, the whole material world is full of many drunkards, in the sense that each and every one of the living entities has something in his mind to enjoy, and everyone desires the fulfillment of his desires very strongly. The almighty Lord, very kind to the living entity, as the father is kind to the son, fulfills the living entity's desire for his childish satisfaction. With such desires in mind, the living entity does not actually enjoy, but he serves the bodily whims unnecessarily, without profit. The drunkard does not derive any profit out of drinking, but because he has become a servant of the drinking habit and does not wish to get out of it, the merciful Lord gives him all facilities to fulfill such desires.

The impersonalists recommend that one should become desireless, and others recommend banishing desires altogether. That is impossible; no one can banish desires altogether because desiring is the living symptom. Without having desires a living entity would be dead, which he is not. Therefore, living conditions and desire go together. Perfection of desires may be achieved when one desires to serve the Lord, and the Lord also desires that every living entity should banish all personal desires and cooperate with the desires of the Lord. That is the last instruction of the *Bhagavad-gītā.* Brahmājī agreed to this proposal, and therefore he is given the responsible post of creating generations in the vacant universe. Oneness with the Lord is therefore to dovetail one's desires with the desires of the Supreme Lord. That makes for the perfection of all desires.

The Lord, as the Supersoul in the heart of every living being, knows what is there in the mind of each living entity, and no one can do anything without the knowledge of the Lord within. By His superior intelligence, the Lord gives everyone the chance to fulfill his desires to the fullest extent, and the resultant reaction is also awarded by the Lord.

TEXT 26

तथापि नाथमानस्य नाथ नाथय नाथितम् ।
परावरे यथा रूपे जानीयां ते त्वरूपिणः ॥२६॥

tathāpi nātha-mānasya
nātha nāthaya nāthitam
parāvare yathā rūpe
jānīyāṁ te tv arūpiṇaḥ

tathā api—in spite of that; *nātha-mānasya*—of the one who is asking for; *nātha*—of the Lord; *nāthaya*—please award; *nāthitam*—as it is desired; *parāvare*—in the matter of mundane and transcendental; *yathā*—as it is; *rūpe*—in the form; *jānīyām*—may it be known; *te*—Your; *tu*—but; *arūpiṇaḥ*—one who is formless.

TRANSLATION

In spite of that, my Lord, I am praying to You, kindly to fulfill my desire. May I please be informed how, in spite of Your transcendental form, You assume the mundane form, although You have no such form at all.

TEXT 27

यथाऽऽत्ममायायोगेन नानाशक्त्युपबृंहितम् ।
विलुम्पन् विसृजन् गृह्णन् बिभ्रदात्मानमात्मना ॥२७॥

yathātma-māyā-yogena
nānā-śakty-upabṛṁhitam
vilumpan visṛjan gṛhṇan
bibhrad ātmānam ātmanā

yathā—as much as; *ātma*—own; *māyā*—potency; *yogena*—by combination; *nānā*—various; *śakti*—energy; *upabṛṁhitam*—by combination and permutation; ***vilumpan***—in the matter of annihilation; ***visṛjan***—in the matter of generation; ***gṛhṇan***—in the matter of acceptance; ***bibhrat***—in the matter of maintenance; ***ātmānam***—own self; ***ātmanā***—by the self.

TRANSLATION

And how You, by Your own Self, manifest different energies for annihilation, generation, acceptance and maintenance by combination and permutation.

PURPORT

The whole manifestation is the Lord Himself by diffusion of His different energies only, namely the internal, external and marginal, just as the sunlight is the manifestation of the energy of the sun planet. Such energy is simultaneously one and different from the Lord, just as the sunshine is simultaneously one and different from the sun planet. The energies are acting by combination and permutation by the indication of the Lord, and the acting agents, like Brahmā, Viṣṇu and Śiva, are also different incarnations of the Lord. In other words, there is nothing but the Lord, and still the Lord is different from all such manifestive activities. How it is so will be explained later on.

TEXT 28

क्रीडस्यमोघसङ्कल्प ऊर्णनाभिर्यथोर्णुते ।
तथा तद्विषयां धेहि मनीषां मयि माधव ॥२८॥

krīḍasy amogha-saṅkalpa
ūrṇanābhir yathorṇute
tathā tad-viṣayāṁ dhehi
manīṣāṁ mayi mādhava

krīḍasi—as You do play; *amogha*—infallible; *saṅkalpa*—determination; *ūrṇābhiḥ*—the spider; *yathā*—as much as; *ūrṇute*—covers; *tathā*—so and so; *tat-viṣayām*—in the subject of all those; *dhehi*—do let me know; *manīṣām*—philosophically; *mayi*—unto me; *mādhava*—O master of all energies.

TRANSLATION

O master of all energies, please tell me philosophically all about them. You play like the spider who covers itself by its own energy, and Your determination is infallible.

PURPORT

By the inconceivable energy of the Lord, every creative element has its own potencies, known as the potency of the element, potency of knowledge and potency of different actions and reactions. By a combination of such potential energies of the Lord there is the manifestation of creation, maintenance and annihilation in due course of time and by different agents like Brahmā, Viṣṇu and Maheśvara. Brahmā creates, Viṣṇu maintains, and Lord Śiva destroys. But all such agents and creative energies are emanations from the Lord, and as such there is nothing except the Lord, or the one supreme source of different diversities. The exact example is the spider and spider's web. The web is created by the spider, and it is maintained by the spider, and as soon as it likes, the whole thing is wound up within the spider. The spider is covered within the web. If an insignificant spider is so powerful as to act according to its will, why can't the Supreme Being act by His supreme will in the creation, maintenance and destruction of the cosmic manifestations? By the grace of the Lord, a devotee like Brahmā, or one in his chain of disciplic succession, can understand the almighty Personality of Godhead eternally engaged in His transcendental pastimes in the region of different energies.

TEXT 29

भगवच्छिक्षितमहं करवाणि ह्यतन्द्रितः ।
नेहमानः प्रजासर्गं बध्येयं यदनुग्रहात् ॥२९॥

bhagavac-chikṣitam ahaṁ
karavāṇi hy atandritaḥ
nehamānaḥ prajā-sargaṁ
badhyeyaṁ yad-anugrahāt

bhagavat—by the Personality of Godhead; *śikṣitam*—taught by; *aham*—myself; *karavāṇi*—be acting; *hi*—certainly; *atandritaḥ*—instrumental; *na*—never; *ihamānaḥ*—although acting; *prajā-sargam*—generation of the living entities; *badhyeyam*—be conditioned; *yat*—as a matter of fact; *anugrahāt*—by the mercy of.

TRANSLATION

Please tell me so that I may be taught in the matter by the instruction of the Personality of Godhead, and thus I may act instrumentally to generate living entities, without being conditioned by such activities.

PURPORT

Brahmājī does not want to become a speculator dependent on the strength of his personal knowledge and conditioned to material bondage. Everyone should know in clear consciousness that one is, in the execution of all activities, an instrument. A conditioned soul is instrumental in the hands of the external energy, *guṇamayī māyā,* or the illusory energy of the Lord, and in the liberated stage the living entity is instrumental to the will of the Personality of Godhead directly. To be instrumental to the direct will of the Lord is the natural constitutional position of the living entity, whereas to be an instrument in the hands of the illusory energy of the Lord is material bondage for the living entity. In that conditioned state, the living entity speculates on the Absolute Truth and His different activities. But in the unconditional stage, the living entity directly receives knowledge from the Lord, and such a liberated soul acts flawlessly, without any speculative habit. The *Bhagavad-gītā* confirms emphatically (Bg. 10.10-11) that the pure devotees, who are constantly engaged in the loving transcendental service of the Lord, are directly advised by the Lord, so much so that the devotee unwaveringly makes progress on the path home, back to Godhead. Pure devotees of the Lord are therefore not proud of their definite progress, whereas the nondevotee speculator is in the darkness of illusory energy and is very much proud of his misleading knowledge based on speculation without any definite path. Lord Brahmā wanted to be saved from that pitfall of pride, although he was posted in the most exalted position within the universe.

TEXT 30

यावत् सखा सख्युरिवेश ते कृतः
प्रजाविसर्गे विभजामि भो जनम् ।
अविक्लवस्ते परिकर्मणि स्थितो
मा मे समुन्नद्धमदोऽजमानिनः ॥३०॥

yāvat sakhā sakhyur iveśa te kṛtaḥ
prajā-visarge vibhajāmi bho janam
aviklavas te parikarmaṇi sthito
mā me samunnaddha-mado 'ja-māninaḥ

yāvat—as it is; *sakhā*—friend; *sakhyuḥ*—unto the friend; *iva*—like that; *īśa*—O Lord; *te*—You; *kṛtaḥ*—have accepted; *prajā*—the living entities; *visarge*—in the matter of creation; *vibhajāmi*—as I shall do it differently; *bhoḥ*—O my Lord; *janam*—those who are born; *aviklavaḥ*—without being perturbed; *te*—Your; *parikarmaṇi*—in the matter of service; *sthitaḥ*—thus situated; *mā*—never it may be; *me*—unto me; *samunnaddha*—resulting arise; *madaḥ*—madness; *aja*—O unborn one; *māninaḥ*—thus being thought of.

TRANSLATION

O my Lord, the unborn, You have shaken hands with me just like a friend does with a friend [as if equal in position]. I shall be engaged in the creation of different types of living entities, and I shall be occupied in Your service. I shall have no perturbation, but I pray that all this may not give rise to pride, as if I were the Supreme.

PURPORT

Lord Brahmā is definitely situated in the humor of friendship with the Lord. Every living being is eternally related with the Personality of Godhead in one of five different transcendental humors, namely *śānta, dāsya, sakhya, vātsalya and mādhurya.* We have already discussed these five kinds of humors in relationship with the Personality of Godhead. It is clearly exhibited herein that Lord Brahmā is related to the Personality of Godhead in the transcendental humor of friendship. A pure devotee may be related with the Lord in any one of the transcendental humors, even in the humor of parenthood, but the devotee of the Lord is always a transcendental servitor. No one is equal to or greater than the Lord. That is the version of the *Bhagavad-gītā.* Brahmājī, although eternally related with the Lord in the transcendental humor of friendship, and although entrusted with the most exalted post of creating different grades of living entities, still is conscious of his position, that he is neither the Supreme Lord nor is supremely powerful. It is possible that some personality, within or without the universe, even though extremely powerful, sometimes shows more power than the Lord Himself. Still the pure devotee knows that this power is a *vibhūti* delegated by the Lord, and such a delegated powerful living entity is never independent. Śrī Hanumānjī crossed the Indian Ocean by jumping over the sea, and Lord Śrī Rāmacandra engaged Himself in marching over the bridge, but this does not mean that Hanumānjī was more powerful than the Lord. Sometimes the Lord gives extraordinary powers to His devotee, but the devotee knows always that the power belongs to the Personality of Godhead and that the devotee is only an instrument. The pure devotee is never puffed up like the nondevotee class of men who falsely think that they are God. It is astonishing to see how a person who is being kicked by the laws of the Lord's illusory energy in every step can falsely think of becoming one with the Lord. Such thinking is the last snare of the illusory energy offered to the conditioned soul. The first illusion is that he wants to become Lord of the material world by accumulating wealth and power, but when he is frustrated in that attempt he wants to be one with the Lord. So both becoming the most powerful man in the material world or desiring to become one with the Lord are different illusory snares. And because the pure devotees of the Lord are surrendered souls, they are above the illusory snares of *māyā*. Because he is a pure devotee, Lord Brahmā, even though the first dominating deity in the material world, and therefore able to do many wonderful things, would never, like the nondevotee with a poor fund of knowledge, have the audacity to think of becoming one with the Lord. People with a poor fund of knowledge should take lessons from Brahmā when they are puffed up with the false notion of becoming God.

Factually Lord Brahmā does not create the living entities. In the beginning of the creation he is empowered to give different bodily shapes to the living entities according to their work during the last millennium. Brahmājī's duty is just to wake the living entities from their slumber and to engage them in their proper duty. The different grades of living entities are not created by Brahmājī by his capricious whims, but he is entrusted with the task of giving the living entities different grades of body so that they can work accordingly. And still he is conscious that he is only instrumental, so that he may not think of himself as the Supreme Powerful Lord.

Devotees of the Lord are engaged in the specific duty offered by the Lord, and such duties are successfully carried out without hindrance because they are ordained by the Lord. The credit of success does not go to the doer but to the Lord. But persons with a poor fund of knowledge take the credit of success into their own accounts and give nothing to the credit of the Lord. That is the symptom of the nondevotee class of men.

TEXT 31

श्रीभगवानुवाच

ज्ञानं परमगुह्यं मे यद् विज्ञानसमन्वितम् ।
सरहस्यं तदङ्गं च गृहाण गदितं मया ॥३१॥

śrī bhagavān uvāca
jñānaṁ parama-guhyaṁ me
yad vijñāna-samanvitam

sa-rahasyaṁ tad-aṅgaṁ ca
gṛhāṇa gaditaṁ mayā

śrī bhagavān uvāca—the Personality of Godhead said; *jñānam*—knowledge acquired; *parama*—extremely; *guhyam*—confidential; *me*—of Mine; *yat*—which is; *vijñāna*—realization; *samanvitam*—coordinated; *sa-rahasyam*—with devotional service; *tat*—of that; *aṅgam ca*—necessary paraphernalia; *gṛhāṇa*—just try to take up; *gaditam*—explained; *mayā*—by Me.

TRANSLATION

The Personality of Godhead said: Knowledge about Me as described in the scriptures is very confidential, and it has to be realized in conjunction with devotional service. The necessary paraphernalia for that process is being explained by Me. You may take it up carefully.

PURPORT

Lord Brahmā is the topmost devotee of the Lord within the universe, and therefore the Personality of Godhead replied to his four principal inquiries in four important statements, which are known as the original *Bhāgavatam* in four verses. These were Brahmā's questions: 1. What are the forms of the Lord both in matter and transcendence? 2. How are the different energies of the Lord working? 3. How does the Lord play with His different energies? 4. How may Brahmā be instructed to discharge the duty entrusted with Him? The prelude to the answers is this verse under discussion, wherein the Lord informs Brahmā that knowledge of Him, the Supreme Absolute Truth, as it is stated in the revealed scriptures, is very subtle and cannot be understood unless one is self-realized by the grace of the Lord. The Lord says that Brahmā may take the answers as He explains them. This means that transcendental knowledge of the absolute Supreme Being can be known if it is made known by the Lord Himself. By the mental speculation of the greatest mundane thinkers, the Absolute Truth cannot be understood. The mental speculators can reach up to the standard of impersonal Brahman realization, but factually, complete knowledge of transcendence is beyond the knowledge of impersonal Brahman. Thus it is called the supreme confidential wisdom. Out of many liberated souls, someone may be qualified to know the Personality of Godhead. In the *Bhagavad-gītā* it is also said by the Lord Himself that out of many hundreds of thousands of people, one may try for perfection in the human life, and out of many liberated souls one may know Him as He is. Therefore, the knowledge of the Personality of Godhead may be attained by devotional service only. *Rahasyam* means devotional service. Lord Kṛṣṇa instructed Arjuna in the *Bhagavad-gītā* because He found Arjuna to be a devotee and friend. Without such qualifications, no one can enter into the mystery of the *Bhagavad-gītā*. Therefore, one cannot understand the Personality of Godhead unless one becomes a devotee and discharges devotional service. This mystery is *love of Godhead*. Therein lies the main qualification for knowing the mystery of the Personality of Godhead. And to attain the stage of transcendental love of Godhead regulative principles of devotional service must be followed. The regulative principles are called *vidhi-bhakti*, or devotional service of the Lord, and they can be practiced by a neophyte with his present senses. Such regulative principles are mainly based on hearing and chanting of the glories of the Lord. And such hearing and chanting of the glories of the Lord can be made possible in the association of devotees only. Lord Caitanya therefore recommended five main principles for attaining perfection in the devotional service of the Lord. The first is association of devotees (hearing); second is chanting the glories of the Lord; third, hearing *Śrīmad-Bhāgavatam* from the pure devotee; fourth, residing in a holy place connected with the Lord; and fifth, worshiping the Deity of the Lord with devotion. Such rules and regulations are parts of devotional service. So, as requested by Lord Brahmā, the Personality of Godhead will explain all about the four questions put forward by Brahmā, and others also which are parts and parcels of the same questions.

TEXT 32

यावानहं यथाभावो यद्रूपगुणकर्मकः ।
तथैव तत्त्वविज्ञानमस्तु ते मदनुग्रहात् ॥३२॥

yāvān ahaṁ yathā-bhāvo
yad-rūpa-guṇa-karmakaḥ
tathaiva tattva-vijñānam
astu te mad-anugrahāt

yāvān—as I am in eternal form; *aham*—Myself; *yathā*—as much as; *bhāvaḥ*—transcendental existence; *yat*—those; *rūpa*—various forms and colors;

guṇa—qualities; *karmakaḥ*—activities; *tathā*—so and so; *eva*—certainly; *tattva-vijñānam*—factual realization; *astu*—let it be unto you; *te*—unto you; *mat*—Mine; *anugrahāt*—by causeless mercy.

TRANSLATION

All of Me, namely My actual eternal form, My transcendental existence, color, qualities and activities—let all be awakened within you by factual realization, out of My causeless mercy.

PURPORT

The secret of success in understanding the intricacies of knowledge of the Absolute Truth, the Personality of Godhead, is the causeless mercy of the Lord. Even in the material world, the father of many sons discloses the secret of his position to the pet sons. The father discloses the confidence unto the son whom he thinks worthy. An important man in the social order can be known by his mercy only. Similarly, one must be very dear to the Lord in order to know the Lord. The Lord is unlimited; no one can know Him completely, but one's advancement in the transcendental loving service of the Lord can make one eligible to know the Lord. Here we can see that the Lord is sufficiently pleased with Brahmājī, and therefore He offers His causeless mercy to him so that Brahmājī may have the factual realization of the Lord by His mercy only.

In the *Vedas* also it is said that a person cannot know the Absolute Truth Personality of Godhead simply by dint of mundane education or intellectual gymnastics. One can know the Supreme Truth if one has unflinching faith in the bona fide spiritual master as well as in the Lord. Such a faithful person, even though illiterate in the mundane sense, can know the Lord automatically by the mercy of the Lord. In the *Bhagavad-gītā* also, it is said that the Lord reserves the right of not being exposed to everyone, and He keeps Himself concealed from the faithless by His *yoga-māyā* potency.

To the faithful the Lord reveals Himself in His form, quality and pastimes. The Lord is not formless, as it is wrongly conceived by the impersonalist, but His form is not like one that we have experienced. The Lord discloses His form, even to the extent of measurement, to His pure devotees, and that is the meaning of *yāvān,* as is explained by Śrīla Jīva Gosvāmī, the greatest scholar of *Śrīmad-Bhāgavatam.*

The Lord discloses His transcendental nature of existence. The mundane wranglers make mundane conceptions of the form of the Lord. It is said in the revealed scriptures that the Lord has no mundane form; therefore persons with a poor fund of knowledge conclude that He must be formless. They cannot distinguish between the mundane form and the spiritual form. According to them, without a mundane form one must be formless. This conclusion is also mundane because formlessness is the opposite conception of form. Negation of the mundane conception does not establish a transcendental fact. In the *Brahma-saṁhitā* it is said that the Lord has a transcendental form and that He can utilize any one of His senses for any purpose. For example, He can eat with His eyes, and He can see with His leg. In the mundane conception of form, no one can eat with one's eyes nor see with his leg. That is the difference between the mundane body and the spiritual body of *sac-cid-ānanda.* Spiritual body does not mean formless, but a different type of body which we cannot conceive with our present mundane senses. Formless therefore means devoid of mundane form, or possessing a spiritual body of which the nondevotee can have no conception by the speculative method.

The Lord discloses to the devotee His unlimited varieties of transcendental bodies, all identical with one another with different kinds of bodily features. Some of the transcendental bodies of the Lord are blackish, and some of them are whitish. Some of them are reddish, and some of them are yellowish. Some of them are four-handed, and some of them are two-handed. Some of them are like the fish, and some of them are like the lion. All these different transcendental bodies of the Lord, without any differential category, are disclosed to the devotees of the Lord by the mercy of the Lord, and thus the impersonalists' false arguments claiming the formlessness of the Supreme Truth do not appeal to a devotee of the Lord, even though such a devotee may not be very advanced in devotional service.

The Lord has unlimited numbers of transcendental qualities, and one of them is His affection for His unalloyed devotee. In the history of the mundane world we can appreciate His transcendental qualities. The Lord incarnates Himself for the protection of His devotees and for the annihilation of the faithless. His activities are in relationship with His devotees, and the *Śrīmad-Bhāgavatam* is full of such activities of the Lord in relationship with His devotees, and the nondevotees have no knowledge of such pastimes. The Lord lifted the Govardhana Hill when He was only seven years old and protected His pure devotees at Vṛndāvana from the wrath of Indra, who was overflooding the place with rain. Now this lifting of the

Govardhana Hill by a seven-year-old boy may be unbelievable for the faithless, but for the devotees it is absolutely believable. The devotee believes in the almighty potency of the Lord, while the faithless say that the Lord is almighty but do not believe it. Such men with a poor fund of knowledge do not know that the Lord is the Lord eternally, and that one cannot become the Lord by meditation for millions of years nor by mental speculation for billions of years.

The impersonal interpretation of the mundane wranglers is completely refuted in this verse because it is clearly stated here that the Supreme Lord has His qualities, form, pastimes, and everything that a person has. All these descriptions of the transcendental nature of the Personality of Godhead are factual realizations by the devotee of the Lord, and by the causeless mercy of the Lord they become revealed to His pure devotee, and to no one else.

TEXT 33

अहमेवासमेवाग्रे नान्यद् यत् सदसत् परम् ।
पश्चादहं यदेतच्च योऽवशिष्येत सोऽस्म्यहम् ॥३३॥

aham evāsam evāgre
nānyad yat sad-asat param
paścād ahaṁ yad etac ca
yo'vaśiṣyeta so'smy aham

aham—I, the Personality of Godhead; *eva*—certainly; *āsam*—existed; *eva*—only; *agre*—before the creation; *na*—never; *anyat*—anything else; *yat*—all those; *sat*—the effect; *asat*—the cause; *param*—the supreme; *paścāt*—at the end; *aham*—I, the Personality of Godhead; *yat*—all these; *etat*—creation; *ca*—also; *yaḥ*—everything; *avaśiṣyeta*—remains; *saḥ*—that; *asmi*—I am; *aham*—I, the Personality of Godhead.

TRANSLATION

Brahmā, it is I, the Personality of Godhead, who was existing before the creation when there was nothing but Myself. Nor was there the material nature, the cause of this creation. That which you see now is also I, the Personality of Godhead, and after annihilation what remains will also be I, the Personality of Godhead.

PURPORT

We should note very carefully that the Personality of Godhead is addressing Lord Brahmā and specifying with great emphasis Himself, pointing out that it is He, the Personality of Godhead, who existed before the creation, it is He only who maintains the creation, and it is He only who remains after the annihilation of the creation. Brahmā is also a creation of the Supreme Lord. The impersonalist puts forth the theory of oneness in the sense that Brahmā, also being the same principle of "I" because he is an emanation from the I, the Absolute Truth, is identical with the Lord, the principle of I, and thus there is nothing more than the principle of I, as explained in this verse. Accepting the argument of the impersonalist, it is to be admitted that the Lord is the creator I, and the Brahmā is the created I. Therefore there is a difference between the two "I's," namely the predominator I and the predominated I. Therefore there are still two I's, even accepting the argument of the impersonalist. But we must note carefully that these two I's are accepted in the Vedic literature *(Kaṭhopaniṣad)* in the sense of quality. The *Kaṭhopaniṣad* says,

nityo nityānāṁ cetanaś cetanānām eko bahūnāṁ yo vidadhāti kāmān
(*Kaṭha* 2.2.13)

The creator "I" and the created "I" are both accepted in the *Vedas* as qualitatively one because both of them are *nityas* and *cetanas.* But the singular "I" is the creator "I," and the created "I's" are of plural number because there are many "I's" like Brahmā and those generated by Brahmā. It is the simple truth. The father creates or begets a son, and the son also creates many other sons, and all of them may be one as human beings, but at the same time from the father, the son and the grandsons are all different. The son cannot take the place of the father, nor can the grandsons. Simultaneously the father, the son and the grandson are one and different also. As human beings they are one, but as relativities they are different. Therefore the relativities of the creator and the created or the predominator and the predominated have been differentiated in the *Vedas* by saying that the predominator "I" is the feeder of the predominated "I's," and thus there is a vast difference between the two principles of "I."

In another feature of this verse, no one can deny the personalities of both the Lord and Brahmā. Therefore in the ultimate issue both the predominator and predominated are persons. This conclusion refutes the conclusion of the impersonalist that in the ultimate issue everything is impersonal. This impersonal feature stressed by the less intelligent impersonalist school is refuted by pointing out that the predominator "I" is the Absolute Truth, and He is a person. The predominated "I," Brahmā, is also a person, but he is not the Absolute. For realization of one's self in spiritual psychology it may be convenient to assume oneself as the same principle as the Absolute Truth, but there is always the difference of the predominated and the predominator, as is clearly pointed out here in this verse, which is grossly misused by the impersonalists. Brahmā is factually seeing eye to eye his predominator Lord who, in His transcendental eternal form, exists even after the annihilation of the material creation. The form of the Lord, as seen by Brahmā, existed before the creation of Brahmā, and the material manifestation with all ingredients and agents of material creation are also energetic expansions of the Lord, and after closing the exhibited energy of the Lord, what remains is the same Personality of Godhead. Therefore the form of the Lord exists in all circumstances of the creation, maintenance and annihilation. The Vedic hymns confirm this fact in the statement, "*vāsudevo vā idam agra āsīn na brahmā na ca śaṅkaraḥ eko vai nārāyaṇa āsīn na brahmā na īśāno, etc.*" Before the creation there was none except Vāsudeva. There was neither Brahmā nor Śaṅkara. Only Nārāyaṇa was there and no one else, neither Brahmā nor Īśāna. Śrīpāda Śaṅkarācārya also confirms in his comments on the *Bhagavad-gītā* that Nārāyaṇa, or the Personality of Godhead, is transcendental to all creation, but the whole creation is the product of *avyakta.* Therefore the difference between the created and the creator is always there, although both the creator and created are of the same quality.

The other feature of the statement is that the supreme truth is Bhagavān, or the Personality of Godhead. The Personality of Godhead and His kingdom have already been explained. The kingdom of Godhead is not void as conceived by the impersonalists. The Vaikuṇṭha planets are full of transcendental variegatedness, including the four-handed residents of those planets, and with great opulence of wealth and prosperity, and there are even airplanes and other amenities required for high-grade personalities. Therefore the Personality of Godhead exists before the creation, and He exists with all transcendental variegatedness in the Vaikuṇṭhalokas. The Vaikuṇṭhalokas, also accepted in the *Bhagavad-gītā* as being of the *sanātana* nature, are not annihilated even after the annihilation of the manifested cosmos. Those transcendental planets are of a different nature altogether, and that nature is not subjected to the rules and regulations of material creation, maintenance or annihilation. The existence of the Personality of Godhead implies the existence of the Vaikuṇṭhalokas, as the existence of a king implies the existence of a kingdom.

In various places of *Śrīmad-Bhāgavatam* and in other revealed scriptures the existence of the Personality of Godhead is mentioned. For example, Mahārāja Parīkṣit asks, "*Sa cāpi yatra puruṣo viśva-sthity-udbhavāpyayaḥ muktvātma-māyāṁ māyeśaḥ śete sarva-guhāśayaḥ?*" How does the Personality of Godhead, the cause of creation, maintenance and annihilation, who is always freed from the influence of the illusory energy and is the controller of the same, lie in everyone's heart? Similar also is a question of Vidura's: "*Tattvānāṁ bhagavaṁs teṣāṁ katidhā pratisaṅkramaḥ tatremaṁ ka upāsīran ka u svid anuśerata.*" Śrīdhara Svāmī explains this in his notes:, "During the annihilation of the creation, who serves the Lord lying on the Śeṣa, etc." This means that the transcendental Lord with all His name, fame, quality and paraphernalia exists eternally. The same confirmation is also in the *Kāśī-Khaṇḍa* in connection with *Dhruva-carita.* It is said there, "*Na cyavante'pi yad-bhaktā mahatyāṁ pralayāpadi ato 'cyuto-khile loke sa ekaḥ sarvago 'vyayaḥ.*" Even the devotees of the Personality of Godhead are not annihilated during the period of the entire annihilation of the material world, not to speak of the Lord Himself. The Lord is ever-existent in all three stages of material change.

The impersonalist adduces no activity in the Supreme, but in this discussion between Brahmā and the Supreme Personality of Godhead the Lord is said to have activities also, as He has His form and quality. The activities of Brahmā and other demigods during the time and maintenance of the creation are to be understood as the activities of the Lord. The king, or the head executive of a state, may not be seen in the government offices, for he may be engaged in royal comforts. Yet it should be understood that everything is being done under his direction, and everything is at his command. The Personality of Godhead is never formless. He may not be visible in His personal form in the material world to the less intelligent class of men, and therefore He may be sometimes called formless. But actually He is always in His eternal form in His Vaikuṇṭha planets as well as in other planets of the universes as different incarnations. The example of the sun is very appropriate in this connection. The sun in the night may not be visible to the eyes of men in the darkness, but the sun is visible wherever it has risen. Because the sun is not visible to the eyes of the inhabitants of a particular part of the earth does not mean that the sun has no form.

In the *Aitareya Upaniṣad* there is the hymn "*ātmaivedam agra āsīt puruṣa-vidhaḥ.*" This *mantra* indicates the Supreme Personality of Godhead (Kṛṣṇa) even before the appearance of the *puruṣa* incarnation. In the *Bhagavad-gītā* it is said (Bg. 15.18) that Lord Kṛṣṇa is *Puruṣottama* because He is the Supreme *Puruṣa,* transcendental even to the *puruṣa akṣara* and the *puruṣa kṣara.* The *akṣara puruṣa,* or the Mahā-Viṣṇu, throws His glance over *prakṛti,* or material nature, but the existence of the Puruṣottama was there even before that. The *Aitareya Upaniṣad* therefore confirms the statement of the *Bhagavad-gītā* that Lord Kṛṣṇa is the Supreme Person *(Puruṣottama).*

In some of the *Vedas* it is also said that in the beginning only the impersonal Brahman was there. But according to this verse, the impersonal Brahman, which is the glowing effulgence of the body of the Supreme Lord, may be called the immediate cause, but the cause of all causes or the remote cause is the Supreme Personality of Godhead. The Lord's impersonal feature is existent in the material world because by material senses or material eyes the Lord cannot be seen or perceived. One has to spiritualize the senses before one can expect to see or perceive the Supreme Lord. But He is always engaged in His personal capacity, and He is eternally visible to the inhabitants of Vaikuṇṭhaloka, eye to eye. Therefore He is materially impersonal, just as the executive head of the state may be impersonal in the government offices, although he is not impersonal in the government house. Similarly, the Lord is not impersonal in His abode, which is always *nirasta-kuhakam,* as is stated in the very beginning of the *Bhāgavatam.* Therefore both the impersonal and personal features of the Lord are acceptable, as mentioned in the revealed scriptures. This Personality of Godhead is very emphatically explained in the *Bhagavad-gītā* in connection with the verse, *"brahmaṇo hi pratiṣṭhāham"* (Bg. 14.27). Therefore in all ways the confidential part of spiritual knowledge is realization of the Personality of Godhead, and not His impersonal Brahman feature. One should therefore have his ultimate aim of realization not in the impersonal feature but in the personal feature of the Absolute Truth. The example of sky within the pot and the sky without the pot may be helpful to the student for his realization of the all-pervading quality of the cosmic consciousness of the Absolute Truth. But that does not mean that the individual part and parcel of the Lord becomes the Supreme by a false claim. It means only that the conditioned soul is a victim of the illusory energy in her last snare. To claim to become one with the cosmic consciousness of the Lord is the last trap set by the illusory energy or *daivi māyā.* Even in the impersonal existence of the Lord, as it is in the material creation, one should be after the personal realization of the Lord, and that is the meaning of *"paścād ahaṁ yad etac ca yo 'vaśiṣyeta so 'smy aham."*

Brahmājī also accepted the same truth when he was instructing Nārada. He said, *"So'yaṁ te 'bhihitas tāta bhagavān viśva-bhāyanaḥ."* (*Bhāg.* 2.7.50). There is no other cause of all causes than the

Supreme Personality of Godhead, Hari, and therefore this verse *aham eva* never indicates anything other than the Supreme Lord, and one should therefore follow the path of *Brahma-sampradāya,* or the path of Brahmājī to Nārada, to Vyāsadeva, etc., and make it a point in life to realize the Supreme Personality of Godhead, Hari, or Lord Kṛṣṇa. This very confidential instruction to the pure devotees of the Lord was also given to Arjuna and to Brahmā in the beginning of the creation. The demigods like Brahmā, Viṣṇu, Maheśvara, Indra, Candra, Varuṇa are undoubtedly different forms of the Lord for execution of different functions; the different elemental ingredients of material creation, as well as the multifarious energies, also may be of the same Personality of Godhead, but the root of all of them is the Supreme Personality of Godhead, Śrī Kṛṣṇa, and one should be attached to the root of everything rather than bewildered by the branches and leaves. That in the instruction given in this verse.

TEXT 34

ऋतेऽर्थं यत् प्रतीयेत न प्रतीयेत चात्मनि ।
तद्विद्यादात्मनो मायां यथाऽऽभासो यथा तमः ॥३४॥

ṛte'rthaṁ yat pratīyeta
na pratīyeta cātmani
tad vidyād ātmano māyāṁ
yathābhāsc yathā tamaḥ

ṛte—without; *artham*—value; *yat*—which; *pratīyeta*—appears to be; *na*—does not; *pratīyeta*—appears to be; *ca*—certainly; *ātmani*—in My relation; *tat*—that; *vidyāt*—must you know; *ātmanaḥ*—Mine; *māyām*—illusory energy; *yathā*—as much as; *ābhāsaḥ*—in reflection; *yathā*—as it is; *tamaḥ*—darkness.

TRANSLATION

O Brahmā, whatever appears to be of any value, if it is without relation to Me, has no reality. Know it as My illusory energy, that reflection which appears to be in darkness.

PURPORT

In the previous verse it has already been concluded that in any stage of the cosmic manifestation—namely its appearance, its sustenance, its growth, its interactions of different energies, its deterioration and its disappearance—all has its basic relation with the existence of the Personality of Godhead. And as such, whenever there is forgetfulness of this prime relation with the Lord, and things are accepted as real without being related with the Lord, that conception is called the product of the illusory energy of the Lord. Because nothing can exist without the Lord, it should be known that the illusory energy is also an energy of the Lord. The right conclusion of dovetailing everything in relationship with the Lord is called *yoga-māyā,* or the energy of union, and the wrong conception of detaching a thing from its relationship with the Lord is called *daivi māyā,* or *mahā-māyā,* of the Lord. Both the *māyās* also have connection with the Lord because nothing can exist without being related with Him. As such, the wrong conception of detaching relationships from the Lord is not false but illusory.

Misconceiving one thing for another thing is called illusion. The example of accepting the rope as a snake is illusion, but it is not false. The rope, as it exists in the front of the illusioned person, is not at all false, but the acceptance is illusory. Therefore the wrong conception of accepting this material manifestation as being divorced from the energy of the Lord is illusion, but it is not false. And this illusory conception is called the reflection of the reality in the darkness of ignorance. Anything that appears as apparently not being "produced out of My energy" is called *māyā.* The conception that the living entity is formless or that the Supreme Lord is formless is also illusion. In the *Bhagavad-gītā* (Bg. 2.12) it is said by the Lord in the midst of the battlefield that the warriors who were standing in front of Arjuna, Arjuna himself, and even the Lord were all existing before, they were existing on the battlefield of Kurukṣetra, and they would all continue to be individual personalities in the future also, even after the annihilation of the present body and even after being liberated from the bondage of material existence. In all circumstances, the Lord and the living entities are individual personalities, and the personal features of both the Lord and living beings are never abolished; only the influence of the illusory energy, the reflection of light in the darkness, can, by the mercy of the Lord, be removed. In the material world, the light of the sun is also not independent, nor is that of the moon. The real source of light is the *brahmajyoti,* which diffuses light from the transcendental body of the Lord, and the same light is reflected in varieties of light: the light of the sun, the light of the moon, the light of the fire, or the light of electricity. So the identity of self as being unconnected with the Supreme Self, the Lord, is also illusion, and the false claim that "*I am the Supreme*" is also the last illusory snare of the same *māyā*, or the external energy of the Lord.

The *Vedānta-sūtra* in the very beginning affirms that everything is born from the Supreme, and thus, as explained in the previous verse, all individual living entities are born from the energy of the supreme living being, the Personality of Godhead, as Brahmā himself was born from the energy of the Lord, and all other living entities are born from the energy of the Lord through the agency of Brahmā, and none of them has any existence without being dovetailed with the Supreme Lord.

The independence of the individual living entity is not real independence, but is just the reflection of the real independence existing in the Supreme Being, the Lord. The false claim of supreme independence by the conditioned souls is illusion, and this conclusion is admitted in this verse.

Persons with a poor fund of knowledge become illusioned, and therefore the so-called scientists, physiologists, empiric philosophers, etc., become dazzled by the glaring reflection of the sun, moon, electricity, etc., and deny the existence of the Supreme Lord, putting forward theories and different speculations about creation, maintenance and annihilation of everything material. The medical practitioner may deny the existence of the soul in the physiological bodily construction of an individual person, but he cannot give life to the dead body, even though all the mechanisms of the body exist even after death. The psychologist makes a serious study of the physiological conditions of the brain, as if the construction of the cerebral lump is the machine of the functioning mind, but in the dead body the psychologist cannot bring back the function of the mind. These scientific studies of the cosmic manifestation or that of the bodily construction independent of the Supreme Lord are different reflective intellectual gymnastics only, but at the end they are all illusion and nothing more. All such advancement of science and knowledge in the present context of material civilization is the action of the covering influence of the illusory energy. The illusory energy has two phases of existence, namely the covering influence and the throwing influence. By the throwing influence the living entities are thrown into the darkness of ignorance, and by the covering influence she covers the eyes of men with a poor fund of knowledge about the existence of the Supreme Person who enlightened the supreme individual living being, Brahmā. The identity of Brahmā with the Supreme Lord is never claimed herein, and therefore such a foolish claim by the man with a poor fund of knowledge is another display of the illusory energy of the Lord. The Lord says in the *Bhagavad-gītā* (Bg. 16.18-20) that demoniac persons who deny the existence of the Lord are thrown more and more into the darkness of ignorance, and thus such demoniac persons transmigrate life after life without any knowledge of the Supreme Personality of Godhead.

The sane man, however, is enlightened in the disciplic succession from Brahmājī, who was personally instructed by the Lord, or in the disciplic succession from Arjuna, who was personally instructed by the Lord in the *Bhagavad-gītā.* He accepts the statement of the Lord, *ahaṁ sarvasya prabhavo mattaḥ sarvaṁ pravartate/ iti matvā bhajante māṁ budhā bhāva-samanvitāḥ*" (Bg.10.8). The Lord is the original source of all emanations, and everything that is created, maintained and annihilated exists by the energy of the Lord. The sane man who knows this is actually learned, and therefore he becomes a pure devotee of the Lord, engaged in the transcendental loving service of the Lord.

Although the reflectory energy of the Lord displays various illusions to the eyes of persons with a poor fund of knowledge, the sane person knows clearly that the Lord can act, even from far, far beyond our vision, by His different energies, just as the fire can diffuse heat and light from a distant place. In the medical science of the ancient sages, known as the *Āyur-veda,* there is definite acceptance of the Lord's supremacy in the following words: "*jagad-yonir anicchasya cid-ānandaika-rūpiṇaḥ puṁso 'sti prakṛtir nityā praticchāyeva bhāsvataḥ acetanāpi caitanya-yogena paramātmanaḥ akarod viśvam akhilam anityam nāṭakā-kṛtim.*" There is one Supreme Person who is the progenitor of this cosmic manifestation, whose energy acts as *prakṛti,* or the material nature, dazzling like the reflection. By such illusory action of the *prakṛti,* even the dead matter is caused to move by the cooperation of living energy of the Lord, and the material world appears like a dramatic performance to the ignorant eyes. The ignorant person, therefore, may even be a scientist or physiologist in the drama of *prakṛti,* while the sane person knows the *prakṛti* as the illusory energy of the Lord. By such a conclusion, and as is confirmed by the *Bhagavad-gītā,* it is clear that the living entities are also a display of the superior energy (*parā prakṛtiḥ*) of the Lord, just as the material world is a display of the inferior energy (*aparā prakṛtiḥ*) of the Lord. The superior energy of the Lord cannot be as good as the Lord, although there is very little difference between the energy and the possessor of the energy, or the fire and the heat. Fire is possessed of heat, but heat is not fire. This simple thing is not understood by the man with a poor fund of knowledge who falsely claims that the fire and heat are the same. This energy of the fire (namely heat) is explained here as a reflection, and not directly fire. Therefore the living energy represented by the living entities is the reflection of the Lord, and never the Lord Himself. And as the reflection of the Lord, the existence of the living entity is dependent on the Supreme Lord, who is the original light. This material energy may be compared with darkness, as actually it is darkness, and the activities of the living entities in the darkness are reflections of the original light. The Lord should be understood by the context of this verse. Nondependence of both the energies of the Lord is explained as *māyā,* or illusion. No one can make a solution of the darkness of ignorance simply by the reflection of light. Similarly, no one can come out of the material existence simply by the reflected light of the common man, but one has to receive the light from the original light itself. The reflection of sunlight in the darkness is unable to drive out the darkness, but the sunlight which is outside the reflection can drive out the darkness completely. In darkness no one can see the things in a room. Therefore a person in the dark is afraid of snakes and scorpions, although there may not be such things. But in the light the things in the room can be clearly seen, and the fear of snakes and scorpions is at once removed. Therefore one has to take shelter of the light of the Lord, as in the *Bhagavad-gītā* or the *Śrīmad-Bhāgavatam,* and not the reflective personalities who have no touch with the Lord. No one should hear *Bhagavad-gītā* or *Śrīmad-Bhāgavatam* from a person who is a nonbeliever in the existence of the Lord. Such a person is already doomed, and any association with such a doomed person makes the associater also doomed.

According to the *Padma Purāṇa,* within the material compass there are innumerable material universes, and all of them are full of darkness. Any living being, beginning from Brahmās (there are innumerable Brahmās also in innumerable universes) to the insignificant ant, are all born in darkness, and they require factual light from the Lord to see Him directly, just as the sun can be seen only by the direct light of the sun. No lamp or man-made torchlight, however powerful it may be, can help one to see the sun. The sun reveals itself. Therefore the action of different energies of the Lord or the Personality of Godhead Himself can be realized by the light manifested by the causeless mercy of the Lord. The impersonalists say that God cannot be seen. God can be seen by the light of God and not by man-made speculations. Here it is specifically mentioned as *vidyāt,* which is an order by the Lord to Brahmā. This direct order of the Lord is a manifestation of His internal energy, and this particular energy is the means of seeing the Lord eye to eye. Not only Brahmā but anyone who may be graced by the Lord to see such merciful direct internal energy can also realize the Personality of Godhead without any mental speculation.

TEXT 35

यथा महान्ति भूतानि भूतेषूच्चावचेष्वनु ।
प्रविष्टान्यप्रविष्टानि तथा तेषु न तेष्वहम् ॥३५॥

yathā mahānti bhūtāni
bhūteṣūccāvaceṣv anu
praviṣṭāny apraviṣṭāni
tathā teṣu na teṣv aham

yathā—as it is; *mahānti*—the universal; *bhūtāni*—elements; *bhūteṣu ucca-avaceṣu*—in the minute and gigantic; *anu*—after; *praviṣṭāni*—entered; *apraviṣṭāni*—not entered; *tathā*—so much so; *teṣu*—in them; *na*—not; *teṣu*—in them; *aham*—Myself.

TRANSLATION

O Brahmā, please know that the universal elements enter into the cosmos and at the same time do not enter into the cosmos; similarly, I Myself also exist within everything created, and at the same time I am outside of everything.

PURPORT

The great elements of material creation, namely earth, water, fire, air and ether, etc., all enter into the body of all manifested entities, namely the seas, mountains, aquatics, plants, reptiles, birds, beasts, human beings, demigods and everyone materially manifested, and at the same time such elements are differently situated. In the developed stage of consciousness, the human being can study both physiological and physical science, but the basic principles of such sciences are nothing but the material elements and nothing more. The body of the human being and the body of the mountain, as also the body of the demigods, including Brahmā, are all of the same ingredients, namely earth, water, etc., and at the same time the elements are beyond the body. The elements were created first, and therefore they entered into the bodily construction later on, but in both circumstances they entered the cosmos as well as not entered. Similarly, the Supreme Lord, by His different energies, namely the internal and external, is within everything in the manifested cosmos, and at the same time He is outside of everything, situated in the kingdom of God (Vaikuṇṭhaloka) as described before. This is very nicely stated in the *Brahma-saṁhitā* as follows:

ānanda-cinmaya-rasa-pratibhāvitābhis
tābhir ya eva nijarūpatayā kalābhiḥ
goloka eva nivasaty akhilātma-bhūto
govindam ādi-puruṣaṁ tam ahaṁ bhajāmi (Bs. 5.37)

"I worship the Personality of Godhead Govinda, who, by expansion of His internal potency of transcendental existence, knowledge and bliss, enjoys in His own and expanded forms. Simultaneously He enters into every atom of the creation."

This expansion of His plenary parts is also more definitely explained in the same *Brahma-saṁhitā* as follows:

eko 'py asau racayituṁ jagad-aṇḍa-koṭiṁ
yac-chaktir asti jagad-aṇḍa-cayā yad-antaḥ
aṇḍāntarastha-paramāṇu-cayāntarasthaṁ
govindam ādi-puruṣaṁ tam ahaṁ bhajāmi (Bs. 5.35)

"I worship the Personality of Godhead Govinda, who, by one of His plenary portions, enters into the existence of every universe and every particle of the atoms and thus manifests His infinite energy all over the material creation unlimitedly."

The impersonalists can imagine or even perceive that the Supreme Brahman is thus all-pervading, and therefore they conclude that there is no possibility of His personal form. Herein lies the mystery of His transcendental knowledge. This mystery is the transcendental love of Godhead, and one who is surcharged with such transcendental love of Godhead can see the Personality of Godhead in every atom and every movable or immovable object without any difficulty. And at the same time he can see the Personality of Godhead in His abode of Goloka, enjoying eternal pastimes with His eternal associates, who are also expansions of His transcendental existence. This vision is the real mystery of spiritual knowledge, as is stated by the Lord in the beginning, "*sa-rahasyaṁ tad-aṅgaṁ ca.*" This mystery is the most confidential part of the knowledge of the Supreme, and it is impossible to be discovered by the mental speculators by dint of intellectual gymnastics. The mystery can be revealed through the process recommended by Brahmājī in his *Brahma-saṁhitā* as follows:

premāñjana-cchurita-bhakti-vilocanena
santaḥ sadaiva hṛdayeṣu vilokayanti
yaṁ śyāmasundaram acintya-guṇa-svarūpaṁ
govindam ādi-puruṣaṁ tam ahaṁ bhajāmi. (Bs. 5.38)

"I worship the original Personality of Godhead, Govinda, whom the pure devotees whose eyes are smeared with the ointment of love of Godhead always observe within their hearts. This Govinda, the original Personality of Godhead, is Śyāmasundara with all transcendental qualities."

Therefore, although He is present in every atom, the Supreme Personality of Godhead may not be visible to the dry speculators; still the mystery is unfolded before the eyes of the pure devotees because their eyes are anointed with love of Godhead. And this love of Godhead can be attained only by the practice of transcendental loving service of the Lord, and nothing else. The vision of the devotees is not ordinary; it is purified by the process of devotional service. In other words, as the universal elements are both within and without, similarly the Lord's name, form, quality, pastimes, entourage, etc., as they are described in the revealed scriptures or as they are being performed in the Vaikuṇṭhalokas, far, far beyond the material cosmic manifestation, are factually being televised in the heart of the devotee. The man with a poor fund of knowledge cannot understand, although by material science one can see things far away by means of television. Factually, the spiritually developed person is able to have the television of the kingdom of God always reflected within his heart. That is the mystery of knowledge of the Personality of Godhead.

The Lord can award anyone and everyone liberation *(mukti)* from the bondage of material existence, yet He rarely awards the privilege of love of Godhead, as is confirmed by Nārada, "*mukti dadhāti karhicit sma na bhakti-yogam.*" This transcendental devotional service of the Lord is so wonderful that the occupation keeps the deserving devotee always rapt in psychological activities, without any deviation from the absolute touch. Thus love of Godhead, developed in the heart of the devotee, is a great mystery. It was previously told by Brahmājī to Nārada that the desires of Brahmājī are never unfulfilled because he is always absorbed in the transcendental loving service of the Lord; nor has he any desire in his heart save and except the transcendental service of the Lord. That is the beauty and mystery of the process of *bhakti-yoga.* As the Lord's desire is infallible, as He is *acyuta,* similarly the desires of the devotees in the transcendental service of the Lord are also *acyuta,* infallible. It is very difficult, however, for the layman to understand without knowledge of the mystery of devotional service, as it is very difficult to know the potency of touchstone. As touchstone is rarely found, a pure devotee of the Lord is also rarely to be seen, even amongst the millions of liberated souls (*katsv api mahāmune*). Out of all kinds of perfections attained by the process of knowledge, *yoga* perfection in devotional service is the highest of all and the most mysterious also, even more mysterious than the eight kinds of mystic perfection attained by the process of yogic performances. In the *Bhagavad-gītā* the Lord therefore advised Arjuna about this *bhakti-yoga:*

sarva-guhyatamaṁ bhūyaḥ
śṛṇu me paramaṁ vacaḥ

"Just hear from Me again about the most confidential part of instructions in the *Bhagavad-gītā*." (Bg. 18.64) The same was confirmed by Brahmājī to Nārada in the following words: *"idaṁ bhāgavataṁ nāma yan me bhagavatoditam/ saṅgraho 'yaṁ vibhūtīnāṁ tvam etad vipulīkuru. Yathā harau bhagavati nṛṇāṁ bhaktir bhaviṣyati."* Brahmājī said to Nārada. "Whatever I have spoken to you about the *Bhāgavatam* was explained to me by the Supreme Personality of Godhead, and I am advising you to expand these topics nicely so that people may easily understand the mysterious *bhakti-yoga* by transcendental loving service to the Lord." It is to be noted here that the mystery of *bhakti-yoga* was disclosed to Brahmājī by the Lord Himself, and the same was explained by Brahmājī to Nārada, and Nārada explained the same to Vyāsa and from Vyāsa to Śukadeva Gosvāmī, and that same knowledge is coming down, in the unalloyed chain of disciplic succession. If one is fortunate enough to have received the knowledge in the transcendental disciplic succession, surely he may have the chance of understanding the mystery of the Lord and that of the *Śrīmad-Bhāgavatam,* the sound incarnation of the Lord.

TEXT 36

एतावदेव जिज्ञास्यं तत्त्वजिज्ञासुनाऽऽत्मनः ।
अन्वयव्यतिरेकाभ्यां यत् स्यात् सर्वत्र सर्वदा ॥३६॥

etāvad eva jijñāsyaṁ
tattva-jijñāsunātmanaḥ
anvaya-vyatirekābhyāṁ
yat syāt sarvatra sarvadā

etāvat—up to this; *eva*—certainly; *jijñāsyam*—is to be required; *tattva*—Absolute Truth; *jijñāsunā*—the student; *ātmanaḥ*—of the Self; *anvaya*—directly; *vyatirekābhyām*—indirectly; *yat*—whatever; *syāt*—it may be; *sarvatra*—in all space and time; *sarvadā*—in all circumstances.

TRANSLATION

A person who is searching after the Supreme Absolute Truth, the Personality of Godhead, has to search it out up to this, certainly in all circumstances, and in all space and time, and both directly and indirectly.

PURPORT

To unfold the mystery of *bhakti-yoga,* as it is explained in the previous verse, is the ultimate stage of all inquiries or the highest objective for the inquisitive. Everyone is searching after self-realization in different ways, namely by *karma-yoga,* by *jñāna-yoga,* by *dhyāna-yoga,* by *rāja-yoga,* or by *bhakti-yoga,* etc. To engage in self-realization is the responsibility of every living entity developed in consciousness. One who is developed in consciousness certainly makes enquiries into the mystery of the self, of the cosmic situation and of the problems of life, in all spheres and fields, namely social, political, economic, cultural, religious, moral, etc., and in their different branches. But here is explained the goal of all such inquiries.

The *Vedānta-sūtra* philosophy begins with this inquiry of life and the *Bhāgavatam* answers such inquiries up to this point, or the mystery of all inquiries. Lord Brahmā wanted to be perfectly educated by the Personality of Godhead, and here is the answer by the Lord finished in four nutshell verses, namely beginning from *aham eva* to this verse, *etāvad eva.* This is the end of all self-realization processes. Men do not know that the ultimate goal of life is Viṣṇu or the Supreme Personality of Godhead due to being bewildered by the glaring reflection in the darkness, and as such everyone is entering into the darkest region of material existence, driven by the uncontrolled senses. The whole material existence has sprung up by sense gratification, desires based principally on the sex desire, and the result is that in spite of all advancement of knowledge, the final goal of all activities of the living entities is sense gratification. But here is the real goal of life, and everyone should know it by inquiries put before a bona fide spiritual master expert in the science of *bhakti-yoga,* or from a living personality of *Bhāgavatam* life. Everyone is engaged in various kinds of scriptural inquiries, but the *Śrīmad-Bhāgavatam* gives answers to all of the various students of self-realization: this ultimate objective of life is not to be searched out without any great labor or perseverance. One who is imbued with such sincere inquiries must ask the bona fide spiritual master in the disciplic succession from Brahmājī, and that is the direction given here. Because the mystery was disclosed before Brahmājī by the Supreme Personality of Godhead, the mystery of all such inquiries regarding self-realization must be put before such a spiritual master who is directly the representative of the Lord, acknowledged in that disciplic succession. Such a bona fide spiritual master is able to clear up the whole thing by evidences from the revealed scriptures, both directly and indirectly. Although everyone is free to consult the revealed scriptures in this connection, still one requires the guidance of a bona fide spiritual master, and that is the direction in this verse. The bona fide spiritual master is the most confidential representative of the Lord, and one must receive direction from the spiritual master in the same spirit as Brahmājī received them from the Personality of Godhead, Lord Kṛṣṇa. The bona fide spiritual master in that bona fide chain of disciplic succession never claims to be the Lord Himself, although such a spiritual master is greater than the Lord in the sense that he can deliver the Lord by his personally realized experience. The Lord is not to be found simply by education or by a good fertile brain, but surely He can be found by the sincere student through the transparent medium of the bona fide spiritual master.

The revealed scriptures give direction directly to this end, but because the bewildered living entities are blinded by the glaring reflection in the darkness, they are unable to find out the truth of the revealed scriptures. For example, in the *Bhagavad-gītā* the whole direction is targetted toward the Personality of Godhead Lord Śrī Kṛṣṇa, but for want of a bona fide spiritual master in the line of Brahmājī or the direct hearer, Arjuna, there are different distortions of the revealed knowledge by many unauthorized persons who just want to satisfy their own whims. Undoubtedly the *Bhagavad-gītā* is accepted as one of the most brilliant stars in the horizon of the spiritual sky, yet the interpretations of the great book of knowledge have so grossly been distorted that every student of the *Bhagavad-gītā* is still in the same darkness of glaring material reflection, and such students are hardly enlightened by the *Bhagavad-gītā*. In the *Gītā* practically the same instruction is imparted as in the four prime verses of the *Bhāgavatam*, but due to wrong and fashionable interpretations by unauthorized persons, one cannot reach the ultimate conclusion. In the *Bhagavad-gītā* (Bg. 18.61) it is clearly said,

īśvaraḥ sarva-bhūtānāṁ hṛd-deśe 'rjuna tiṣṭhati
bhrāmayan sarva-bhūtāni yantrārūḍhāni māyayā

The Lord is situated in the heart of all living beings (as Paramātmā), and He is controlling all of them in the material world under the agency of His external energy. Therefore it is clearly mentioned that the Lord is the supreme controller and that the living entities are controlled by the Lord. In the same *Bhagavad-gītā* (Bg. 18.65) the Lord directs as follows:

manmanā bhava mad-bhakto
madyājī māṁ namaskuru
mām evaiṣyasi satyaṁ te
pratijāne priyo 'si me

It is clear in this verse of the *Bhagavad-gītā* that the direction of the Lord is that one should be Godminded, a devotee of the Lord, a worshiper of the Lord, and must offer all obeisances unto Lord Kṛṣṇa, and by so doing, the devotee will undoubtedly go back to Godhead, back to home.

Indirectly it is said that the whole Vedic social construction of human society is so made that everyone acts as the part and parcel of the complete body of the Lord. The intelligent class of men, or the *brāhmaṇas,* are situated on the face of the Lord; the administrative class of men, or the *kṣatriyas,* are situated on the arms of the Lord; the productive class of men, or the *vaiśyas,* are situated on the belt of the Lord; and the laborer class of men, or the *śūdras,* are situated on the legs of the Lord. Therefore the complete social construction is the body of the Lord, and each and every part of the body, namely the *brāhmaṇas,* the *kṣatriyas,* the *vaiśyas* and the *śūdras,* is meant to serve the Lord's whole body conjointly; otherwise it becomes unfit to be coordinated with the supreme consciousness of oneness. Universal consciousness is factually achieved by coordinated service of all concerned to the Supreme Personality of Godhead, and that alone can insure total perfection.

Therefore even the great scientists, the great philosophers, the great mental speculators, the great politicians, the great industrialists and the great social reformers, etc., cannot give any relief to the restless society of the material world because they do not know the secret of success as mentioned in this verse of the *Bhāgavatam,* namely that one must know the mystery of *bhakti-yoga.* In the *Bhagavad-gītā* also it is said,

na māṁ duṣkṛtino mūḍhāḥ prapadyante narādhamāḥ
māyayā 'pahṛta-jñānā āsuraṁ bhāvam āśritāḥ (Bg. 7.15)

The so-called great leaders of human society, because they are ignorant of this great knowledge of *bhakti-yoga* and are always engaged in the ignoble acts of sense gratification, bewildered by the external energy of the Lord, are stubborn rebels against the supremacy of the Supreme Personality of Godhead, and they never agree to surrender unto Him because they are fools, miscreants and the lowest type of human beings. Such faithless nonbelievers may be highly educated in the material sense of the term, but factually they are the greatest fools of the world because by the influence of the external material nature all their so-called acquisition of knowledge has been made null and void. Therefore all advancement of knowledge in the present context of things is being misused in terms of the cats and dogs fighting with one another for sense gratification, and all acquisition of knowledge in science, philosophy, fine arts, nationality, economic development, religiousness and great activities are being spoiled by being used as dresses for dead men. There is no utility in the dresses used for covering a coffin of the dead body save getting a false applause from the ignorant public. The *Śrīmad-Bhāgavatam* therefore says again and again that without attainment of the status of *bhakti-yoga,* all activities of the human society are to be considered as absolute failures only. It is said:

parābhavas tāvad abodha-jāto
yāvan na jijñāsata ātma-tattvam
yāvat kriyās tāvad idaṁ mano vai
karmātmakaṁ yena śarīra-bandhaḥ (*Bhāg.* 5.5.5)

As long as one is blind to inquiring after self-realization, all material activities, however great they may be, are all different kinds of defeat because the aim of human life is not fulfilled by such unwanted and profitless activities. The function of the human body is to attain freedom from the material bondage, but as long as one is fully absorbed in material activities, his mind will be overwhelmed in the whirlpool of matter, and thus he will continue to be encaged in the material bodies life after life.

evaṁ manaḥ karma-vaśaṁ prayuṅkte
avidyayātmany upadhīyamāne
prītir na yāvan mayi vāsudeve
na mucyate deha-yogena tāvat (*Bhāg.* 5.5.6)

It is one's mind that generates different kinds of bodies for suffering different kinds of material pangs. Therefore as long as the mind is absorbed in fruitive activities, it is to be understood that the mind is absorbed in nescience, and thus one is sure to again and again be subjected to material bondage in different bodies until one develops a transcendental love of Godhead, Vāsudeva, the Supreme Person. To become absorbed in the transcendental name, quality, form and activities of the Supreme Person, Vāsudeva, means to change the temper of the mind from matter to absolute knowledge, which leads one to the path of absolute realization and thus frees one from the bondage of material contact and encagements in different material bodies.

Śrīla Jīva Gosvāmī Prabhupāda therefore comments on the words *sarvatra sarvadā* in the sense that the principles of *bhakti-yoga,* or devotional service to the Lord, are apt in all circumstances, i.e., it is recommended in all the revealed scriptures, it is performed by all authorities, it is important in all places, it is useful in all causes and effects, etc. As far as all the revealed scriptures are concerned, he quotes from the *Skanda Purāṇa* on the topics of Brahmā and Nārada as follows:

saṁsāre 'smin mahā-ghore janma-mṛtyu-samākule
pūjanaṁ vāsudevasya tārakaṁ vādibhiḥ smṛtam.

In the material world, which is full of darkness and dangers, combined with birth and death and full with different anxieties, the only way to get out of the great entanglement is to accept loving transcendental devotional service of the Lord Vāsudeva. This is accepted by all classes of philosophers.

Śrīla Jīva Gosvāmī also quotes another common passage which is found in three *Purāṇas,* namely the *Padma Purāṇa,* the *Skanda Purāṇa* and *Linga Purāṇa.* It runs as follows:

āloḍya sarva-śāstrāni vicārya ca punaḥ punaḥ
idam ekaṁ suniṣpannaṁ dhyeyo nārāyaṇaḥ sadā.

"By scrutinizingly reviewing all the revealed scriptures and judging them again and again, it is now concluded that Lord Nārāyaṇa is the Supreme Absolute Truth, and thus He alone should be worshiped."

The same truth is also indirectly described as follows:

pāraṁ gato 'pi vedānāṁ sarva-śāstrārtha-vedyapi
yo na sarvesvare bhaktas taṁ vidyāt puruṣādhamam.

"Even though one may have gone to the other side of all the *Vedas,* and even though one is well versed in all the revealed scriptures, if one is not a devotee of the Supreme Lord, he must be considered to be the lowest of mankind." Similarly, it is also stated indirectly as follows:

yasyāsti bhaktir bhagavaty akiñcanā
sarvair guṇais tatra samāsate suraḥ
harāv abhakteṣu kuto mahat-guṇa-
mano-rathenāsato dhāvato yahi.

One who has unflinching devotion unto the Supreme Personality of Godhead must have all the good qualities of the demigods, and contrarily one who is not a devotee of the Lord must be hovering in the darkness of mental speculation and thus must be engaged in the material impermanence.

It is also said in the Eleventh Canto of *Śrīmad-Bhāgavatam:*

śabda brahmaṇi niṣṇāto na niṣṇāyāt pare yadi
śravas tasya śrama-phalo hy adhenum iva rakṣataḥ

"One may be well versed in all the transcendental literature of the *Vedas,* but if he fails to be acquainted with the Supreme, then it must be concluded that all of his education is like the burden of the beast or as one's keeping a cow without milking capacity."

Similarly, the liberty of discharging loving transcendental service to the Lord is invested in everyone, even the women, the *śūdras,* the forest tribes, or any other living beings who are born in sinful conditions.

te vai vidanty atitaranti ca deva-māyāṁ
strī-śūdra-hūṇa-śabarā api pāpa-jīvāḥ
yady adbhūta-krama-parāyaṇa-śīlaśikṣās
tiryag-janā api kimu śruta-dhāraṇā ye
(*Bhāg.* 2.7.46)

The lowest of human beings can be elevated to the highest stage of devotional life if they are trained up by the bona fide spiritual master well versed in the transcendental loving service of the Lord. If the lowest can be so elevated, then what to speak of the highest who are well versed in the Vedic knowledge? The conclusion is that devotional service of the Lord is open for all, regardless of who they are. That is the confirmation of its application for all kinds of performers of the service.

Therefore devotional service of the Lord with perfect knowledge through the training of a bona fide spiritual master is advised for everyone, even if they happen not to be human beings. This is confirmed in the *Garuḍa Purāṇa* as follows:

kīṭa-pakṣi-mṛgāṇāṁ ca harau sannyasta-karmaṇām
ūrdhvam eva gatiṁ manye kiṁ punar jñāninām nṛṇām

"Even the worms, birds and beasts are assured of elevation to the highest perfectional life if they are completely surrendered to the transcendental loving service of the Lord, so what to speak of those philosophers amongst the human beings?"

Therefore there is no need to seek properly qualified candidates for discharging devotional service of the Lord. Let them be either well behaved or ill trained, let them be either learned or fools, let them be either grossly attached or in the renounced order of life, let them be liberated souls or desirous of salvation, let them be inexpert in the discharge of devotional service or expert in the same, all of them can be elevated to the supreme position by discharge of devotional service under the proper guidance. This is also confirmed in the *Bhagavad-gītā* as follows:

api cet sudurācāro bhajate mām ananya-bhāk
sādhur eva sa mantavyaḥ samyag vyavasito hi saḥ

māṁ hi pārtha vyapāśritya ye 'pi syuḥ pāpa-yonayaḥ
striyo vaiśyās tathā śūdrās te 'pi yānti parāṁ gatim
(Bg. 9.30,32)

Even if a person is fully addicted to all sorts of sinful acts, if he happens to be engaged in the loving transcendental service of the Lord under proper guidance, he is to be considered the most perfect holy man without a doubt. And thus any person, whatsoever and whosoever he or she may be—even the fallen woman, the less intelligent laborer class or the dull mercantile type of men, or even men lower than all these—can attain the highest perfection of life by going back home, back to Godhead, provided he or she takes shelter of the lotus feet of the Lord in all earnestness. This sincere earnestness is the only qualification that can lead one to the highest perfectional stage of life, and unless and until such real earnestness is aroused, there is a difference between cleanliness or uncleanliness, learning or nonlearning in the material estimation. The fire is always fire, and thus if someone touches the fire, knowingly or unknowingly, the fire will act in its own way without any discrimination. The principle is: *harir harati pāpāni duṣṭa-cittair api smṛtaḥ.* The all-powerful Lord can purify the devotee of all sinful reactions, just as the sun can sterilize all sorts of infections by its powerful rays. "Attraction of material enjoyment cannot act upon a pure devotee of the Lord." There are hundreds and thousands of aphorisms in the revealed scriptures. *Ātmārāmāś ca munayaḥ.* Even the self-realized souls are also attracted by the transcendental loving service of the Lord. *Kecit kevalayā bhaktyā vāsudeva-parāyaṇā*: "Simply by hearing and chanting, one becomes a great devotee of Lord Vāsudeva." *Na calati bhagavat-padāravindāl lavanimiṣārdham api sa vaiṣṇavāgryaḥ:* "A person who does not move from the lotus feet of the Lord even for a moment or a second is to be considered the greatest of all Vaiṣṇavas." *Bhagavat-pārṣadatāṁ prāpte mat-sevayā pratītaṁ te:* "The pure devotees are convinced of attaining the association of the Personality of Godhead, and thus they are always engaged in the transcendental loving service of the Lord." Therefore in all continents, in all planets, in all universes, there is currency of devotional service of the Lord, or *bhakti-yoga,* and that is the statement of the *Śrīmad-Bhāgavatam* and allied scriptures. Everywhere means in every part of the creation of the Lord. The Lord can be served by all the senses, or even simply by the mind. The South Indian *brāhmaṇa* who served the Lord simply on the strength of his mind also factually realized the Lord. Success is guaranteed for a devotee who fully engages any one of his senses in the mode of devotional service. The Lord can be served by any ingredient, even the most common commodities—a flower, a leaf, a fruit or a little water, which are available in any part of the universe and without any cost—and thus the Lord is served universally by the universal entities. He can be served simply by hearing, He can be served simply by chanting or reading about His activities, He can be served simply by adoring Him and accepting Him.

In the *Bhagavad-gītā* it is stated that one can serve the Lord by offering the result of one's own work; it does not matter what one does. Generally men may say that whatever they are doing is inspired by God, but that is not all. One should actually work on behalf of God as a servant of God. The Lord says in the *Bhagavad-gītā:* (Bg. 9.27)

yat karoṣi yad aśnāsi yaj juhoṣi dadāsi yat
yat tapasyasi kaunteya tat kuruṣva mad-arpaṇam

Do whatever you like or whatever may be easier for you to do, eat whatever you may eat, sacrifice whatever you can sacrifice, give whatever you may give in charity, and do whatever you may undertake in penance, but everything must be done for Him only. If you do business or if you accept some employment, do so on behalf of the Lord. Whatever you may eat, you may offer the same to the Lord and be assured that He will return the food after eating it Himself. He is the complete whole, and therefore whatever He may eat as offered by the devotee is accepted because of the devotee's love, but again it is returned as *prasādam* for the devotee so that he can be happy by eating. In other words, be a servant of God and live peacefully in that consciousness, ultimately returning home, back to Godhead.

It is said, *yasya smṛtyā ca nāmoktyā tapo-yajña-kriyādiṣu nūnaṁ sampūrṇatāmeti sadyo vandetam acyutam.* I offer my obeisances unto Him, the infallible, because simply by either remembering Him or vibrating His holy name one can attain the perfection of all penances, sacrifices or fruitive activities, and this process can be universally followed. It is enjoined, *akāmaḥ sarva-kāmo vā mokṣa-kāma udarādhiḥ tibreṇa bhakti-yogena yajeta puruṣaṁ param:* "A person, though he may be full of desires or may have no desires, may follow this path of infallible *bhakti-yoga* for complete perfection." One need not be anxious to propitiate each and every demigod and goddess because the root of all of them is the Personality of Godhead. As by pouring water on the root of the tree all the branches and leaves are served and enlivened, so by rendering service unto the Supreme Lord every god and goddess becomes automatically served without extraneous effort. The Lord is all-pervading, and therefore service unto Him is also all-pervading. This fact is corroborated in the *Skanda Purāṇa* as follows: *"arcite deva-deveśe śaṅkha-cakra-gadādhare. arcitaḥ sarva-devaḥ syur yataḥ sarva-gato hariḥ."* When the Supreme Lord, the Personality of Godhead, who carries in His hands a conchshell, wheel, club, and lotus flower, is worshiped, certainly all other demigods are worshiped automatically because Hari the Personality of Godhead is all-pervading. Therefore, in all cases, namely nominative, objective, causative, dative, ablative, possessive and supportive, everyone is benefitted by such transcendental loving service of the Lord. The man who worships the Lord, the Lord Himself who is worshiped, the cause for which the Lord is worshiped, the source of supply, the place where such worship is done, etc.—everything is benefitted by such an action.

Even during the annihilation of the material world, the process of *bhakti-yoga* can be applied. *Kālena naṣṭā pralaye vāṇīyam:* the Lord is worshiped in devastation because He protects the *Vedas* from being annihilated. He is worshiped in every millennium or *yuga*, as it is said,

kṛte yad dhyāyato viṣṇuṁ tretāyāṁ yajato makhaiḥ
dvāpare paricaryāyāṁ kalau taddhari-kīrtanāt

In the *Viṣṇu Purāṇa* it is written: "*sa hānis tan-mahacchidram sa mohaḥ sa ca vibhramaḥ yan-muhūrtaṁ kṣaṇaṁ vāpi vāsudevaṁ na cintayet.*" If even for a moment remembrance of Vāsudeva, the Supreme Personality of Godhead, is missed, that is the greatest loss, that is the greatest illusion, and that is the greatest anomaly. The Lord can be worshiped in all stages of life. For instance, even in the womb of their mothers Mahārāja Prahlāda and Mahārāja Parīkṣit worshiped the Lord; even in his very childhood, at the age of only five years, Dhruva Mahārāja worshiped the Lord; even in full youth, Mahārāja Ambarīṣa worshiped the Lord; and even at the last stage of his frustration and old age Mahārāja Dhṛtarāṣṭra worshiped the Lord. Ajāmila worshiped the Lord even at the point of death, and the Lord was worshiped by Citraketu even in heaven and in hell. In the *Narasiṁha Purāṇa* it is said that as the hellish inhabitants began to chant the holy name of the Lord they began to be elevated from hell towards heaven. Durvāsā Muni has also supported this view: "*mucyeta yan-nāmny udite nārako 'pi.*" Simply by chanting the holy name of the Lord the inhabitants of hell became released from their hellish persecution. So the conclusion of *Śrīmad-Bhāgavatam,* as given by Śukadeva Gosvāmī to Mahārāja Parīkṣit, is: *etad nirvidyā manānām icchatam akuto-bhayam yoginānam api nirṇītam harer nāmānukīrtanam:* "O King, it is finally decided that everyone, namely those in the renounced order of life, the mystics, and the enjoyers of fruitive work, should chant the holy name of the Lord fearlessly to achieve the desired success in their pursuits."

Similarly, it is indicated indirectly in various places of revealed scriptures:

1. Even though one is well versed in all the *Vedas* and scriptures, if one is not a devotee of the Supreme Lord, the Personality of Godhead, he is considered to be the lowest of mankind.

2. In the *Garuḍa Purāṇa, Bṛhad-Nāradīya Purāṇa* and *Padma Purāṇa,* the same is repeated: What is the use of Vedic knowledge and penances for one who is devoid of devotional service of the Lord?

3. What is the comparison of thousands of Prajāpatis with one devotee of the Lord?

4. Śukadeva Gosvāmī said (*Bhāg.* 2.4.17) that neither the ascetic, nor one who is greatly munificent, nor one who is famous, nor the great

philosopher, nor the great occultist, nor anyone else can achieve the desired result without being engaged in the service of the Lord.

5. Even if a place is more glorious than heaven, if there is no glorification of the Lord of Vaikuṇṭha nor His pure devotee, it should be at once quitted.

6. The pure devotee refuses to accept all the five different types of liberation in order to be engaged in the service of the Lord.

The final conclusion, therefore, is that the glories of the Lord must be always and everywhere proclaimed, one should hear about His glories, one should chant about His glories, and one should always remember His glories because that is the highest perfectional stage of life. As far as fruitive work is concerned, it is limited to an enjoyable body; as far as *yoga* is concerned, it is limited to the acquirement of mystic power; as far as empiric philosophy is concerned, it is limited to the attainment of transcendental knowledge; and as far as transcendental knowledge is concerned, it is limited to attainment of salvation. Even if they are adopted, there is every chance of discrepencies in discharging the particular type of functions. But adoptation of the transcendental devotional service of the Lord has no limit, nor is there fear of falling down. The process reaches automatically to the final stage by the grace of the Lord. In the preliminary stage of devotional service there is an apparent requisition of knowledge, but in the higher stage there is no necessity of such knowledge. The best and guaranteed path of progress is therefore engagement in *bhakti-yoga*, pure devotional service.

The cream of *Śrīmad-Bhāgavatam* in the foregoing four *ślokas* is sometimes squeezed out by the impersonalist for different interpretations in their favor, but it should be carefully noted that the four *ślokas* were first described by the Personality of Godhead Himself, and thus the impersonalist has no scope to enter into them because he has no conception of the Personality of Godhead. Therefore, the impersonalist may squeeze out any interpretations from them, but such interpretations will never be accepted by those who are taught in the disciplic succession from Brahmā, as will be cleared up in the following verses. Besides that, the *Śruti* confirms that the Supreme Truth Absolute Personality of Godhead never reveals Himself to anyone who is falsely proud of his academic knowledge. The *Śruti mantra* clearly says:

nāyam ātmā pravacanena labhyo na medhayā na bahudhā śrutena
yam evaiṣa vṛṇute tena labhyas tasyaiṣa ātmā vivṛṇute tanuṁ svām

The whole matter is explained by the Lord Himself, and one who has no approach to the Lord in His personal feature can rarely understand the purport of *Śrīmad-Bhāgavatam* without being taught by the *bhāgavatas* in the disciplic succession.

TEXT 37

एतन्मतं समातिष्ठ परमेण समाधिना ।
भवान् कल्पविकल्पेषु न विमुह्यति कर्हिचित् ॥३७॥

etan mataṁ samātiṣṭha
parameṇa samādhinā
bhavān kalpa-vikalpeṣu
na vimuhyati karhicit

etat—this is; *matam*—the conclusion; *samātiṣṭha*—remain fixed up; *parameṇa*—by the Supreme; *samādhinā*—concentration of the mind; *bhavān*—yourself; *kalpa*—intermediate devastation; *vikalpeṣu*—in the final devastation; *na vimuhyati*—will never bewilder; *karhicit*—anything like complacence.

TRANSLATION

O Brahmā, just follow this conclusion by fixed concentration of mind, and no pride will disturb you, neither in the partial nor final devastations."

PURPORT

As in the *Bhagavad-gītā*, Tenth Chapter, the Personality of Godhead, Lord Kṛṣṇa, has summarized the whole text in four verses, namely, *"ahaṁ sarvasya prabhavaḥ,"* etc., so also the complete *Śrīmad-Bhāgavatam* also has been summarized in four verses, as *aham evāsam evāgre*, etc., and the secret purpose of the most important *Bhāgavatite* conclusion is explained by the original speaker of the *Śrīmad-Bhāgavatam*, who was also the original speaker of the *Bhagavad-gītā*, the Personality of Godhead, Lord Śrī Kṛṣṇa. There are many grammarians and nondevotee material wranglers who have tried to present false interpretations of these four verses of the *Śrīmad-Bhāgavatam*, but the Lord Himself advised Brahmājī not to be deviated from the fixed conclusion the Lord taught him. The Lord was the teacher of the nucleus four verses of *Śrīmad-Bhāgavatam,* and Brahmā was the receiver of the knowledge. Misinterpretation of the word *aham* by the word jugglery of the impersonalist should not disturb the mind of the strict followers of the *Śrīmad-Bhāgavatam. Śrīmad-Bhāgavatam* is the text of the Personality of Godhead and His unalloyed devotees, who are also known as the *Bhāgavatas,* and any outsider should have no access to this confidential literature of devotional service. But unfortunately the impersonalist, who has no relation with the Supreme Personality of Godhead, sometime tries to interpret *Śrīmad-Bhāgavatam* by his poor fund of knowledge in grammar and dry speculation. Therefore, the Lord warns Brahmā (and, through Brahmā, all future devotees of the Lord in the disciplic succession of Brahmā) that one should never be misled by the conclusion of the so-called grammarians or by other men with a poor fund of knowledge, but must always fix the mind properly, via the *paramparā* system. No one should try to give a new interpretation by dint of mundane knowledge. And the first thing, therefore, in pursuance of the system of knowledge received by Brahmā is to approach a bona fide *guru* who is the representative of the Lord following the *paramparā* system. No one should try to squeeze out his own meaning by imperfect mundane knowledge. The *guru,* or the bona fide spiritual master, is competent to teach the disciple in the right path with reference to the context of all authentic Vedic literature. He does not attempt to juggle words to bewilder the student. The bona fide spiritual master, by his personal activities, teaches the disciple the principles of devotional service. Without personal service, like the impersonalist and dry speculators, one would go on speculating life after life and would be unable to reach the final conclusion. By following the instructions of the bona fide spiritual master in conjunction with the principles of revealed scriptures, the student will rise to the plane of complete knowledge, which will be exhibited by development of detachment from the world of sense gratification. The mundane wranglers are surprised as to how one can detach himself from the world of sense gratification, and thus any attempt to be fixed in God realization appears to them to be mysticism. This detachment from the sensory world is called the *brahma-bhūta stage of realization,* the preliminary stage of transcendental devotional life (*parā bhaktiḥ*). The *brahma-bhūta* stage of life is also known as the *ātmārāma* stage, in which one is fully self-satisfied and does not hanker for the world of sense enjoyment. This stage of full satisfaction is the proper situation for understanding the transcendental knowledge of the Personality of Godhead. The *Śrīmad-Bhāgavatam* affirms this:

evaṁ prasanna-manaso bhagavat-bhakti-yogataḥ
bhagavat-tattva-vijñānaṁ mukta-saṅgasya jayate.(*Bhāg.* 1.2.20)

Thus in the completely satisfied stage of life, exhibited by full detachment from the world of sense enjoyment as the result of performing devotional service, one can understand the science of God in the liberated stage.

In this stage of full satisfaction and detachment from the sensory world, one can know the mystery of the science of God with all its confidential intricacies, and not by grammar or academic speculation. And because Brahmā qualified himself for such reception, the Lord was pleased to disclose the purpose of *Śrīmad-Bhāgavatam.* This direct instruction by the Lord to any devotee who is detached from the world of sense gratification is possible, as is stated in the *Bhagavad-gītā:*

teṣāṁ satata-yuktānāṁ bhajatāṁ prīti-pūrvakam
dadāmi buddhi-yogaṁ taṁ yena mām upayanti te. (Bg. 10.10)

Unto the devotees who are constantly engaged in the transcendental loving service *(prīti-pūrvakam)* of the Lord, the Lord out of His causeless mercy upon the devotee gives direct instructions so that the devotee may make accurate progress on the path of returning home, back to Godhead. One should not, therefore, try to understand these four verses of *Śrīmad-Bhāgavatam* by mental speculation. Rather, by direct perception of the Supreme Personality of Godhead, one is able to know all about His abode, Vaikuṇṭha, as was seen and experienced by Brahmājī. Such Vaikuṇṭha realization is possible by any devotee of the Lord situated in the transcendental position as a result of devotional service.

In the *Gopāla-tāpanī Upaniṣad (Śruti)* it is said that the Lord appeared before Brahmājī as *"gopa-veśome purastād āvirbhūvaḥ":* the Lord appeared before Brahmā as a cowboy, that is, as the original Personality of Godhead, Lord Śrī Kṛṣṇa, Govinda, who is later described by Brahmājī in his *Brahma-saṁhitā:*

cintāmaṇi-prakara-sadmasu kalpavṛkṣa-
lakṣāvṛteṣu surabhīr abhipālayantam
lakṣmī-sahasra-śata-sambhrama-sevyamānaṁ
govindam ādi-puruṣaṁ tam ahaṁ bhajāmi. (Bs. 5.29)

Brahmājī desires to worship the original Personality of Godhead, Lord Śrī Kṛṣṇa, who resides in the topmost Vaikuṇṭha planet, known as Goloka

Vṛndāvana, and where He is in the habit of keeping *surabhi* cows as a cowboy, and where He is served by hundreds and thousands of goddesses of fortune (the *gopīs)* with love and respect.

Therefore Lord Śrī Kṛṣṇa is the original form of the Supreme Lord *(kṛṣṇas tu bhagavān svayam).* This is also clear in this instruction. The Supreme Personality of Godhead is Lord Kṛṣṇa, and not directly *Nārāyaṇa or puruṣa-avatāras* because such manifestations are subsequent. Therefore *Śrīmad-Bhāgavatam* means consciousness of the Supreme Personality of Godhead Lord Śrī Kṛṣṇa, and *Śrīmad-Bhāgavatam* is the sound representation of the Lord as much as the *Bhagavad-gītā* is. Thus the conclusion is that *Śrīmad-Bhāgavatam* is the science of the Lord in which the Lord and His abode are perfectly realized.

TEXT 38

श्रीशुक उवाच
सम्प्रदिश्यैवमजनो जनानां परमेष्ठिनम् ।
पश्यतस्तस्य तद् रूपमात्मनो न्यरुणद्धरिः ॥३८॥

śrī śuka uvāca
sampradiśyaivam ajano
janānāṁ parameṣṭhinam
paśyatas tasya tad-rūpam
ātmano nyaruṇaddhariḥ

śrī śukaḥ uvāca—Śrī Śukadeva Gosvāmī said; *sampradiśya*—thus fully instructing Brahmājī; *evam*—thus; *ajanaḥ*—the Supreme Lord; *janānām*—of the living entities; *parameṣṭhinam*—unto the supreme leader, Brahmā; *paśyataḥ*—while he was seeing; *tasya*—His; *tat-rūpam*—that transcendental form; *ātmanaḥ*—of the Absolute; *nyaruṇat*—disappeared; *hariḥ*—the Lord, the Personality of Godhead.

TRANSLATION

The Supreme Personality of Godhead, Hari, after being seen in His transcendental form, instructing Brahmājī, the leader of the living entities, disappeared," said Śukadeva Gosvāmī to Mahārāja Parīkṣit.

PURPORT

In this verse it is clearly mentioned that the Lord is *ajanaḥ,* or the Supreme Person, and He was showing His transcendental form *(ātmano rūpam)* to Brahmājī while He was instructing him in the summarization of *Śrīmad-Bhāgavatam* in four verses. He is *ajanaḥ,* or the Supreme Person amongst *janānām,* or all persons. All living entities are individual persons, and amongst all such persons Lord Hari is Supreme, as it is confirmed in the *Śruti mantra, nityo nityānāṁ cetanaś cetanānām.* So there is no place for impersonal features in the transcendental world as there are impersonal features in the material world. Whenever there is *cetana,* or knowledge, the personal feature comes in. In the spiritual world everything is full of knowledge, and therefore everything in the transcendental world is personal; nothing is impersonal there. In the transcendental world, the land, the water, the tree, the mountain, the river, the man, the animal, the bird and everything are all of the same quality, namely *cetana,* and therefore everything there is individual and personal. *Śrīmad-Bhāgavatam* gives us this information as the supreme Vedic literature, and it was personally instructed by the Supreme Personality of Godhead to Brahmājī so that the leader of the living entities might broadcast the message to all in the universe in order to teach the supreme knowledge of *bhakti-yoga.* Brahmājī in his turn instructed Nārada, his beloved son, the same message of *Śrīmad-Bhāgavatam,* and Nārada, in his turn, taught the same to Vyāsadeva, who again taught it to Śukadeva Gosvāmī, and through Śukadeva Gosvāmī's grace and by the mercy of Mahārāja Parīkṣit we are all given *Śrīmad-Bhāgavatam* perpetually to learn the science of the Absolute Personality of Godhead, Lord Kṛṣṇa.

TEXT 39

अन्तर्हितेन्द्रियार्थाय हरये विहिताञ्जलिः ।
सर्वभूतमयो विश्वं ससर्जेदं स पूर्ववत् ।।३९।।

antarhitendriyārthāya
haraye vihitāñjaliḥ
sarva-bhūtamayo viśvaṁ
sasarjedaṁ sa pūrvavat

antarhita—on disappearance; *indriya-arthāya*—unto the Personality of Godhead, the objective of all senses; *haraye*—unto the Lord; *vihita-añjaliḥ*—

in folded hands; *sarva-bhūta*—all living entities; *mayaḥ*—full of; *viśvam*—the universe; *sasarja*—created; *idam*—this; *saḥ*—he, Brahmājī; *pūrvavat*—exactly like before.

TRANSLATION

On the disappearance of the Supreme Personality of Godhead, Hari, who is the object of transcendental enjoyment for the senses of devotees, Brahmā, with folded hands, began to recreate the universe full with living entities, as it was previously.

PURPORT

The Supreme Personality of Godhead, Hari, is the object for fulfilling the senses of all living entities. Illusioned by the glaring reflection of the external energy, the living entities worship the senses instead of engaging them properly in fulfilling the desires of the Supreme.

In the *Hari-bhakti-sudhodaya* there is the following verse:

akṣinoḥ phalaṁ tvādṛśaṁ darśanaṁ hi
tanoḥ phalaṁ tvādṛśa-gatra-saṅgaḥ
jihvā-phalaṁ tvādṛśa-kīrtanaṁ hi
sudurlabha-bhāgavataṁ hi loke.

"O devotee of the Lord, the purpose of the visual sense is fulfilled simply by seeing you, and to touch your body is the fulfillment of this bodily touch. The tongue is meant for glorifying your qualifies because in this world it is very difficult to find a pure devotee of the Lord."

Originally the senses of the living entity were awarded for this purpose, namely to engage them in the transcendental loving service of the Lord or that of His devotees, but the conditioned souls, illusioned by the material energy, became captivated by sense enjoyment. Therefore the whole process of God consciousness is meant to rectify the conditional activities of the senses and to re-engage them in the direct service of the Lord. Lord Brahmā thus engaged his senses in the Lord by recreating the conditioned living entities to act in the recreated universe. This material universe is thus created and annihilated by the will of the Lord. It is created to give a chance to the conditioned soul to act to return home, back to Godhead, and servants like Brahmājī, Nāradajī, Vyāsajī and their company become busy with the same purpose of the Lord: to reclaim the conditioned souls from the field of sense gratification and return them to the normal stage of engaging the senses in service of the Lord. Instead of doing so, i.e. converting the actions of the senses, the impersonalists began to make the conditioned souls sense-less, and the Lord also sense-less. That is improper treatment for the conditioned souls. The diseased condition of the senses may be treated by curing the defect, but not uprooting it altogether. When there is some disease in the eyes, the eyes may be cured to see properly. Plucking out the eyes is no treatment. Similarly, the whole material disease is based on the process of sense gratification, and liberation from the diseased condition is to re-engage the senses to see the beauty of the Lord, hear His glories, and act on His account. Thus Brahmājī recreated the universal activities again.

TEXT 40

प्रजापतिर्धर्मपतिरेकदा नियमान् यमान् ।
भद्रं प्रजानामन्विच्छन्नातिष्ठत् स्वार्थकाम्यया ॥३९॥

prajāpatir dharmapatir
ekadā niyamān yamān
bhadraṁ prajānām anvicchann
ātiṣṭhat svārtha-kāmyayā

prajā-patiḥ—the forefather of all living entities; *dharma-patiḥ*—the father of religious life; *ekadā*—once upon a time; *niyamān*—rules and regulations; *yamān*—principles of control; *bhadram*—welfare; *prajānām*—of the living beings; *anvicchan*—desiring; *ātiṣṭhat*—situated; *sva-artha*—own interest; *kāmyayā*—so desiring.

TRANSLATION

Thus once upon a time the forefather of living entities and the father of religiousness, Lord Brahmā, situated himself in the acts of regulative principles, desiring self-interest for the welfare of all living entities.

PURPORT

No one can be situated in an exalted position without having undertaken a regulative life of rules and regulations. An unrestricted life of sense gratification is animal life, and Lord Brahmā, in order to teach all concerned within the jurisdiction of his generations, taught the same principles of sense control for executing higher duties. He desired the welfare of everyone as servants of God, and anyone desiring the welfare of the members of his family and generations must conduct a moral, religious life. The highest life of moral principles is to become a devotee of the Lord because one who is a pure devotee of the Lord has all the good qualities of the Lord. On the other hand, one who is not a devotee of the Lord, however qualified he may be in the mundane sense of the term, cannot be qualified with any good quality worthy of the name. The pure devotees of the Lord, like Brahmā and persons in the chain of disciplic succession, do not do anything to instruct their subordinates without acting accordingly themselves.

TEXT 41

तं नारदः प्रियतमो रिक्थादानामनुव्रतः ।
शुश्रूषमाणः शीलेन प्रश्रयेण दमेन च ॥४०॥

taṁ nāradaḥ priyatamo
rikthādānām anuvrataḥ
śuśrūṣamāṇaḥ śīlena
praśrayeṇa damena ca

tam—unto him; *nāradaḥ*—the great sage Nārada; *priyatamaḥ*—very dear; *rikthādānām*—of the inheritor sons; *anuvrataḥ*—very obedient; *śuśrūṣamāṇaḥ*—always ready to serve; *śīlena*—by good behavior; *praśrayeṇa*—by meekness; *damena*—by sense control; *ca*—also.

TRANSLATION

Nārada, the most dear of the inheritor sons of Brahmā, always ready to serve his father, strictly follows the instructions of his father by his mannerly behavior, meekness and sense control.

TEXT 42

मायां विविदिषन् विष्णोर्मायेशस्य महामुनिः ।
महाभागवतो राजन् पितरं पर्यतोषयत् ॥४१॥

māyāṁ vividiṣan viṣṇor
māyeśasya mahā-muniḥ
mahā-bhāgavato rājan
pitaraṁ paryatoṣayat

māyām—energies; *vividiṣan*—desiring to know; *viṣṇoḥ*—of the Personality of Godhead; *māyā-īśasya*—of the master of all energies; *mahā-muniḥ*—the great sage; *mahā-bhāgavataḥ*—the first-class devotee of the Lord; *rājan*—O King; *pitaram*—unto his father; *paryatoṣayat*—very much pleased.

TRANSLATION

Nārada very much pleased his father and desired to know all about the energies of Viṣṇu, the master of all energies, for he [Nārada] was the greatest of all sages and greatest of all devotees, O King.

PURPORT

Lord Brahmā, being the creator of all living beings in the universe, is originally the father of several well-known sons, like Dakṣa, the Sanakas, and Nārada. In three departments of human knowledge, namely fruitive work (*karma-kāṇḍa*), transcendental knowledge (*jñāna-kāṇḍa*), and devotional service (*upāsanā-kāṇḍa*), disseminated by the *Vedas,* Devarṣi Nārada inherited from his father Brahmā devotional service, whereas the Dakṣas inherited from their father fruitive work, and Sanaka, Sanātana, etc., inherited from their father information about *jñāna-kāṇḍa,* or transcendental knowledge. But out of them all, Nārada is described here as the most beloved son of Brahmā because of good behavior, obedience, meekness and readiness to render service unto the father. And Nārada is famous as the greatest of all sages because of his being the greatest of all devotees. Nārada is the spiritual master of many famous devotees of the Lord. He is spiritual master of Prahlāda, Dhruva and Vyāsa, down to the forest animal hunter Kirāṭa. His only business is to turn everyone to the transcendental loving service of the Lord. Therefore all these features of Nārada make him the dearmost son of his father, and all this is due to Nārada's being a first-class devotee of the Lord. The devotees are always anxious to know more and more about the Supreme Lord, the master of all energies. As is confirmed in the *Bhagavad-gītā*:

mac-cittā mad-gata-prāṇā bodhayantaḥ parasparam
kathayantaś ca māṁ nityaṁ tuṣyanti ca ramanti ca
(Bg. 10.9)

The Supreme Lord is unlimited, and His energies are also unlimited. No one can know them completely. Brahmājī, being the greatest living entity within this universe and being directly instructed by the Lord, must know more than anyone within this universe, although such knowledge may not be complete, and thus it is the duty of everyone to ask about the unlimited Lord from the spiritual master in the disciplic succession of Brahmā, which descends from Nārada to Vyāsa, from Vyāsa to Śukadeva and so on.

TEXT 43

तुष्टं निशाम्य पितरं लोकानां प्रपितामहम् ।
देवर्षिः परिपप्रच्छ भवान् यन्मानुपृच्छति ॥४३॥

tuṣṭaṁ niśāmya pitaraṁ
lokānāṁ prapitāmaham
devarṣiḥ paripapraccha
bhavān yan mānupṛcchati

tuṣṭam—satisfied; *niśāmya*—after seeing; *pitaram*—the father; *lokānām*—of the whole universe; *prapitāmaham*—the great-grandfather; *devarṣiḥ*—the great sage Nārada; *paripapraccha*—inquired; *bhavān*—yourself; *yat*—as it is; *mā*—from me; *anupṛcchati*—inquiring.

TRANSLATION

The great sage Nārada also inquired in detail from his father Brahmā, the great-grandfather of all the universe, after seeing him well satisfied.

PURPORT

The process of understanding spiritual or transcendental knowledge from the realized person is not exactly like asking an ordinary question from the schoolmaster. The schoolmasters in the modern days are paid agents for giving some information, but the spiritual master is not a paid agent. Nor can he impart instruction without being authorized. In the *Bhagavad-gītā,* the process of understanding transcendental knowledge is directed as follows:

tad viddhi praṇipātena paripraśnena sevayā
upadekṣyanti te jñānaṁ jñāninas tattva-darśinaḥ

Arjuna was advised to receive transcendental knowledge from the realized person by surrender, questions and service. Receiving transcendental knowledge is not like exchanging dollars; such knowledge has to be received by service to the spiritual master. As Brahmājī received the knowledge directly from the Lord by satisfying Him fully, similarly one has to receive the transcendental knowledge from the spiritual master by satisfying him. The spiritual master's satisfaction is the means of assimilating transcendental knowledge. One cannot understand transcendental knowledge simply by becoming a grammarian. The *Vedas* declared:

yasya deve parā bhaktir yathā deve tathā gurau
tasyaite kathitā hy arthaḥ prakāśante mahātmanaḥ

"Only unto one who has unflinching devotion to the Lord and to the spiritual master does transcendental knowledge become automatically revealed." Such a relationship between the disciple and the spiritual master is eternal. One who is now the disciple is the next spiritual master. And one cannot be a bona fide and authorized spiritual master unless one has been strictly obedient to his spiritual master. Brahmājī, as disciple of the Supreme Lord, received the real knowledge and imparted it to his dear disciple Nārada, and similarly Nārada, as spiritual master, handed over this knowledge to Vyāsa and so on. Therefore the so-called formal spiritual master and disciple are not facsimiles of Brahmā and Nārada or Nārada or Vyāsa. The relationship between Brahmā and Nārada is reality, while the so-called formality is the relation between the cheater and cheated. It is clearly mentioned herewith that Nārada is not only well behaved, meek and obedient, but is also self-controlled. One who is not self-controlled, specifically in sex life, can neither become a disciple nor a spiritual master. One must have disciplinary training in controlling speaking, anger, tongue, mind, belly and the genitals. One who has controlled the particular senses mentioned above is called a *gosvāmī.* Without becoming a *gosvāmī* one can neither become a disciple nor a spiritual master. The so-called spiritual master without sense control is certainly the cheater, and the disciple of such a so-called spiritual master is the cheated.

One should not think of Brahmājī as a dead great-grandfather, as we have experience in this planet. He is the oldest great-grandfather, and he is still living, and Nārada is also living. The age of the inhabitants of the Brahmaloka planet is mentioned in the *Bhagavad-gītā.* The inhabitants of this small planet earth can hardly calculate even the duration of one day of Brahmā.

TEXT 44

तस्मा इदं भागवतं पुराणं दशलक्षणम् ।
प्रोक्तं भगवता प्राह प्रीतः पुत्राय भूतकृत् ॥४४॥

tasmā idaṁ bhāgavataṁ
purāṇaṁ daśa-lakṣaṇam
proktaṁ bhagavatā prāha
prītaḥ putrāya bhūta-kṛt

tasmai—thereupon; *idam*—this; *bhāgavatam*—the glories of the Lord or the science of the Lord; *purāṇam*—Vedic supplementary; *daśa-lakṣaṇam*—ten characteristics; *proktam*—described; *bhagavatā*—by the Personality of Godhead; *prāha*—said; *prītaḥ*—in satisfaction; *putrāya*—unto the son; *bhūta-kṛt*—the creator of the universe.

TRANSLATION

Thereupon the supplementary Vedic literature, Śrīmad-Bhāgavatam, which was described by the Personality of Godhead and contains ten characteristics, was told by the father [Brahmā] to his son Nārada with satisfaction.

PURPORT

Although the *Śrīmad-Bhāgavatam* was spoken in four verses, it had ten characteristics which will be explained in the next chapter. In the four verses it is first said that the Lord existed before the creation, and thus the beginning of the *Śrīmad-Bhāgavatam* includes the *Vedānta* aphorism, *janmādyasya. Janmādyasya* is the beginning, yet the four verses in which it is said that the Lord is the root of everything that be, beginning from the creation up to the supreme abode of the Lord, naturally explain the ten characteristics. One should not misunderstand by wrong interpretations that the Lord spoke only four verses, and therefore all the rest of the 17,994 verses are all useless. The ten characteristics, as will be explained in the next chapter, require so many verses just to explain them properly. Brahmājī also advised Nārada previously that he should expand the idea that he had heard from Brahmājī. Śrī Caitanya Mahāprabhu instructed this to Śrīla Rūpa Gosvāmī in a nutshell, but the disciple Rūpa Gosvāmī expanded this very elaborately, and the same subject was further expanded by Jīva Gosvāmī and even further by Śrī Viśvanātha Cakravartī Ṭhākur. We are just trying to follow in the footsteps of all these authorities. So *Śrīmad-Bhāgavatam* is not like ordinary fiction or mundane literature. It is unlimited in strength, and however one may expand it to one's own capacity, *Bhāgavatam* still cannot be finished by such expansion. *Śrīmad-Bhāgavatam,* being the sound representation of the Lord, is simultaneously explained in four verses, as well as in four billions of verses all the same, inasmuch as the Lord is smaller than the atom and bigger than the unlimited sky. Such is the potency of *Śrīmad-Bhāgavatam.*

TEXT 45

नारदः प्राह मुनये सरस्वत्यास्तटे नृप ।
ध्यायते ब्रह्म परमं व्यासायामिततेजसे ॥४५॥

nāradaḥ prāha munaye
sarasvatyās taṭe nṛpa
dhyāyate brahma paramaṁ
vyāsāyāmita-tejase

nāradaḥ—the great sage Nārada; *prāha*—instructed; *munaye*—unto the great sage; *sarasvatyāḥ*—of the River Sarasvatī; *taṭe*—on the bank; *nṛpa*—O King; *dhyāyate*—unto the meditative; *brahma*—Absolute Truth; *paramam*—the Supreme; *vyāsāya*—unto Śrīla Vyāsadeva; *amita*—unlimited; *tejase*—unto the powerful.

TRANSLATION

In succession, O King, the great sage, Nārada, instructed Śrīmad-Bhāgavatam unto the unlimitedly powerful Vyāsadeva, who meditated in devotional service upon the Supreme Personality of Godhead, the Absolute Truth, on the bank of the River Sarasvatī.

PURPORT

In the Fifth Chapter of the First Canto of *Śrīmad-Bhāgavatam,* Nārada instructed the great sage Vyāsadeva as follows:

atho mahā-bhāga bhavān amogha-dṛk
śuci-śravāḥ satya-rato dhṛta-vrataḥ
urukramas yākhila-bandha-muktaye
samādhinānusmara tad viceṣṭitam

"O greatly fortunate, pious philosopher, your name and fame are universal, and you are fixed in the Absolute Truth with spotless character and infallible vision. I ask you to meditate upon the activities of the Personality of Godhead, whose activities are unparalleled."

So in the disciplic succession of the Brahma-sampradāya, the practice of *yoga* meditation is not neglected. But because the devotees are *bhakti-yogīs,* they do not undertake the trouble to meditate upon the impersonal Brahman, but, as is indicated here, on Brahma Paramam or the Supreme Brahman. Brahman realization begins from the impersonal effulgence, but by further progress of such meditation, manifestation of the Supreme Soul, Paramātmā realization, takes place. And progressing further, realization of the Supreme Personality of Godhead is fixed. Śrī Nārada Muni, as the spiritual master of Vyāsadeva, knew very well the position of Vyāsadeva, and thus he certified the qualities of Śrīla Vyāsadeva as fixed in the Absolute Truth with great vow, etc. He advised meditation upon the transcendental activities of the Lord. Impersonal Brahman has no activities, but the Personality of Godhead has many activities, and all such activities are transcendental without any tinge of material quality. If the activities of the Supreme Brahman would have been material activities, then Nārada would not have advised Vyāsadeva to meditate upon them. And the *Param Brahman* is Lord Śrī Kṛṣṇa, as is confirmed in the *Bhagavad-gītā.* In the Tenth Chapter of the *Bhagavad-gītā,* when Arjuna realized the factual position of Lord Kṛṣṇa, he addressed Lord Kṛṣṇa in the following words:

paraṁ brahma paraṁ dhāma pavitraṁ paramaṁ bhavān
puruṣaṁ śāśvataṁ divyam ādi-devam ajaṁ vibhum
āhus tvām ṛṣayaḥ sarve devarṣir nāradas tathā
asito devalo vyāsaḥ svayaṁ caiva bravīṣi me (Bg. 10.12-13)

Arjuna summarized the purpose of the *Bhagavad-gītā* by his realization of Lord Śrī Kṛṣṇa and thus said, "My dear Personality of Godhead, You are the Supreme Absolute Truth, the Original Person in the eternal form of bliss and knowledge, and this is confirmed by Nārada, Asita, Devala and Vyāsadeva, and, above all, Your personal self has also confirmed it."

When Vyāsadeva fixed his mind in meditation, he did it in *bhakti-yoga* trance and actually saw the Supreme Person with *māyā,* the illusory energy, in contraposition. As we have discussed before, the Lord's *māyā* or illusion is also a representation because *māyā* has no existence without the Lord. Darkness is not independent of light. Without light, no one can experience the contraposition of darkness. But this *māyā* or illusion cannot overcome the Supreme Personality of Godhead, but stands apart from Him (*apāśrayam*).

Therefore, perfection of meditation is to realize the Personality of Godhead along with His transcendental activities. Meditation on the impersonal Brahman is a troublesome business for the meditator, as is confirmed in the *Bhagavad-gītā:*

kleśo 'dhikataras teṣām avyaktāsakta-cetasām
(Bg. 12.5)

TEXT 46

यदुताहं त्वया पृष्टो वैराजात् पुरुषादिदम् ।
यथाऽऽसीत्तदुपाख्यास्ते प्रश्नानन्यांश्च कृत्स्नशः ।।४६।।

yad utāhaṁ tvayā pṛṣṭo
vairājāt puruṣād idam
yathāsīt tad upākhyāste
praśnān anyāṁś ca kṛtsnaśaḥ

yat—what; *uta*—is, however; *aham*—I; *tvayā*—by you; *pṛṣṭaḥ*—I am asked; *vairājāt*—from the universal form; *puruṣāt*—from the Personality of Godhead; *idam*—this world; *yathā*—as it; *āsīt*—was; *tat*—that; *upākhyāste*—I shall explain; *praśnān*—all the questions; *anyān*—others; *ca*—as well as; *kṛtsnaśaḥ*—in great detail.

TRANSLATION

O King, your questions as to how the universe became manifested from the gigantic form of the Personality of Godhead, as well as other questions, I shall answer in detail by the explanation of the four verses already mentioned.

PURPORT

As stated in the beginning of the *Śrīmad-Bhāgavatam,* this great transcendental literature is the ripened fruit of the tree of Vedic knowledge, and therefore all questions that can be humanly possible regarding the universal affairs, beginning from its creation, are all answered in the *Śrīmad-Bhāgavatam.* It depends only on the qualification of the person who explains. The ten divisions of *Śrīmad-Bhāgavatam,* as explained by the great speaker Śrīla Śukadeva Gosvāmī, are the limitation of all questions, and intelligent persons will derive all intellectual benefits from them by proper utilization.

Thus end the Bhaktivedanta purports of the Second Canto, Ninth Chapter, of the Śrīmad-Bhāgavatam, *entitled "Answers by Citing the Lord's Version."*

CHAPTER TEN

Bhāgavatam is the Answer to All Questions

TEXT 1

श्रीशुक उवाच
अत्र सर्गो विसर्गश्च स्थानं पोषणमूतयः ।
मन्वन्तरेशानुकथा निरोधो मुक्तिराश्रयः ॥ १ ॥

śrī śuka uvāca
atra sargo visargaś ca
sthānaṁ poṣaṇam ūtayaḥ
manvantareśānukathā
nirodho muktir āśrayaḥ

śrī śukaḥ uvāca—Śukadeva Gosvāmī said; *atra*—in this *Śrīmad-Bhāgavatam; sargaḥ*—statement of the creation of the universe; *visargaḥ*—statement of subcreation; *ca*—also; *sthānam*—the planetary system; *poṣaṇam*—protection; *ūtayaḥ*—creative impetus; *manvantara*—changes of Manus; *īśa-anukathāḥ*—science of God; *nirodhaḥ*—going back home, back to Godhead; *muktiḥ*—liberation; *āśrayaḥ*—the *summum bonum.*

TRANSLATION

Śukadeva Gosvāmī said: "In the Śrīmad-Bhāgavatam there are ten divisions of statements regarding the following: creation of the universe, subcreation, planetary systems, protection by the Lord, creative impetus, change of Manus, science of God, return to home, back to Godhead, liberation, and the summum bonum.

TEXT 2

दशमस्य विशुद्ध्यर्थं नवानामिह लक्षणम् ।
वर्णयन्ति महात्मानः श्रुतेनार्थेन चाञ्जसा ॥ २ ॥

daśamasya viśuddhy-arthaṁ
navānām iha lakṣaṇam
varṇayanti mahātmānaḥ
śrutenārthena cāñjasā

daśamasya—of the *summum bonum; viśuddhi*—isolation; *artham*—purpose; *navānām*—of the other nine; *iha*—in this *Śrīmad-Bhāgavatam; lakṣaṇam*—symptoms; *varṇayanti*—they describe; *mahā-ātmānaḥ*—the great sages; *śrutena*—by Vedic evidences; *arthena*—by direct explanation; *ca*—or; *añjasā*—summarily.

TRANSLATION

In order to eliminate transcendence of the summum bonum, the symptoms of the rest are described sometimes by Vedic inference, sometimes by direct explanation, and sometimes by summary explanation given by the great sages.

TEXT 3

भूतमात्रेन्द्रियधियां जन्म सर्ग उदाहृतः ।
ब्रह्मणो गुणवैषम्याद्विसर्गः पौरुषः स्मृतः ॥ ३ ॥

bhūta-mātrendriya-dhiyāṁ
janma sarga udāhṛtaḥ
brahmaṇo guṇa-vaiṣamyād
visargaḥ pauruṣaḥ smṛtaḥ

bhūta—the five gross elements like the sky, etc.; *mātrā*—objects perceived by the senses; *indriya*—the senses; *dhiyām*—of the mind; *janma*—creation; *sargaḥ*—manifestation; *udāhṛtaḥ*—is called the creation; *brahmaṇaḥ*—of Brahmā, the first *puruṣa; guṇa-vaiṣamyāt*—by interaction of the three modes of nature; *visargaḥ*—recreation; *pauruṣaḥ*—resultant activities; *smṛtaḥ*—it is so known.

TRANSLATION

The elementary creation of sixteen items of matter—namely the five elements [fire, water, land, air and sky], sound, form, taste, smell, touch, eyes, ears, nose, tongue, skin and mind—is known as sarga, whereas subsequent resultant interaction of the modes of material nature is called visarga.

PURPORT

In order to explain the ten divisional symptoms of the *Śrīmad-Bhāgavatam,* there are seven continuous verses. The first of these under reference pertains to the sixteen elementary manifestations of earth, water, etc., with material ego composed of material intelligence and mind, and the subsequent creation is a result of the reactions of the above-mentioned sixteen energies of the first *puruṣa,* the Mahā-Viṣṇu incarnation of Govinda, as is later on explained by Brahmā in his treatise the *Brahma-saṁhitā* as follows:

yaḥ kāraṇārṇava-jale bhajati sma yoga-
nidrām ananta-jagadaṇḍa-saromakūpaḥ
ādhāra-śaktim avalambya parāṁ sva-mūrtiṁ
govindam ādi-puruṣaṁ tamahaṁ bhajāmi (B.s. 5.47)

The first *puruṣa* incarnation of Govinda, Lord Kṛṣṇa, known as the Mahā-Viṣṇu, goes into a *yoga-nidrā* mystic sleep, and the innumerable universes are situated in potency in each and every hair hole of His transcendental body.

As is mentioned in the previous verse, *śrutena* (or with reference to the Vedic conclusions), the creation is made possible from the Supreme Personality of Godhead directly by manifestation of His particular energies. Without such a Vedic reference, the creation appears to be a product of material nature, and this conclusion comes from a poor fund of knowledge. From Vedic reference it is concluded that the origin of all energies (namely internal, external, and marginal) is the Supreme Personality of Godhead. And as has been explained hereinbefore, the illusory conclusion is that creation is made by the inert material nature. The Vedic conclusion is transcendental light, whereas the non-Vedic conclusion is material darkness. The internal potency of the Supreme Lord is identical with the Supreme Lord, and the external potency is enlivened in contact with the internal potency. The parts and parcels of the internal potency which react in contact with the external potency are called the marginal potency, or the living entities.

Thus the original creation is directly from the Supreme Personality of Godhead, or *Param Brahman,* and the secondary creation, as reactionary resultant of the original ingredients, is made by Brahmā, and the activities of the whole universe are thus started.

TEXT 4

स्थितिर्वैकुण्ठविजयः पोषणं तदनुग्रहः ।
मन्वन्तराणि सद्धर्म ऊतयः कर्मवासनाः ॥ ४ ॥

sthitir vaikuṇṭha-vijayaḥ
poṣaṇaṁ tad-anugrahaḥ
manvantarāṇi sad-dharma
ūtayaḥ karma-vāsanāḥ

sthitiḥ—right situation; *vaikuṇṭha-vijayaḥ*—victory of the Lord of Vaikuṇṭha; *poṣaṇam*—maintenance; *tat-anugrahaḥ*—His causeless mercy; *manvantarāṇi*—reign of the Manus; *sat-dharmaḥ*—perfect occupational duty; *ūtayaḥ*—impetus to work; *karma-vāsanāḥ*—desire for fruitive work.

TRANSLATION

The right situation for the living entities is to obey the laws of the Lord and thus be in perfect peace of mind under the protection of the Supreme Personality of Godhead. The Manus and their laws are meant to give right direction in life. The impetus of activity is the desire for fruitive work.

PURPORT

This material world is created, maintained for some time, and again annihilated by the will of the Lord. The ingredients for creation and the subordinate creator, Brahmā, are first created by Lord Viṣṇu in His first and second incarnations. The first *Puruṣa* incarnation is Mahā-Viṣṇu, and the second *Puruṣa* incarnation is the Garbhodakaśāyī Viṣṇu, from whom Brahmā is created. The third *Puruṣa avatāra* is the Kṣīrodakaśāyī Viṣṇu, who lives as the Supersoul of everything in the universe and maintains the creation generated by Brahmā. Śiva is one of the many sons of Brahmā, and he annihilates the creation. Therefore the original creator of the universe is Viṣṇu, and He is also maintainer of the created beings by His causeless mercy. As such, it is the duty of all conditioned souls to acknowledge the victory of the Lord and thus become pure devotees and live peacefully in this world where miseries and dangers of life are always in existence. The conditioned souls who take this material creation as the place for satisfaction of the senses, and thus are illusioned by the external energy of Viṣṇu, remain again to be subjected to laws of material nature, creation and destruction.

In the *Bhagavad-gītā* it is said that beginning from the topmost planet of this universe down to the lowest planet, the Pātālaloka, all are destructible, and the conditioned souls may travel in space either by good or bad work or by the modern spacecraft, but they are sure to die everywhere, although the duration of life in different planets is different. The only means to attain eternal life is to go back home, back to Godhead, where there is no more rebirth as in the material planets. The conditioned souls, being unaware of this very simple fact by forgetting the relationship with the Lord of Vaikuṇṭha, try to plan out a permanent life in this material world, being illusioned by the external energy, and thus become engaged in various types of economic and religious development of life, forgetting that they are meant for going back home, back to Godhead. This forgetfulness is so strong due to the influence of *māyā* that the conditioned souls do not at all want to go back to Godhead. By sense enjoyment they become victims of birth and death repeatedly and thus spoil human lives which are chances for going back to Viṣṇu. The directive scriptures made by the Manus at different ages and millenniums are called *sad-dharma,* good guidance for the human beings, who should take up the advantage of all the revealed scriptures on their own interest to make life's successful termination. The creation is not false, but it is a temporary manifestation just to give a chance for the conditioned souls to go back to Godhead. And the desire to go back to Godhead and functions performed in that direction are the right path of work. When such a regulative path is accepted, the Lord gives all protection to His devotees by His causeless mercy, while the nondevotees risk their own activities to bind themselves up in the chain of fruitive reactions. The word *sad-dharma* is significant in this connection. *Sad-dharma,* or duty performed for going back to Godhead and thus becoming His unalloyed devotee, is the only pious activity; all others may be pretendingly pious, but actually they are not so. It is for this reason only that the Lord advises in the *Bhagavad-gītā* to give up all so-called religious activities and be completely engaged in the devotional service of the Lord in order to become free from all anxieties due to the dangerous life of material existence. To work situated in the *sad-dharma* is the right direction of life. One's aim of life should be to go back home, back to Godhead, and not be subjected to repeated births and deaths in the material world by getting good or bad bodies for temporary existence. Herein lies the intelligence of human life, and one should desire the activities of life in that way.

TEXT 5

अवतारानुचरितं हरेश्चास्यानुवर्तिनाम् ।
पुंसामीशकथाः प्रोक्ता नानाख्यानोपबृंहिताः ॥ ५ ॥

avatārānucaritaṁ
hareś cāsyānuvartinām
puṁsām īśa-kathāḥ proktā
nānākhyānopabṛṁhitāḥ

avatāra—incarnation of Godhead; *anucaritam*—activities; *hareḥ*—of the Personality of Godhead; *ca*—also; *asya*—of His; *anuvartinām*—followers; *puṁsām*—of the persons; *īśa-kathāḥ*—science of God; *proktāḥ*—is said; *nānā*—various; *ākhyāna*—narrations; *upabṛṁhitāḥ*—described.

TRANSLATION

The science of God describes the incarnations of the Personality of Godhead and His different activities together with the activities of His great devotees.

PURPORT

During the course of existence of the cosmic manifestation, the chronology of history is created, recording the activities of the living entities. People in general have a tendency to learn history and narrations of different men and times, but due to lack of knowledge in the science of Godhead, they are not apt to study the history of the incarnations of the Personality of Godhead. It should always be remembered that the material creation is created for the salvation of the conditioned souls. The merciful Lord, out of His causeless mercy, descends in the material world to various planets and acts for the salvation of the conditioned souls. That makes the history and narrations worth reading. *Śrīmad-Bhāgavatam* offers such transcendental topics of the Lord in relationship with great devotees. Therefore the topics of the devotees and the Lord are to be given respectful aural reception.

TEXT 6

निरोधोऽस्यानुशयनमात्मनः सह शक्तिभिः ।
मुक्तिर्हित्वान्यथारूपं स्वरूपेण व्यवस्थितिः ॥ ६ ॥

nirodho 'syānuśayanam
ātmanaḥ saha śaktibhiḥ
muktir hitvānyathā rūpaṁ
sva-rūpeṇa vyavasthitiḥ

nirodhaḥ—winding up of the cosmic manifestation; *asya*—of His; *anuśayanam*—lying down of the Puruṣa incarnation Mahā-Viṣṇu in mystic slumber; *ātmanaḥ*—of the living entities; *saha*—along with; *śaktibhiḥ*—with the energies; *muktiḥ*—liberation; *hitvā*—giving up; *anyathā*—otherwise; *rūpam*—form; *sva-rūpeṇa*—in constitutional form; *vyavasthitiḥ*—permanent situation.

TRANSLATION

When the living entity, along with his conditional living tendency, merges with the mystic lying down of the Mahā-Viṣṇu, it is called the winding up of the cosmic manifestation. Liberation is the permanent situation of the form of the living entity after giving up the changeable material gross and subtle bodies.

PURPORT

As we have discussed several times, there are two types of living entities. Most of them are ever liberated, or *nitya-muktas,* while some of them are ever conditioned. The ever conditioned souls are apt to develop a mentality of lording over the material nature, and therefore the material cosmic creation is manifested to give the ever conditioned souls two kinds of facilities. One facility is that the conditioned soul can act according to his tendency to lord it over the cosmic manifestation, and the other facility is to give a chance to the conditioned soul to come back to Godhead. So after the winding up of the cosmic manifestation, most of the conditioned souls merge into the existence of the Mahā-Viṣṇu Personality of Godhead, lying in His mystic slumber, to be recreated again when there will be the next creation. But some of the conditioned souls, who follow the transcendental sound in the form of Vedic literatures and are thus able to go back to Godhead, attain spiritual and original bodies after quitting the material conditional gross and subtle bodies. The material conditional bodies develop out of the living entities' forgetfulness of the relationship with Godhead, and during the course of the cosmic manifestation, the conditioned souls are given a chance to revive their original status of life by the help of revealed scriptures, so mercifully compiled by the Lord in His different incarnations. Reading or hearing of such transcendental literatures helps one to become liberated even in the conditional state of material existence. The whole Vedic literatures aim at devotional service of the Personality of Godhead, and as soon as one is fixed to this point, he at once becomes liberated from the conditional life. The material gross and subtle forms are simply due to ignorance of the conditioned soul, and as soon as he is fixed in the devotional service of the Lord, he becomes eligible to be freed from the conditioned state. This devotional service is transcendental attraction for the Supreme on account of the latter's being the source of all pleasing humors. Everyone is after some pleasure of humor for enjoyment, but does not know the supreme source of all attraction *(raso vai sa rasaṁ hy evāyaṁ labdhvānandī bhavati)*. The Vedic hymns inform everyone about the supreme source of all pleasure; the unlimited fountainhead of all pleasure is the Personality of Godhead, and one who is fortunate enough to get this information through the transcendental literatures like *Śrīmad-Bhāgavatam* becomes permanently liberated to occupy one's proper place in the kingdom of God.

TEXT 7

आभासश्च निरोधश्च यतो ऽस्त्यध्यवसीयते ।
स आश्रयः परं ब्रह्म परमात्मेति शब्द्यते ॥ ७ ॥

ābhāsaś ca nirodhaś ca
yato 'sty adhyavasīyate
sa āśrayaḥ paraṁ brahma
paramātmeti śabdyate

ābhāsaḥ—the cosmic manifestation; *ca*—and; *nirodhaḥ*—and its winding up; *ca*—also; *yataḥ*—from the source; *asti*—is; *adhyavasīyate*—become manifested; *saḥ*—He; *āśrayaḥ*—reservoir; *param*—the Supreme; *brahma*—Being; *paramātmā*—the Supersoul; *iti*—thus; *śabdyate*—called.

TRANSLATION

The supreme one who is celebrated as the Supreme Being or the Supreme Soul is the supreme source of the cosmic manifestation as well as its reservoir and winding up. Thus He is the Supreme Fountainhead Absolute Truth.

PURPORT

Synonyms of the supreme source of all energies, as explained in the very beginning of the *Śrīmad-Bhāgatavam*, are *janmādyasya yataḥ, vadanti tat tattvavidas tattvaṁ yaj jñānam advayam, brahmeti paramātmeti bhagavān iti śabdyate,* called Param Brahma, Paramātmā or Bhagavān. The word *iti* used here in the verse completes the synonyms and thus indicates Bhagavān. This will be further explained in the later verses, but this Bhagavān means ultimately Lord Kṛṣṇa because the *Śrīmad-Bhāgavatam* has already accepted the Supreme Personality of Godhead as Kṛṣṇa. *Kṛṣṇas tu bhagavān svayam.* The original source of all energies or the *summum bonum* is the Absolute Truth which is called Param Brahma, etc., and Bhagavān is the last word of the Absolute Truth. But even with the synonyms of Bhagavān, such as Nārāyaṇa, Viṣṇu, Puruṣa, etc., the last word is Kṛṣṇa, as confirmed in the *Bhagavad-gītā: ahaṁ sarvasya prabhavo mattaḥ sarvaṁ pravartate,* etc. Besides that, the *Śrīmad-Bhāgavatam* is the representation of Lord Kṛṣṇa as sound incarnation of the Lord. *Kṛṣṇe sva-dhāmopagate dharma-jñānādibhiḥ saha/ kalau naṣṭa-dṛśām eṣaḥ purāṇārko'dhunoditaḥ.* Thus by general conclusion Lord Kṛṣṇa is the ultimate source of all energies, and the word Kṛṣṇa means that. And to explain Kṛṣṇa or the science of Kṛṣṇa, the *Śrīmad-Bhāgavatam* has been prepared. In the First Canto of *Śrīmad-Bhāgavatam* this truth is indicated in the questions and answers by Sūta Gosvāmī and great sages like Śaunaka, etc., and in the First and Second Chapters of the canto this is explained. In the Third Chapter this subject is more explicit, and in the Fourth Chapter even more explicit. In the Second Canto the Absolute Truth as the Personality of Godhead is further emphasized, and the indication is the Supreme Lord Kṛṣṇa. The summary of *Śrīmad-Bhāgavatam* in four verses, as we have already discussed, is succinct. This Supreme Personality of Godhead in the ultimate issue is confirmed by Brahmā in his *Brahma-saṁhitā* as *īśvaraḥ paramaḥ kṛṣṇaḥ sac-cid-ānanda-vigrahaḥ.* So it is concluded in the Third Canto of the *Śrīmad-Bhāgavatam.* The complete subject matter is elaborately explained in the Tenth and Eleventh Cantos of the *Śrīmad-Bhāgavatam.* In the matter of changes of the Manus of *manvantaras,* such as the *Svāyambhuva manvantara* and *Cākṣuṣa manvantara,* as they are discussed in the Third, Fourth, Fifth, Sixth and Seventh Cantos of *Śrīmad-Bhāgavatam,* Lord Kṛṣṇa is indicated. In the Eighth Canto Vaivasvata *manvantara* explains the same subject indirectly, and in the Ninth Canto the same purport is there. In the Twelfth Canto the same is further explained, specifically regarding the different incarnations of the Lord. Thus it is concluded by studying the complete *Śrīmad-Bhāgavatam* that Lord Śrī Kṛṣṇa is the ultimate *summum bonum,* or the ultimate source of all energy. And according to the grades of worshipers, the indications of the nomenclature may be differently explained as Nārāyaṇa, Brahmā, Paramātmā, etc.

TEXT 8

योऽध्यात्मिकोऽयं पुरुषः सोऽसावेवाधिदैविकः ।
यस्तत्रोभयविच्छेदः पुरुषो ह्याधिभौतिकः ॥ ८ ॥

yo 'dhyātmiko 'yaṁ puruṣaḥ
so 'sāv evādhidaivikaḥ
yas tatrobhayavicchedaḥ
puruṣo hyādhibhautikaḥ

yaḥ—one who; *adhyātmikaḥ*—is possessed of the sense organs; *ayam*—this; *puruṣaḥ*—personality; *saḥ*—he; *asau*—that; *eva*—also; *adhidaivikaḥ*—controlling deity; *yaḥ*—that which; *tatra*—there; *ubhaya*—of both; *vicchedaḥ*—separation; *puruṣaḥ*—person; *hi*—for; *ādhibhautikaḥ*—the visible body or the embodied living entity.

TRANSLATION

The individual person possessing different instruments of senses is called the adhyātmic person, and the individual controlling deity of the senses is called adhidaivic. And the embodiment which is seen on the eyeballs is called the adhibhautic person.

PURPORT

The supreme controlling *summum bonum* is the Personality of Godhead in His plenary portion of Paramātmā or the Supersoul manifestation. In the *Bhagavad-gītā* it is said:

athavā bahunaitena kiṁ jñātena tavārjuna
viṣṭabhyāham idaṁ kṛtsnam ekāṁśena sthito jagat

"All the controlling deities like Viṣṇu, Brahmā and Śiva are different manifestations of the Paramātmā feature of the Supreme Personality of Godhead Śrī Kṛṣṇa, and He exhibits himself in such manners by entering into each and every universe generated from Him." (Bg. 10.42) But still apparently there are divisions of the controller and controlled. For example, in the food-controlling department the controller of food is a person made of the same ingredients as the person who is controlled. Similarly, each and every individual in the material world is controlled by the higher demigods. For example, we have our senses, but the senses are controlled by superior controlling deities. We cannot see without light, and the supreme controller of light is the sun. The sun-god is in the sun planet, and we, the individual human beings or any other being on this earth, are all controlled by the sun-god as far as our eyes are concerned. Similarly, all the senses that we have are controlled by the superior demigods, who are also as much living entities as we are, but one is empowered while the other is controlled. The controlled living entity is called the *adhyātmic* person, and the controller is called the *adhidaivic* person. All these positions in the material world are due to different fruitive activities. Any individual living being can become the sun-god or even Brahmā or any other god in the upper planetary system by a higher grade of pious work, and similarly one becomes controlled by the higher demigods by lower grades of fruitive activities. So every individual living entity is subject to the supreme control of the Paramātmā, who puts everyone in different positions of the controller and the controlled.

That which distinguishes the controller and controlled, i.e. the material body, is called the *adhibhautic puruṣa.* The body is sometimes called *puruṣa,* as is confirmed in the *Vedas* in the following hymn: "*sa vā eṣa puruṣo 'nna-rasamaya.*" This body is called *anna-rasa* embodiment. This body depends on food. The living entity which is embodied does not eat anything, however, because the owner is spirit in essence. The material body requires replacement of matters for the wearing and tearing of the mechanical body. Therefore the distinction between the individual living entity and controlling planetary deities is in the *anna-rasamaya* body. The sun may have a gigantic body, and the man may have a smaller body, but all these visible bodies are made of matter; nonetheless, the sun-god and the individual person related as the controller and the controlled are the same spiritual parts and parcels of the Supreme Being, and it is the Supreme Being who places different parts and parcels in different positions. And thus the conclusion is that the Supreme Person is the shelter of all.

TEXT 9

एकमेकतराभावे यदा नोपलभामहे ।
त्रितयं तत्र यो वेद स आत्मा स्वाश्रयाश्रयः ॥ ९ ॥

ekam ekatarābhāve
yadā nopalabhāmahe

tritayaṁ tatra yo veda
sa ātmā svāśrayāśrayaḥ

ekam—one; *ekatara*—another; *abhāve*—in the absence of; *yadā*—because; *na*—does not; *upalabhāmahe*—perceptible; *tritayam*—in three stages; *tatra*—there; *yaḥ*—the one; *veda*—who knows; *saḥ ātmā*—the Supersoul; *sva*—own; *āśraya*—shelter; *āśrayaḥ*—of the shelter.

TRANSLATION

All the above-mentioned three stages of different living entities are interdependent. In the absence of one, the other is not understood. And the Supreme Being who is seeing every one of them as the shelter of the shelter is independent of all, and therefore He is the supreme shelter.

PURPORT

So there are innumerable living entities, one dependent on the other in the relationship of the controlled and the controller. But without the medium of perception, no one can know or understand who is the controlled and who is the controller. For example, the sun controls the power of our vision, and we can see the sun because the sun has its body, and the sunlight is useful only because we have eyes. Without our having eyes, the sunlight is useless, and without sunlight the eyes are useless. Thus they are interdependent, and neither of them is independent. Therefore the natural question arises concerning who made them interdependent, and one who has made such a relationship of interdependence must be ultimately completely independent. As it is stated in the beginning of the *Śrīmad-Bhāgavatam,* the ultimate source of all interdependent objectives is the complete independent subject. This ultimate source of all interdependence is the Supreme Truth or Paramātmā, the Supersoul, who is not dependent on anything else. He is *svāśrayāśrayaḥ*. He is only dependent on His self, and thus He is the supreme shelter of everything. Although Paramātmā or Brahman are subordinate to Bhagavān, because Bhagavān is Puruṣottama or the Superperson, He is the source of the Supersoul also. In the *Bhagavad-gītā* (Bg. 15.18) Lord Kṛṣṇa says that He is the Puruṣottama and the source of everything, and thus it is concluded that Śrī Kṛṣṇa is the ultimate source and shelter of all entities including the Supersoul or Supreme Brahman. Even accepting that there is no difference between the

Supersoul and the individual soul, the individual soul is dependent on the Supersoul for being liberated from the illusion of material energy. The individual is under the clutches of illusory energy, and therefore although qualitatively one with the Supersoul, he is under the illusion of identifying himself with matter. And to get out of this illusory conception of factual life, the individual soul has to depend on the Supersoul to be recognized as one with Him. In that sense also the Supersoul is the supreme shelter. And there is no doubt about it.

The individual living entity or the *jīva* is always dependent on the Supersoul Paramātmā because the individual soul forgets his spiritual identity whereas the Supersoul Paramātmā does not forget His transcendental position. In the *Bhagavad-gītā* these separate positions of the *jīva-ātmā* and the *paramātmā* are specifically mentioned. In the Fourth Chapter, Arjuna, the *jīva* soul, is represented as forgetful of his many, many previous births, but the Lord, the Supersoul, is not forgetful. The Lord even remembers when He taught the *Bhagavad-gītā* to the sun-god some billions of years before. The Lord can remember such millions and billions of years, as is stated in the *Bhagavad-gītā* as follows:

vedāhaṁ samatītāni vartamānāni cārjuna
bhaviṣyāṇi ca bhūtāni māṁ tu veda na kaścana

The Lord in His eternal blissful body of knowledge is fully aware of all that happened in the past, and that which is going on at the present as well as what will happen in the future. And in spite of His becoming the shelter of both the Paramātmā and Brahman, persons with a poor fund of knowledge are unable to understand Him as He is.

The propaganda of the identity of cosmic consciousness with the consciousness of the individual living entities is completely misleading because even a person or individual soul like Arjuna could not remember his past deeds, although he is always with the Lord. And what can the tiny ordinary man know about his past, present and future, falsely claiming to be one with the cosmic consciousness.

TEXT 10

पुरुषोऽण्डं विनिर्भिद्य यदासौ स विनिर्गतः ।
आत्मनोऽयनमन्विच्छन्नपोऽस्राक्षीच्छुचिः शुचीः॥१०

puruṣo 'ṇḍaṁ vinirbhidya
yadāsau sa vinirgataḥ
ātmano 'yanam anvicchann
apo 'srākṣīcchuciḥ śucīḥ

puruṣaḥ—the Supreme Person, Paramātmā; *aṇḍam*—the universes; *vinirbhidya*—making them each separately situated; *yadā*—when; *asau*—the same; *saḥ*—He (the Lord); *vinirgataḥ*—came out; *ātmanaḥ*—of Himself; *ayanam*—lying in place; *anvicchan*—desiring; *apaḥ*—water; *asrākṣīt*—created; *śuciḥ*—the most pure; *śucīḥ*—transcendental.

TRANSLATION

The gigantic universal form of the Lord [Mahā-Viṣṇu], which came out of the causal ocean, the place of appearance of the first puruṣa-avatāra, after separating the different universes, entered into each of the separate universes, desiring to lie on the created transcendental water [Garbhodaka].

PURPORT

After analysis of the living entities and the Supreme Lord Paramātmā, the independent source of all other living beings, Śrīla Śukadeva Gosvāmī is now presenting the prime necessity for devotional service of the Lord, which is the only occupational business of all living entities. The Supreme Lord Śrī Kṛṣṇa and all His plenary portions and extensions of plenary portions are nondifferent from one another, and thus the supreme independence is there in each and every one of them. In order to prove this, Śukadeva Gosvāmī (as promised to King Parīkṣit) describes herein the independence of the *Puruṣa-Avatāra* Personality of Godhead, even in the sphere of the material creation. Such activities of the Lord are also transcendental, and therefore they are also *līlā,* or pastimes, of the absolute Lord. Such pastimes of the Lord are very conducive to the hearers for self-realization in the field of devotional service. Some may argue, why not then relish the transcendental *līlā* of the Lord as exhibited in the land of Mathurā and Vṛndāvana, which are sweeter than anything in the world? Śrīla Viśvanātha Cakravarti Ṭhākur replies that the pastimes of the Lord in Vṛndāvana are meant to be relished by advanced devotees of the Lord. Neophyte devotees will misunderstand such supreme transcendental activities of the Lord, and therefore for the neophyte the Lord's pastimes in the material sphere related to creation, maintenance and destruction are verily relishable by the *prākṛta,* or mundane devotees of the Lord. As the *yoga* system mainly based on bodily exercises is meant for the person who is too much attached to the bodily conception of existence, similarly the pastimes of the Lord related to creation and destruction of the material world are for those who are too much materially attached. For such mundane creatures the functions of the body as well as the functions of the cosmic world by physical laws in relationship with the Lord are also therefore included in understanding the lawmaker, the Supreme Personality of Godhead. The scientists explain the material functions by so many technological terms of material law, but such blind scientists forget the lawmaker. The *Śrīmad-Bhāgavatam* points out the lawmaker. One should not be amazed by the mechanical arrangement of the complicated engine or dynamo, but one should be praising the engineer who creates such a wonderful working machine. That is the difference between the devotee and nondevotee. Devotees are always full with praising the Lord who directs the physical laws. In the *Bhagavad-gītā* the direction of the Lord upon the material nature is described as follows:

mayādhyakṣena prakṛtiḥ sūyate sacarācaram
hetunānena kaunteya jagad viparivartate.

"The material nature full of physical laws is one of My different energies; therefore it is neither independent nor blind. Because I am transcendentally all-powerful, simply by My glancing over the material nature, the physical laws of nature work so wonderfully. The actions and reactions of the physical laws work on that account, and thus the material world is created, maintained and annihilated again and again."

Men with poor fund of knowledge, however, become astonished by studying the physical laws both within the construction of the individual body as well as the cosmic manifestation and foolishly decry the existence of God, taking it for granted that the physical laws are independent without any metaphysical control. The *Bhagavad-gītā* replies to this foolishness in the following words:

avajānanti māṁ mūḍha mānuṣīṁ tanum āśritam
paraṁ bhāvam ajānanto mama bhūta-maheśvaram.

"The foolish men *[mūḍhāḥ]* do not know the Personality of Godhead in His eternal form of bliss and knowledge." The foolish man thinks of the transcendental body of the Lord as something like his own, and therefore he cannot think of the Lord's unlimited power of control, even though He is not visible in the acting of the physical laws. The Lord is, however, visible to the naked eyes of the people in general when He descends Himself by His own personal potency. Lord Kṛṣṇa incarnated Himself as He is and played very wonderful parts as the Lord Himself, and the *Bhagavad-gītā* concerns such wonderful actions and knowledge, and yet foolish men will not accept Lord Kṛṣṇa as the Supreme Lord. Generally they consider the infinitesimal and infinite features of the Lord because they themselves are unable to become either the infinitesimal or the infinite, but one should know that the infinite and infinitesimal sizes of the Lord are not His highest glories. The most wonderful manifestation of the Lord's power is exhibited when the infinite Lord becomes visible to our eyes as one of us. Yet His activities are different from those of the finite beings. To lift a mountain at the age of six years or to marry sixteen thousand wives in His prime of youth are some of the examples of His infinite energy, but the *mūḍhas,* after seeing them or hearing about them, decry them as legendary and take the Lord as one of them. They cannot understand that the Lord Śri Kṛṣṇa, although in the form of a human being by His own potency, is still the Supreme Lord with full potency as supreme controller.

When, however, the *mūḍhas* give submissive aural reception to the messages of the Lord as in the *Śrīmad-Bhagavad-gītā* or in the *Śrīmad-Bhāgavatam* through the channel of disciplic succession, such *mūḍhas* also become devotees of the Lord by the grace of His pure devotees. And for this reason only, either in the *Bhagavad-gītā* or in the *Śrīmad-Bhāgavatam,* the pastimes of the Lord in the material world are delineated for the benefit of those men with a poor fund of knowledge.

TEXT 11

ताखवात्सीत् स्वसृष्टासु सहस्रंपरिवत्सरान् ।
तेन नारायणो नाम यदापः पुरुषोद्भवाः ॥११॥

tāsv avātsīt sva-sṛṣṭāsu
sahasraṁ parivatsarān
tena nārāyaṇo nāma
yad āpaḥ puruṣodbhavāḥ

tāsu—in that; *avātsīt*—resided; *sva*—own; *sṛṣṭāsu*—in the matter of creation; *sahasram*—one thousand; *parivatsarān*—years of His measurement; *tena*—for that reason; *nārāyaṇaḥ*—the Personality of Godhead named Nārāyaṇa; *nāma*—name; *yat*—because; *āpaḥ*—water; *puruṣa-udbhavāḥ*—emanated from the Supreme Person.

TRANSLATION

That Supreme Person is not impersonal and therefore is distinctively a nara, or person. Therefore the transcendental water created from the Supreme Nara is known as nāra. And because He lies down on that water, He is known as Nārāyaṇa.

TEXT 12

द्रव्यं कर्म च कालश्च स्वभावो जीव एव च ।
यदनुग्रहतः सन्ति न सन्ति यदुपेक्षया ॥१२॥

dravyaṁ karma ca kālaś ca
sva-bhāvo jīva eva ca
yad-anugrahataḥ santi
na santi yad-upekṣayā

dravyam—physical elements; *karma*—action; *ca*—and; *kālaḥ*—time; *ca*—also; *sva-bhāvaḥ jīvaḥ*—the living entities; *eva*—certainly; *ca*—also; *yat*—whose; *anugrahataḥ*—by the mercy of; *santi*—exist; *na*—does not; *santi*—exist; *yat-upekṣayā*—by negligence.

TRANSLATION

One should know definitely that all material ingredients, activities, time, modes, and the living entities who are meant to enjoy them all, exist by His mercy only, and as soon as He does not care for them, everything becomes nonexistent.

PURPORT

The living entities are the enjoyers of the material ingredients, time, modes, etc., because they want to lord it over the material nature. The

Lord is the supreme enjoyer, and the living entities are meant to assist the Lord in His enjoyment and thus participate in the transcendental enjoyment of everyone. The enjoyer and the enjoyed both participate in enjoyment, but, deluded by the illusory energy, the living entities want to become the enjoyer like the Lord, although they are not meant for such enjoyment. The *jīvas* or the living entities are mentioned in the *Bhagavad-gītā* as the superior nature or *parā prakṛti* of the Lord, and so also it is mentioned in the *Viṣṇu Purāṇa.* Therefore the living entities are never the *puruṣas,* or the factual enjoyers. As such, the spirit of enjoyment by the living entity in the material world is false. In the spiritual world the living entities are pure in nature, and therefore they are associates in the enjoyment of the Supreme Lord. In the material world the spirit of enjoyment by the living entities by dint of their own actions *(karma)* becomes gradually faded by the laws of nature, and thus the illusory energy dictates in the ear of the conditioned souls to become one with the Lord. This is the last snare of the illusory energy. When the last illusion is also cleared off by the mercy of the Lord, the living entity again becomes reinstated in his original position and thus becomes actually liberated. And for this attainment of liberation from the material clutches, the Lord creates the material world, maintains it for some time (one thousand years of His measurement, as is stated in the previous verse), and then again annihilates it by His will. The living entities are therefore completely dependent on the mercy of the Lord, and all their so-called enjoyments by scientific improvement are crushed into dust when the Lord desires.

TEXT 13

एको नानात्वमन्विच्छन् योगतल्पात् समुत्थितः ।
वीर्यं हिरण्मयं देवो मायया व्यसृजत् त्रिधा ॥१३॥

eko nānātvam anvicchan
yoga-talpāt samutthitaḥ
vīryaṁ hiraṇmayaṁ devo
māyayā vyasṛjat tridhā

ekaḥ—He, one alone; *nānātvam*—varieties; *anvicchan*—so desiring; *yoga-talpāt*—from the bedstead of mystic slumber; *samutthitaḥ*—thus generated; *vīryam*—the semina; *hiraṇmayam*—golden hue; *devaḥ*—the demigod; *māyayā*—by the external energy; *vyasṛjat*—perfectly created; *tridhā*—in three features.

TRANSLATION

The Lord, while lying on His bed of mystic slumber, generated the seminal symbol, golden in hue, through external energy out of His desire to manifest varieties of living entities from Himself alone.

PURPORT

In the *Bhagavad-gītā* the creation and annihilation of the material world are stated as follows:

sarva-bhūtāni kaunteya prakṛtiṁ yānti māmikām
kalpakṣaye punas tāni kalpādau visṛjāmy aham
prakṛtiṁ svām avaṣṭabhya visṛjāmi punaḥ punaḥ
bhūta-grāmam imaṁ kṛtsnam avaśaṁ prakṛter vaśāt.
(Bg. 9.7-8)

"At the end of each millennium the creative forces, namely the material nature as well as the living entities who struggle in the material nature, all merge together into the transcendental body of the Lord, and again when the Lord desires to manifest them, all of them are again displayed by the Lord.

"Therefore the material nature is working under the control of the Lord. All of them, under the agency of material nature and under the control of the Lord, are thus repeatedly created and annihilated by the will of the Lord."

As such, before the creation or manifestation of the material cosmic world, the Lord exists as total energy *(mahāsamasti),* and thus desiring Himself to be diffused to many, He expands Himself further into multi-total energy *(samasti),* and from the multi-total energy He further expands Himself into individuals in three dimensions, namely *adhyātmic, adhidaivic* and *adhibhautic,* as explained before *(vyasti).* As such, the whole creation and the creative energies are nondifferent and different simultaneously. Because everything is an emanation from Him (the Mahā-Viṣṇu or Mahāsamasti), nothing of the cosmic energies is different from Him; but all such expanded energies have specific functions and display as designed by the Lord, and therefore they are simultaneously different from the Lord. The living entities are also similar energy (marginal potency) of the Lord, and thus they are simultaneously one and different from Him.

At the stage of nonmanifestation, the living energies remain potent in the Lord, and when they are let loose in the cosmic manifestation they are exhibited differently in terms of different desires under the modes of nature. Such differential manifestations of the living energies are conditional states of the living entities. The liberated living entities, however, in the *sanātana* or eternal manifestation, are unconditionally surrendered souls, and therefore they are not subject to the conditions of creation and annihilation. So this creation takes place by the glance of the Lord from His bedstead of mystic slumber. And thus all the universes and the lord of the universe, Brahmā, are again and again manifested and annihilated.

TEXT 14

अधिदैवमथाध्यात्ममधिभूतमिति प्रभुः ।
अथैकं पौरुषं वीर्यं त्रिधाभिद्यत तच्छृणु ॥१४॥

adhidaivam athādhyātmam
adhibhūtam iti prabhuḥ
athaikaṁ pauruṣaṁ vīryaṁ
tridhābhidyata tac chṛṇu

adhidaivam—the controlling entities; *atha*—now; *adhyātmam*—the controlled entities; *adhibhūtam*—the material bodies; *iti*—thus; *prabhuḥ*—the Lord; *atha*—in this way; *ekam*—one only; *pauruṣam*—of His Lordship; *vīryam*—potency; *tridhā*—in three; *abhidyata*—divided; *tat*—that; *śṛṇu*—just hear from me.

TRANSLATION

Just hear from me how the potency of His Lordship divides one into three, called by the names controlling entities, controlled entities and the material bodies, in the manner mentioned above.

TEXT 15

अन्तःशरीर आकाशात् पुरुषस्य विचेष्टतः ।
ओजः सहो बलं जज्ञे ततः प्राणो महानसुः ॥१५॥

antaḥ śarīra ākāśāt
puruṣasya viceṣṭataḥ
ojaḥ saho balaṁ jajñe
tataḥ prāṇo mahān asuḥ

antaḥ śarīre—within the body; *ākāśāt*—from the sky; *puruṣasya*—of Mahā-Viṣṇu; *viceṣṭataḥ*—while so trying, or willing; *ojaḥ*—energy of the senses; *sahaḥ*—mental force; *balam*—bodily strength; *jajñe*—generated; *tataḥ*—thereafter; *prāṇaḥ*—living force; *mahān asuḥ*—the fountainhead of everyone's life.

TRANSLATION

From the sky situated within the transcendental body of the manifesting Mahā-Viṣṇu, sense energy, mental force and bodily strength are all generated, as well as the sum total of the fountainhead of the total living force.

TEXT 16

अनुप्राणन्ति यं प्राणाः प्राणन्तं सर्वजन्तुषु ।
अपानन्तमपानन्ति नरदेवमिवानुगाः ॥१६॥

anu prāṇanti yaṁ prāṇāḥ
prāṇantaṁ sarva-jantuṣu
apānantam apānanti
nara-devam ivānugāḥ

anu prāṇanti—follow the living symptoms; *yam*—whom; *prāṇāḥ*—senses; *prāṇantam*—endeavoring; *sarva-jantuṣu*—in all living entities; *apānantam*—stop endeavoring; *apānanti*—all others stop; *nara-devam*—the king; *iva*—like; *anugāḥ*—the followers.

TRANSLATION

As the followers of the king follow their lord, similarly when the total energy is in motion, all other living entities move, and when the total energy stops endeavoring, all other living entities stop sense activities.

PURPORT

The individual living entities are completely dependent on the total energy of the supreme *puruṣa.* No one has independent existence, just as no electric lamp has independent effulgence. Each and every electrical instrument depends fully on the total powerhouse; the total powerhouse depends on the electric generating water reservation; water depends on the cloud; the cloud depends on the sun; the sun depends on creation, and the creation depends on the movement of the Supreme Personality of Godhead. Thus the Supreme Personality of Godhead is the cause of all causes.

TEXT 17

प्राणेनाक्षिपता क्षुत् तृडन्तरा जायते विभोः ।
पिपासतो जक्षतश्च प्राङ्मुखं निरभिद्यत ॥१७॥

prāṇenākṣipatā kṣut-tṛḍ
antarā jāyate vibhoḥ
pipāsato jakṣataś ca
prāṅ mukhaṁ nirabhidyata

prāṇena—by the living force; *ākṣipatā*—being agitated; *kṣut*—hunger; *tṛṭ*—thirst; *antarā*—from within; *jāyate*—generates; *vibhoḥ*—of the Supreme; *pipāsataḥ*—being desirous to quench the thirst; *jakṣataḥ*—being desirous to eat; *ca*—and; *prāk*—at first; *mukham*—mouth; *nirabhidyata*—was opened.

TRANSLATION

The living force, being agitated by the virāṭa puruṣa, generated hunger and thirst, and when He desired to drink and eat, the mouth opened.

PURPORT

The process functioning for all living beings in the womb of the mother to develop the sense organs and sense perceptions appears to follow the same principles in the case of *virāṭa puruṣa,* the sum total of all living entities. Therefore the supreme cause of all generation is not impersonal or without desire. The desires for all kinds of sense perception and sense organs are there in the Supreme, and they take place in the individual persons. And this desire is the nature of the supreme living being, the Absolute Truth. Because He has the sum total of all mouths, the individual living entities have mouths. Similarly with all other senses and sense organs. Here the mouth is the symbolic representation of all sense organs, and the same principle is applicable in others also.

TEXT 18

मुखतस्तालु निर्भिन्नं जिह्वा तत्रोपजायते ।
ततो नानारसो जज्ञे जिह्वया योऽधिगम्यते ॥१८॥

mukhatas tālu nirbhinnaṁ
jihvā tatropajāyate
tato nānā-raso jajñe
jihvayā yo 'dhigamyate

mukhataḥ—from the mouth; *tālu*—the palate; *nirbhinnam*—being generated; *jihvā*—the tongue; *tatra*—thereupon; *upajāyate*—becomes manifested; *tataḥ*—thereupon; *nānā-rasaḥ*—various tastes; *jajñe*—became manifested; *jihvayā*—by the tongue; *yaḥ*—which; *adhigamyate*—become relished.

TRANSLATION

From the mouth the palate became manifested, and thereupon the tongue was also generated. After this all the different tastes came into existence so that the tongue can relish them.

PURPORT

This gradual process of evolution suggests the explanation of the controlling deities *(adhidaiva)* because Varuṇa is the controlling deity for all relishable juices. Therefore the mouth becomes the resting place for the tongue, which tastes all the different juices of which the controlling deity is the Varuṇa. It suggests, therefore, that Varuṇa was also generated along with the development of the tongue. The tongue and the palate, being instrumental, are *adhibhūtam,* or the forms of matter, but the functioning deity who is a living entity is *adhidaiva,* whereas the person undergoing the function is *adhyātmic,* and thus the three categories are also explained as to their birth after the opening of the mouth of the *virāṭa puruṣa.* The four principles mentioned here in this verse serve to explain the three main principles, namely the *adhyātma, adhidaiva* and *adhibhūtam,* as explained before.

TEXT 19

विवक्षोर्मुखतो भूम्नो वह्निर्वाग् व्याहृतं तयोः ।
जले चै तस्य सुचिरं निरोधः समजायत ॥१९॥

vivakṣor mukhato bhūmno
vahnir vāg vyāhṛtaṁ tayoḥ
jale caitasya suciraṁ
nirodhaḥ samajāyata

vivakṣoḥ—when there was a need to speak; *mukhataḥ*—from the mouth; *bhūmnaḥ*—of the Supreme; *vahniḥ*—the fire or the controlling deity of fire; *vāk*—vibration; *vyāhṛtam*—speeches; *tayoḥ*—by both; *jale*—in the water; *ca*—however; *etasya*—of all these; *suciram*—very, very long time; *nirodhaḥ*—suspension; *samajāyata*—did continue.

TRANSLATION

When the Supreme desired to speak, there was vibration of speeches from the mouth. Then the controlling deity Fire generated from the mouth. But when He was lying in the water, all these functions remained suspended.

PURPORT

The peculiarity of the gradual development of the different senses is simultaneously being supported by their controlling deities. It is to be understood, therefore, that the activities of the sense organs are controlled by the will of the Supreme. The senses are, so to speak, offering a license for the conditioned souls, and they are to use them properly under the control of the controlling deity deputed by the Supreme Lord. One who violates such controlling regulations has to be punished by degradation to the lower status of life. Take, for example, the tongue and its controlling deity Varuṇa. The tongue is meant for eating, and men, animals and birds each have their different tastes because of different licenses. The taste of the human beings and that of the swine are not on the same level. The controlling deity, however, awards or certifies a particular type of body when the particular living entity develops a taste in terms of different modes of nature. If the human being develops taste without discrimination, as does the swine, then the controlling deity is certainly certified for the next term to award him the body of a swine. The swine accepts any kind of foodstuff, including stools, and a human being who has developed such indiscriminate taste must be prepared for a degraded life in the next life. Such life is also God's grace because the conditioned soul desired a body like that for perfectly tasting a particular type of foodstuff, and if a man gets the body of a swine it must be considered the grace of the Lord because He awards the facility. After death the body is offered by superior control, and not blindly. A human being, therefore, must be on his guard as to what sort of body he is going to have in the next life. Irresponsible life of indiscrimination is risky, and that is the declaration of all scriptures.

TEXT 20

नासिके निरभिद्येतां दोधूयति नभस्वति ।
तत्र वायुर्गन्धवहो घ्राणो नसि जिघृक्षतः ॥२०॥

nāsike nirabhidyetāṁ
dodhūyati nabhasvati
tatra vāyur gandha-vaho
ghrāṇo nasi jighṛkṣataḥ

nāsike—in the nostrils; *nirabhidyetām*—being developed; *dodhūyate*—rapidly blowing; *nabhasvati*—air respiration; *tatra*—thereupon; *vāyuḥ*—air; *gandha-vahaḥ*—smelling odor; *ghrāṇaḥ*—sense of smell; *nasi*—in the nose; *jighṛkṣataḥ*—desiring to smell odors.

TRANSLATION

Thereafter, when the supreme puruṣa desired to smell odors, the nostrils and respiration generated, the nasal instrument and odors came into existence, and the controlling deity of air, carrying smell, also became manifested.

PURPORT

The nasal instrument, odor, and the controlling deity air, smelling, etc., all became manifested simultaneously when the Lord desired to smell. The Vedic *mantras* confirm this statement in the *Upaniṣads'* statement that everything is first desired by the Supreme, and then the subordinate living entity can act upon it. The living entity can see only when the Lord sees, the living entity can smell when the Lord smells, and so on. The idea is that the living entity cannot do anything independently. He can simply think of doing something independently, but he cannot act independently. This independence of thinking is there by the grace of the Lord, but the thinking can be given shape by the grace of the Lord, and therefore the common saying is that man proposes and God disposes. The whole explanation is on the subject of absolute dependence of the living entities and absolute independence of the Supreme Lord. Less intelligent persons, claiming to be on an equal level with God, first of all must prove themselves to be absolute and independent, and then they must substantiate their claim as one with God.

TEXT 21

यदाऽऽत्मनि निरालोकमात्मानं च दिदृक्षतः ।
निर्भिन्ने ह्यक्षिणी तस्य ज्योतिश्चक्षुर्गुणग्रहः ॥२१॥

yadātmani nirālokam
ātmānaṁ ca didṛkṣataḥ
nirbhinne akṣiṇī tasya
jyotiś cakṣur guṇa-grahaḥ

yadā—while; *ātmani*—unto Himself; *nirālokam*—without any light; *ātmānam*—His own transcendental body; *ca*—also other bodily forms; *didṛkṣataḥ*—desired to look upon; *nirbhinne*—due to being sprouted; *akṣiṇī*—of the eyes; *tasya*—of Him; *jyotiḥ*—the sun; *cakṣuḥ*—the eyes; *guṇa-grahaḥ*—the power of seeing.

TRANSLATION

Thus when everything existed in darkness, the Lord desired to see Himself and all that was created. Then the eyes, the illuminating god Sun, the power of vision and the object of sight all became manifested.

PURPORT

The universe is by nature dense darkness, and therefore the total creation is called *tamas* or darkness. The night is the real feature of the universe, for then no one can see anything, including oneself. The Lord, out of His causeless mercy, first desired to see Himself and all the creation as well, and thus the sun became manifested, the power of vision of all living entities became possible, and the objects of vision were also manifested. This means the whole phenomenal world became visible after the creation of the sun.

TEXT 22

बोध्यमानस्य ऋषिभिरात्मनस्तज्जिघृक्षतः ।
कर्णौ च निरभिद्येतां दिशः श्रोत्रं गुणग्रहः ॥२२॥

bodhyamānasya ṛṣibhir
ātmanas taj jighṛkṣataḥ
karṇau ca nirabhidyetāṁ
diśaḥ śrotraṁ guṇa-grahaḥ

bodhyamānasya—desiring to understand; *ṛṣibhiḥ* by the authorities; *ātmanaḥ*—of the Supreme Being; *tat*—that; *jighṛkṣataḥ*—when he desired to take up; *karṇau*—the ears; *ca*—also; *nirabhidyetām*—became manifested; *diśaḥ*—the direction or the god of air; *śrotram*—the power of hearing; *guṇa-grahaḥ*—and the objects of hearing.

TRANSLATION

By development of the desire of the great sages to know, the ears, the power of hearing, the controlling deity of hearing, and the objects of hearing became manifested. The great sages desired to hear about the Self.

PURPORT

As is stated in the *Bhagavad-gītā,* one should try to know by advancement of knowledge about the Supreme Lord, the *summum bonum* of everything. Knowledge does not mean to know the laws of nature or of physical knowledge that are working by the direction of the Lord. The scientists are eager to hear about the physical laws that are working in the material nature. They are eager to hear through the medium of radio and television about the things which are taking place far away from them in other planets, but they should know that the power of hearing and the instruments for hearing were given to them by the Lord for hearing about the Self, or about the Lord. Unfortunately the power of hearing is misused in hearing the vibrations of mundane affairs. The great sages were interested to hear about the Lord through Vedic knowledge and nothing more. And that is the beginning of aural reception of knowledge.

TEXT 23

वस्तुनो मृदुकाठिन्यलघुगुर्वोष्णशीतताम् ।
जिघृक्षतस्त्वङ् निर्भिन्ना तस्यां रोममहीरुहाः ।
तत्र चान्तर्बहिर्वातस्त्वचा लब्धगुणो वृतः ॥२३॥

vastuno mṛdu-kāṭhinya-
laghu-gurvoṣṇa-śītatām
jighṛkṣatas tvaṅ nirbhinnā
tasyāṁ roma-mahīruhāḥ
tatra cāntar bahir vātas
tvacā labdha-guṇo vṛtaḥ

vastunaḥ—of all matters; *mṛdu*—softness; *kāṭhinya*—hardness; *laghu*—lightness; *guru*—heaviness; *oṣṇa*—warmness; *śītatām*—coldness; *jighṛkṣataḥ*—desiring to perceive; *tvak*—touch sensation; *nirbhinnā*—distributed; *tasyām*—in the skin; *roma*—hairs on the body; *mahī-ruhāḥ*—as well as the trees, the controlling deities; *tatra*—there; *ca*—also; *antaḥ*—within; *bahiḥ*—outside; *vātaḥ tvacā*—sense of touch or the skin; *labdha*—having been perceived; *guṇaḥ*—objects of sense perception; *vṛtaḥ*—generated.

TRANSLATION

When there was a desire to perceive the physical characteristics of matter, as softness, hardness, warmth, cold, lightness, heaviness, etc., the background of sensation, skin, the skin pores, the hairs on the body and their controlling deities (the trees) were generated. Within and without the skin there is an air covering through which sense perception became prominent.

PURPORT

The physical characteristics of matter, as softness, etc., are subject of the sense perception, and thus physical knowledge is the subject matter of the touch sensation. One can measure the temperature of matter by touching with the hand, and one can measure the weight of a matter by lifting with the hand and thus estimate its heaviness or lightness. The skin, the skin pores and the hairs on the body are all interdependent with touch sensation. The air blowing within and without the skin is also an object of sense perception. This sense perception is also the source of knowledge, and therefore it is suggested here that physical or physiological knowledge are subordinate to the knowledge of the Self, as above mentioned. Knowledge of Self can expand to the knowledge of phenomena, but physical knowledge cannot lead to the knowledge of Self.

There is, however, intimate relation between the hairs on the body and the vegetation on the body of the earth. The vegetables are nourishment for the skin both as food and medicine, as is stated in the Third Canto: *"tvacam asya vinirbhinnāṁ viviśur dhiṣṇyam oṣadhīḥ."*

TEXT 24

हस्तौ रुरुहतुस्तस्य नानाकर्मचिकीर्षया ।
तयोस्तु बलवानिन्द्र आदानमुभयाश्रयम् ॥२४॥

hastau ruruhatus tasya
nānā-karma-cikīrṣayā
tayos tu balavān indra
ādānam ubhayāśrayam

hastau—the hands; *ruruhatuḥ*—manifested; *tasya*—His; *nānā*—various; *karma*—work; *cikīrṣayā*—being so desirous; *tayoḥ*—of them; *tu*—however; *balavān*—to give strength; *indraḥ*—the demigod in heaven; *ādānam*—activities of the hand; *ubhaya-āśrayam*—dependent on both the demigod and the hand.

TRANSLATION

Thereafter when the Supreme Person desired to perform varieties of work, the two hands and their controlling strength, and Indra, the demigod in heaven, became manifested, as also the acts dependent on both the hands and the demigod.

PURPORT

In every item we can note with profit that the sense organs of the living entity are never independent in any stage. The Lord is known as the Lord of the senses *(Hṛṣīkeśa)*, and thus the sense organs of the living entities become manifested by the will of the Lord, and each organ is controlled by a certain type of demigod. No one, therefore, can claim any proprietorship of the senses. The living entity is controlled by the senses, the senses are controlled by the demigods, and the demigods are the servants of the Supreme Lord. That is the arrangement in the system of creation. The whole thing is controlled ultimately by the Supreme Lord, and there is no independence either of the material nature or of the living entity. The illusioned living entity who claims to be the lord of his senses is under the clutches of the external energy of the Lord, and as long as a living entity continues to be puffed up by his tiny existence, he is to be understood to be under the stringent control of the external energy of the Lord, and there is no question of liberation from the clutches of illusion (*māyā*), however much one may declare himself a liberated soul.

TEXT 25

गतिं जिगीषतः पादौ रुरुहातेऽभिकामिकाम् ।
पद्भ्यां यज्ञः स्वयं हव्यं कर्मभिः क्रियते नृभिः ॥२५॥

gatiṁ jigīṣataḥ pādau
ruruhāte 'bhikāmikām
padbhyāṁ yajñaḥ svayaṁ havyaṁ
karmabhiḥ kriyate nṛbhiḥ

gatim—movement; *jigīṣataḥ*—so desiring; *pādau*—the legs; *ruruhāte*—being manifested; *abhikāmikām*—purposeful; *padbhyām*—from the legs; *yajñaḥ*—a certain demigod of the name Viṣṇu; *svayam*—personally Himself; *havyam*—the duties; *karmabhiḥ*—by one's occupational duty; *kriyate*—caused to be done; *nṛbhiḥ*—by different human beings.

TRANSLATION

Thereupon, by so desiring to control movement, His legs became manifested, and from the legs the controlling deity named Viṣṇu generated. By His personal supervision of this act, all varieties of human being are busily engaged in dutiful occupational sacrifice.

PURPORT

Every human being is engaged in his particular occupational duty, and such activities are visible as men go hither and thither. This is very prominently visible in big cities of the world: people are going all over the cities with great concern, from one place to another. This movement is not only limited within the cities but is also visible outside the cities from one place to another, or from one city to another, by different means of vehicles. They are moving by cars and rails on the roads, by subways within the earth and by planes in the sky for the purpose of business success. But in all these movements the real purpose is to earn wealth for comfortable life. And for this comfortable life the scientist is engaged, the artist is engaged, the engineer is engaged, the technician is engaged, all in different branches of human activity. But they do not know how to make the activities purposeful to fulfill the mission of human life. Without knowing this secret, all their activities are targetted towards the goal of sense gratification without any control, and therefore by all this business they are unknowingly entering into the deep regions of darkness.

Because they have been captivated by the external energy of the Supreme Lord, they have completely forgotten the Supreme Lord Viṣṇu, and thus they have taken it for granted that this life, as presently manifested under the conditions of material nature, is all in all for enjoying the highest amount of sense gratification. But such a wrong conception of life cannot give anyone the desired peace of mind, and thus in spite of all advancement of knowledge by using the resources of nature, no one is happy in this material civilization. The secret is that in every step they should try to execute sacrifices towards the path of world peace. The *Bhagavad-gītā* also advises the same secret in the following verses.

sve sve karmaṇy abhirataḥ saṁsiddhiṁ labhate naraḥ
sva-karmanir ataḥ siddhiṁ yathā vindati tac chṛṇu
yataḥ pravṛttir bhūtānāṁ yena sarvam idaṁ tatam
sva-karmaṇā tam abhyarcya siddhiṁ vindati mānavaḥ

The Lord said to Arjuna, "Just hear from Me how one can attain the highest perfection in life simply by discharging his specified occupational duty.

"Man can attain the highest perfection of life by worshiping the Supreme Lord and by performing sacrifice for the sake of the Supreme Lord Viṣṇu, who is all-pervading, and by whose control every living being acquires his desired facilities, according to his personal propensity."

There is no harm in having different propensities in life because every human being is proportionately independent to chalk out the plan of his life by different occupations, but he should make it a point in his life to know perfectly well that he is not independent absolutely. He is certainly under the control of the Supreme Lord and under different agencies. And knowing this, he should make it a point that by his work and the result of his labor he serves the Supreme Lord as it is prescribed by the authorities expert in the transcendental loving service of the Supreme Lord Viṣṇu. And for performing such occupational duties of life the leg is the most important instrument of the body because without the help of the legs no one can move from one place to another, and therefore the Lord has special control over the legs of all human beings, which are meant for performing *yajñas*.

TEXT 26

निरभिद्यत शिश्नो वै प्रजानन्दामृतार्थिनः ।
उपस्थ आसीत् कामानां प्रियं तदुभयाश्रयम् ॥२६॥

nirabhidyata śiśno vai
prajānandāmṛtārthinaḥ
upastha āsīt kāmānāṁ
priyaṁ tad-ubhayāśrayam

nirabhidyata—came out; *śiśnaḥ*—the genitals; *vai*—certainly; *prajā-ānanda*—sex pleasure; *amṛta-arthinaḥ*—aspiring to taste the nectar; *upasthaḥ*—the male or female organ; *āsīt*—came into existence; *kāmānām*—of the lustful; *priyam*—very dear; *tat*—that; *ubhaya-āśrayam*—shelter for both.

TRANSLATION

Thereupon, for sex pleasure, begetting offspring and tasting heavenly nectar, the Lord developed the genitals, and thus there is the genital organ and its controlling deity, the Prajāpati. The object of sex pleasure and the controlling deity are under the control of the genitals of the Lord.

PURPORT

The heavenly pleasure for the conditioned soul is sex pleasure, and this pleasure is tasted by the genitals. The woman is the object of sex pleasure, and both the sense perception of sex pleasure and the woman are controlled by the Prajāpati, who is under the control of the Lord's genitals. The impersonalist must know from this verse that the Lord is not impersonal because he has His genitals on which all the pleasurable objects of sex depend. No one would have taken the trouble to maintain children if there were no taste of the heavenly nectar by means of sexual intercourse. This material world is created to give a chance to the conditioned souls for rejuvenation for going back home, back to Godhead, and therefore generation of the living being is necessary for upkeep of the purpose of creation. The sex pleasure is an impetus for such action, and as such one can even serve the Lord in the act of such sex pleasure. The service is counted when the children born out of such sex pleasure are properly trained in God consciousness. The whole idea of material creation is to revive the dormant God consciousness of the living entity. In other forms of life, besides the human form, the sex pleasure is prominent only without any motive of service for the mission of the Lord. But in the human form of life the conditioned soul can render service to the Lord by creating progeny suitable for the attainment of salvation. One can beget hundreds of children and enjoy the celestial pleasure of sexual intercourse provided he is able to train up the children in God consciousness. Otherwise begetting children is on the level of the swine. Rather, the swine is more expert that the human being because the swine can beget a dozen piglets at a time, whereas the human being can give birth to one only at a time. So one should always remember that the genitals, sex pleasure, the woman, and the offspring are all related in the service of the Lord, and one who forgets this relationship in the service of the Supreme Lord becomes subjected to the threefold miseries of material existence by the laws of nature. Perception of sex pleasure is there even in the body of the dog, but there is no sense of God consciousness. The human form of life is distinct from that of the dog by the perception of God consciousness.

TEXT 27

उत्सिसृक्षोर्धातुमलं निरभिद्यत वै गुदम् ।
ततः पायुस्ततो मित्र उत्सर्ग उभयाश्रयः ॥२७॥

utsisṛkṣor dhātu-malaṁ
nirabhidyata vai gudam
tataḥ pāyus tato mitra
utsarga ubhayāśrayaḥ

utsisṛkṣoḥ—desiring to evacuate; *dhātu-malam*—refuse of eatables; *nirabhidyata*—became open; *vai*—certainly; *gudam*—the evacuating hole; *tataḥ*—thereafter; *pāyuḥ*—the evacuating sense organ; *tataḥ*—thereafter; *mitraḥ*—the controlling demigod; *utsargaḥ*—the substance evacuated; *ubhaya*—both; *āśrayaḥ*—shelter.

TRANSLATION

Thereafter, desiring to evacuate the refuse of eatables, the evacuating hole, anus, and the sensory organ thereof developed along with the controlling deity Mitra. The sensory organ and the evacuating substance are both under the shelter of the controlling deity.

PURPORT

Even in the matter of evacuating stool, the refuse is controlled, so how can the living entity claim to be independent?

TEXT 28

आसिसृप्सोः पुरः पुर्या नाभिद्वारमपानतः ।
तत्रापानस्ततो मृत्युः पृथक्त्वमुभयाश्रयम् ॥२८॥

āsisṛpsoḥ puraḥ puryā
nābhi-dvāram apānataḥ
tatrāpānas tato mṛtyuḥ
pṛthaktvam ubhayāśrayam

āsisṛpsoḥ—desiring to go everywhere; *puraḥ*—in different bodies; *puryāḥ*—from one body; *nābhi-dvāram*—the navel or abdominal hole; *apānataḥ*—was manifested; *tatra*—thereupon; *apānaḥ*—stopping of the vital force; *tataḥ*—thereafter; *mṛtyuḥ*—death; *pṛthaktvam*—separately; *ubhaya*—both; *āśrayam*—shelter.

TRANSLATION

Thereafter, desiring to move from one body to another, the navel and the air of departure and death were combinedly created. The navel is the shelter for both, namely death and the separating force.

PURPORT

The *prāṇa-vāyu* continues the life, and the *apāna-vāyu* stops the living force. And both the vibrations are generated from the abdominal hole, navel. This navel is the joint from one body to the other. Lord Brahmā was born out of the abdominal hole of Garbhodakaśāyī Viṣṇu as a separate body, and the same principle is followed even in the birth of any ordinary body. The body of the child develops from the body of the mother, and when the child is separated from the body of the mother, it is separated by cutting the navel joint. And that is the way the Supreme Lord manifested Himself as separated many. The living entities are therefore separated parts, and thus they have no independence.

TEXT 29

आदित्सोरन्नपानानामासन् कुक्ष्यन्त्रनाडयः ।
नद्यः समुद्राश्च तयोस्तुष्टिः पुष्टिस्तदाश्रये ॥२९॥

āditsor anna-pānānām
āsan kukṣy-antra-nāḍayaḥ
nadyaḥ samudrāś ca tayos
tuṣṭiḥ puṣṭis tad-āśraye

āditsoḥ—desiring to have; *anna-pānānām*—of food and drink; *āsan*—there became; *kukṣi*—abdomen; *antra*—intestines; *nāḍayaḥ*—and the artery; *nadyaḥ*—the rivers; *samudrāḥ*—seas; *ca*—also; *tayoḥ*—of them; *tuṣṭiḥ*—sustenance; *puṣṭiḥ*—metabolism; *tat*—of them; *āśraye*—the source.

TRANSLATION

When there was desire to have food and drink, the abdomen and the intestines and also the arteries became manifested. The rivers and the seas are the source of their sustenance and metabolism.

PURPORT

The controlling deities of the intestines are rivers, and those of the arteries, the seas. Fulfillment of the belly with food and drink is the cause of sustenance, and the metabolism of the food and drink replaces the waste of the bodily energies. Therefore, the body's health is dependent on healthy actions of the intestines and the arteries. The rivers and the seas, being the controlling deities of the two, keep the intestines and the arteries in healthy order.

TEXT 30

निदिध्यासोरात्ममायां हृदयं निरभिद्यत ।
ततो मनश्चन्द्र इति सङ्कल्पः काम एव च ॥३०॥

nididhyāsor ātma-māyāṁ
hṛdayaṁ nirabhidyata
tato manaś candra iti
saṅkalpaḥ kāma eva ca

nididhyāsoḥ—being desirious to know; *ātma-māyām*—own energy; *hṛdayam*—the location of the mind; *nirabhidyata*—was manifested; *tataḥ*—thereafter; *manaḥ*—the mind; *candraḥ*—the controlling deity of the mind, the moon; *iti*—thus; *saṅkalpaḥ*—determination; *kāmaḥ*—desire; *eva*—as much as; *ca*—also.

TRANSLATION

When there was a desire to think about the activities of His own energy, then the heart, the seat of the mind, the mind, the moon, determination and all desire became manifested.

PURPORT

The heart of every living entity is the seat of the Supersoul Paramātmā, a plenary expansion of the Supreme Personality of Godhead. Without His presence the living entity cannot get into the working energy according to his past deeds. The living entities who are conditioned in the material world are manifested in the creation in terms of respective inclinations inherent in them, and the requisite material body is offered to each and every one of them by the material energy under the direction of the Supersoul. This is explained in the *Bhagavad-gītā* (Bg. 9.10). When, therefore, the Supersoul is situated in the heart of the conditioned soul, the requisite mind is manifested in the conditioned soul, and he becomes conscious of his occupation as one is conscious of his duty after waking up from slumber. Therefore the material mind of the living entity develops when the Supersoul sits on his heart, after which the mind, the controlling deity, moon, and then the activities of the mind (namely thinking, feeling, and willing) all take place. The activities of the mind cannot begin without the manifestation of the heart, and the heart becomes manifested when the Lord wants to see the activities of the material creation.

TEXT 31

त्वक्चर्ममांसरुधिरमेदोमज्जास्थिधातवः ।
भूम्यप्तेजोमयाः सप्त प्राणो व्योमाम्बुवायुभिः ॥३१॥

tvak-carma-māṁsa-rudhira-
medo-majjāsthi-dhātavaḥ
bhūmy-ap-tejomayāḥ sapta
prāṇo vyomāmbu-vāyubhiḥ

tvak—the thin layer on the skin; *carma*—skin; *māṁsa*—flesh; *rudhira*—blood; *medaḥ*—fat; *majjā*—marrow; *asthi*—bone; *dhātavaḥ*—elements; *bhūmi*—earth; *ap*—water; *tejaḥ*—fire; *mayāḥ*—predominating; *sapta*—seven; *prāṇaḥ*—breathing air; *vyoma*—sky; *ambu*—water; *vāyubhiḥ*—by the air.

TRANSLATION

The seven elements of the body, namely the thin layer on the skin, the skin, the flesh, the blood, fat, the marrow and the bone, are all made of earth, water and fire, whereas the life breathing air is produced by the sky, water and air.

PURPORT

Construction of the whole material world is prominently made by three elements, namely earth, water and fire. But the living force is produced by sky, air, and water. So water is the common element both in the gross and subtle forms of all material creation, and it should be noted herewith that due to necessity, water, being most prominent in the material creation, is the principal element of all the five. This material body is thus an embodiment of the five elements, and the gross manifestation is perceived because of three, namely, earth, water, and fire. Sensation of touch is perceived due to the thin layer on the skin, and bone is as good as hard stone. Since the breathing air of life is produced of sky, air and water, open air, regular bath and ample space to live in are favorable for healthy vitality. Fresh produce of the earth like grains and vegetables, fresh water and heat are good for the upkeep of the gross body.

TEXT 32

गुणात्मकानीन्द्रियाणि भूतादिप्रभवा गुणाः ।
मनः सर्वविकारात्मा बुद्धिर्विज्ञानरूपिणी ॥३२॥

guṇātmakānīndriyāṇi
bhūtādi-prabhavā guṇāḥ
manaḥ sarva-vikārātmā
buddhir vijñāna-rūpiṇī

guṇa-ātmakāni—attached to the qualities; *indriyāṇi*—senses; *bhūtādi*—material ego; *prabhavāḥ*—influenced by; *guṇāḥ*—modes of material nature; *manaḥ*—the mind; *sarva*—all; *vikāra*—affection (happiness and distress); *ātmā*—form; *buddhiḥ*—intelligence; *vijñāna*—deliberation; *rūpiṇī*—featuring.

TRANSLATION

The sense organs are attached to the modes of material nature, and the modes of material nature are products of the false ego. Mind is subjected to all kinds of material experiences (happiness and distress), and the intelligence is the feature of mind's deliberation.

PURPORT

Illusioned by the material nature, the living entity identifies with false ego. More clearly, when the living entity is entrapped by the material body he at once identifies with the bodily relationships, forgetting his own identity as spirit soul. This false ego associates with different modes of material nature, and thus the senses become attached to the modes of material nature. Mind is the instrument for feeling different material experiences, but intelligence is deliberative and can change everything for the better. The intelligent person, therefore, can attain salvation from the illusion of material existence by proper use of intelligence. An intelligent person can detect the awkward position of material existence and thus begin to inquire as to what he is, why he is subjected to different kinds of miseries, how to get rid of all miseries, and thus, by good association, an advanced intelligent person can turn towards the better life of self-realization. It is advised, therefore, that an intelligent person associate with great sages and saints who are on the path of salvation. By such association, one can receive instructions which are able to slacken the conditioned soul's attachment for matter, and thus gradually the intelligent man gets rid of the illusion of matter and false ego and is promoted to the real life of eternity, knowledge and blissfulness.

TEXT 33

एतद्भगवतो रूपं स्थूलं ते व्याहृतं मया ।
मह्यादिभिश्चावरणैरष्टभिर्बहिरावृतम् ॥३३॥

etad bhagavato rūpaṁ
sthūlaṁ te vyāhṛtaṁ mayā
mahy-ādibhiś cāvaraṇair
aṣṭabhir bahir āvṛtam

etat—all these; *bhagavataḥ*—of the Personality of Godhead; *rūpam*—form; *sthūlam*—gross; *te*—unto you; *vyāhṛtam*—explained; *mayā*—by me; *mahī*—the planets; *ādibhiḥ*—et cetera; *ca*—unlimitedly; *avaraṇaiḥ*—by coverings; *aṣṭabhiḥ*—by eight; *bahiḥ*—external; *āvṛtam*—covered.

TRANSLATION

Thus by all this, the external feature of the Personality of Godhead is covered by gross forms of planets, et cetera, which were explained to you by me.

PURPORT

As explained in the *Bhagavad-gītā* (Bg. 7.4) the separated material energy of the Personality of Godhead is covered by eight kinds of material coverings: namely earth, water, fire, air, sky, mind, intelligence and false ego. All these are emanations from the Personality of Godhead as His external energy. These coverings are just like the covering of clouds for the sun. The cloud is a creation of the sun, yet it actually covers the eyes so that one cannot see the sun. The sun cannot be covered by the clouds. The cloud can at utmost extend a few hundreds of miles in the sky, but the sun is far greater than millions of miles. So a hundred-mile covering is not competent to cover millions of miles. Therefore, one of the various energies of the Supreme Personality of Godhead cannot, of course, cover the Lord. But these coverings are created by Him to cover the eyes of the conditioned souls who want to lord it over the material nature. Actually the conditioned souls are covered by the illusory creative cloud of matter, and the Lord reserves the right of not being exposed to the eyes of the conditioned souls. And because they have no eyes of transcendental vision and because they cannot see the Personality of Godhead, they therefore deny the existence of the Lord as well as the transcendental form of the Lord. The covering of the gigantic material feature is accepted by such men with poor fund of knowledge, and how it becomes so is explained in the following verse.

TEXT 34

अतः परं सूक्ष्मतममव्यक्तं निर्विशेषणम् ।
अनादिमध्यनिधनं नित्यं वाङ्मनसः परम् ॥३४॥

ataḥ paraṁ sūkṣmatamam
avyaktaṁ nirviśeṣaṇam
anādi-madhya-nidhanaṁ
nityaṁ vāṅ-manasaḥ param

ataḥ—therefore; *param*—transcendental; *sūkṣmatamam*—finer than the finest; *avyaktam*—unmanifested; *nirviśeṣaṇam*—without material features; *anādi*—without beginning; *madhya*—without an intermediate stage; *nidhanam*—without end; *nityam*—eternal; *vāk*—words; *manasaḥ*—of the mind; *param*—transcendental.

TRANSLATION

Therefore beyond this [gross manifestation] there is a transcendental manifestation finer than the finest form, which has no beginning, no intermediate stage and no end; therefore it is beyond the limits of expression or mental speculation and is distinct from the material conception.

PURPORT

The gross external body of the Supreme is manifested at certain intervals, and thus the external feature or form of the Supreme Personality of Godhead is not the eternal form of the Lord, which has no beginning, no intermediate stage and no end. Anything which has beginning, interim and end is called material. The material world is begun from the Lord, and thus the form of the Lord, before the beginning of the material world, is certainly transcendental to the finest or the finer material conception. The ether in the material world is considered to be the finest. Finer than the ether is mind, intelligence, and false ego. But all the eight outward coverings are explained as outer coverings of the Absolute Truth. The Absolute Truth is therefore beyond the expression and speculation of the material conception, He is certainly transcendental to all material conceptions. This is called *nirviśeṣaṇam.* One should not, however, misunderstand *nirviśeṣaṇam* as being without any transcendental qualifications. *Viśeṣaṇam* means qualities. Therefore *nir* added with it means that He has no material qualities or variegatedness. This nullifying expression is described in four transcendental qualifications, namely unmanifested, transcendental, eternal and beyond the conception of mind or word. Beyond the limits of words means negation of the material conception, and unless one is transcendentally situated, it is not possible to know the transcendental form of the Lord.

TEXT 35

अमुनी भगवद्रूपे मया ते ह्यनुवर्णिते ।
उभे अपि न गृह्णन्ति मायासृष्टे विपश्चितः ॥३५॥

amunī bhagavad-rūpe
mayā te hy anuvarṇite
ubhe api na gṛhṇanti
māyā-sṛṣṭe vipaś-citaḥ

amunī—all these; *bhagavat*—unto the Supreme Personality of Godhead; *rūpe*—in the forms; *mayā*—by me; *te*—unto you; *hi*—certainly; *anuvarṇite*—described respectively; *ubhe*—both; *api*—also; *na*—never; *gṛhṇanti*—accepts; *māyā*—external; *sṛṣṭe*—being so manifested; *vipaś-citaḥ*—the learned one who knows.

TRANSLATION

Both the above forms of the Lord, as just described unto you from the material angle of vision, are not accepted by the pure devotees of the Lord who know Him well.

PURPORT

The impersonalists think of the Absolute Personality of Godhead in two different ways, as above mentioned. On the one hand they worship the

Lord in His *viśva-rūpa* or all-pervading universal form, and on the other they think of the Lord's unmanifested, indescribable, subtle form. The theories of pantheism and monism are respectively applicable to these two conceptions of the Supreme as gross and subtle, but both of them are rejected by the learned pure devotees of the Lord because they are aware of the factual position. This is very clearly mentioned in the Eleventh Chapter of the *Bhagavad-gītā*, Arjuna's experience of the *viśva-rūpa* of the Supreme Lord Śrī Kṛṣṇa.

adṛṣṭa-pūrvaṁ hṛṣito 'smi dṛṣṭvā
bhayena ca pravyathitaṁ mano me
tad eva me darśaya deva rūpaṁ
prasīda deveśa jagannivāsa (Bg. 11.45)

Arjuna, as a pure devotee of the Lord, never previously saw the contemplated universal form of the Lord *(viśva-rūpa)*, but when he did see, his curiosities became satisfied. But he was not happy to see such a form of the Lord because of his attachment as a pure devotee. He was therefore afraid to see the gigantic form of the Lord. He therefore prayed to the Lord to assume His fourhanded Nārāyaṇa or Kṛṣṇa form, which alone could please him (Arjuna). Undoubtedly the Lord has the supreme potency to exhibit Himself in multifarious forms, but the pure devotees of the Lord are interested in His forms as are eternally exhibited in the abode of the Lord, known as the *tripād-vibhūti* or kingdom of God. The Lord in the *tripād-vibhūti* abode exhibits Himself in two forms, either with four hands or with two hands. The *viśva-rūpa* exhibited in the material manifestation has unlimited hands and unlimited dimensions with everything unlimited. The pure devotees of the Lord worship Him in His Vaikuṇṭha forms as Nārāyaṇa or Kṛṣṇa. Sometimes the same Vaikuṇṭha forms of the Lord are in the material world also by His grace as Śrī Rāma, Srī Kṛṣṇa, Śrī Narasiṁhadeva, etc., and thus the pure devotees also worship them. Usually the features shown in the material world have no existence in the Vaikuṇṭha planets, and thus they are not accepted by the pure devotees. What the pure devotees worship from the very beginning are eternal forms of the Lord existing in the Vaikuṇṭha planets. The nondevotee impersonalists imagine the material forms of the Lord, and ultimately they merge in the impersonal *brahmajyoti* of the Lord, whereas the pure devotees of the Lord are worshipers of the Lord both in the beginning and also in the perfect stage of salvation, eternally. The worship of the pure devotee never stops, whereas the worship of the impersonalist stops after his attainment of salvation, being merged in the impersonal form of the Lord known as *brahmajyoti.* Therefore the pure devotees of the Lord are described here as *vipaścita,* or the learned who are in the knowledge of the Lord perfectly.

TEXT 36

स वाच्यवाचकतया भगवान् ब्रह्मरूपधृक्।
नामरूपक्रिया धत्ते सकर्माकर्मकः परः ॥३६॥

sa vācya-vācakatayā
bhagavān brahma-rūpa-dhṛk
nāma-rūpa-kriyā dhatte
sa-karmākarmakaḥ paraḥ

saḥ—He; *vācya*—by His forms and activities; *vācakatayā*—by His transcendental qualities and entourage; *bhagavān*—the Personality of Godhead; *brahma*—absolute; *rūpa-dhṛk*—by accepting visible forms; *nāma*—name; *rūpa*—form; *kriyā*—pastimes; *dhatte*—accepts; *sa-karma*—engaged in work; *akarmakaḥ*—without being affected; *paraḥ*—transcendence.

TRANSLATION

He, the Personality of Godhead, manifests Himself in a transcendental form, being the subject of His transcendental name, quality, pastimes, entourage and transcendental variegatedness. Although He is unaffected by all such activities, He appears to be so engaged.

PURPORT

Whenever there is need of material creation, the transcendental Personality of Godhead accepts forms in the material world for creation, maintenance and destruction, and one should be intelligent enough to know His activities in truth without being biased to conclude that He descends in the material world by accepting a form created by material nature. Any form accepted from the material nature has its affection to everything done in the material world. A conditioned soul who accepts the material form for undergoing a certain term of material activities is subjected to the laws of matter. But here in this verse it is clearly stated that the forms and activities of the Lord, although they appear to be the same as those of another conditioned soul, are supernatural and impossible for the conditioned soul. He, the Supreme Personality of Godhead, is always unaffected by such activities. In the *Bhagavad-gītā* the Lord says:

na māṁ karmāṇi limpanti na me karma-phale spṛhā
iti māṁ yo'bhijānāti karmabhir na sa baddhyati
(Bg. 4.14)

The Lord is never affected by the activities which He apparently performs by His different incarnations and personalities, nor does He have any desire to achieve success by fruitive activities. The Lord is full by His different potencies of wealth, strength, fame, beauty, knowledge and renunciation, and thus He has no reason for physical exertion like the conditioned soul. Therefore an intelligent person who can distinguish between the transcendental activities of the Lord and those of the conditioned souls also is not bound by the reactions of activities. The Lord as Viṣṇu, Brahmā and Śiva conducts the three modes of material nature. From Viṣṇu is born Brahmā, and from Brahmā is born Śiva. Sometimes Brahmā is a separated part of Viṣṇu, and sometimes Brahmā is Viṣṇu Himself. Thus Brahmā creates the different species of life all over the universe, which means that the Lord creates the whole manifestation either Himself or through the agency of His authorized deputies.

TEXTS 37-40

प्रजापतीन्मनून् देवानृषीन् पितृगणान् पृथक् ।
सिद्धचारणगन्धर्वान् विद्याध्रासुरगुह्यकान् ॥३७॥
किन्नराप्सरसो नागान् सर्पान् किम्पुरुषान्नरान् ।
मातृ रक्षःपिशाचांश्च प्रेतभूतविनायकान् ॥३८॥
कूष्माण्डोन्मादवेतालान् यातुधानान् ग्रहानपि ।
खगान्मृगान् पशून् वृक्षान् गिरीन्नृप सरीसृपान् ॥३९॥
द्विविधाश्चतुर्विधा येऽन्ये जलस्थलनभौकसः ।
कुशलाकुशला मिश्राः कर्मणां गतयस्त्विमाः ॥४०॥

prajā-patīn manūn devān
ṛṣīn pitṛ-gaṇān pṛthak
siddha-cāraṇa-gandharvān
vidyādhrāsura-guhyakān

kinnarāpsaraso nāgān
sarpān kimpuruṣān narān
mātṝ rakṣaḥ piśācāṁś ca
preta-bhūta-vināyakān
kūṣmāṇḍonmāda-vetālān
yātudhānān grahān api
khagān mṛgān paśūn vṛkṣān
girīn nṛpa sarīsṛpān
dvi-vidhāś catur-vidhā ye'nye
jala-sthala-nabhaukasaḥ
kuśalākuśalā miśrāḥ
karmaṇāṁ gatayas tv imāḥ

prajā-patīn—Brahmā and his sons like Dakṣa and others; *manūn*—the periodical heads like Vaivasvata Manu, etc.; *devān*—like Indra, Candra, Varuṇa, etc.; *ṛṣīn*—like Bhṛgu, Vasiṣṭha, etc.; *pitṛgaṇān*—the inhabitants of the Pitā planets; *pṛthak*—separately; *siddha*—the inhabitants of the Siddha planet; *cāraṇa*—inhabitants of the Cāraṇa planet; *gandharvān*—inhabitants of the Gandharva planets; *vidyādhra*—inhabitants of the same planet; *asura*—the atheists; *guhyakān*—the inhabitants of the Yakṣa planet; *kinnara*—the inhabitants of the Kinnara planet; *apsarasaḥ*—the beautiful angels of the Apsara planet; *nāgān*—the inhabitants of the Nāgaloka (serpentine); *sarpān*—inhabitants of the Sarpaloka (snakes); *kimpuruṣān*—monkey-shaped inhabitants of the Kimpuruṣa planet; *narān*—inhabitants of the earth; *mātṝ*—inhabitants of the Mātṛloka; *rakṣaḥ*—inhabitants of the demoniac planet; *piśācān*—inhabitants of the Piśācaloka; *ca*—also; *preta*—inhabitants of Pretaloka; *bhūta*—the evil spirits; *vināyakān*—the goblins; *kūsmāṇḍa*—will o' the wisp; *unmāda*—lunatics; *vetālān*—the jinn; *yātudhānān*—a particular type of evil spirit; *grahān*—the good and evil stars; *api*—also; *khagān*—the birds; *mṛgān*—the forest animals; *paśūn*—the household animals; *vṛkṣān*—the ghosts; *girīn*—the mountains; *nṛpa*—O King; *sarīsṛpān*—reptiles; *dvi-vidhāḥ*—the moving and the standing living entities; *catur-vidhāḥ*—living entities born in the embryo, in eggs, in perspiration and in seeds; *ye*—others; *anye*—all; *jala*—water; *sthala*—land; *nabhaukasaḥ*—birds; *kuśala*—in happiness; *akuśalāḥ*—in distress; *miśrāḥ*—in mixed happiness and distress; *karmaṇām*—according to one's own past deeds; *gatayaḥ*—as result of; *tu*—but; *imāḥ*—all of them.

TRANSLATION

O King, know from me that Brahmā and his sons, like Dakṣa, and the periodical heads like Vaivasvata Manu, etc., demigods like

Indra, Candra, Varuṇa, etc., great sages like Bhṛgu, Vyāsa, Vasiṣṭha, etc., the inhabitants of the Pitṛloka, the inhabitants of the Siddhaloka, the Cāraṇas, Gandharvas, Vidyādharas, Asuras, Yakṣas, Kinnaras, Angels, the serpentines, the monkey-shaped Kimpuruṣas, the human beings, the inhabitants of Mātṛloka, the demons, Piśācas, ghosts, spirits, lunatics, evil spirits, good and evil stars, the goblins, the animals in the forest, the birds, the household animals, the reptiles, the mountains, the moving and standing living entities, the living entities who are born in embryos, in eggs, in perspiration and in seeds, and all others who may be in the water, land and sky, who may be in happiness or in distress or in mixed happiness and distress, according to past deeds, are all created by the Supreme Lord.

PURPORT

The varieties of living entities are mentioned in this list, and, with no exception from the highest topmost planet down to the lowest planet of the universe, all of them in different species of life are created by the Almighty Father Viṣṇu, and therefore no one is independent of the Supreme Personality of Godhead. In the *Bhagavad-gītā* the Lord therefore claims all living entities as His offsprings in the following verse:

sarva-yoniṣu kaunteya mūrtayaḥ sambhavanti yāḥ
tāsāṁ brahma mahad yonir ahaṁ bīja-pradaḥ pitā
(Bg. 14.4)

The material nature is compared to the mother. Although every living being is seen to be coming out of the mother's body, still it is a fact that the mother is not the ultimate cause of such a birth. The father is the ultimate cause of birth. Without the father's seed, no mother can give birth to a child. Therefore the living beings that are within the innumerable universes in different varieties of forms and position are all born out of the seeds of the Almighty Father, Personality of Godhead, and only to the man with a poor fund of knowledge does it appear that they are born out of the material nature. Being under the material energy of the Supreme Lord, all living entities beginning from Brahmā down to the insignificant ant are manifested in different bodies according to their past deeds.

The material nature is one of the energies of the Lord (Bg. 7.4). The material nature is inferior in comparison to the living entities, the superior nature. The superior nature and inferior nature of the Lord combined together to manifest the whole universal affairs.

Some of the living entities are relatively happy and in better conditions of life, whereas others are in distressed conditions of life. But factually none of them are actually happy in the material conditional life. No one can be happy in prison life, although one is a first-class prisoner and the other is a third-class prisoner. The intelligent person should not try to be promoted from third-class prison life to first-class prison life, but should try to be released from the prison altogether. One may be promoted to first-class prisoner, but the same first-class prisoner is again degraded to a third-class prisoner in the next term. One should try to be free from prison life and go back to home, back to Godhead. That is the real goal for all types of living entities.

TEXT 41

सत्त्वं रजस्तम इति तिस्रः सुरनृनारकाः ।
तत्राप्येकैकशो राजन् भिद्यन्ते गतयस्त्रिधा ।
यदैकैकतरोऽन्याभ्यां स्वभाव उपहन्यते ॥४१॥

sattvaṁ rajas tama iti
tisraḥ suranṛnārakāḥ
tatrāpy ekaikaśo rājan
bhidyante gatayas tridhā
yadaikaikataro'nyābhyāṁ
sva-bhāva upahanyate

sattvam—the mode of goodness; *rajaḥ*—the mode of passion; *tamaḥ*—the mode of darkness; *iti*—thus; *tisraḥ*—trio; *sura*—demigod; *nṛ*—human being; *nārakāḥ*—one who is suffering hellish conditions; *tatra api*—even there; *ekaikaśaḥ*—another; *rājan*—O King; *bhidyante*—divide into; *gatayaḥ*—movements; *tridhā*—three; *yadā*—at that time; *ekaikataraḥ*—one in relation with another; *anyābhyām*—from the other; *sva-bhāvaḥ*—habit; *upahanyate*—develops.

TRANSLATION

According to the different modes of material nature—the mode of goodness, the mode of passion and the mode of darkness—there are different living creatures, who are known as demigods, human beings and hellish living entities. O King, even a particular mode of nature, being mixed with the other two, is divided into three, and thus each kind of living creature is influenced by the other modes and acquires its habits also.

PURPORT

The living entities individually are being conducted by a particular mode of nature, but at the same time there is every chance of being influenced by the other two. Generally, all conditioned souls in the material encagement are influenced by the mode of passion because every one of them is trying to lord it over the material nature to fulfill individual desire. But in spite of the individual mode of passion, there is always the chance of being influenced by other modes of nature by association. If one is in good association he can develop the modes of goodness, and if he is in bad association he may develop the modes of darkness or ignorance. Nothing is stereotyped. One can change his habit by good or bad association, and one has to become intelligent enough to discriminate between good and bad. The best association is the service of the devotees of the Lord, and by that association one can become the highest qualified man by the grace of pure devotees of the Lord. As we have already seen in the life of Śrīla Nārada Muni, he became the topmost devotee of the Lord simply by the association of pure devotees of the Lord. By birth he was the son of a maidservant and had no knowledge of his father and no academic education, even of the lowest status. But simply by associating with the devotees and by eating the remnants of their foodstuff, he gradually developed the transcendental qualities of the devotees. By such association, his taste for chanting and hearing the transcendental glories of the Lord became prominent, and because the glories of the Lord are nondifferent from the Lord, he got direct association with the Lord by means of sound representation. Similarly, there is the life of Ajāmila (Sixth Canto), who was the son of a *brāhmaṇa* and was educated and trained properly in the discharge of the duties of a *brāhmaṇa* but in spite of all this, because he contacted the bad association of a prostitute, was put into the path of the lowest quality of *caṇḍāla,* or the last position of human beings. Therefore the *Bhāgavatam* recommends always the association of the *mahat,* or the great soul, for opening the gate of salvation. And to associate with persons engaged in lording it over the material world means to enter into the darkest region of hell. One should try to raise himself by the association of the great soul, and that is the way of perfection of life.

TEXT 42

स एवेदं जगद्धाता भगवान् धर्मरूपधृक् ।
पुष्णाति स्थापयन् विश्वं तिर्यङ्नरसुरादिभिः ॥४२॥

sa evedaṁ jagad-dhātā
bhagavān dharma-rūpa-dhṛk
puṣṇāti sthāpayan viśvaṁ
tiryaṅ-nara-surādibhiḥ

saḥ—He; *eva*—certainly; *idam*—this; *jagat-dhātā*—the maintainer of the entire universe; *bhagavān*—the Personality of Godhead; *dharma-rūpa-dhṛk*—assuming the form of religious principles; *puṣṇāti*—maintains; *sthāpayan*—after establishing; *viśvam*—the universes; *tiryak*—living entities lower than the human beings; *nara*—the human beings; *sura-ādibhiḥ*—by the demigodly incarnations.

TRANSLATION

He, the Personality of Godhead, as maintainer of all in the universe, appears in different incarnations after establishing the creation, and thus He reclaims all kinds of conditioned souls amongst the humans, nonhumans and the demigods.

PURPORT

The Supreme Personality of Godhead Viṣṇu incarnates Himself in different societies of living entities to reclaim them from the clutches of illusion, and such activities of the Lord are not limited only to the human society. He incarnates Himself even as a fish, hog, tree and many other forms, but less intelligent persons who have no knowledge of Him deride Him even if He is in the human society as a human being. The Lord therefore says in the *Bhagavad-gītā:*

avajānanti māṁ mūḍhā mānuṣīṁ tanum āśritam
paraṁ bhāvam ajānante mama bhūta-maheśvaram. (Bg. 9.11)

As we have already discussed in the previous verses, it is concluded that the Lord is never a product of the material creation. His transcendental position is always unchanged. He is the eternal form of knowledge and bliss, and He executes His almighty will by His different energies. As such He is never the subject of reaction for all His acts. He is transcendental to all such conceptions of action and reactions. Even if He is visible in the material world, the exhibition is only of His internal energy, for He is above the good and bad conceptions of this material world. In the material world the fish or the hog may be considered lower than the man, but when the Lord appears as a fish or hog, He is neither of them in the material conception. It is His causeless mercy that He appears in every society or species of life, but He is never to be considered one of them. Conceptions of the material world such as good and bad, lower and upper, important and insignificant are estimations of the material energy, and the Supreme Lord is transcendental to all such conceptions. The word *paraṁ bhāvam,* or transcendental nature, can never be compared with the material conception. We should not forget that the potencies of the Almighty Lord are always the same and do not decrease because the Lord assumes the form of a lower animal. There is no difference between Lord Śrī Rāma, Lord Śrī Kṛṣṇa or His incarnations of fish and hogs. He is all-pervading and simultaneously localized at any and every place. But the foolish person with a poor fund of knowledge, for want of that *paraṁ bhāvam* of the Lord, cannot understand how the Supreme Lord can take the form of a man or a fish. Everything is compared to its own standard of knowledge, as the frog in the well considers the sea to be one like the well. The frog in the well cannot even think of the sea, and when such a frog is informed of the greatness of the sea it takes the conception of the sea as a little greater than the well. As such, one who is foolish in the transcendental science of the Lord will find it difficult to understand how Lord Viṣṇu can equally manifest Himself in every society of living entities.

TEXT 43

ततः कालाग्निरुद्रात्मा यत्सृष्टमिदमात्मनः ।
संनियच्छति तत् काले घनानीकमिवानिलः ॥४३॥

tataḥ kālāgni-rudrātmā
yat sṛṣṭam idam ātmanaḥ
sanniyacchati tat kāle
ghanānīkam ivānilaḥ

tataḥ—thereafter at the end; *kāla*—destruction; *agni*—fire; *rudra-ātmā*—in the form of Rudra; *yat*—whatever; *sṛṣṭam*—created; *idam*—all these; *ātmanaḥ*—of His own; *sam*—completely; *niyacchati*—annihilates; *tat kāle*—at the end of the millennium; *ghana-anīkam*—bunches of clouds; *iva*—like that of; *anilaḥ*—air.

TRANSLATION

Thereafter, at the end of the millennium, the Lord Himself in the form of Rudra, the destroyer, will annihilate the complete creation as the wind displaces the clouds.

PURPORT

This creation is very appropriately compared to the clouds. The clouds are created or situated in the sky, and when they are displaced they remain in the same sky without manifestation. Similarly, the whole creation is made by the Supreme Personality of God in His form of Brahmā, it is maintained by Him in the form of Viṣṇu, and it is destroyed by Him in the form of Rudra or Śiva, all in due course. This creation, maintenance and destruction are nicely explained in the *Bhagavad-gītā* as follows:

bhūta-grāmaḥ sa evāyaṁ bhūtvā bhūtvā pralīyate
rātryāgame 'vaśaḥ pārtha prabhavaty ahar āgame
paras tasmāt tu bhāvo 'nyo 'vyakto 'vyaktāt sanātanaḥ
yaḥ sa sarveṣu bhūteṣu naśyatsu na vinaśyati (Bg. 8.19-20)

The nature of the material world is that it is first created very nicely, develops very nicely, stays for a great number of years (even beyond the calculation of the greatest mathematician), but after that it is again destroyed during the night of Brahmā without any resistance, and again at the end of the night of Brahmā the same is again manifested as creation to follow the same principles of maintenance and destruction. The foolish conditioned soul who has taken this temporary world as a permanent settlement has to learn intelligently why such creation and destruction take place. The fruitive actors in the material world are very enthusiastic in the creation of big enterprises, big houses, big empires, big industries and so many big, big things out of the energy and ingredients supplied by the material agent of the Supreme Lord. With such resources, and at the cost of valuable energy, the conditioned soul creates, satisfies his whims, but unwillingly has to depart from all his creations and enter into another phase of life to create again and again. And to give hope to such foolish conditioned souls who waste their energy in this temporary material world, the Lord gives information that there is another nature which is eternally existent without being occasionally created or destroyed, and the conditioned soul can understand what he should do and how his valuable energy may be utilized. Instead of wasting his energy in matter, which is sure to be destroyed in due course by the supreme will, he (the conditioned soul) should utilize his energy in devotional service of the Lord so that he can be transferred to the other, eternal nature where there is no birth, no death, no creation, no destruction, but permanent life instead, full of knowledge and unlimited bliss. This temporary creation is thus exhibited and destroyed just to give information to the conditioned soul who is attached to temporary things. It is meant also to give him a chance for self-realization, and not for sense gratification, which is the prime aim of all fruitive actors.

TEXT 44

इत्थंभावेन कथितो भगवान् भगवत्तमः ।
नेत्थंभावेन हि परं द्रष्टुमर्हन्ति सूरयः ॥४४॥

itthambhāvena kathito
bhagavān bhagavattamaḥ
netthambhāvena hi paraṁ
draṣṭum arhanti sūrayaḥ

ittham—in these features; *bhāvena*—matter of creation and destruction; *kathitaḥ*—described; *bhagavān*—the Personality of Godhead; *bhagavattamaḥ*—by the great transcendentalists; *na*—not; *ittham*—in this; *bhāvena*—features; *hi*—only; *param*—most glorious; *draṣṭum*—to see; *arhanti*—deserve; *sūrayaḥ*—great devotees.

TRANSLATION

The great transcendentalists thus describe the activities of the Supreme Personality of Godhead, but the pure devotees deserve to see more glorious things in transcendence, beyond these features.

PURPORT

The Lord is not only creator and destroyer of the material manifestations of His different energies. He is more than simple creator and destroyer, for there is His feature of *ānanda,* or His pleasure feature. This pleasure feature of the Lord is understood by the pure devotees only, and not by others. The impersonalist is satisfied simply by understanding the all-pervasive influence of the Lord, called Brahman realization. Greater than the impersonalist is the mystic who sees the Lord situated in his heart as Paramātmā, the partial representation of the Lord. But there are pure devotees who take part in the direct pleasure *(ānanda)* potency of the Lord by factual reciprocation of loving service. The Lord in His abode called the Vaikuṇṭha planets, which are eternal manifestations, always remains with His associates and enjoys transcendental loving services by His pure devotees in different transcendental humors. The pure devotees of the Lord thus undergo a practice of that devotional service of the Lord during the manifestation of the creation and take full advantage of the manifestation by qualifying themselves to enter into the kingdom of God. The *Bhagavad-gītā* confirms this:

bhaktyā mām abhijānāti yāvān yaś cāsmi tattvataḥ
tato māṁ tattvato jñātvā viśate tad anantaram. (Bg. 18.55)

By development of pure devotional service one can know factually the Lord as He is and thus become trained in the bona fide service of the Lord and be allowed to enter into the direct association of the Lord in so many capacities. And the highest glorious association with the Lord is made possible in the planet of Goloka Vṛndāvana, where Lord Kṛṣṇa enjoys Himself with the *gopīs* and His favorite animals, the *surabhi* cows. Description of this transcendental land of Kṛṣṇa is given in the *Brahma-saṁhitā,* considered by Lord Śrī Caitanya to be the most authentic literature in this connection.

TEXT 45

नास्य कर्मणि जन्मादौ परस्यानुविधीयते ।
कर्तृत्वप्रतिषेधार्थं माययारोपितं हि तत् ॥४५॥

nāsya karmaṇi janmādau
parasyānuvidhīyate
kartṛtva-pratiṣedhārthaṁ
māyayāropitaṁ hi tat

na—never; *asya*—of the creation; *karmaṇi*—in the matter of; *janma-ādau*—creation and destruction; *parasya*—of the Supreme; *anuvidhīyate*—it is so described; *kartṛtva*—engineering; *pratiṣedha-artham*—counteract; *māyayā*—by the external energy; *āropitam*—is manifested; *hi*—for; *tat*—the creator.

TRANSLATION

There is no direct engineering by the Lord for the creation and destruction of the material world. What is described in the Vedas about His direct interference is simply to counteract the idea that material nature is the creator.

PURPORT

The Vedic direction for creation, maintenance and destruction of the material world is this: "*yato vā imāni bhūtāni jāyante yena jātāni jīvanti yat prayanty abhisaṁviśanti,*" i.e. everything is created by Brahman, and after creation everything is maintained by Brahman, and after annihilation everything is conserved in Brahman. Gross materialists without any knowledge of Brahman, Paramātmā or Bhagavān conclude material nature to be the ultimate cause of the material manifestation, and the modern scientist also shares this view that material nature is the ultimate cause of all manifestations of the material world. This view is refuted by all Vedic literature. The *Vedānta* philosophy mentions that Brahman is the fountainhead of all creation, maintenance and destruction, and *Śrīmad-Bhāgavatam,* the natural commentation on the *Vedānta* philosophy, says, "*janmādy asya yato 'nvayād itarataś cārtheṣv abhijñaḥ svarāṭ,*" etc.

Inert matter is potential energy undoubtedly by interactions, but it has no initiative of its own. *Śrīmad-Bhāgavatam* therefore comments on the aphorism of *janmādyasya* as *abhijñaḥ* and *svarāṭ,* i.e. the Supreme Brahman is not inert matter, but He is supreme consciousness and is independent. Therefore inert matter cannot be the ultimate cause of the creation, maintenance and destruction of the material world. Superficially it appears that the material nature is the cause of creation, maintenance and destruction, but material nature is set into motion for creation by the supreme conscious being, the Personality of Godhead. He is the background of all creation, maintenance and destruction, and this is confirmed in the *Bhagavad-gītā:*

> *mayādhyakṣeṇa prakṛtiḥ sūyate sacarācaram*
> *hetunānena kaunteya jagad viparivartate* (Bg. 9.10)

The material nature is one of the energies of the Lord, and she can work under the direction of the Lord *(adhyakṣeṇa)*. When the Lord throws His transcendental glance over the material nature, then only can the material nature act, as the father contacts the mother, and then the mother is able to conceive a child. The material nature therefore produces the moving and standing manifestations of the material world after being contacted by the supreme father, and not independently. Therefore although it appears, to the layman, that the mother gives birth to the child, the experienced man knows that the father gives birth to the child. To consider material nature as the cause of creation, maintenance, etc., is called the "logic of nipples on the neck of the goat." The *Caitanya-caritāmṛta* by Śrīla Kṛṣṇadāsa Kavirāja Gosvāmī describes this logic of *ajagalastana* as follows (as explained by His Divine Grace Śrī Śrīmad Bhaktisiddhānta Sarasvatī Gosvāmī Mahārāja): "The material nature, as the material cause, is known as *pradhāna,* and as efficient cause is known as *māyā.* But being inert matter, it is not the remote cause of creation." Kavirāja Gosvāmī states as follows:

ataeva kṛṣṇa mul, jagat karan
prakṛti karan jaichhe ajagalastan (C.c., *Ādi* 5.61)

Because the Kāraṇārṇavaśāyī Viṣṇu is a plenary expansion of Kṛṣṇa, it is He who electrifies the matter to be in motion. The example of electrification is quite appropriate. A piece of iron is certainly not fire, but when the iron is made red-hot, certainly it has the quality of fire through its burning capacity. Matter is compared with the piece of iron, and it is electrified or made red-hot by the glance or manipulation of the supreme consciousness of Viṣṇu. By such electrification only does the energy of matter become displayed by various actions and reactions. Therefore the inert matter is neither efficient nor is it the material cause of the cosmic manifestation. Śrī Kapiladeva has said:

yatholmukād visphuliṅgād dhūmād vāpi svasambhavāt
apy ātma-tvenābhimatād yathāgniḥ pṛthag ulmukāt
(*Bhāg.* 3.28.40)

The original fire, its flame, its sparks, and its smoke are all one, as fire is still fire yet is different from the flame, flame is different from sparks, and sparks are different from the smoke. In every one of them, namely in the flames, in the sparks and in the smoke, the integrity of fire is present, and still all of them and each and every one of them are differently situated with different positions. The cosmic manifestation is compared to the smoke (when the smoke passes over the sky so many forms appear resembling many known and unknown manifestations), the sparks are compared to living entities, and the flames are compared to material nature, *pradhāna.* One must know that each and every one of them is effective simply by being empowered by the quality of fire (original). Therefore every one of them, namely the material nature, the cosmic manifestation and the living entities, are all but different energies of the Lord (fire). Therefore those who accept the material nature as the original cause (*prakṛti,* the cause of creation according to Sāṅkhya philosophy) of cosmic manifestation are not correct in their conclusion. The material nature has no separate existence without the Lord. Therefore, setting aside the Supreme Lord as the cause of all causes is the logic of *ajagalastan,* or trying to milk the nipples on the neck of the goat. The nipples on the neck of a goat may seem like sources of milk, but it will be foolish to try to get milk from such nipples.

TEXT 46

अयं तु ब्रह्मणः कल्पः सविकल्प उदाहृतः ।
विधिः साधारणो यत्र सर्गाः प्राकृतवैकृताः ॥४६॥

ayaṁ tu brahmaṇaḥ kalpaḥ
sa-vikalpa udāhṛtaḥ
vidhiḥ sādhāraṇo yatra
sargāḥ prākṛta-vaikṛtāḥ

ayam—this process of creation and annihilation; *tu*—but; *brahmaṇaḥ*—of Brahmā; *kalpaḥ*—his one day; *sa-vikalpaḥ*—along with the duration of the universes; *udāhrtaḥ*—exemplified; *vidhiḥ*—regulative principles; *sādhāraṇaḥ*—in summary; *yatra*—wherein; *sargāḥ*—creation; *prākṛta*—in the matter of material nature; *vaikṛtāḥ*—disbursement.

TRANSLATION

This process of creation and annihilation described herein is in summary the regulative principle during the duration of Brahmā's one day, as well as the creation of mahat in which the material nature is dispersed.

PURPORT

There are three different types of creation, called *mahākalpa, vikalpa* and *kalpa.* In the *mahākalpa* the Lord assumes the first incarnation of

Puruṣa as Kāraṇodakaśāyī Viṣṇu with all the potencies of *mahat-tattva* and the sixteen principles of creative matter and instruments. The creative instruments are eleven, and the ingredients are five, and all of them are products of *mahat* or materialistic ego, and these creations by the Lord in His feature of Kāraṇodakaśāyī Viṣṇu are called *mahākalpa*. Creation of Brahmā and dispersion of the material ingredients are called *vikalpa*, and creation by Brahmā in each day of his life is called *kalpa*. Therefore each day of Brahmā is called a *kalpa*, and there are thirty *kalpas* in terms of Brahmā's days, which is also confirmed in the *Bhagavad-gītā* as follows:

sahasra-yuga-paryantam ahar yad brahmaṇo viduḥ
rātriṁ yuga-sahasrāntāṁ te 'horātravido janāḥ (Bg. 8.17)

In the upper planetary system the duration of one complete day and night is equal to one complete year of this earth. This is accepted even by the modern scientist and testified by the astronauts. Similarly, in the region of still higher planetary systems, the duration of day and night is still greater than in the heavenly planets. The four *yugas* are calculated in terms of the heavenly calendars and accordingly are twelve thousand years in terms of the heavenly planets. This is called *divya-yuga*, and one thousand *divya-yugas* make one day of Brahmā. Creation during the day of Brahmā is called *kalpa*, and creation of Brahmā is called *vikalpa*, and when *vikalpas* are made possible by the breathing of Maha-Viṣṇu they are called *mahākalpa*. There are regular and systematic cycles of these *mahākalpas*, *vikalpas* and *kalpas*, and in answer to Mahārāja Parīkṣit's question about them, Śukadeva Gosvāmī answered in the Prabhāsa-khaṇḍa of the *Skanda Purāṇa*, and they are as follows:

prathamaḥ śvetakalpas tu dvitīyo nīlalohitaḥ
vāmadevas tṛtīyas tu tato gāthāntaroparaḥ
rauravaḥ pañcamaḥ proktaḥ ṣaṣṭhaḥ prāṇa iti smṛtaḥ
saptamo 'tha bṛhatkalpaḥ kandarpo 'ṣṭamaḥ ucyate
savyotha navamaḥ prokta īśāno daśamaḥ smṛtaḥ
dhyāna ekādaśaḥ proktas tathā sārasvato 'paraḥ
trayodaśa udānas tu garuḍo 'tha caturdaśaḥ
kaurmaḥ pañcadaśo jñeyaḥ paurṇamāsī prajāpateḥ
ṣoḍaśo nārasiṁhas tu samādhis tu tato 'paraḥ
āgneyo viṣṇujaḥ sauraḥ somakalpas tato'paraḥ
dvāviṁśo bhāvanaḥ proktaḥ supumān iti cāparaḥ
vaikuṇṭhaś cārciṣas tadvat vallīkalpas tato'paraḥ

saptaviṁśo'tha vairājo gaurīkalpas tathāparaḥ
māheśvaras tathā proktas tripuro yatra ghātitaḥ
pitṛkalpas tathā cānte yaḥ kuhur brahmaṇaḥ smṛtaḥ

Therefore the thirty *kalpas* of Brahmā are: 1. Śvetakalpa, 2. Nīlalohita, 3. Vāmadeva, 4. Gāthāntara, 5. Raurava, 6. Prāṇa, 7. Bṛhatkalpa, 8. Kandarpa, 9. Savyotha, 10. Īśāna, 11. Dhyāna, 12. Sārasvata, 13. Udāna, 14. Garuḍa, 15. Kaurma, 16. Nārasiṁha, 17. Samādhi, 18. Āgneya, 19. Viṣṇuja, 20. Saura, 21. Somakalpa, 22. Bhāvana, 23. Supuma, 24. Vaikuṇṭha, 25. Arciṣa, 26. Vallīkalpa, 27. Vairāja, 28. Gaurīkalpa, 29. Māheśvara, 30. Paitṛkalpa.

These are Brahmā's days only, and he has to live months and years up to one hundred, so we can just imagine how many creations there are in *kalpas* only. Then again there are *vikalpas* which are generated by the breathing of Mahā-Viṣṇu, as is stated in the *Brahma-saṁhitā (yasyaika-niśvasita-kālam athāvalambya jīvanti lomavilajā jagadaṇḍa-nāthāḥ).* The Brahmās live only during the breathing period of Mahā-Viṣṇu. So the exhaling and inhaling of Viṣṇu are *mahākalpas,* and all these are due to the Supreme Personality of Godhead, for no one else is the master of all creations.

TEXT 47

परिमाणं च कालस्य कल्पलक्षणविग्रहम् ।
यथा पुरस्ताद्व्याख्यास्ये पाद्मं कल्पमथो शृणु ॥४७॥

parimāṇaṁ ca kālasya
kalpa-lakṣaṇa-vigraham
yathā purastād vyākhyāsye
pādmaṁ kalpam atho śṛṇu

parimāṇam—measurement; *ca*—also; *kālasya*—of time; *kalpa*—day of Brahmā; *lakṣaṇa*—symptoms; *vigraham*—form; *yathā*—as much as; *purastāt*—hereafter; *vyākhyāsye*—shall be explained; *pādmam*—by the name Pādma; *kalpam*—duration of day; *atho*—thus; *śṛṇu*—just hear.

TRANSLATION

O King, I shall in due course explain the measurement of time in its gross and subtle features with specific symptoms of each of them, but for the present let me explain unto you the Pādma-kalpa.

PURPORT

The present duration of a *kalpa* of Brahmā is called Varāha-kalpa or Śvetavarāha-kalpa because the incarnation of the Lord as Varāha took place during the creation of Brahmā, who was born on the lotus coming out of the abdomen of Viṣṇu. Therefore this Varāha-kalpa is also called Pādma-kalpa, and this is testified by *ācāryas* like Jīva Gosvāmī as well as Viśvanātha Cakravartī Ṭhākur in pursuance of the first commentator, Svāmī Śrīdhara. So there is no contradiction between the Varāha and the Pādma-kalpa of Brahmā.

TEXT 48

शौनक उवाच
यदाह नो भवान् सूत क्षत्ता भागवतोत्तमः ।
चचार तीर्थानि भुवस्त्यक्त्वा बन्धून् सुदुस्त्यजान् ॥४८॥

śaunaka uvāca
yadāha no bhavān sūta
kṣattā bhāgavatottamaḥ
cacāra tīrthāni bhuvas
tyaktvā bandhūn su-dustyajān

śaunakaḥ uvāca—Śrī Śaunaka Muni said; *yat*—as; *āha*—you said; *naḥ*—unto us; *bhavān*—your good self; *sūta*—O Sūta; *kṣattā*—Vidura; *bhāgavata-uttamaḥ*—one of the topmost devotees of the Lord; *cacāra*—practiced; *tīrthāni*—places of pilgrimage; *bhuvaḥ*—on the earth; *tyaktvā* leaving aside; *bandhūn*—all relatives; *su-dustyajān*—very difficult to give up.

TRANSLATION

Śaunaka Ṛṣi, after hearing all about the creation, inquired from Sūta Gosvāmī about Vidura, as Sūta Gosvāmī previously informed him how Vidura left home, leaving aside all relatives who were very difficult to leave.

PURPORT

The Ṛṣis headed by Śaunaka were more anxious to know about Vidura, who met Maitreya Ṛṣi while traveling in the pilgrimage sites of the world.

TEXTS 49-50

क्षत्तुः कौशारवेस्तस्य संवादोऽध्यात्मसंश्रितः ।
यद्वा स भगवांस्तस्मै पृष्टस्तत्त्वमुवाच ह ॥४९॥
ब्रूहि नस्तदिदं सौम्य विदुरस्य विचेष्टितम् ।
बन्धुत्यागनिमित्तं च यथैवागतवान् पुनः ॥५०॥

kṣattuḥ kauśāraves tasya
saṁvādo 'dhyātma-saṁśritaḥ
yad vā sa bhagavāṁs tasmai
pṛṣṭas tattvam uvāca ha
brūhi nas tad idaṁ saumya
vidurasya viceṣṭitam
bandhu-tyāga-nimittaṁ ca
yathaivāgatavān punaḥ

kṣattuḥ—of Vidura; *kauśāraveḥ*—as that of Maitreya; *tasya*—their; *saṁvādaḥ*—news; *adhyātma*—in the matter of transcendental knowledge; *saṁśritaḥ*—full of; *yat*—which; *vā*—anything else; *saḥ*—he; *bhagavān*—his grace; *tasmai*—unto him; *pṛṣṭaḥ*—inquired; *tattvam*—the truth; *uvāca*—answered; *ha*—in the past; *brūhi*—please tell; *naḥ*—unto us; *tat*—those matters; *idam*—here; *saumya*—O gentle one; *vidurasya*—of Vidura; *viceṣṭitam*—activities; *bandhu-tyāga*—renouncing the friends; *nimittam*—cause of; *ca*—also; *yathā*—as; *eva*—also; *āgatavān*—came back; *punaḥ*—again (at home).

TRANSLATION

Śaunaka Ṛṣi said: Let us know, please, what topics were discussed between Vidura and Maitreya, who talked on transcendental subjects, and what was inquired by Vidura and replied by Maitreya. Also please let us know what was the reason for Vidura's giving up the connection of family members, and why he again came home, and please also let us know the activities of Vidura while he was in the places of pilgrimage.

PURPORT

Śrī Sūta Gosvāmī was narrating the topics of creation and destruction of the material world, but it appears that the *ṛṣis* headed by Śaunaka were more inclined to hear of transcendental subjects which are on a higher level than the physical. There are two classes of men, namely those too much addicted to the gross body and the material world, and the others, on the higher level, who are interested more in transcendental knowledge. *Śrīmad-Bhāgavatam* gives facility to everyone, both to the materialist and the transcendentalist. And by hearing *Śrīmad-Bhāgavatam,* in the matter of the Lord's glorious activities both in the material world and in the transcendental world, men can derive equal benefit. The materialists are more interested in the physical laws, how they are acting, and they see wonders in those physical glamours. Sometimes, due to physical glamours, they forget the glories of the Lord. They should know definitely that physical activities and their wonders are all initiated by the Lord. The rose flower in the garden gradually takes its shape and color to become beautiful and sweet not by a blind physical law, although it appears like that. Behind that physical law there is the direction of the complete consciousness of the Supreme Lord, otherwise things cannot take shape so systematically. The artist draws a picture of a rose very nicely with all attention and artistic sense, and yet it does not become as perfect as the real rose. If that is the real fact, how can we say that the real rose has taken its shape without intelligence behind the beauty? This sort of conclusion is due to a poor fund of knowledge. One must know from the above description of creation and annihilation that the supreme consciousness is so omnipresent that it can take care of everything with perfect attention. That is the fact of the omnipresence of the Supreme Lord. There are persons, however, still more foolish than the gross materialists, who claim to be transcendentalists, and they claim to have such supreme all-pervading consciousness, but offer no proof. Such foolish persons cannot know what is going on behind the next wall, yet they are falsely proud of possessing the cosmic all-pervading consciousness of the Supreme Person. For them also, hearing of *Śrīmad-Bhāgavatam* is a great help to open their eyes that by simply claiming supreme consciousness one does not become so, but actually one has to prove in the physical world that he has such supreme consciousness. The *ṛṣis* of Naimiṣāraṇya, however, were above the gross materialists and the false transcendentalists, and thus they are always anxious to know the real truth in transcendental matters, as they are discussed by authorities.

TEXT 51

सूत उवाच

राज्ञा परीक्षिता पृष्टो यद्वोचन्महामुनिः ।
तद्वोऽभिधास्ये शृणुत राज्ञः प्रश्नानुसारतः ॥५१॥

sūta uvāca
rājñā parīkṣitā pṛṣṭo
yad avocan mahā-muniḥ
tad vo 'bhidhāsye śṛṇuta
rājñaḥ praśnānusārataḥ

śrī sūtaḥ uvāca—Śrī Sūta Gosvāmī replied; *rājñā*—by the King; *parīkṣitā*—by Parīkṣit; *pṛṣṭaḥ*—as asked; *yat*—what; *avocat*—spoke; *mahā-muniḥ*—the great sage; *tat*—that very thing; *vaḥ*—unto you; *abhidhāsye*—I shall explain; *śṛṇuta*—please hear; *rājñaḥ*—by the King; *praśna*—question; *anusārataḥ* in accordance with.

TRANSLATION

Śrī Sūta Gosvāmī explained: I shall now explain to you the very subjects which were explained by the great sage in answer to King Parīkṣit's inquiries. Please hear them attentively.

PURPORT

Any question that is put forward may be answered by quoting the authority, and that satisfies the saner section. That is the system even in the law court. The best lawyer gives evidence from the past judgement of the court without taking much trouble to establish his case. This is called the *paramparā* system, and learned authorities follow it without manufacturing rubbish interpretations.

īśvaraḥ paramaḥ kṛṣṇaḥ sac-cid-ānanda-vigrahaḥ
anādir ādir govindaḥ sarva-kāraṇa-kāraṇam

Let us all obey the Supreme Lord whose hand is in everything, without exception.

Thus ends the Bhaktivedanta purports of the Second Canto, Tenth Chapter, of the Śrīmad-Bhāgavatam, *entitled "Bhāgavatam is the Answer."*

END OF THE SECOND CANTO

References

The purports of *Śrīmad-Bhāgavatam* are all confirmed by standard Vedic authorities. The following authentic scriptural sources are specifically cited in the Second Canto.

Bhagavad-gītā
Śrīmad-Bhāgavatam
Aitareya Upaniṣad
Bhagavat-sandarbha
Bhakti-rasāmṛta-sindhu
Brahma-saṁhitā
Brahma-vaivarta Purāṇa
Nārada-pañcarātra
Garuḍa Purāṇa
Hari-bhakti-sudhodaya
Īśopaniṣad
Kaṭhopaniṣad
Mahābhārata
Mārkaṇḍeya Purāṇa
Matsya Purāṇa
Narasiṁha Purāṇa
Nirukti (Vedic dictionary)
Padma Purāṇa
Sāṅkhya-kaumudī
Skanda Purāṇa
Śvetāśvatara Upaniṣad
Vaiṣṇava Tantras
Vāmana Purāṇa
Vedānta-sūtras
Viṣṇu-jāmala Tantra
Viṣṇu Purāṇa

Glossary

A

Ācārya—an authorized teacher of a particular cult.
Acyuta-kathā—the message of the infallible Lord.
Ādi—Kṛṣṇa, the origin of all.
Advaita—the nondual nature of Kṛṣṇa's forms.
Ahaṅkara—the meeting point of matter and spirit.
Ajita—Kṛṣṇa, the unconquerable.
Akāmaḥ—one who has no material desire.
Anartha—unwanted habit.
Apsaras—the society girls of heaven.
Arcā—a form of the Lord manifested through a material agency such as mind, metal, earth, paint, wood, stone, jewel or drawing. It is accepted as an incarnation of Godhead and worshiped according to regulations.
Aśrama—orders of life in connection with self-realization.
Aṣṭa-siddhi—the eightfold mystic perfections.
Asura—one who is against the service of the Lord.
Arthadam—that which can deliver values.
Ātma-māyā—Kṛṣṇa's internal potency.
Ātmārāma—self-satisfied in spiritual values.
Ātma-tattva—knowledge concerning liberation.
Avaroha-panthā—the process of receiving transcendental knowledge through bona fide disciplic succession.
Avatāra—(lit., one who descends) an incarnation of God.
Aveṣa—an incarnation of Godhead partially empowered.

B

Bhakti—activities of the purified senses.
Bhakti-yoga—direct attachment to Kṛṣṇa.
Bhāva—the stage of transcendental ecstacy experienced after transcendental affection.
Bhūtas—powerful created demigods who manage universal affairs.
Brahmā—the first created being of a universe.

Brahma-bhūta—self-satisfaction.

Brahmacarya—student life of celibacy and study of *śāstras* under a spiritual master.

Brahmajyoti—the impersonal bodily effulgence of the Personality of Godhead.

Brahmaloka—the planet of Lord Brahmā.

Brāhmaṇa—a person in the mode of goodness.

Brahma-sampradāya—the disciplic succession descending from Lord Brahmā.

C

Candraloka—the moon.

Catuḥśloki-Bhāgavatam— the four essential verses of *Śrīmad-Bhāgavatam* spoken by the Lord to Brahmā.

Cintāmaṇi-dhāma—the abode of the Lord, Kṛṣṇaloka.

D

Daivī-sampada—spiritual assets.

Deva—a demigod or godly person.

Dharma—the capacity to render service, which is the essential quality of a living being.

Divyam—transcendental.

Durgā-śakti—the material energy.

E

Ekapāda-vibhūti—the material manifestation.

G

Gandharvas—the celestial singers of the heavenly planets.

Garbhodakaśāyī Viṣṇu—the Viṣṇu expansion who enters each universe to create diversity.

Goloka—a name of the planet of Kṛṣṇa.

Gosvāmī—master of the senses.

Gṛhamedhīs—envious householders who live only for family benefit.

Gṛhastha—householder life aimed at transcendental realization.

H

Hiraṇyākṣa—a demon killed by the Lord in His boar incarnation.

Hlādhinī—the potency of the Supreme Personality of Godhead for spiritual bliss.

I

Indra—the King of the heavenly planets.
Īśvara—controller.

J

Jaḍa-yoga—a method of subduing the senses by voluntary infliction of pain to one's body.
Jīva—the soul or atomic living entity.
Jñāna—transcendental knowledge.
Jñāna-yoga—the empirical process of linking with the Supreme.
Jñānī—one engaged in the cultivation of knowledge.

K

Kāla—eternal time.
Kali-yuga—the age in which quarrel is a common affair.
Kāraṇārṇavaśāyī Viṣṇu—another name of Kāraṇodakaśāyī Viṣṇu.
Kāraṇodakaśāyī Viṣṇu—the Viṣṇu expansion from whom all the material universes emanate.
Karma—material activities subject to reaction.
Karma-kāṇḍīya—the conception of life in which regulated religion, economic development and sense gratification are prominent.
Karmī—a fruitive laborer.
Kṛṣṇa-kathā—narrations spoken by or about Kṛṣṇa.
Kṣatriya—the martial caste, which is in the mode of passion.
Kṣīrodakaśāyī Viṣṇu—the Supersoul.
Kūṭa-yogīs—pseudo transcendentalists with ulterior motives.

L

Labdhopaśānti—the state of being unaffected by material circumstances.
Lakṣmī—the goddess of fortune, consort of the Supreme Lord, Nārāyaṇa.
Līlā—transcendental pastimes of the Lord.
Loka—planet.

M

Mahāpauruṣika—one who deserves to approach Kṛṣṇa.
Mahāpuruṣa—Kṛṣṇa, the supreme enjoyer.
Mahātmā—a devotee of the Lord constantly engaged in His service.
Mahat-tattva—the total material energy.
Maheśvara—Kṛṣṇa, creator of the controllers.

Mantras—transcendental sound or Vedic hymns.
Manu—the father of mankind.
Manu-saṁhitā—the lawbook for humanity.
Māyā—the external illusory energy of the Lord.
Māyāvāda—the system of philosophy propounded by the impersonalists.
Medhī—jealousy of others.
Mukti—recovery from material existence and reinstatement in one's original form.
Muni—a sage or self-realized soul.

N

Nārāyaṇa—the four-handed expansion of the Supreme Lord Kṛṣṇa.
Nārāyaṇa-smṛti—constant remembrance of Kṛṣṇa.
Nirvāṇa—cessation of material existence.
Nitya-siddhas—souls liberated from birth.
Nivṛtta—the state of being freed from material existence.

O

Omkāra—the seed of all transcendental sound.

P

Pāda-vibhūti (ekapāda-vibhūti)—the material manifestation.
Paramahaṁsa—the topmost class of God-realized devotees.
Paramātmā—the Supersoul, or localized aspect of the Lord.
Param Brahma—the Supreme Brahman, the Personality of Godhead.
Paramparā—disciplic succession.
Paravyoma—the spiritual sky.
Prakṛta-sahajiyā—mundane devotee.
Prakṛti—energy or nature, especially the material nature.
Prāṇa—the living energy.
Prāṇāyāma—the yogic process of fully controlling the breathing air.
Praśāntas—unalloyed devotees of Kṛṣṇa.
Puruṣa—an incarnation of Godhead for material manifestation.

R

Rājarṣis—saintly kings.
Rasa—a spiritual relationship through spiritual sense perception.
Rāsa-līlā—the pastimes of Lord Kṛṣṇa with the *gopīs*.

S

Sac-cid-ānanda vigraha—the eternal form of the Lord, full of bliss and knowledge.

Sad-dharma—duty performed for going back to Godhead.

Sādhana-siddha—one who develops a tendency towards devotional service by association.

Śaktas—worshipers of great powers.

Samādhi—trance, or absorption in the service of the Lord.

Saṁsāra—repetition of birth, death, old age and disease.

Sanātana-dharma—man's eternal engagement.

Sandhinī—the eternal existence potency of the Lord.

Sannyāsa—the renounced order of life for spiritual culture.

Śāstras—revealed scriptures or Vedic literatures.

Satyaloka—the topmost planetary system within the universe.

Sāyujya—impersonal liberation.

Śiva—the predominating deity of the mode of ignorance.

Śravaṇa—hearing.

Śṛṅgāra—decoration and dressing of the Deity.

Śruti—direct Vedic injunctions.

Śūdras—persons in the mode of ignorance, the laborer class.

T

Tapasya—voluntary acceptance of some material trouble for progress in spiritual life.

Tatastha-śakti—the marginal potency of the Lord.

Tīrthas—propounders of Vedic knowledge.

Tripāda-vibhūti—the spiritual sky.

U

Umā—the wife of Lord Śiva.

Urvaśī—the society girls of heaven.

V

Vaikuṇṭha—the spiritual world, where there is no anxiety.

Vairāgya—detachment from unwanted things.

Vaiṣṇavas—devotees of the Lord.

Vaiśya—the mercantile caste, who are in the modes of passion and ignorance.

Varṇas—castes or sections of society in terms of qualification and occupation.

Varṇāśrama-dharma—classification of society into four social orders and four spiritual orders according to their qualities and work.

Vāsudeva-parāyaṇaḥ—a devotee of Vāsudeva, Lord Kṛṣṇa.

Veda-vāda-ratas—those who claim to follow the *Vedas* but are against the Vedic conclusion.

Vidhi-bhakti—regulated devotional service.
Virāṭa-rūpa (viśva-rūpa)—the universal form of the Lord.
Viṣṇu-tattva—the status of Godhead.

Y

Yajña—sacrifice.
Yamarāja—the demigod who punishes sinful living entities after death.
Yoga—that which links with the Supreme.
Yogamāyā—the internal potency of the Lord.
Yoga-nidrā—the mystic slumber of Mahā-Viṣṇu.
Yuga—one of the four ages of the universe.

Sanskrit Pronunciation Guide

Vowels

अ a आ ā इ i ई ī उ u ऊ ū ऋ ṛ ॠ ṝ
ऌ ḷ ए e ऐ ai ओ o औ au

ं ṁ *(anusvāra)* ः ḥ *(visarga)*

Consonants

Gutturals:	क ka	ख kha	ग ga	घ gha	ङ ṅa
Palatals:	च ca	छ cha	ज ja	झ jha	ञ ña
Cerebrals:	ट ṭa	ठ ṭha	ड ḍa	ढ ḍha	ण ṇa
Dentals:	त ta	थ tha	द da	ध dha	न na
Labials:	प pa	फ pha	ब ba	भ bha	म ma
Semivowels:	य ya	र ra	ल la	व va	
Sibilants:	श śa	ष ṣa	स sa		
Aspirate:	ह ha	ऽ = ' *(avagraha)* - the apostrophe			

The vowels above should be pronounced as follows:

a – like the *a* in org*a*n or the *u* in b*u*t.
ā – like the *ā* in f*a*r but held twice as long as *a*.

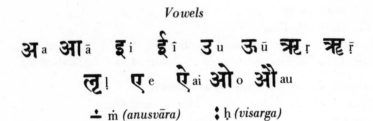

i – like the *i* in p*i*n.
ī – like the *ī* in p*i*que but held twice as long as *i*.
u – like the *u* in p*u*sh.
ū – like the *ū* in r*u*le but held twice as long as *u*.
ṛ – like the *ri* in *Ri*ta (but more like French *ru*).
ṝ – same as *ṛi* but held twice as long.
ḷ – like *lree (lruu)*.
e – like the *e* in th*e*y.
ai – like the *ai* in *ai*sle.
o – like the *o* in g*o*.
au – like the *ow* in h*ow*.
ṁ *(anusvāra)* – a resonant nasal like the *n* in the French word *bon*.
ḥ *(visarga)* – a final *h*-sound: *aḥ* is pronounced like *aha; iḥ* like *ihi.*

The consonants are pronounced as follows:

k – as in *k*ite	kh – as in Ec*kh*art
g – as in *g*ive	gh – as in di*g-h*ard
ṅ – as in si*ng*	c – as in *ch*air
ch – as in staun*ch-h*eart	j – as in *j*oy
jh – as in he*dgeh*og	ñ – as in ca*n*yon
ṭ – as in *t*ub	ṭh – as in ligh*t-h*eart
ṇ – as r*n*a (prepare to say the *r* and say *na*).	ḍha- as in re*d-h*ot
	ḍ – as in *d*ove

Cerebrals are pronounced with tongue to roof of mouth, but the following dentals are pronounced with tongue against teeth:

t – as in *t*ub but with tongue against teeth.
th – as in ligh*t-h*eart but tongue against teeth.
d – as in *d*ove but tongue against teeth.
dh – as in re*d-h*ot but with tongue against teeth.
n – as in *n*ut but with tongue in between teeth.

p – as in *p*ine	ph – as in u*p-h*ill (not *f*)
b – as in *b*ird	bh – as in ru*b-h*ard
m – as in *m*other	y – as in *y*es
r – as in *r*un	l – as in *l*ight
v – as in *v*ine.	s – as in *s*un

ś (palatal) – as in the *s* in the German word *sprechen*
ṣ (cerebral) – as the *sh* in *sh*ine
h – as in *h*ome

There is no strong accentuation of syllables in Sanskrit, only a flowing of short and long (twice as long as the short) syllables.

Index of Sanskrit Verses

This index constitutes a complete listing of the first and third lines of each of the Sanskrit verses of *Śrīmad-Bhāgavatam,* Second Canto, arranged in English alphabetical order. In the first column the Sanskrit transliteration is given, and in the second and third columns respectively the chapter-verse references and page number for each verse are to be found.

A

E

G

H

I

General Index
to the Second Canto

Numerals in boldface type indicate references to translations of the verses of *Śrīmad-Bhāgavatam.*

B

Body
- human body desired by demigods, 154
- meant to be eaten by dogs, **403**
- of a Vaiṣṇava changes transcendentally, 203
- overcast with five kinds of miseries, 473
- spiritual body not formless, 506
- *See also* Form of Kṛṣṇa, Material body

Brahmā
- afraid of pitfall of pride, 500-502
- always correct to the letter, 313
- as direct creator of manifested universe, 223
- as example of service in liberation, 62
- as lord of mode of passion, 249, 400
- as predominated "I," 509
- attains liberation after cosmic annihilation, 284
- believed in art of *bhakti-yoga,* 486
- born without father and mother, 300
- cited as example of forgetfulness, 61
- dependent on Kṛṣṇa, 22, 213-214, 240
- describes creation of universe, 236-262
- did not exist before creation, 60
- generates all beings in material world, **50,** 262
- granted benediction to Hiraṇyakaśipu, 359
- greatest of all ascetics, **471**
- hears four essential verses of *Bhāgavatam,* **507**-532
- his discourse with Nārāyaṇa, **488**-535
- his nondeceptive vow of devotion, 464
- his self-sufficiency compared with spider's, **225**
- impregnated with Vedic knowledge from birth, 116, 218, 309
- initiated into Kṛṣṇa *mantra,* 468
- inspired with knowledge within his heart, **213**
- is not cause of all causes, 232
- known as father of all fathers, 317
- most pure being in universe, 470
- questioned by Nārada, **218**-228
- resides in Satyaloka system, 46
- situated in humor of friendship, 501
- studied *Vedas* three times, **119**
- subject to death, 291
- taught us the way of sacrifice, 305
- transcendental to all pretensions, **205**

Brahma-bhūtaḥ prasannātmā
- verses quoted, 315

Brahmacarya
- as training of celibacy, 294-295, 346-347

Brahmajyoti
- as eternity and knowledge only, 90
- as effect of Supreme Brahman, 135, 311
- as limitless and all-pervasive, 193, 233
- as potential seed of creation, **232-233**
- as rays of Vaikuṇṭha planets, 92, 193
- as real source of light, 513
- attained by demons, **393**
- dependent on Personality of Godhead, 92, 233,311
- same quality as Kṛṣṇa's body, 381
- surpassed by *bhakti* creeper, 111
- unlimited, unfathomed, all-pervasive, 192, 233
- veils Godhead from view, 194

Brahmaloka (Satyaloka)
- as topmost planet, **98, 101,** 103
- attained by spiritual prefection, 107
- duration of life on, **103**
- free from pain, **104**
- travel to, **101**

Brahman
- Absolute Truth first realized as, 14
- as feeling of eternal existence, 409
- as immediate cause of creation, 511, 602
- as partial representation of Nārāyaṇa, 240
- as rays of Kṛṣṇa's body, 190
- distinct from material variegatedness, 408-409
- has no activities, 545

Brāhmaṇas
- as face of universal form, **55**
- as mouth of universal form, **266**
- as natural guardians of society, 352
- austerity as wealth of, 467
- consulted by *kṣatriyas,* 352
- expert *brāhmaṇas* rare in age of Kali, 302
- must be expert in performing sacrifices, 56, 266
- *See also Varṇāśrama-dharma*

Brāhmaṇo 'sya mukham
- verses quoted, 267

Brahma-saṁhitā
- authorized by Lord Caitanya, 601
- cited, 51, 163, 180, 183, 185, 207, 211, 256, 316, 387, 506
- quoted, 179, 233, 234, 299, 311, 313, 324, 330, 468, 518, 519, 534, 551, 557, 606

Creation
its symmetry suggests intelligence behind it, 223
made possible by potential power of *brahmajyoti,* **232**, 233, 511
merges within body of Nārāyaṇa, 247
Nārāyaṇa as transcendental to all, 509
nondifferent from Kṛṣṇa, 323
not blind or accidental, 488
not decried by devotees, 446, 476
process of creation as subject of Chapter Four, 169-219
secondary creation made by Brahmā, **61**, 551
takes place at a historical date, 246
takes place by glance of Kṛṣṇa, 60, 568
three types described, 604-605
Cupid
failed to break vows of Lord, **346-348**
incurred wrath of Lord Śiva, 349

D

Daśaratha
as father of Lord Rāmacandra, **375**-376
Dattātreya
as incarnation of Lord, **343-344**
Death
as problem of life, 73
as symptom of material infection, 149
can be controlled by yogic exercises, 256
compared to sleeping, 26
defined as change of body, 26, 213
duty at time of death prescribed, **24-39**
exists as misery in all universes, 7, 63
inevitable for intelligent and foolish alike, 132
not feared by Mahārāja Parīkṣit, 453
one should not be afraid of, **25**
Deity
identical with Lord Viṣṇu, 33
meditated upon in temples, 83
must be visited and bowed to, 157
nondifferent from *omkāra,* 33
not considered an idol by devotee, 203, 204
not respected by nondevotees, 162
shows favor to fallen souls, 158
spiritual master teaches worship of, 159-160
supreme worshipable Deity is Nārāyaṇa, 238
Deity
worshiped by child Parīkṣit, **145-146**
worshiped by proper decoration, 160
See also Ārcanā
Demigods
annihilated at period of devastation, 139
appeased by worship of Kṛṣṇa, 47
as arms of universal form, **46-47**
as controllers of senses, 559
as manifested personalities, 306
as parts and parcels of Kṛṣṇa, 22, 55, **238**, 280, 529, 577
bewildered by Kṛṣṇa's creative energy, 178
controlled by devastating time, **89**
envious of *brahmacārīs,* 347
headed by Indra, **46**
manage different departments of universe, 138, 390
modes of worship of, 131
represent musical rhythm of Lord, **54**
sometimes aspire after human body, 154
their fears vanquished by Narasiṁhadeva, **359**
which ones to worship for various boons, **130-134**
worshiped by materialists, 74
See also Brahmā, Devotees, Indra, Śiva
Demons
have civilization of materialistic advancement, 66
represent prowess of Lord, **54**
See also Atheists, Nondevotees
Desires
as diseases of heart, 116
as living symptom, 496
based on false ego, 94
changed from material to spiritual, 27
develop according to engagement of mind, 30
of living being are eternal, 27, 205
that bind to the cycle of birth and death, 37
Devotees
above all pretensions, 205
all accept *mahā-mantra,* 468
always consider themselves instruments of Kṛṣṇa, 215
always full with praising God, 563
always protected by Kṛṣṇa, 70, 453
are able authorities on world leadership, 202

K

.ṛṣṇa
ever young with permanent youthful energy, 185, 381
full in six opulences, 309
full of unlimited bliss without grief, **408**
has unlimited number of father-devotees, 343
His activities are unfathomed, 184, 242
His appearance on earth described, **380-393**
His body and soul nondifferent, 33, 381, 430
See also Supreme Lord, Govinda
.ṛṣṇadāsa Kavirāja
cited, 142
.ṣatriyas
as arms of universal form, **55, 266**
as representatives of Kṛṣṇa, 374
uprooted by Paraśurāma, 374
.ṣetrajñaṁ cāpi māṁ viddhi
verses quoted, 296
.ṣīrodakaśāyī Viṣṇu
acts as Supersoul in every living being, 46
lives in Satyaloka system, 46
.umāras
as incarnations of Kṛṣṇa's knowledge, 345
their incarnation described, **345**-346

L

.aws of nature
are not blind, 438
as manifestation of Kṛṣṇa's control, 564
award material bodies, 26
condition living entities, 85, 137
do not affect Kṛṣṇa, 440-441
materialists become victims of, 27
work by Kṛṣṇa's glance, 563
See also Material energy, Material existence, Material nature, Material world, Modes of nature.
.eaders
adored by men like dogs and hogs, **152-154**
as stubborn rebels against God's supremacy, 524
blind and incompetent, 73
make appeals to the body, 26
must reform social order, 398
nonsensical, 134

Leaders
should hear about all-auspicious Lord, 200
See also King, Politicians
Liberated souls
as instruments of Kṛṣṇa's will, 499-500
enjoy discussing Kṛṣṇa's pastimes, 11, 327, 411
exactly like the Lord, 430
not devoid of senses, 409-410
not to be imitated by conditioned souls, 419
of many one may know God as He is, 504
without speculative habit, 500
See also Devotees
Liberation
as freedom from illusory bodily attachments, 171
as path of Kapila, **340**
as release from slumber of forgetfulness, 62
awarded only by Śrī Kṛṣṇa, 135
desired by *karmīs,* 205
from conception of false egoism, 21
from material coverings, 107
is easiest through devotional service, 62, 80, 272, 274, 462
offered to souls in every millennium, 345
refused by pure devotees, 136, 316, 531
surpasses regulated principles, 11
through meditation upon universal form, 57
Living beings
afraid of Satanic influence, 89
all born in darkness, 516
all maintained by Supreme Lord, 181, 566
all struggling for existence, 7
apt to fall into atmosphere of noneternity, 345
as class A., B. or C. prisoners, 75
as dominating factors over material elements, 216, 253, 565
as marginal potency of Kṛṣṇa, 85, 237, 288
as offshoots of internal potency, 237
as subordinate parts and parcels of Kṛṣṇa, 205, 247, 261, 266, 284, 370, 382
as susceptible to modes of nature, 137, 326, 343
as unborn, **412,** 413

Living beings
- born from energy of Kṛṣṇa, 514
- can never become God, 383
- cannot conceive of the unlimited, 184
- can possess percentage of full knowledge, 213
- cleansed of material contamination, 109
- compact in fearfulness, 291
- compared to small children, 261
- constitutionally spiritual sparks, 148, 327
- controlled by demigods, 47
- controlled by senses, 577
- create their own bodies, 460
- dependent on direction of Supersoul, 122
- encaged by propensity for overlordship, 493
- enchanted by form of woman, 347
- eternally servants of Kṛṣṇa, 135, 212, 310, 573, 583
- ever-liberated and ever-conditioned, 448
- forgetful due to false egoism, 61, 62, 296
- have never been produced by matter, 121
- identify with false ego, 586
- in 8,400,000 species, 226
- limited in every respect, 349
- many varieties listed, **593-594**
- meant for service activities, 27, 274
- meant to satisfy Kṛṣṇa's senses, 462
- must surrender either to Kṛṣṇa or material nature, 318
- naturally attracted to devotional service, 370
- neither absolute nor independent, 278
- not endowed equally with intelligence, 208-209
- perpetually unhappy, 88
- purely conscious in pure state, 457
- separate from car of body, 260
- some in heaven, some hell, 75
- spiritually as good as God, 341
- sterilized by contact with Kṛṣṇa, 327
- subjected to many transmigrations, 430
- their desires eternal, 27
- their hearts changed by devotional service, 164
- their identity never lost, 26
- their intelligence overseen by Kṛṣṇa, 242
- undergo terms of encagement, 110
- worship the senses, 537
- *See also* Human beings

Lotus feet of Kṛṣṇa
- as first object of meditation, 81-82
- as goal of Vedic adventure, 169
- caught hold of by Brahmā, **312**
- deliver one from birth and death, **317**
- entrance into network of, 211
- firmly accepted by Mahārāja Parīkṣit, 175
- placed over hearts of great mystics, **78**
- serve as protection from all fear, **280**
- should be taken shelter of, 445
- taken into heart of pure devotee, **91, 428**

M

Mac-cittā mad-gata-prāṇa
- verses quoted, 541

Mad-dhāma gatvā
- verse quoted, 149

Mādhavendra Purī
- quoted, 174, 175

Mahābhārata
- cited, 374, 380
- recommended for less intelligent classes, 143

Mahātmās
- depend wholly on Kṛṣṇa, 174
- never return to material world, 114
- open gate of salvation, 596
- take pleasure in Kṛṣṇa's pastimes, 381
- *See also* Devotees

Mahā-Viṣṇu
- as expansion of Govinda, 324, 330
- as master of eternal time, space, etc., **329**
- as original cause of creation, 255
- assumed *virāṭa-rūpa* form, **264**
- creates manifested cosmos, **323-325**
- electrifies matter to be in motion, 603
- generates universes with His breathing, 42, 262
- lies in causal water of *mahat-tattva,* 255-256

Māṁ ca yo 'vyabhicāreṇa
- verses quoted, 313, 342, 463

Manmanā bhava mad-bhaktaḥ
- verses quoted, 196, 523

Manu
- as father of mankind, **339**
- characterized by his glorious fame, **371**
- his incarnation described, **371-372**

Modern civilization
creates intolerable existence for everyone, 73
following the way of phantasmagoria, 65
like decoration of a dead body, 7
manifested by huge accumulation of materials, 252
spoils human life, 202
Modes of nature
absent in spiritual world, **475**-477
accepted by Kṛṣṇa through external energy, **242**
act under Kṛṣṇa's direction, 51
as products of false ego, **586**
conducted by Brahmā, Viṣṇu, Śiva, 592
contaminate material activities, 274
divisions of, **595**-596
do not affect devotee, 89
drive the conditioned souls, 51
evolution of, **248**-252
manifest as matter, knowledge and activities, **244**
never affect Kṛṣṇa, 44
products of, **257**-260
See also Material energy, Material nature, Material world, Laws of nature
Mugdhaṁ māṁ nigadantu
verses quoted, 175
Mukti dadhati karhicit
verse quoted, 519
Mystic powers
attained by Kṛṣṇa's parents and relatives, 343
described, 443-444
description of eightfold perfections, 98
desired by materialists, 39
mystic *yogīs* encumbered by, 39, 114
used to reach higher planets, 10
See also Yogīs

N

Na 'haṁ prakāśaḥ
verse quoted, 380
Na māṁ duṣkṛtinaḥ
verses quoted, 524
Na māṁ karmāṇi
verses quoted, 592
Nārada Muni
as spiritual master of Dhruva Mahārāja, 350
distributes transcendental knowledge, 312, **421**-422
follows instructions of Brahmā, **539**
his appearance as good as Kṛṣṇa's, 421
inquires from Brahmā, **218**-229, **541**-543
instructed by Brahmā, **229**-420, **543**-544
instructed Vyāsadeva, **545**
ordered to preach in missionary spirit, 418
pleased Brahmā, **540**
unique in history of devotional service, 146
was formerly son of a maidservant, 231
Nārada-pañcarātra
cited, 476
quoted, 274
Nara-Nārāyaṇa
exhibited way of austerity and penance, **346**
their incarnation described, **346**-348
Narasiṁhadeva
His incarnation described, **359**-360
Narasiṁha Purāṇa
cited, 530
Nārāyaṇa
as goal of sacrificial results, 304
as subsequent manifestation, 535
as ultimate destination, **239**-240
exists apart from impersonal creative energy, 247
He alone should be worshiped, 525
His discourse with Lord Brahmā, **488**-535
lies down on transcendental water, **565**
no one is independent but Him, 452
transcendental to all material creation, 10, 60, 304, 509
Na tad bhāsayate sūryaḥ
verses quoted, 193
Na tatra sūryo bhāti
verses quoted, 193
Na vyavante'pi vad-bhaktā
verses quoted, 510
Nāyam ātma pravacanena
verses quoted, 531
Nectar of Devotion
cited, 165

controlled by intelligence, **31**
engaged in mundane affairs, 156
generation of, **259, 298**
Kṛṣṇa beyond perception of, **245**
Kṛṣṇa's free from contamination, 409
materialized cannot perceive Kṛṣṇa, 120
of devotees as without grief, 410
of devotees enjoy Hari, **537**
offer license to conditioned soul, 572
of Kṛṣṇa as interchangeable, 506
produced out of Kṛṣṇa's reservoir of senses, 274
purified by devotional service, 87, 155, 188, 252, 258, 313, 322, 327, 472, 528, 538
revival of their original purity, 99, 110
subdued by *jaḍa-yoga,* 354
supplied to us by material nature, 120-121
worshiped by living beings, 537

Service
See *Bhakti-yoga,* Devotional Service

Śeṣa
cannot estimate Kṛṣṇa's potencies, 402
His incarnation described, **402**

Sex
as cause of many distresses, 281
as nighttime activity of envious householders, **5**
as phantasmagoria pleasure potency, 207
as principle of present civilization, **5-6**
as profit, adoration and distinction, 81
as very strong desire, 347
binds conditioned soul, 80, 294
compared to sucking one's own blood, 153
condemned in renounced order of life, 295
considered suicidal for transcendentalist, 6, 29
impelled by pleasure-giving substance, **280-281**
rascals indulge in in name of *Bhāgavatam,* 82
used to serve Kṛṣṇa, 581
worship of Indra for, **130**

Sītā
as internal potency of Kṛṣṇa, **376**
meant to be worshiped by living beings, 376

Śiva
as all-powerful, **405**
as fragment of potency of Lord, **332**
as greatest *yogī,* 444
as initiator for materialistic life, 249
as lord of mode of ignorance, 249, 400
could not ascertain limits of spiritual happiness, **320**
destroys, **309**
did not exist before creation, 60, 509
in universal form, **53,** 286
knows potencies of Lord, **405**
not equal to Kṛṣṇa, 22
not free from his own wrath, **348**
resides in Satyaloka systems, 46
transcendental to all pretensions, **205**
worshiped to become great hero, **130**
worshiped to become learned, **131**
worships Kṛṣṇa, **205**

Skanda Purāṇa
cited, 442
quoted, 525, 529, 605-606

Soul
always different from material nature, 7, **429**
as eternal servitor of Kṛṣṇa, 241
dependent on Supersoul, 561
devotional service is dynamic force of, 155
entangled in chain of birth and death, 8
influenced by external energy, 457
nature of, 64
relieved of repetition of birth and death, 294, 373
See also Living beings

Spiritual master
always prepared to impart knowledge, 450
as direct representative of Kṛṣṇa, 111, 470, 522
as transparent via medium, 212, 522
engages disciples in Deity worship, 160
his order as sustenance of life, 16, 170, 428, 471
is not a theoretical speculator, 214
is not ordinary man, 204
must be satisfied, 16
never claims to be God, 227, 522
not a paid agent, 223, 542
original spiritual master is Kṛṣṇa, 214
real knowledge depends on his mercy, 16

Universes
inconceivable even by demigods, 177
Kṛṣṇa is proprietor of all, 19
See also Material World, Planets, Spiritual sky, Vaikuṇṭha,
Upaniṣads
cited, 181, 208, 209, 241, 362, 406
quoted, 176, 194, 508

V

Vaikuṇṭhas
achieved by demons, 393
adored by all self-realized persons, 472
as eternity, bliss and knowledge, 90
as supreme residential place, 92
as unalloyed goodness only, 476
enriched with transcendental qualities, 476
free from lust and hankering, 475
its inhabitants described, 478-481
manifested to Brahmā, 472-488
not reached by mechanical means, 486
planets all self-illuminating in, 193
reached by *bhakti-yoga,* 90, 108
ruled by Nārāyaṇa, 290
See also Kingdom of God, Spiritual sky
Vaiṣṇava Tantras
cited, 159
Vāmanadeva
became doorman of Bali Mahārāja, 366
expanded His leg beyond topmost planet, 401
His incarnation described, 365-369, 400-401
Vāmana Purāṇa
cited, 353
Varṇāśrama-dharma
culminates in detachment from sex life, 294
four castes described, 55-56, 266-267
is no longer regular, 203
its procedure for making human life perfect, 27
recommends voluntary renunciation, 68
requires householders to give alms, 69
trains one from beginning to depend on Lord, 70
See also Brāhmaṇas, Kṣatriyas, etc.
Vasati daśana-śikhare
verses quoted, 338
Vāsudevaḥ sarvam iti
quoted, 310
Vāsudevāt paro brahman
verse quoted, 310
Vāsudevo vā idam
verses quoted, 509
Vedāhaṁ samatītāni
verses quoted, 561
Vedaiś ca sarvair aham
verse quoted, 149
Vedānta-sūtras
cited, 238
quoted, 291
Vedas
as our mother, 321
as source of all knowledge, 373
cited, 51, 277, 505
divided by Vyāsadeva, 394-395
Kṛṣṇa is personification of, 204
means knowledge that leads to the Lord, 85, 238, 258
not imparted by any created being, 214
prohibit offering meat to Kṛṣṇa, 152
quoted, 193, 267, 310, 317, 326, 327, 559
recommend demigod worship, 138
revealed only by disciplic succession, 219
saved by fish incarnation, 356-357
studied three times by Brahmā, 119
to revive lost memory of fallen souls, 217
Vedic version is eternal truth, 116, 216
Vedic hymns
as cerebral passage of the Lord, 49
cited, 233
generated from skin of *virāṭa-rūpa,* 273
give new life to sacrificed animal, 300
meant for sacrifices to demigods, 356
meant to please Nārāyaṇa, 304
not understood by mundane scholars, 214
quoted, 509
reveal supreme source of all pleasure, 556
Vena Mahārāja
delivered by Pṛthu, 352-353
Viracaya mayi daṇḍam
verses quoted, 174
Virāṭa-rūpa
See Universal form
Viṣṇu
as Almighty Father, 594